LUDWIG II OF BAVARIA

The Man and the Mystery

By the same author

Heinrich Schliemann – For Gold or Glory

LUDWIG II OF BAVARIA

The Man and the Mystery

by

KATERINA VON BURG

WINDSOR PUBLICATIONS

British Library Cataloguing in Publication Data
Burg, Katerina von
    Ludwig II of Bavaria : The Man and the Mystery
    1. West Germany. Bavaria. Ludwig II, King of Bavaria

I. Title
943' .308'0924

ISBN 1-870417-02-X

Printed by Antony Rowe Ltd, Chippenham, England

CONTENTS

LIST OF ILLUSTRATIONS

Between Pages 152 and 153

CHAPTER ONE

THE CROWN PRINCE

ENIGMATIC, fascinating and much maligned, King Ludwig II of Bavaria was undoubtedly one of the most charismatic figures of the 19th Century. Even today, a century after his mysterious death, he is revered and discussed as if he were still living. Ask a Bavarian what he thinks of Ludwig and he will offer superlatives: noble, generous, deeply aware of his people. Only by the uninformed is he still erroneously described as "mad King Ludwig".

Ludwig Friedrich Wilhelm von Wittelsbach was a perfect paradox; he shuddered at the very word "duty" yet he adored his peasant subjects and they adored him. He built three magnificent palaces which were neither residences nor follies, yet preferred to live frugally in a hunting lodge. He was apolitical yet better informed on world affairs than most, and he was addicted equally to nature and the arts. Even his sexual predilections were ambiguous, although a close examination of his life shows him to be bi-sexual rather than homosexual. He was, on his own admission, "an eternal enigma even to myself", offering us not only a most apposite epitaph but also an element of prophecy.

He was born at Schloss Nymphenburg on the outskirts of Munich on August 25th, 1845, the first son of Crown Prince Maximilian and his wife, Marie. His arrival was warmly received, the more so since his mother had previously miscarried. Joyfully, the proud father wrote to his brother-in-law, Prince Adalbert of Prussia, "These lines bring you the happy news that our dear Marie has been blessed with a fine, strong little boy, and on my father's birthday too, which pleased him greatly (...) You can imagine that I myself scarcely left her bed of suffering - and indeed, I suffered myself during these long hours." He added triumphantly, "It certainly is a splendid feeling to be a father." This appears to have been the extent of his paternal pride, for as he was later to reveal, he cared little for his son and if ever a boy was later to cry out for love it was Ludwig, who was never to receive it.

In the first instance he was called Otto, but this was changed shortly afterwards to Ludwig and the original choice of name was later given to the little brother who was to follow. Shortly after Ludwig's birth, he and his mother were removed from Munich to escape a fever epidemic which was causing havoc in the hot Bavarian summer. The favourite refuge of the Royal family was in the Allgäu where, at the foot of the Säuling, stood Schloss Hohenschwangau. In company with Otto, who

was born in 1848, Ludwig spent most of his childhood here and the boys
were scarcely ever seen or recognised in the Bavarian capital. Ludwig's
lifetime rapport with the peasants undoubtedly had its root in these
early days, as did some of his more individual characteristics which
were to provoke such acrimony and criticism in later years.

In 1848, his grandfather, Ludwig I, was forced to abdicate partly
following public indignation over his blatant and expensive affaire with
the Irish dancer who called herself Lola Montez, but basically as a
result of the revolution which had swept Bavaria as it had erupted
elsewhere in Europe. Ludwig's father unexpectedly became King
Maximilian II and the two year old toddler thus became Crown Prince.
From that moment on, he ceased to be treated like an ordinary child
and became an object of awe and adulation. As he grew older, to his
naturally democratic feeling towards the peasants was forcibly added
the idea, fostered by those in charge of his upbringing, that he was a
being superior to everyone else except God and his parents.

Unsurprisingly, his overburdened young mind quickly developed
into a labyrinth of paradox and confusion. His mother was little help
to him. Queen Marie, a Hohenzollern Princess from Berlin and a niece
of King Friedrich Wilhelm of Prussia, had been accepted by the
Bavarian people despite the spontaneous comment, "Another Prussian!" following her betrothal to Max. Physically at least she was
admired and her father-in-law, who had an eye for the ladies, considered her worthy of inclusion in his famous *Schönheitsgalerie.* * Her
beauty soon faded, leaving a plump, square-jawed, somewhat stolid-
looking creature who found it hard to hold a conversation on any but
the most basic of levels, and who enjoyed nothing better than to gossip
with her ladies. In later years, when Ludwig tried to engage her on
some more erudite topic, she would explain away her failure to respond
by confessing placidly, "I never read anything. I cannot understand
why people always want to be reading!"

Paradoxically, she seemed proud of Ludwig's intellectual mind and
in the family chronicle, which she sporadically remembered to update,
she wrote in 1851, "Pleasure in art has developed early in Ludwig; he
likes to build, especially churches, monasteries and the like." This
particular interest of the young prince also pleased his grandfather who
wrote to King Otto of Greece**, "At Christmas 1852, Ludwig got the
Siegestor made of building bricks so that he might build, and he does
so with surprising excellence. I very much liked a building that he had
made." In the same letter, the perceptive grandfather also observed,
more ominously, "I recognise a striking resemblance in the future

---

*A portrait collection of beauties which was housed in the Residenz and is now at
Schloss Nymphenburg.   ** His elder son.

Ludwig II to the politically dead Ludwig I; I also see myself again in his dependence upon his governess........"

Some of Ludwig's other interests were also recorded by his mother: "He (...) likes to dress himself as a nun, shows pleasure in playing at theatres, loves pictures and the like, enjoys reading aloud and telling stories and right from childhood gladly gave away things and money from his own purse." This comment shows a somewhat thoughtless streak in Marie, for the unfortunate princes were both kept extremely short of pocket money by their parsimonious father; their pitiful monthly 12 Gulden had not only to be exactly accounted for but also had to be stretched far beyond the limits expected of more lowly-born children. This early frugality was undoubtedly the reason why Ludwig threw monetary caution to the winds in later years.

It was also said that, as part of their disciplinary upbringing, the Princes' food was kept to a minimum and it was apparently not unusual for the sympathetic domestics in the Royal Household to supplement the boys' diet from their own more liberal rations. Possibly Marie, who left her sons' upbringing to others, was not even aware of all this and did not see enough of her sons to learn of it, living as she did in her prosaic world of nothingness. Her own interests, such as they were, centred around botany, needlework and, more surprisingly, walking and climbing. She followed this latter pursuit in an outlandish garb consisting of a knee-length crinoline and ankle-length men's trews and, trailing her brood behind her, took to what was considered a most unladylike pastime with gusto. Most of the present-day forest and mountain paths at Hohenschwangau, including the lovely Alpenrosen-weg, were originally marked out by Marie. As she grew older and stouter, however, she abandoned not only the climbing and the cos-tume, but sadly also the brood. Max, who preferred more formal landscaping, was responsible for the Schlosspark and Schwanseepark which today stretch almost as far as the village of Horn, some two miles distant in the direction of Füssen. A passionate huntsman, Max also created hunting paths higher into the mountains.

With all her failings, Marie seems at least to have loved her adopted country and rarely left it except to make the occasional visit to France or Italy. Although she was always ready to receive visitors from the Prussian court in Berlin, it is noticeable that she never put herself out to visit them. Did she, to some extent, avoid her family, as if trying to forget that they existed? If she did, it was not without reason, for she brought considerably more than a comely face and figure to Bavaria. She also carried with her a heritage of mental instability ranging from mild eccentricity to incurable insanity and almost all of her immediate family were affected in some manner. The commonplace Marie herself showed none of the familiar symptoms.

While Ludwig did his best to be as loving and attentive as his patience would allow, he found her company so irritating that, throughout his adult life, he tried to avoid living under the same roof with her. Franz von Pfistermeister, King Max's secretary who later served Ludwig in the same capacity, had some interesting comments to make upon the Royal family in this regard. A schoolmaster's son with some basic idea of child psychology, he observed that "the Queen had little knowledge as to how to draw her little sons to her. She visited them only fleetingly in their rooms, and scarcely even knew how to treat them as children ought to be treated. Nor did the little sons know how to treat their mother." Nevertheless, up to the time when Ludwig and Otto were old enough to go their own ways she did her best to present to the world a reasonably united if ill-matched family.

At Bleckenau, a few miles into the Highlands from Hohenschwangau, Max had built a small hunting lodge* in the heart of the dense pine forest; Marie formed a deep attachment for this solitary place and her boys were often obliged to go with her when she set off on one of her periodic treks there. She spent a good deal of time at Bleckenau without a single servant in attendance, cooking and cleaning for her family with all the vigour and satisfaction of a peasant woman. When members of the court were also coerced into joining the party, they were nonplussed to find a high-born, arrogant Prussian contentedly preparing the food as if it was her life's work.

If Marie had little to offer the Crown Prince his father was even more of a loss to him. A cold, over-practical man with a deep interest in science and education, he had more affection for his subjects than for his own family. From an impetuous, immoral youth he had changed almost overnight into a heartless stickler for protocol and was so ill-acquainted with his sons that he would refuse to converse with them because he "could think of nothing to say." Later, it was decided that Ludwig should accompany Max on his constitutional in the Englischer Garten in Munich with a view to improving their relationship, but doubtless to Ludwig's own relief he soon abandoned the idea, with the excuse "What should I talk about to the young man? He is not interested in anything I do." This was by no means true, for Ludwig had inherited many of Max's interests in science and education, nature and the arts, and would have much appreciated an opportunity to participate at the celebrated gatherings of his father's academic friends, but Max remained cold and unbending and was a stranger to his son until the end.

*Now a restaurant.

Ludwig never forgot his father's attitude and years later told Crown Prince Rudolf of Austria, "You are to be congratulated on having enjoyed such a thoroughly excellent and enlightened education, and it is a further piece of good luck that the Emperor so ardently interests himself personally in your instruction. Unfortunately, it was very different with my father, who always talked down to me and at the most honoured me, *en passant*, with a few polite, cold words." As it happened, Ludwig was mistaken on this point: Rudolf's relationship with Franz-Josef was even worse and certainly sowed the seeds which grew into the Mayerling tragedy.

Pfistermeister also confirmed that "the King saw his little sons, the Princes Ludwig and Otto, only once or twice a day; at noon for second breakfast and in the evening for dinner; but he only very rarely went into the rooms where they grew up. Therefore, he usually shook hands on greeting and removed himself with all haste."

Despite these uncomfortable parents, the Princes developed into charming and reasonably well-behaved children, although predictably both were extremely shy. To Marie's discredit, if she felt deeply about her children at all, her preference fell on Otto, a fact which Ludwig understandably resented although in later years he accepted the situation with his usual gracious magnanimity and became deeply attached to the brother with whom he had so little in common. Neither boy was spared the harsh disciplines inflicted upon them, and although it was not anticipated that Otto would ever wear the crown, he was subjected to the same rigorous routines as his elder brother.

At the age of eight months, Ludwig had received his first shock of human disappointment when his wetnurse died of typhoid fever. His second traumatic experience came when his beloved Governess, Baroness Sybille von Meilhaus, was dismissed in favour of a Governor, a 54 year old former cavalry officer, Theodore, Count Bassalet de la Rosée, a strict disciplinarian who terrified the shy ten year old. From that moment Ludwig's life became a lonely and miserable void of toil and reprimand and it is not hard to guess how things were when we find La Rosée writing to the Queen with grim satisfaction, "I had many a battle to fight with the Crown Prince before we established the existing relationship." That is to say, before he succeeded in almost breaking the boy's spirit. An even heavier burden was placed on both children's shoulders when, in the following year, they were given a military instructor and companion in the shape of Emil von Wülffen, another somewhat unfortunate choice since this moody and unstable gentleman was to take his own life before their horrified eyes by jumping from one of the promontaries above Hohenschwangau.

Not long after this dreadful occurrence, the boys were separated so that the Crown Prince might concentrate on more advanced studies for as well as being older than Otto he was also considerably brighter and was already showing signs of the remarkable intellect which was later so admired. Ludwig's day was now almost as long and arduous as that of any artisan, beginning at 5.30 am and ending officially at 8.00 pm, after which time the exhausted boy could do as he pleased if he still had the energy to do anything. Accustomed to spending all their leisure time together, the Princes had no particular longing for the company of outsiders but as part of their general instruction, a few carefully selected playmates were found for them, notably their young Wittelsbach cousins from Possenhofen on Lake Starnberg, Toni, Count Arco and Max, Count Holnstein, the latter of whom was to play a portentious part in Ludwig's later life. Also invited was the son of the family physician, Max von Gietl. Dr. Gietl himself later reminisced: "There was always a struggle to get rid of the innate shyness of both Princes. War games and games of soldiers were therefore considered especially beneficial (...) It was forbidden for the invited boys to kiss the hands of the Princes and call them 'Your Royal Highness', but guests who did not behave politely would be passed over at the next invitation, as once was Count Toni Arco because he boxed the ears of the Crown Prince."

La Rosée seemingly had no idea of the damage he did by pressing both democratic and autocratic ideas simultaneously on his charge. By the time the "playmates" had appeared on the scene, Ludwig had already been so brainwashed as to his own importance by La Rosée that he must have found it difficult to behave naturally with anyone. Paradoxically and revealingly, he enjoyed a warm intimacy with the gardener's son Peter, with whom no such problems of status and etiquette arose. This particular problem and Ludwig's solution to it reappeared at intervals throughout his life.

For most of the time, the brothers relied on each other for company, and like all small boys they occasionally fought and quarrelled. Their happier moments together may not have been so carefully recorded as their discordant ones, but the detailed reports of their contretemps found their way into many a memoir, as on the occasion when Ludwig, imbued in the strange teachings of La Rosée, tied up his younger brother in the garden of their summer home at Berchtesgaden, put a gag into his mouth and pronounced Otto to be his "vassal" before pretending to execute his captive by tying a kerchief around his neck and twisting it with a stick. Since Otto's screams were audible through the gag, it cannot have been a very serious attempt at execution but Ludwig was soundly thrashed for it. His punishment instilled into him a dislike of Berchtesgaden which was never to leave him. He was at that time still slightly jealous of his brother, and presumably he hoped to take his revenge in this way. There is no doubt that as a small boy he was frequently naughty, but the truth behind the story of his going into a shop and pocketing an object without paying for it was that his seeming dishonesty stemmed only from inexperience in that, like most Royals, he carried no money on his person and had not even been instructed in the basic principles of commerce. Ludwig was severely punished for his "shoplifting" but as a result of this incident he and his brother were allotted pocket money.

Bullied and made thoroughly miserable by La Rosée and by King Max, who thought very highly of the tutor, it is hardly surprising that Ludwig took full advantage of the very few pleasures available to him. Like all boys he loved to swim and fish and to observe the wildlife in the highlands and mountains, but most of all, he liked to read and contemplate the paintings and murals which graced Schloss Berg, the Munich Residenz and Schloss Hohenschwangau. On the walls of the latter were fresh and charming tempera frescoes by Moritz von Schwind depicting some of Ludwig's favourite legends. Prominent among these was that of Lohengrin, the Knight of the Swan, after whom the region was named. Since these frescoes were almost identical to those at the Residenz scarcely a day passed when Ludwig could not indulge himself. It was said that his imagination was so strong that, when he had stared for some time at a picture, he could imagine himself to be a part of it. This was borne out by a friend of his mother, Marie Schültze, who described him as having, at about this time, "a very lively imagination, lofty flights of fancy and high aspirations. His spirit occupied itself preferably with poetic things: everything ugly, of course, lay far from his idealistic nature and affected him distressingly. Not merely distressingly but actually painfully because, in his world of ideals, he could not understand them. In such cases he went into his shell. Added to this, he had an unusually strong inclination towards self-esteem."

In 1856, the Crown Prince began riding lessons and soon developed the proficiency and love of horses characteristic of all the Wittelsbachs, a passion he was later to share actively with his cousin, Empress Elisabeth of Austria. But in 1861 everything else was overshadowed when he was taken to see a performance of *Lohengrin* at the Royal Court Theatre in Munich. This event had a deep effect upon his future development. His childhood governess had been enthusiastic about the first production of this opera in 1859 and, listening with rapt attention to her descriptions of the musical version of his favourite legend, the desire was born in him to hear *Lohengrin* for himself. He never forgot that performance or, indeed, the opera itself and years later described his feeling for it in a letter to its composer: "The worse things were, the more I began to recognise the meaning of this immortal work. In this performance was the germ of our love and friendship unto death; from then onward, the spark of our sacred ideals was ignited to a flame in me."

There is a certain irony in the fact that, in this same year, La Rosée recommended that Ludwig's piano lessons should be curtailed because "the Crown Prince has neither the talent for music, nor does he like it." The truth was that he realised Ludwig liked it all too well and was determined that, as a discipline, he should be denied even this pleasure. There was no doubt about Ludwig's reaction to the opera, however, after which he "cried tears of the highest rapture". Richard Wagner had captivated Ludwig and as well as knowing the text of all his published works by heart he had also memorised great tracts of the composer's somewhat verbose prose.

With the same short-sightedness which marked all the other pronouncements on his character and upbringing, Ludwig's interest was dismissed as "a passing fancy" of the type to which 15 year olds are prone, but it was far more than that. Wagner's interpretations of the old legends spoke to Ludwig's lonely soul and brought him a measure of comfort such as he was never to find elsewhere.

Although he was now permitted to go to the theatre to see classic dramas and operas (probably under pressure on his parents by his erudite grandfather Ludwig I), the boy desperately lacked a congenial friend of his own choosing or even a selected one who might share some of his interests. Consequently, he preferred his own company to that of the young philistines among whom he was sporadically thrown. Instead of becoming more gregarious as was intended by his unthinking instructors, he became progressively more shy and introverted. Afraid of La Rosée and a stranger to his parents, he sought refuge in his own private world. Luise von Kobell, another understanding friend of the Queen, had already noticed this hypersensitivity, realising that the reaction of Ludwig's family to his behaviour was doing more harm than good. "It was like a stab through the heart of the young Wittelsbach," she observed, "when he was laughed at in the family because of some 'eccentricity': a mundane word from his mother falling on to his ecstasy would vex him to the marrow. It was hard for him to forget a disagreeable remark or incident and where he could, he avoided people, even places, which had unpleasant memories for him."

Ludwig did not make his first official appearance in public until 1862 when, on his 17th birthday, he was installed as a Knight of the Order of St. Hubertus by his father, who held the hereditary position of Grand Master, a post which Ludwig himself would later fill. When he came

officially of age the following year, the birthday celebrations were at
Hohenschwangau, where he was treated to a serenade by the Füssen
choir who sang their greeting from the courtyard framed in Bengal
lights. Earlier, he had gone fishing and caught a 9 1/2 lb. trout in the
Alpsee, dined with a delegation from Munich and visited the
Schweizerhaus, one of the nearby hunting lodges; he spent the rest of
the time admiring his presents, which included some pictures of the
Nibelungen saga by Ludwig von Schnorr and a swan shaped pin. This
was hardly a swinging birthday by anybody's standards and one cannot
help wondering if, apart from the fishing expedition, Ludwig truly
enjoyed any of it. He did receive one "perk" in the form of a modest
suite of his own to denote his coming of age, including two aides de
camp and his own apartments in the Munich Residenz. These were
situated on the floor above his parents' quarters which were known as
the Hofgartenzimmer.

It was Ludwig's first opportunity to furnish and decorate his accom-
modations to his own taste although, in fact, with the exception of his
much-commented-on clockwork moon and stars which moved across
his bedroom ceiling, his rooms looked no different from those of any
other reasonably well-to-do person in the 19th Century. Ludwig was
very proud of his little paradise, however, and boasted to Meilhaus, the
Governess with whom he was still in close correspondence, "My new
dressing room is dark blue and my study light blue; the bedroom and
the corner room overlook the Theatinerkirche and in the Salon and the
Study - which is the room I like most - there are carved ruins and castles
from the neighbourhood of Hohenschwangau, and there are pictures
of the Knight of the Swan (as they are painted on the walls at Hohenschwangau), reproductions of Schnorr's '*Nibelungen*' pictures, a portrait
of Beethoven and one of Shakespeare."

Of his aides de camp, Ludwig preferred the lively and handsome
Prince Paul of Thurn und Taxis to the more sober Lt. Baron Karl
Theodor von Sauer and the two quickly forged a close friendship.
Prince Paul came of an old and aristocratic family whose activities
included the formation of the Bavarian Postal Service in the early 19th
Century (the first in Germany) and the operation of a Munich brewery
which still flourishes today. The family was wealthier even than the
Wittelsbachs and from all accounts considerably more autocratic in its
outlook. Their official seat was in Regensburg but the family owned
many other imposing houses and estates throughout Southern Germany.

Paul, a charming and erudite extrovert, was well able to share
Ludwig's outdoor and cultural pursuits and it was hoped that he would
succeed in bringing the Crown Prince out of his shell. Ludwig had

never had such a companion before and was bowled over by him. Since
Paul was known to have an eye for the ladies, the idea was that he would
propel Ludwig in this direction. It occurred to no one that Paul and
Ludwig would form an almost romantic attachment for each other but
in the event, this was exactly what happened. The two were packed off
to the family's summer home at Berchtesgaden for a holiday and there
the friendship, warm from its inception, quickly reached boiling point.

To a lesser degree or rather, for a shorter period of time, Ludwig
was also on close terms with one of his cousins, Duke Karl Theodor,
or "Gackl" as he was known, the middle son of Duke Max in Bavaria
and brother of the Empress of Austria. These "poor relations" led an
enviably carefree existence and Ludwig enjoyed their company occasionally, but on the whole, with his romantic optimism, he rarely
showed any great wisdom in his choice of friends: he invariably saw
something in them which was either not there or was not observed and
appreciated by others. When he discovered his error, usually the hard
way, he would reject the person concerned with ruthless totality. Yet
he never learned and despite an inherent cynical distrust of his ministers which never ceased to aggravate them, in his personal relationships
he remained as blind as the proverbial bat and continued to make the
same mistakes over and over again.

More shy and introspective in his teens than he had been as a small
child, Ludwig was the type to lavish body and soul on one person and
he expected the object of his affections to reciprocate in like manner.
At the height of his friendship with Gackl, for instance, he wrote
enthusiastically, "He is hated and misunderstood by almost everybody,
but I know him better and I know that he has a good heart and soul."
This confidence, like many others, was addressed to his former governess who, after leaving Royal service, had married an Army officer,
Baron von Leonrod, and gone to live in Ansbach. Her correspondence
with her former charge, of whom she was deeply fond, continued until
her death in 1881 and Ludwig never got over the loss of her society.
He often felt desperately lonely and over the years sent his "dear
Meilhaus" an endless stream of letters. Most of these were concerned
with his cultural activities but occasionally he would recount family
gossip or pour out his troubles to this sympathetic lady, secure in the
knowledge that his confidence would not be betrayed.

Ludwig's only personal confrontation with Otto von Bismarck came
in 1863 when, in the company of King Wilhelm of Prussia the Iron
Chancellor visited Munich *en route* for Baden Baden. Ludwig found
Bismarck "very interesting" but the Chancellor's impressions of the
Crown Prince seem somewhat ambiguous. During the visit, Bismarck's
table companions were Ludwig and his mother and he was later to

observe that, during this time, the Crown Prince's thoughts seemed "... far away from the table and only now and then did he remember his intention to talk to me. Our conversation did not go beyond the ordinary Court subjects but even so, I thought I recognised in his remarks a talent, a vitality and a good sense which was to come to fruition in his future career. In the pauses during the conversation, he looked past his mother to the ceiling, now and again hastily emptying the champagne glass, the refilling of which, or so it seemed to me, was, on his mother's instruction, somewhat slowly performed. Thus it happened that the Crown Prince very often held his glass over his shoulder behind him, where it was hesitantly refilled. Neither then, nor later, did he overstep the bounds of moderation in drinking, but I had the feeling that his surroundings bored him."

Bismarck, of course, wrote this description for public consumption, and in view of his subsequent two-faced behaviour, his cordiality towards Ludwig can only have been false. His generous verbal and written reference was probably merely a cover for his shabby treatment, as was to be demonstrated many times when Ludwig later found himself in political difficulties. Nevertheless he accurately assessed Ludwig's ennui although apparently did not seek the reason for it. In fact, only the tedium of court ceremonial and endless formalities of public functions bored Ludwig to distraction: in his personal pursuits, where time permitted he had much with which to occupy himself not only in the realms of music, literature and the plastic arts but also in more scientific spheres. It had been planned that, shortly after his coming of age, Ludwig should attend some University courses in Munich, where he was to have benefited from the teaching of such illustrious men as the famous Professor Liebig, Professor Jolly and Professor Steininger for science, physics and the history of philosophy respectively. Unfortunately, the plan was at first postponed owing to Ludwig's poor health and abandoned completely when he unexpectedly ascended the Throne.

He was scarcely developing into a social animal, and one detects a hint of satisfaction in a note written to Baroness Leonrod during the winter of 1862-63, telling her of his health problems, "This carnival is positively one of the last balls I shall attend; I am not allowed to dance because it is bad for my throat (...) Although I have not been allowed to leave my room for many weeks, I am still happy and content: I read a great deal, which I enjoy more than all the balls." This was not to say he was dull. Prince Hohenlohe, later to become one of Ludwig's Prime Ministers, found him at this time to be "...lively, intelligent, courageous and accomplished in the arts, sciences and equestrian pursuits." Already Ludwig's riding was commented upon within the family circle as "reckless" - the same word currently used to describe the equestrian style of his cousin, Elisabeth of Austria.

Having returned to Munich from the country for the winter, his favourite companion was still Paul of Taxis. To another of his cousins, Princess Anna of Hesse, he confided "After dinner (on the 22nd) I went to see Prince Taxis.* I only got to know him properly in Berchtesgaden and have grown very fond of him." It was not only Paul who caused Ludwig to neglect his correspondence, but also the many futile, time-consuming activities forced upon him to keep him out of mischief. "If in future I should not be able to write to you so often," he wrote plaintively to Leonrod, "please do not think it is because I feel cold towards you. Let me assure you that I shall always foster with the same sincerity the feelings of gratitude and true love which I bear for you in my heart."

Busy or not, he found time to listen to gossip which circulated concerning his friend Taxis, whose weakness for the feminine sex frequently led him into difficulty. Ludwig could not bear to think that he had a rival, male or female, for Paul's affections and when, possibly from Pfistermeister or Leinfelder**, neither of whom was above carrying tales, he heard that Paul was leading "a frivolous life" in Regensburg, he was quick to show his displeasure in writing. Indignantly, Taxis wrote back, "You have scarcely given me your confidence and already you see how everybody tries to bring me into disfavour with you (...) I only ask one thing: don't believe too many of the flattering speeches of others, but try to form your own opinion of those around you. If the conclusion is that people are correct in their opinion of me, well, you shall have the right to judge me. But you may be sure that I would not dare to use this free and sincere language if I had not a serene and clear conscience." And on this occasion at least, Ludwig chose to believe him.

---

* Prince Taxis, who was allowed to live outside the Residenz, had rooms in the nearby Türkenstrasse.

** Franz Leinfelder, The Court Archivist.

CHAPTER TWO

THE YOUTHFUL KING

AT the end of January King Max, in defiance of medical advice, hurried back to crisis-bound Munich from Italy where he had been wintering in an attempt to boost his deteriorating health. The crisis in question had been building up for some time. With the death of King Friedrich VII of Denmark, a bitter dispute had erupted between the Confederation of German States, the Austro-Hungarian Empire and Denmark herself as to the rightful ownership of the twin Duchies of Schleswig and Holstein, which lay between North Germany and Denmark.

Maximilian had participated at a meeting of Princes called at Frankfurt by Emperor Franz Josef of Austria the previous year. Despite much *brouhaha*, little of constructive value had been achieved and the verbal battle for supremacy had continued between the old rival powers, Prussia and Austria, until the situation became so abrasive that war seemed inevitable.

Disturbing reports of a new Prussian ultimatum to Denmark now brought the 53 year old Max rushing home in a panic. Never a man to leave his ministers to do his work for him, he preferred to attend to such matters personally. His attitude towards the capabilities of his sons, now 19 and 17, was no better, being reminiscent of that of Queen Victoria of England towards the unfortunate Prince of Wales who was left to languish in idleness until late middle age, by which time he had virtually lost interest. Although the Bavarian King saw to it that his sons were kept occupied, he never allowed them to perform even the most trivial of functions in public and kept them in strict ignorance of what was going on in the country and at Court.

Now that the Crown Prince had come of age, he might reasonably have been expected to involve himself in State affairs but he was given no opportunity to do so. Erroneously, Max had little faith in Ludwig but was always the first to complain when the Crown Prince, dispirited by his father's attitude, returned to his own pursuits. Thus while Ludwig was less than interested in politics he could recite the plays of Schiller, Goethe and Shakespeare by heart. He was the despair of his parents but the darling of the theatricals and academics, always ready for a stimulating discussion on music, literature or, indeed, anything of an aesthetic nature. He was also much loved and revered by the foresters, farmers and gamekeepers on the royal estates with whom he felt a great affinity, and with whom he shared a love of Bavaria which would have greatly surprised his unseeing father who considered him to be totally feckless.

As a result of the curious educational methods employed by La Rosée, Ludwig's character was by this time an unfortunate and mystifying collection of contradictions and paradoxes. Since his early childhood, he had been made over-conscious of his unique and exalted status by La Rosée to the extent where he could scarcely bring himself to pass the time of day with aristocrats and court officials. Yet when his own personality asserted itself, he was happy to share a peasant's frugal meal of cheese and ale and engage him in animated conversation concerning his life and livelihood.

Notoriously soft hearted, a favourite story circulated to the effect that, on one occasion, he insisted upon having a chair brought for an ailing guard on palace duty. Another anecdote, dating from his early childhood, told of the request to his father that he might put some of his own meagre dinner into the pocket of another sentry who appeared to have a hungry interest in the royal dinner table. These small acts of kindness, together with much larger ones, were well documented throughout his life and his attitude towards those less fortunate than himself never changed. Yet his staff and ministerium never stopped complaining about his cold unapproachability. He was already the complete enigma. His moods and his affections changed like quicksilver but after the bitterest quarrel with a friend or counsellor, he would go out of his way to do some special favour for that person and was always the first to make amends. In later life, he dismissed staff with some frequency but invariably ensured that some other post or a generous pension was arranged for the offender. He certainly never learned to do this from his parents' example for although Ludwig and his brother always received suitable presents on his birthday and at Christmas, Max and Marie were not noted for their efforts to gladden their sons' childhood.

The moment Maximilian set foot in Munich in January, he retired to a sick bed from which he was never to rise. Ludwig found it hard to sympathise with the father he scarcely knew and created a sensation by appearing at the opera when most of the Court stayed away in deference to the King's indisposition. He refused to be cheated out of the pleasure of hearing the tenor, Albert Niemann, who was to make a guest appearance in *Lohengrin*, an event from which fifty stricken fathers could not have kept him. From Niemann's first enthralling entrance, Ludwig was blind to the portly, self-esteeming tenor and saw only the living Knight of the Swan. Lohengrin was superhuman, a perfect, romantic being who would not destroy his illusions and to the hypersensitive young man that was, perhaps, the most important thing

of all. Despite his youth, Ludwig had already experienced the bitterness of disappointment when those he thought to be devoted to him
were shown to be no more than ambitious sycophants or fair weather
friends. Small wonder that he went overboard for Niemann.

Against all advice, Ludwig attended every performance of the opera
in which Niemann appeared, granted him long private audiences and
showered him with gifts. Inevitably, tongues began to wag, but Ludwig
ignored them, safe in the knowledge that the Crown Prince was born
to break the rules as well as make them, or so he thought. In a state of
euphoria, he wrote to his cousin Anna of Hesse, "The other night I got
someone to throw him lots of flowers, and I sent him a pair of cufflinks
with swans and brilliants. Also a cross, which gave him great pleasure.
Gardez-vous silence! Je vous supplié!"

The request for silence was superfluous since by this time everyone
in the Munich Residenz was aware of the young man's interest in the
tenor and lost no time in acquainting their friends with the details.

Despite the optimism of the official bulletins, Maximilian II died on
March 9th 1864 with his wife at his side. Stupid and empty-headed as
she was, Marie had loved him in her way, although her entry in her
family chronicle rings suspiciously of bathos: "I felt that I myself was
dead and had passed into the next world. Even if death separates us,
our hearts cling together" which, in view of their respective natures,
sounds highly unlikely. As for Ludwig himself, it is improbable that he
felt any great sorrow since they had been almost strangers and indeed,
Ludwig had little for which to thank his father.

There was more than an element of hypocrisy about Max's death,
for what was euphemistically termed "a catarrh of the nose, throat and
trachea" was in fact the harvest of wild oats sown in his youth. The root
cause of Max's many ailments, namely, syphillis, was discreetly ignored
by all and in particular by the family physicians who had no desire to
lose their very lucrative posts; nevertheless, they were all old enough
to remember his scandalous affaires with common prostitutes when he
was still under age. At one stage, he had been as wild and immoral as
his much-criticised father, Ludwig I ever was, but had been effectively
tamed by the early contraction of venereal disease during a visit to
Hungary. Burdened with this unpleasant affliction, it had obviously
not been too difficult for him to develop into a blameless and respected
monarch, but it would be interesting to know if Marie ever realised
exactly what she had married and, indeed, it is worth speculating
further on the effects of his illness on his sons and whether he had
infected his wife as well. Incredibly, no word of reproach was heard
against this remarkably charmless and inconsiderate man.

Not quite 19 years old, Ludwig was now King and, full of enthusiasm for his new role, he expected life to change overnight. For months before his coming of age, he had hardly been able to contain his impatience at the prospect of being his own master, but although he had been granted a few miserly concessions, he had still found himself disappointingly lacking in the hoped-for freedom to do exactly as he pleased and the influence of Count la Rosée still held him more or less in check. With his accession, poor Ludwig discovered all too soon that his leisure and freedom was to be even more restricted than before.

La Rosée, appears to have been uncertain as to what he wanted from his charge, and their relationship continued to be strained and abrasive. It was his duty to produce a future King capable of command and decision as well as of deep understanding of his country and the Government; if he failed to do so after so many years of effort he would have been regarded as a failure himself. Yet even while he constantly reminded the staff of the Royal household that they must behave with great deference towards the King and persuaded Ludwig himself that he was a superior being, he had a deep-seated, perhaps subconscious, desire to remain superior to the boy and even to sublimate his will. He could not have it both ways and it was undoubtedly this curious dilemma which resulted in Ludwig's later difficulties in his personal relationships.

While the body of King Maximilian II lay in state in the private chapel at the Residenz, his features set in the same mould of cold indifference as they had worn in life, his heir stood in another part of the building waiting nervously for the Taking of the Oath. Although there was no coronation ceremonial as such in Bavaria, the occasion of the taking of the Oath was a most solemn and awe-inspiring one and Ludwig was deeply affected by it. Had it been any more spectacular than it was, the excessively shy Prince might well have recoiled at the thought of being stared at by a thousand pairs of eyes and developed one of the sudden diplomatic ailments so beloved of the Wittelsbachs as a means of avoiding or at least postponing it. His terror of the funeral procession which obliged him to go on foot through the streets of Munich had already resulted in a 24 hour postponement ; the sympathetic public assumed that he had been too griefstricken to appear and his apparent display of filial love was much admired. But those same fickle Burghers were capable of instantaneous reversals of mood. Fortunately, possibly because of his own mercurial nature, Ludwig appears to have sensed this very early on.

The Oathtaking was neither long nor complex and when Ludwig spoke the words he meant sincerely to stand by what he promised: "Almighty God has called my dear, much beloved father from this earth; I cannot express the feelings which stir in my breast. The task is great and heavy. I shall call on God to send me light and strength so that I might fulfil it. I shall reign true to the Oath which I am taking and in the spirit of our constitution which has been tested now for almost half a century. The well-being of my beloved Bavarian people and Germany's greatness are the aim of my endeavours. Support me, all of you, in my difficult duty!"

And support him they did. Ludwig was their darling. On March 14th, Max was duly interred and the moment the public saw their new King they forgot the old one. Most of them who came to pay their respects to Max had never laid eyes on Ludwig before and the sight of him walking with his younger brother in the cortège created a sensation. The Crown Prince was by this time a towering six feet four inches, taller than his father had been and taller, in fact, than most Bavarians. Slim and upright and elegant, he was so handsome that even the most blasé of men found him fascinating. Because of his constant exposure to the Alpine air his skin was lightly tanned although his nervousness made him appear paler than usual. His full lips were perhaps a shade effeminate in their sensuality, but this did not detract from the beauty of his youthful freshness. His deepset eyes were dark blue with a dreamy expression which all but his ministers found irresistible. He rarely looked directly at those about him but, like an actor, would fix his gaze high above him on some distant object or, on occasions, on the ground. The picture was completed by his shock of dark hair which was carefully curled and coiffed away from his face to disguise the fact that his ears were a little too large for his head and his head a little too small for his body.

For the funeral, he wore the uniform of an infantry colonel and despite the bitter weather walked with his head uncovered. With his unusual height he towered above the other members of the cortège, commanding the attention of all. By comparison, his brother Otto seemed as weak and unformed as a child although in fact the 17 year old was of an athletic and pleasing build and his physical constitution was stronger than that of Ludwig, who was prone to colds, toothaches and throat infections.

As much a stranger at this time to the Munich public as Ludwig, Prince Otto could not hope to match the good looks or magnetic charm of his elder brother, but he was nevertheless an attractive youth who soon became very popular. He had reddish gold hair, the same nervous, oversensitive lips and the same large and lustrous eyes. His brows were straight and more finely drawn than those of his brother, and elongated features lent him a deceptively intellectual appearance. Deceptive, because Otto was cast in a very different mould from Ludwig; he already enjoyed the rough masculine company of the army officers attached to the Royal household and that of his Wittelsbach cousins with whom he was on friendly terms. He did not change greatly and a few years later Ludwig was to write of him in response to a written comment from Cosima von Bülow, "You said you imagined my brother to be an understanding and companionable friend to me; oh no, dear *Freundin*! He is a thoroughly commonplace person, completely without feeling for anything noble or beautiful. He often hunts all day, spends a lot of time with my dull and superficial cousins and spends his evenings mostly at the music hall where what he enjoys most is the ballet." In other words, all the things which Ludwig himself despised. Nobody minded, least of all Ludwig. Since the latter was young and comparatively healthy, it was considered unlikely that Otto would ever become King and his development was therefore considered to be highly satisfactory.

Since childhood, the younger Wittelsbach had shown a marked interest in things military, keen on toy soldiers and the like while Ludwig's preference was for books and building bricks. To a psychologist these childhood interests might well have offered some clue as to the boys' future development but to Max such observations would have meant nothing. He was interested only in facts and the more obvious aspects of life. Otto had been a thin and sensitive child, lively and affectionate and although slightly more outgoing than Ludwig, had still been very shy. Now that he was approaching manhood, he had acquired at least a veneer of gaiety and bonhomie but hidden deep inside him lay a nervous and highly strung temperament. His moodiness and tendency to become over-excited was totally ignored although such traits would scarcely seem the most obvious attributes for an army officer. His father remained of the opinion that discipline mends all ills, bends all wills, and was quite satisfied with what appeared on the surface.

Both young men initially made a good impression on the crowd who had turned out in force to enjoy a good funeral, but it was Ludwig who won their almost hysterical love. Their obvious delight and approval came as a complete surprise to him and although he was too timid to acknowledge their enthusiastic welcome, he was certainly warmed by it.

Ludwig quickly became accustomed to his new status and although he was initially disappointed because he would not now be able to attend the University, looked forward instead to doing other things which had hitherto been denied him. To his credit, although he had never enjoyed a good rapport with his Governor, he kept La Rosée on his staff "for life" and promoted him to the rank of Major General although his sense of what was correct may well have been spiced with the knowledge that, since La Rosée was already a sick and, indeed, a dying man, he would not have to suffer him for very long. In the event, La Rosée died soon afterwards.

In the first euphoria of becoming King, Ludwig was extremely conscious of his duty. As he rather touchingly wrote to his former Governess, "I carry my heart to the Throne – a heart which beats for my people and which glows for their welfare – all Bavarians *may be sure of that*. I will do everything in my power to make my people happy; their welfare, their peace, are the conditions of my own happiness." Yet despite La Rosée's rigorous teaching, or possibly because of it, Ludwig had still to grapple with a sense of inferiority as well as his innate dislike for too much formality and constriction. The truth was that, despite his childish love of dressing up, he was too much of an intellectual rebel to appreciate the trappings of Monarchy and like most of the Wittelsbachs, he heartily loathed the empty social activities with which he was expected to occupy himself.

By mid-April, some of the euphoria had worn off and his demanding new schedule had already become a tiresome chore. Hinting to Leonrod that the new life was scarcely different from the old one, he described the tedium of an average day which was evidently quite a strain as well as a bore even for one who had been trained with such a task in mind: "In the morning, the secretaries come at 1/2 10 o'clock, and then I go out; dinner is at 4 o'clock and at 6 o'clock one of the secretaries comes alternately and then Leinfelder reads the papers out loud, whch lasts until around 8 o'clock; then comes tea."

Small wonder that after only a few weeks, the novelty of becoming King and dwindled to the despairing realisation that, far from being free to do as he pleased, he had lost what little freedom he had. Unable to bear the prospect of being condemned forever to a life of social functions and rigid protocol, he decided that he might as well take advantage of his position to carry out a plan which had lain dormant for some time; he resolved to bring his idol, the poet-composer Richard Wagner, to Munich.

To this end he enlisted the aid of the secretary whom he had inherited from his father. For weeks Ludwig had scrutinised the Munich Strangers' List in vain and at last asked Pfistermeister why Wagner's name never appeared on it. Pfistermeister's offhand reply that "Wagner is a common name - which one does Majesty have in mind?" elicited the haughty but passionate rejoinder, "There is only one Wagner" which must have struck a chill into the secretary's heart, for there is no doubt that Pfistermeister was only too well aware who Ludwig meant.

At 34, Franz von Pfistermeister had a reasonably secure place at

Court, was reasonably well liked and was, in short, a reasonable man. He had known Ludwig from childhood and, being accustomed to the ways of the Wittelsbachs, must have had some idea what lay before him under the new King. He therefore set off for Vienna somewhat reluctantly to find Richard Wagner, a gargantuan task since that gentleman was well known, among other things, for his elusiveness. Everyone at Court was aware of Ludwig's passion for the works of Wagner although at this time he was better known among the masses for his political rather than his aesthetic works. To Ludwig's more worldly associates, Wagner was a dangerous man, an unsavoury upstart and political rebel with a penchant for preying on other men's wives and worse, on other men's bank accounts. He had already spent many years in exile, following involvement in a plot to set fire to the Royal Palace in Dresden, for which he was remembered far more vividly than for his opera *Tannhäuser*.

Having abandoned his neglected although not entirely blameless wife, Minna, in Vienna, Wagner at this time was as usual awaiting rescue in a squalid lodging. He was eternally falling into some financial abyss yet when he did find himself in funds, lived beyond his means. His customary means of support was his current mistress but at the moment he was without such comfort since he was on the brink of a far more meaningful affaire with a woman of a totally different type. Many of his earlier mistresses had been upper class women with wealthy and apparently blind husbands but he had squandered every chance which came his way. Thus, in the spring of 1864, he found himself pursued by the usual howling pack of creditors and by the time Pfistermeister arrived in Vienna, Wagner had already fled. With some relief, the secretary made his way back to Munich with his negative report, presumably hoping that the young King's whim was already forgotten. Unfortunately for him, he had underestimated the power of Ludwig's longing to meet his hero: the King was furious and despatched the reluctant Pfistermeister forthwith to pick up the trail.

The composer was again in hiding at Penzing, near Vienna, but when the secretary arrived Wagner's manservant, Mrasek, told him that Wagner had "gone to Russia". Pfistermeister naturally took this information with a pinch of salt and with the aid of a bribe, extracted from him the name of a certain Dr. Uhl* as the likely host of the elusive composer. Dr. Uhl's scruples troubled him not at all and Wagner was at last traced at the home of another of his mistresses, Frau Doctor Elise Wille. Since his tendency to become involved in emotional as well as political and financial intrigues was also well known, Pfistermister could scarcely have been surprised.

---

* Editor of the Süddeutscher Botschafter.

Meantime, with a blend of sadness and irritation the King had learned of the death of his aunt, Princess Luitpold, an event which plunged the Court into mourning. Pfistermeister arrived back in Munich to find everyone shrouded in black and Ludwig sulking in his room in a mood of the same colour, claiming to have "catarrh" in order to avoid attending his aunt's funeral. Whether or not his sufferings were genuine, he remained chained to his room for another nine days, but he was not too ill to write a long letter to Wagner, an effusion steeped in flattery and admiration calculated to bring the composer running. In his near-ecstatic fan letter he expressed the wish to meet personally the composer who had given him such pleasure and spiritual uplift with his wonderful works and, in particular, with his opera *Lohengrin*. As an enticement, he enclosed a gold and ruby ring and a signed photograph of himself. Wagner obligingly accepted everything.

Pfistermeister's efforts to find Wagner helped to keep him in office. The composer had led him an exasperating dance across half Europe and had received him with extreme rudeness before finally accepting his credentials. When the ill-assorted pair arrived in the Bavarian capital, the composer took advantage of his unexpected good fortune by engaging the best suite at the Hotel Bayerischerhof, naturally at the King's expense. Pfistermeister was outraged but his hands were tied; he could only pay up cheerfully on the King's behalf and hope that he would take a dislike to the boastful and greedy Saxon.

When Ludwig received his hero for the first time the following day he was so nervous that he kept him waiting for some time while he controlled himself. At last Wagner was ushered into the blue and gold audience chamber with its blue velvet rondell and plethora of exotic plants but found the room apparently empty. Ludwig then emerged from behind the miniature jungle having first scrutinised his guest without being subjected to the same torture. He stood staring at Wagner for some time with a slightly quizzical smile on his lips. If he had been shocked by the composer's dreadful physical appearance, he was either too polite or too astounded to show it. The reality must nevertheless have been very different from his dreams.

Richard Wagner was 51 years of age at this time but looked somewhat older. He was raddled and racked with excess of various kinds, with a stocky body surmounted by a large head. His hair, receding from a high domed forehead, flowed into a long, lank mane and his little eyes, bright and embedded deep in the loose folds of flesh, resembled those of an elephant. He was heavily perfumed with Chypre, this embellishment being a last minute effort both to disguise his unwashed state and to beguile the King whose fondness for this particular scent was well known. A sybaritic adventurer and a political firebrand,

Wagner nevertheless possessed a personal magnetism and worldly charm which throughout his life he used outrageously to further his own ends. During this first meeting with the King, he employed all of these wiles to their full degree.

As he stood before Ludwig, his head was bowed respectfully but his eyes, gazing boldly up at the King from under his brows, betrayed his impudence. This boldness should have cautioned Ludwig but he was apparently too thrilled to notice. The Monarch who rarely offered more than two outstretched fingers in greeting because he hated the physical contact of handshaking even paid Wagner the unprecedented honour of a warm embrace. Wagner took it as his right.

King and composer launched themselves immediately into an animated conversation which culminated with the wily composer extracting from his 19 year old admirer all manner of extravagant promises. Wagner had waited for years in a vortex of poverty and discontent for a wealthy patron to appear. All his life he had been dependent upon others for his survival, his prey consisting mainly of rich and lonely women. Many of these ladies had furthered his career, given him encouragement, introductions, a roof over his head, more love and admiration than he deserved and, above all, money, which had invariably been squandered on fripperies with no thought of settling his outstanding debts. Male benefactors had been treated with the same disregard and when they had served their purpose he left them all without remorse or gratitude.

All previous acts of charity, friendship and love now paled as he basked in the warmth of feeling which exhuded from the young King. He saw himself sequestered at last under Royal patronage and was doubtless already dreaming of the benefits which such patronage could bring. In the preface to one of his works, he had prayed for a saviour with an open hand. As he gazed up at the eager young man before him, he realised that his prayer had been answered. A man well versed in the ways of the world, he did not believe that the King had sought him out and brought him to Munich merely to praise his work. Instinct told him that he might expect tangible expression of the King's all too obvious admiration.

Ludwig on his side was determined to do all he could to further the career of the middle-aged degenerate who now stood before him. Despite Wagner's obvious shortcomings, he recognised genius when he saw it and thought the world should not be denied the fruits of that genius. Unfortunately, in common with many others, Wagner misconstrued Ludwig's motives and assumed that his natural warmth and over-effusive manner of expressing his wishes indicated something more personal than the enthusiastic love of the arts which it actually was. Wagner deceived himself fundamentally as to the true nature of their relationship and in all the years they knew each other, he was never to put it into its true perspective.

Ludwig may have worshipped the artist but he was far from smitten by the debauched, decaying reprobate: how could he have been when his life revolved around beauty in its various forms? Most of the things which Ludwig cherished and respected stemmed not from the prosaic ugliness of the 19th Century but from the ethics and aesthetics of earlier centuries and mythology. His heroes in the modern world were few and less real to him than the noble personages of the old Germanic legends. Only poetry and music could lend a spark of warmth and happiness to Ludwig's sad and rather empty young life and he did not appreciate his enviable position in society. With the exception of Paul of Taxis, he had no real friends and had little in common with his brother. It was inevitable that he would grasp eagerly at the man who had come bearing such an attractive cornucopia of brilliantly coloured dreams. "I feel," he told the delighted composer, "As if we had changed places, you and I, for you seem to be more like the King while I am the man of the theatre. It is *you* to whom *I* must pay homage." Wagner was naturally in complete agreement.

That first audience lasted for an hour and three quarters, thus creating a sensation in the Residenz; most mortals were given only a few minutes of the King's time and even this somewhat grudgingly conceded. Ludwig was deliriously happy to meet the man whose work he had for so long admired, and Wagner was equally pleased to discuss that rivetingly fascinating subject, himself. In a letter to his cousin, Princess Sophie in Bavaria, who professed to have a great interest in Wagner's work (mainly, one suspects, to attract Ludwig's attention), the King enthused, "If only you had been a witness as to how his thanks embarrassed me as I reassured him, by giving him my hand, that his great *Nibelungen* would not only be completed, but that a production, as he wants it, will take place, that I shall carry all the responsibility! Then he bowed low over my hand and seemed moved by it, which was so natural that he stayed for a long time in this position without speaking. I had the sensation that we had changed roles. I moved closer towards him with the feeling in my heart that I was taking an oath to be bound faithfully to him for all time."

Wagner's own account of their first meeting in a letter to the long-suffering Elisa Wille, makes interesting reading: "I would be an ungrateful creature if I did not write to you immediately to tell you of my boundless happiness! You know that the young King of Bavaria has been searching for me. Today, I shall go to him. He is unfortunately so handsome and brilliant, so soulful and fine, that I fear his life must dissolve like a winged dream of the Gods in this mundane world. He loves me with the tenderness and fervour of a first love. He knows all about me and understands my soul as I do myself. He wants me to work, rest and produce my works; he wants to give me everything that I need for it. I shall finish the *Nibelung* and he will produce it the way I want it. I shall be my own master, not a conductor, nothing but myself and his friend. And he understands everything serious, as when you and I speak together. All need shall be taken from me. I shall have all I want. I have only to stay with him. What do you say to that? Is it not unbelievable? Can it be anything but a dream? You can imagine the mood I am in (...) My happiness is so great that I am quite shattered. You can have no idea of the magic of his eyes; it is an unheard of miracle."

Unfortunately, Ludwig appeared to confirm Wagner's extravagant claims by offering his assurance that "everything is arranged" and by repeating in a letter his verbal promises that Pfistermeister should find him somewhere suitable to live. The additional comforting reassurance that his financial worries were at an end was music in Wagner's ears, for if there was anything he loved more than he loved himself, it was money. Ludwig concluded his letter with words which he later had good cause to regret: "Oh, how I have looked forward to the time when I could do this! I hardly dared to indulge myself in the hope of being able so soon to prove my love to you."

This particular sentiment was probably the only one he truly shared with Wagner.

CHAPTER THREE

ELISABETH

FOR five days Ludwig was in ecstasy, bathed in the magical atmosphere created by Wagner. His infatuation was not for Wagner the man. Far from it. He had quickly found the composer to be devious, irritating and mendacious. He was beguiled by the man's artistic genius and it was this alone which claimed his attention.

The bond of mutual admiration which had been forged between the two was like a sparkling stream in which the composer was content for the moment to immerse himself. What Wagner most admired in the young King, apart from his good looks, was his wealth and generosity and to the chagrin of Ludwig's anxious advisers, the impecunious Saxon was showered with gifts, not the least of which were monetary. He found it surprisingly easy to convince the King that he could not work with a collection of debts hanging over his head and that his dire need of money overshadowed his creative genius. Ludwig's own finances had improved with his accession but he knew all too well from his childhood experiences what it was like to be without funds and was ready to lend a sympathetic ear to his new friend.

Each time Wagner left the Residenz, his rewards were such that a lackey was sent to help him carry off his spoils. The endless presents from the adoring King flowed unremittingly forth and with his customary rapacity, Wagner greedily accepted everything without thought of reciprocation unless, of course, he regarded his poetry readings and piano recitals to be sufficient return. The opportunity to talk unrestrainedly about himself and to be paid for doing so made him sublimely happy. He was highly flattered to find that his young listener already knew by heart whole chapters of his written works on the arts and every word of his published libretti. So ardent an admirer was usually feminine and to be held in such high esteem by a member of his own sex was intoxicating indeed.

"If I had any idea that I would find a youth as wonderful as the King!" he enthused in a letter to a friend, "No topic, however remote, ever wearies him; for hours on end I talk with him about art and his enthusiasm becomes stronger all the time. The King is still so young, and has so little yearning to be amused, to have amusement to pass the time. His wonderful eyes must be the mirror of a heavenly soul; sometimes I find a rare luminosity in them which quite astonishes me. It has nothing to do with that particular moment, but seems of quite a different world." This was strong stuff from the man who was later to claim that all the affection was on Ludwig's side!

The greedy opportunist took full advantage of the new friendship and soon found himself surrounded by enemies in the Residenz. Gossip flourished about the strange and unsuitable relationship which looked like becoming even more scandalous than Ludwig's earlier warm friendship with the singer, Albert Niemann.

Ludwig's advisers were so worried by the way the wind was blowing that they even asked the Queen Mother to intervene, but Marie had so little influence over her son that she had no idea how to go about doing so. Throughout her husband's reign no one had known her place as well as Marie, and while her prosaic domesticity and forbearance from interfering in anything but general household matters may have endeared her to some court officials, it was freely acknowledged by others that as a mother she was totally useless. Now that she no longer sat on the Throne, she receded even further into the background; no one meeting her in the Hofgarten or in the street, where she frequently walked unattended, would have supposed her to be anything but a fairly well-to-do if somewhat provincial housewife. In her later years, she occasionally liked to sit for an hour or two in the Hofbräuhaus in Munich with a measure of ale before her* and only here can we see a sign of the abnormal in her makeup: while other Hesses and Hohenzollerns spent their years locked in padded cells or indulging in their flights of fancy, Marie's eccentricity lay merely in a penchant for emulating the common man in the local or to work like a kitchen maid in the privacy of the hut at Bleckenau (and for an arrogant Hohenzollern, this was most assuredly eccentric). Yet she was ever the first to criticise her elder son, whose own foibles at least produced tangible and, indeed, breathtaking results.

Marie's lack of comprehension drove Ludwig to distraction and by the time he had been on the Throne for a few weeks, he had successfully learned the art of avoiding her, paring down their encounters to one visit for tea per week and as, with the exception of the Countess Fugger, he did not enjoy the company of her ladies, made certain that he could always plead a prior engagement as a means of escape.

Meantime, the friendship between the King and Wagner flourished unchecked. Their talks together were animated and searching, their discussions on music, philosophy and the arts rewarding to the King beyond his wildest dreams. Never before had he had such an opportunity to stretch his brain; he thus declared himself the "slave" of the "Great Friend" as he termed Wagner, and so far that gentleman had wisely refrained from discussing politics with the impressionable young

---

* Empress Elisabeth of Austria also habitually did this when she visited her family in Bavaria.

man. Evidently he had decided that there would be time enough for this later and contented himself the present with answering the King's endless questions on the arts.Wagner's earlier political ambitions still flourished and he somewhat over-confidently saw himself as the potential ruler of Bavaria opposed only by Ludwig's outraged Ministerium. To a confidante he boasted, "And then there is the delightful way he cares for me, the attractive chastity of his heart, of his every feature, when he assures me of his happiness in possessing me. So we often sit there, gazing dumbly, lost in each other's eyes. He does not talk to me; we are simply and utterly one. Thus the Court stands completely open to me. If I wanted to take an ambitious role there, he would not deny me." This was nonsense although Ludwig did make him one irresistible offer and when the composer returned to Vienna it was only to settle his affairs before returning to Bavaria on a "temporarily permanent" basis, to live and work under Royal patronage.

Because of his increasingly interesting private life, the facts of which he had neglected to tell Ludwig, Wagner had no great desire to commit himself too deeply, but at the same time he would have been a fool to forego so golden an opportunity. With his inherent nomadic streak and the continual need for flight from his creditors, the chances are that he would have left Vienna in any case; he therefore regarded Ludwig's invitation merely as an unanticipated bonus to be accepted without any expectation of having to honour his promises.

It was Ludwig's custom to spend the months of May and June at Schloss Berg on Lake Starnberg and Pfistermeister, albeit unwillingly, had arranged for Wagner to rent the Villa Seehaus at nearby Percha, a charming summer residence owned by the Count Pellet. Starnberg then as now was a popular haunt for holidaymakers and the inhabitants of the expensive villas and summer houses were to a large extent wealthy aristocrats who came only to spend weekends and summer holidays at the lakeside.

The composer's initial disappointment at not being invited to stay in the Royal residence itself soon evaporated when he discovered that he had the best of the bargain. Schloss Berg was small, square and comparatively simply furnished in the popular Biedermeyer style. Another visitor was to describe it somewhat critically as being "...almost devoid of personnel and unguarded; there was a single Gendarme to be seen at the main gate but no porter, no officials, no servants. The rooms, simply appointed with old furniture, were almost unheated. In the corridors and anterooms were all sorts of domestics, kitchen boys and chambermaids milling around in an assortment of garbs. The whole house smelled unpleasantly of photographic fluid*. Ludwig was

* Ludwig was a keen photographer .

very fond of the place, however, and spent something like half the year there. When he was in Munich he usually spent his weekends there as well.

The King enjoyed taking Wagner to his favourite haunts in Starnberg and the nearby Ammerland, but his pleasure was somewhat one-sided; the womanising Wagner, who had a new love, was aching for feminine company despite his proud boast to Elise Wille, "He is completely aware of who I am and what I need." Nor had he any compunction about writing "Not a word have I to waste about my situation. He feels that a King's prerogative must assuredly suffice to keep all common cares from me so that I can give myself totally to my muse, and procure for me every means to produce my works how and when I want. At present, he resides mostly in a little castle near to me. In ten minutes the carriage takes me there. He sends once or twice daily; then I fly as if to a lover. It is a fascinating interview. This thirst for instruction, this comprehension, this quiver and glow! I have never encountered such splendid unrestraint."

But even as he penned this eulogy to one who certainly knew him well enough to read between the lines, he was dying of boredom without his rowdy crew of satellites and pining for the caresses of a more exciting companion than the young King. Unable to endure Ludwig's hero worship any longer, Wagner had already summoned his clique to join him at Percha: Peter Cornelius, Hans von Bülow and his wife Cosima, together with their two children. Ludwig of course had no idea that he was now extending his hospitality to six people instead of one. Ungratefully, Wagner trampled on his kindness, even though he had just been granted a stipend of 40,000 Gulden, to be paid in advance, with the additional benefit of free accommodation in a luxurious villa to which he could never otherwise have aspired. Yet after only a few days, he was already grumbling openly to his cronies that he regarded the audiences with the King as a tedious and inavoidable chore. Ever ready to complain, he grumbled to Frau Wille, "I think only about myself and my advantages and am so well hidden that nobody can disturb me, but nevertheless there is something wrong with my composition and I attribute this to my close companionship with the King."

Almost simultaneously and quite illogically, he wrote to another long-suffering confessor, Julius Froebel, "In political matters, the complete immaturity of the young Sovereign has now become so clear to me that I have given up all attempts for the time being to alter his opinions (...) The art of governing has once again fallen into the domain of common bureaucrats. This youth, full of fantasies, is afraid of the repulsive machinery and his fear expresses itself quickly in a kind of shy respect for it (...) It is so difficult to comprehend to the full the development of this greatly talented Prince who might well become the saviour of the German people when he matures; my belief in him - but only in him - remains unshakeable. This is the key which Herr von der Pfordten* does not possess, I can assure you of that."

Wagner was wrong about Ludwig even in this. At no time was he ever "immature" in the matter of politics. He was in fact most astute, quick to grasp a situation and to see the best possible solution. What he lacked was the impetus and the encouragement of others to take action against what was going on around him. He began his reign on the wrong foot by allowing his Ministerium too much freedom and by not imposing change to suit his own far from feeble ideas. His attitude and gradual loss of interest was undoubtedly hardened by the fact that they refused to take him seriously. Contrary to what many people thought, he was far from ignorant of the political situation and was probably better informed than his Ministers. Not until the last years of his life did his finger leave the political pulse of Bavaria, but it suited him to give the impression that he neither knew nor cared about what was going on.

The situation was not improved when Wagner began to boast to anyone who would listen that he held Ludwig in the palm of his hand, a statement which was both erroneous and foolhardy. The King was not so besotted that he did not know the effect on his reputation if the extent of his generosity to the arrogant composer should become public. He therefore sent Pfistermeister to him to say that, if he felt obliged to discuss the matter of his stipend at all, he was to mention a sum considerably lower than the actual amount. Wagner agreed although he had in fact already boasted extensively of his good fortune. Ludwig was justifiably annoyed when he discovered this but he became really angry and left for Munich in a huff when Wagner's friends arrived *en masse* in response to his invitation. The composer thus had his first taste of the Royal rage. The King was bitterly disappointed by the abrupt end to his idyll but was not foolish enough to regard the relationship as being at an end because Wagner's manners could not match his talent.

With Ludwig safely back in the Residenz Wagner had more time to devote to his guests and, in particular, to his latest inamorata, the fascinating and intellectual wife of his friend, Hans von Bülow. His illicit relationship with Cosima had ripened quickly and easily while poor Bülow sat bowed over Wagner's scores, painstakingly making copies of these lengthy works because the Master himself was too lazy to turn his hand to such laborious tasks.

Cosima von Bülow was tall, thin, auburn haired and elegant with a

---

* Ludwig von der Pfordten, the Prime Minister.

strong facial resemblance to her father, the much-acclaimed composer, Franz Liszt, and with the sheer force of her personality she soon dominated even the ebullient Wagner. "That red haired person", as Queen Marie, who disliked her intensely, was to call her, soon made herself as unpopular at Court as Wagner himself. The latter, ever a man to flout convention, was unconcerned at the idea of making a fool and a cuckold of the little Prussian who, with the exception of Ludwig, had done more to help him than anyone else. Bülow was a fine musician in his own right, a conductor and pianist of merit who believed in Wagner's genius to the extent where he was prepared to sublimate his own talent to further the Master's cause. He was also charmless and ugly with a genius for saying the wrong thing and, like Wagner, he left a trail of enemies behind him wherever he went.

Fortunately for the composer, Ludwig's anger was short-lived. Determined not to let Wagner out of his sight until he had completed and produced the promised *Meistersinger von Nürnberg* and, as agreed, had supervised the first production of *Tristan und Isolde*, he did everything he could to please his irritating genius; Wagner was given a carriage and horses and an imposing town house, the Villa Gôtham, in Munich's fashionable Briennerstrasse. Unblushingly, Wagner pointed out that to maintain so luxurious an establishment he would need a larger stipend; although he had actually already frittered away most of the 40,000 had already received, he assured the King that it had gone to pay his creditors. A hopeless spendthrift, Wagner went through life incurring debts which he could not settle in the confident expectation that someone with an open hand would turn up at the last moment to put things right.

He liked to live well, even opulently: he would buy vast quantities of fine silks and satins, draping the walls and windows of his current abode, and also his person, with whole bales of brilliant scarlet, gold and purple. He would then parade before the mirror in these strange plumes, declaring that he could not compose a note without them. Despite his reputation for being quick tempered, Ludwig showed remarkable patience in tolerating him for as long as he did, for basically he was an unscrupulous confidence trickster with no idea of time, morals or money. He was the complete egocentric; he loved to be fêted and admired, seeing himself as some brilliant candle around which less richly endowed moths must hover. He genuinely believed himself to be a genius, which he was, and said so without reservation whenever he discussed himself, which was often.

Naturally sceptical and highly perceptive, Ludwig was certainly not blind to Wagner's many faults, but nevertheless allowed himself to be swept along on the tide of Wagner's flamboyance, giving in more and

more to his outrageous demands. All attempts to discourage the King
in his new friendship fell on seemingly deaf ears. It seemed not to occur
to his irate advisers that he was employing the most likely means of
persuading Wagner to work. With this aim in view, Ludwig ignored his
own instincts and chose to believe whatever Wagner told him. For
another opera of the importance of *Lohengrin, Tannhäuser* or *Der
Fliegende Holländer,* he was prepared to endure almost anything.

It was Pfistermeister's unhappy duty to take care of Wagner's
finances. Powerless to stop the young King from giving away his
money, the furious secretary could only console himself with loud
predictions of impending disaster. His efforts proved to be unnecessary
for in July Ludwig suddenly departed for Bad Kissingen without a word
of farewell to "The Great Friend".

The King found Kissingen so agreeable that he momentarily forgot
everything else. Europe's most prolific and eloquent correspondant
stayed at the Spa for a whole month without sending so much as a
postcard to his forgotten genius. So much for his "love unto death".

The official reason for Ludwig's visit was the discreet inspection of
the daughter of the Tzar of Russia as a prospective bride, but since
Marie was only ten years old at the time, he could scarcely be blamed
for dismissing the idea and concentrating instead on the more mature
ladies who were foregathered. With typical contrariness, he developed
a tendresse for Maria's mother, the Tzaritza Maria Alexandrowna,
although his feeling for her was undoubtedly more filial than amorous.
When, after anxiously watching Ludwig as he loaded her with expensive
gifts, Pfistermeister felt bound to remind him that the Tzaritza was not
only a married lady but was also old enough to be his mother, his
impassioned reply was "Oh, I wish she were!" Nevertheless, he accepted the reproof and thereafter sent only flowers and books to the
lovely Maria Alexandrowna.

Here again, Ludwig's capitulation was not all it seemed, for the truth
was that he had found mettle more attractive in another visitor: his
second cousin, the Empress Elisabeth of Austria. There has been
much speculation as to the relationship between Ludwig and Elisabeth
and while there is little remaining personal documentary evidence to
link them romantically, there was an undeniable bond between them
which has been well documented by their contemporaries and by
disapproving members of their respective staffs.

For Elisabeth, or Sisi, as she was known by her family, Kissingen was
only one of many Spas purporting to cure almost any ailment, and she
was a regular visitor. Aside from the medicinal properties of its waters,
it was a popular meeting place for members of Europe's royal houses.

Unlike most, however, the Empress had a restless temperament and rarely stayed anywhere for more than a few days.

At 26, she was an extremely beautiful woman with a mane of hip-length chestnut brown hair which she wore braided around her head like a coronet, but it was so heavy that in private she would wear it loose to relieve the fierce headaches which resulted from its weight. Her eyes, golden dark and luminous, gazed dreamily away from her surroundings in much the same way as Ludwig's. Tall, slender and supple; she had a penchant for gymnastics far ahead of her time and a great belief in walking as a healthy exercise. This belief was not shared by her ladies-in-waiting, since a stroll with Elisabeth might well last for anything up to seven hours and as she walked very fast, her companions often found it difficult to keep up with her. Riding was her greatest passion and she was said to be the best horsewoman in Europe, a pronouncement unpleasing to her sister Empress, Eugénie of France, who considered herself to be the rightful holder of that title. She also wrote poetry and in many of her verses is clearly to be seen her misery and loneliness. She thus had much in common with Ludwig, who adored her.

The cousins shared many characteristics, including a slightly imperious manner which concealed acute shyness and hypersensitivity. An unkind word or slight would send her into a deep depression which would make her physically ill for days, but when she was among friends, her charm and wit sparkled like crystal and her kindnesses belied her reputation for selfish indifference.

Originally, Elisabeth's elder sister had been chosen to be Franz Josef's Empress, but the moment he laid eyes on Elisabeth poor Hélène, pretty but prosaic, received scarcely a second glance. Although it was obvious to all that they were totally incompatible, the Emperor went against the wishes of his mother, who had no time for Elisabeth, in his determination to have her; Elisabeth's mother* agreed willingly enough since the Imperial Crown would still be in the family but Elisabeth was doomed. From the moment the 16 year old Princess arrived in Vienna, Archduchess Sophie did all she could to make her life a misery. The girl who had enjoyed a happy and liberated childhood had no idea how to behave as an Empress and, overcome by the open hostility of her mother-in-law and the inevitable acolytes, soon became cowed by the stiff formalities and open contempt of the Hofburg court.

Forbidden to follow her own pursuits or even to be alone with her husband except on the nights when Franz Josef chose to claim his conjugal rights (which she loathed), Elisabeth, for reasons unspecified but which provoked endless speculation, at last took flight and travelled

---

* Duchess Ludovika was the sister of Archduchess Sophie of Austria.

to Madeira. The official reason given for her absence was ill health and certainly she suffered endless coughs and chest complaints as well as swollen joints, but wagging tongues had it that her mysterious ailment was actually a venereal infection transmitted to her by her husband. In the light of circumstance, this is by no means unlikely. By this time, all Vienna knew of the marital differences and endless quarrels which electrified the Hofburg and while she received little sympathy most of her critics must have been aware of her difficult existence with her mother-in-law and that the Imperial newlyweds already had virtually nothing to say to each other.

The scandal of Sisi's departure was never to be forgotten. Four years later, her every move was avidly watched and commented upon by her enemies who were all too ready to run to Sophie with tales about the moody, capricious and bewildered Empress.

Elisabeth fanned the flames further by escaping from Vienna for a second time in 1863, this time to Corfu, where she was later to build an elegant villa, the Achilleion, whose lavish style owed much to the influence of her great uncle, Ludwig I of Bavaria. As on her previous trip to the sundrenched freedoms of other climes, she returned glowing with her former good health, looks and vitality, but after only a few hours in Vienna was reported to look as ill and miserable as before.

When the Empress appeared at Bad Kissingen in 1864, although she looked beautiful it was apparent that all was not well with her. The climate on Corfu coupled with the revolutionary slimming cures with which she had become obsessed had left a certain puffiness in her skin which betrayed a deficiency both of vitamins and happiness. Her weight loss was the talk of the Spa where most of the other ladies taking the more orthodox cure were of a more portly build. Franz Josef did nothing to aid her recovery. Cold and undemonstrative by nature, he had no patience with Elisabeth's misery and did not believe in meeting her halfway. The Emperor was selfish and stubborn, as prosaic as Ludwig's parents yet openly lustful, lecherous and blatantly unfaithful. He even left the shy and inexperienced Elisabeth to meditate alone on their wedding night to seek satisfaction in a brothel, but nevertheless expected her to play the dutiful wife. Elisabeth did not object to his infidelity since when he was with other women she was afforded respite from his unwelcome physical demands, but she was deeply upset by his lack of discretion and disgusted by his diseased body.

Despite his endless protestations of undying love for Elisabeth, the Emperor failed totally to understand her. Throughout their marriage he was fascinated by her unattainable beauty and showered her with gifts to enhance it but had no time for her aesthetic pursuits. Why did he continue to indulge her whims when to the casual onlooker it was she who had broken their marriage vows? Probably from a deepseated guilt for having contaminated her with the fruits of his own pursuits. He was promiscuous but not affectionate and he did not know the meaning of true love. His relationships centred entirely around lust or duty and his heart remained as cold as stone. As far as Elisabeth was concerned, her only obligation was to provide him with an heir and she had, in fact, presented him with a son and two daughters.*

Meeting her cousin Ludwig for the first time in several years, at Bad Kissingen, Elisabeth found herself totally in accord with the erudite and charming young man who in turn was all too obviously smitten by her and, despite a seven year age difference, they spent most of their time together. In such sympathetic company Ludwig, who had only intended to spend two or three days at the spa, found it hard to tear himself away and remained for a whole month. Elisabeth herself wrote home "I am entranced by our affinity during the many hours we have spent together." Ludwig himself was equally entranced and was to remain so until his death.

En route to Kissingen, the King had called on his grandfather, the deposed Ludwig I at his residence, the Johannisburg at Aschaffenburg. Their discussion had encompassed the younger Ludwig's marriage prospects and the note which the old man afterwards wrote to his grandson is illuminating:

"Dear Ludwig,

"You know how fond I am of you; I cannot therefore suppress my innermost wish to say that you ought not tie yourself by marriage. At your age, one is far too young for matrimonial life and, considering that you grew up so very quickly, it is doubtful whether marriage would be good for your health. If you give your promise to marry, you deprive yourself of the liberty of seeing other Princesses. Later on, many things appear differently from the way they did at the beginning. What you are deciding now is your happiness for life; therefore, do not act quickly but keep a hand free.

"I am convinced of this, beloved grandson, and wishing you everything that is best, I remain,

"Your affectionate grandfather, Ludwig."

The affection was mutual, the advice sound. Ludwig often went to this worldly, understanding man who had given him his first building bricks and took a deep and sincere interest in everything he did. Ludwig's personal affairs were not the only objects of the old man's observations; he also kept an eye on political events being of the

* The eldest, Sophie, had died of typhus at the age of 2. In 1868 she gave birth to another girl, Marie-Valerie.

opinion that some of the leading politicians proposed to use his grandson's youthful inexperience in order to weaken the country; his assessment of the situation proved to be all too accurate.

At this moment in time the Landtag was adamant in its favour of a
short-term financial plan as opposed to retaining the prescribed six
year plan of which both Ludwigs were in favour. When the young King
asked the reason for the proposed change and was told by the Ministers
that the long term policy had been adhered to "out of faithful devotion
to Your Majesty's blessed father, who preferred the six year period,"
he confounded them with the rejoinder "How can a ruler learn the truth
if his advisers judge one way today and differently tomorrow?" Whatever Ludwig thought of his father personally, he respected Max's ability
to rule and, determined to carry out his duties thoroughly and without
making too many mistakes, would ask when faced with some difficult
problem, "What would my father have done?"

Unfortunately, he did not apply the same logic to his personal life
and would never tolerate interference in his friendships although he
occasionally allowed his secretary to make a few gentle suggestions.
Pfistermeister's point concerning the Tzaritza had been taken but he
pointedly ignored comments about his relationship with the Empress
of Austria and began to disappear with her at frequent intervals.
Together, Ludwig and Elisabeth explored the Ammerland and Allgäu
on horseback, usually without even a groom in attendance.

Refreshed from visits to various German cities and a courtesy call
on the Tzaritza who was now in Bad Schwalbach, Ludwig returned to
Munich eager to see how *Die Meistersinger* was progressing. The first
thing he did was to visit the Villa Gôtham where Wagner was holding
his own court.

The composer had already transformed the house into something
resembling a Parisian brothel, having covered every wall with gaudily
coloured fabrics. The room known as the Grail Room was particularly
horrible, a nightmare of yellow satin, plaster cupids and artificial roses.
In the garden strutted peacocks whose colourful splendour was only
marginally less flamboyant than that of their owner. Although Ludwig
loved the opulence of a castle or palace, he actually preferred to live
in simple, almost spartan surroundings. The authority on architecture
and *objéts d'art* who talked endlessly of producing theatrical works of
exquisite beauty and unrivalled spectacle was content to live in a shack
furnished only with a bed, chairs and a table. Even after he had built
his three castles, Ludwig rarely slept in any of them but preferred to
rest his head at Berg, Hohenschwangau (if his mother was not there)
or in some remote hunting lodge. While Neuschwanstein was being
built, he would often sleep in the gatehouse rather than under the roof

of his mother across the road at Hohenschwangau which would indicate that he regarded his castles more as shrines or theatrical sets than
as homes.

However splendid his castles were, they were never tasteless and his
first glimpse of Wagner's new home must have come as something of
a shock. It is possible that in all the excitement he did not even notice
for his visit was basically to finalise agreement between himself and the
composer whereby Wagner was officially commissioned to complete
the *Ring des Nibelungen* cycle on which he had been working sporadically for several years. At the same time, the production rights to this
gargantuan work were to be made over to King Ludwig*; the sum
offered in exchange for the epic was 30,000 Gulden - another vast sum
which would be dissipated within weeks by the spendthrift composer.

Having heard nothing from the King for so long, Wagner must have
been relieved to see him. The hiatus should have stood as a warning
that he should tread carefully, yet he continued to boast openly that the
young King was his "willing slave". This audacious statement appeared
to have the ring of truth when he arranged for Hans von Bülow's
appointment as official performer to the King at a salary of 2,000
Gulden a year, although his helpful suggestion that Bülow's wife might
be appointed as "official reader" to the King was vetoed on the direct
instruction of the Queen Mother who had no time for Cosima. Marie
was well aware of the gossip surrounding Bülow's wife, on which basis
alone her appearance at court in any capacity would be unthinkable.
The prosaic Marie was certainly not prepared to have her on the
payroll.

Wagner had not recommended Bülow from any genuine desire to
help his friend but because he wanted Cosima to have a legitimate
independent reason for remaining in Munich. To all intents and purposes she was still Bülow's faithful spouse, but before long she was
installed in Wagner's home in the guise of "secretary" to the composer
although, in the 1860s, even this must have caused a considerable stir.
With his cronies comfortably settled around him, Wagner wrote com-
placently of the King, "He is and remains of magical beauty and
kindness." He had yet to learn that in the long term, Ludwig, who was
nobody's fool, paid only kindness with kindness.

Blissfully unaware that he could ever put a foot wrong, on Ludwig's
20th birthday Wagner transported a whole orchestra to Hohenschwangau with the notion of serenading his patron with the *Hüldigungsmarsch*
which he had composed for the occasion. The gesture brought swift
protective action from the Queen Mother who sent him packing the
moment she heard of his arrival.

---

* In fact Wagner had already sold the rights twice to friends in exchange for financial
assistance; the earlier recipients nobly conceded their rights to Ludwig.

Marie was by no means Wagner's only opponent: with the exception of Prince Taxis, most of Ludwig's circle were against him and the Ministers had their heads together trying to think of a way of getting rid of him. They were worried that Wagner would corrupt the young man and some of them even thought that Ludwig had been hypnotised by him. Wagner himself seems also to have been of this opinion for he wrote to one of his erstwhile mistresses, "Among all these unfavourable influences, only the favour of the young King remains constant. He loves me sincerely and beautifully. He denies me nothing as long as I do not go. He is almost childishly grateful for the smallest thing that I tell him. He is at once strong and regal yet unbelievably naïve. A piece of living poetry!"

Unfortunately, Ludwig's effusive letters to Wagner appeared to confirm his extravagant claims. The King's rather purple prose was well known to everyone, but Wagner chose to take every word literally. One such letter at least was intended to be taken at its face value: immediately after the agreement concerning the *Ring* Cycle had been signed, Ludwig wrote, "It is impossible for me to let this day pass without assuring you again that I am happier in my mind knowing that you are happy! The fulfillment of our dreams shall now approach, the work for which for the whole of your life you have scarcely dared to hope to see realised shall be produced and definitely the way you want it - which I on my side also wish you to do. (...) We shall make a present of this wonderful work to the German people as well as showing other Nations of what German art is capable."

This was a surprising aspiration for so young a man, even one of Ludwig's intellectual maturity, but the egotistical Wagner misinterpreted his sincere intentions, believing the arrangement to be mere camouflage to enable him to lavish gifts on his idol without exciting further comment.

In fact, Wagner was very far from being Ludwig's only interest. Deeply conscious of his duty, the young King was devoted to his people as well as to the arts and his Ministers maligned him if they thought that he was not. Prince Chlodwig von Hohenlohe-Schillingfürst, who was to have much contact with Ludwig in later years, noted in his diary that he had seen the King at the theatre during the first week in October: "He looks well," he wrote, "But I could not help thinking that he is beginning to take on his father's distrustful expression." Hohenlohe, who himself frequently provoked comment which swung from one extreme to the other, was to observe in his journal a year later, "It becomes more and more obvious that the neglect and the mistakes of which the King has been accused are really due to the Cabinet. My instincts were not deceived: it is true that Pfistermeister and Lutz purposely keep the King in isolation in order that they might pursue their protection policy undisturbed in conjunction with Pfordten and Bomhard." This is a most interesting comment if one goes on to look at the change in Ludwig's attitudes between the years of 1863 and 1866, and still further to the state of affairs by 1886 when Lutz had become Prime Minister.

Eduard von Bomhard, the new Minister for Justice, was actually opposed to some of Ludwig's open-minded policies and in later years involved himself in the many intrigues against the King, yet he was greatly taken with Ludwig personally and during 1864 Ludwig often sought his advice. Bomhard was received initially at Hohenschwangau where Ludwig was always at his best. "The 19 year old youth, brimming over with charm and youthful beauty, noble in countenance and figure, with luxuriant thick brown hair and truly magnificent eyes full of spirit and soul, was dressed in a formal black suit with a star-shaped order on his breast. He received me graciously with the words "Now you may see my view at last." He opened the window and showed me the magnificent surroundings of the Hochgebirge, with its two deepest lakes picturesquely placed."

Bomhard was astounded by Ludwig's wide knowledge on a variety of subjects including current political affairs, which the Minister had not been led to expect. Nevertheless, he was quick to sense the melancholy with which the King was already afflicted, but which few people took a deep enough interest in the young man to notice. "I was very soon struck by the fact that, while his eyes (and, indeed, his whole being), showed graciousness and good nature, he suddenly raised them upwards and, with an earnest, even severe gaze, took on a gloomy air in complete contrast with his gracefully youthful appearance."

Moody or not, Ludwig certainly knew how to please his guest. After dinner he took Bomhard on to the terrace so that they could further enjoy the incomparable view, and later drove him through the region in a four in hand which "really whizzed along." They enjoyed a pleasant enough relationship at that time and Bomhard recalled with obvious affection, "Especially during interesting conversations, I liked to look into those beautiful, wide open eyes. Even if I had never met him I would have selected him from a collection of hundreds and pronounced 'This is the King'."

Ludwig's effect upon people in general was extraordinary. No one was indifferent towards him, and just as with the prominent of today, he was either passionately loved or violently hated. Peter Cornelius, the writer and composer who met him through Wagner, said of his first audience with him, "Actually, I didn't know what I saw when I first stood before him, except for the eyes which were like those of a lion

one wants to tame. I no longer knew if he wore epaulettes and a star
or some other similar decoration. All the details melted into a single
impression of an unchanging good soul, an unclouded innocent, an
earnest, lofty ideal." The poet, Paul Hyse, also commented about
Ludwig's eyes which were evidently the focal point of his whole being:
"The huge, powerfully beautiful eyes of the King slid constantly around
and never stayed firmly in one place. But when they did gaze into mine
for a moment, I saw in them a peculiar expression, strange and puzzling.
It was as if some inner turmoil possessed the King, a turmoil which I
would finally feel myself." But Count Blome, the Austrian Ambassador who clearly disliked him, wrote, "His great, deep eyes gazed with
demoniac power, their gaze even at that time carrying more the impression of staring autocracy than of kindly affability." Like many
others, Blome was never to discover that Ludwig treated people as they
treated him.

In the first autumn of his reign Ludwig, together with Otto, carried
on Max's tradition by appearing at the Munich Oktoberfest. The
brothers again received a rapturous welcome not only from the burghers but from the thousands of country people who flocked to the
annual beer festival. Karl von Hegel's explanation for public reaction
to the King was simple: "On his way to the Royal tent he was greeted
with cheers such as he had never heard before. No victory garlands
graced his brow; he had never had any particular success. The people
cheered him because they loved him."

Sure now of his popularity, Ludwig blossomed; he began to display
a new dignity and assurance, a new maturity. His discussion groups at
official functions and at private supper parties became the talk of
Munich because of their lively atmosphere and clever combination of
widely different guests and opinions. He was becoming proficient in
his official duties also and even told Baroness Leonrod, "I am growing
fonder and fonder of my occupation." Sadly, he was unable to sustain
such a lifestyle for very long and at every opportunity would ride off to
Berg or Hohenschwangau. This upset the Prime Minister, Baron von
der Pfordten, who could never find him when he was wanted.

Pfordten was one of the old school, a man cast very much in the same
mould as Ludwig's former governor, Count de la Rosée and had no
patience with the aesthetic King. "I find it highly disquieting that HM
goes away [from Munich] for such long periods," he wrote to Pfistermeister, "I can only beg you earnestly to see that the King attends to
his career and not merely to his inclinations." Despite Ludwig's many
attempts to explain his relationship with Wagner, Pfordten continued
to find it inexplicable. Nor would he ever concede a single virtue in the
composer, professionally or otherwise. The actor, Emil Devrient, one

of the many artists who had ample opportunity to observe how things were, later wrote in his memoirs, "In Pfordten was blended personal antipathy towards Wagner and (...) his opinion of the man's works (...) The statesman who criticised with a fundamentally narrow outlook said that the arrogance of the personality as it manifested itself in Richard Wagner heralded the destruction of our present day life and political system, and if the critics would only co-operate a little, as the democrats did, then Wagnerian music would never be played."

The more moderate Ministers were just beginning to form a more favourable opinion of the King when, shortly after Wagner took up permanent residence in Munich, Ludwig's new rapport with his staff was threatened by an unpleasant article commenting on Wagner's bad influence on the young King appeared in the *Augsburger Abendzeitung*. To see in cold print what had long been on the tip of every tongue served only to inflame public opinion the more. The capricious burghers blamed not only the parasite, as they regarded him, but also the young King off whom he fed. Those who only weeks before had openly worshipped him were suddenly all too ready to criticise.

At this untimely moment, Prussia declared war on Schleswig-Holstein and with these hostilities began a series of terrible wars from which Europe never recovered. Totally inexperienced in such a sphere and receiving little or no real encouragement from his so-called advisers, Ludwig decided that the best thing to do was to leave the important decisions concerning the war to the Ministerium while he applied himself to pursuits within his scope, namely, the arts. It was the wrong attitude but he could scarcely be blamed for it.

Nevertheless, he did not neglect to read the Ministerial reports but these upset him so much that the only way he could maintain his equilibrium was to turn to Wagner's work for spiritual comfort. He contrived to look calm and assured before the public, probably by pretending they were not there, but he remained painfully shy. It was torment for him to have to endure audiences with unsympathetic strangers and to give his ear to those advisers who, having pushed him into his present position, reminded him with typical duplicity that he should be spending his time and money in quite different ways.

CHAPTER FOUR

WAGNER AND TRISTAN

EARLY in his reign Ludwig began to dislike Munich and its associations and the Residenz itself with all its connotations of representational life made him depressed and irritable. He dreamed hopeless dreams of spending all his time at Berg and Hohenschwangau until he was able to build castles of his own even further from the despised capital, yearning to create something which would endure for posterity like his grandfather's gracious buildings. His first opportunity to build came when Wagner, still with an eye to the main chance, presented him with the rough plans for a theatre. He too had dreams of building. Originally, the title had read "A Project for the Organisation of a German National Theatre for the Kingdom of Saxony", but having fallen foul of everyone in Dresden, he now found it expedient to substitute the word "Bavaria" for "Saxony" and offer the same building to Ludwig.

Although on the King's own admission, Wagner's voice, with its barely intelligable Saxon accent, gave him a headache, he listened eagerly enough on this occasion. Wagner visualised a stone edifice on the banks of the Isar, with massive portals and a good deal of gold and marble decoration. Apart from the Residenz itself, it would be the focal point of Munich, and needless to say it was intended primarily as a temple to the God Wagner. He had even chosen the architect to carry his dreams to reality, namely, Gottfried Semper, a popular creator of 19th Century horrors throughout Europe and the luckless Pfistermeister was despatched to seek him out.

The secretary was becoming increasingly anxious about Ludwig's ideas, possibly because he had plans of his own which showed no signs of coming to fruition, but there was little he could do but obey or at least give the appearance of so doing. Despite his intrigues he was genuinely fond of Ludwig and was appalled to see him apparently falling ever deeper under the composer's spell and retreating daily further into a make believe world of myth and legend as Wagner led him deliberately into a precarious fairyland.

As a child at Hohenschwangau, Ludwig had spent hours gazing at his favourite hero, the Knight of the Swan. As a young adult, he gave every impression of seeing himself as a kind of 19th Century Lohengrin, an immortal, autocratic being who scorns to sully his hands with modern warfare or to stain his fine intellect with affairs of the Treasury. Ludwig's real problem was that he was living in the wrong century, something which happens to many of us and to the less privileged there is no course but to endure it. For Ludwig there was an alternative and even if he and Wagner had never met it was inevitable that he would have taken refuge in some other dream world. It was the only way he could survive. When the composer arrived on the scene at a such a psychologically important moment, Ludwig predictably grasped at him like a sinking man to a piece of driftwood.

Wagner's own life meantime was becoming increasingly complicated, for Bülow's wife Cosima was pregnant and Wagner was popularly supposed to be the child's father. At this particular time only Ludwig refused to believe it although he was later to change his mind. He had met Cosima in her capacity as Bülow's wife during the idyll at Starnberg and while he was not particularly taken by her, he was disgusted by the unpleasant gossip about her affaire with the composer which was being bandied about the city.

The lurid tales about Liszt's daughter were Heavensent and gave Pfistermeister an excuse to regale Ludwig with something even more likely to upset the sensitive King. Wagner had commissioned one of his artist friends, Friedrich Pecht, to paint a portrait of him and send it to the King. Believing it to be a gift, the delighted Ludwig hung the picture prominently in the Residenz. His fury when Pfistermeister joyfully produced the artist's bill for the work was enough to encourage him to tell the King that, not content with this, Wagner was swaggering around Munich referring loudly to the King as his "Young lad" and his "boy". This was too much for Ludwig who was quick to convey his displeasure by refusing to see him. He attended the performance of *Der Fliegende Holländer* as planned and magnanimously penned a note of appreciation to the composer, indicating that despite what people thought, he regarded the man and the artist as separate beings: "I grasp my pen, still quite stirred by yesterday's performance, in order to express to you my deepest thanks for the true happiness of soul and strength which you have given me."

Eager to get back into the King's good books, Wagner replied with a wild effusion which led to another lengthy exchange of almost tropical correspondence, but still Ludwig did not suggest a meeting. Meantime, Gottfried Semper had been engaged to carry through the designs for the new theatre and, anxious for Ludwig's patronage, he dropped all his other prospects and hurried to Munich for an audience with the King. Wagner was less fortunate for despite the apparent warmth of Ludwig's letters, when he tried to see him personally, he was told that the King had left Munich with Prince Taxis.

After all this somewhat public emotion, it was widely felt that marriage would be the best means of keeping Ludwig out of mischief and to this end a constant stream of eligibles trooped daily through the Residenz in the hope of meeting and winning the heart of the handsome King. Many of these young ladies wore in their lockets all kinds of curious trophies such as hairs from his horse and even wilted flower petals which had been crushed under his feet. But although he could barely move without tripping over one of these young hopefuls, he remained aggravatingly blind to their charms. Only to Empress Elisabeth and one or two other females older than himself was he susceptible although he was always gallant towards the ladies. His friendship with his aide de camp, on the other hand, was again becoming so warm as to excite comment, although Paul's basic interests remained with the opposite sex.

Ludwig was never able to appreciate that for Taxis, life without a woman's love was nothing; to the aesthetic King, such liaisons as Paul enjoyed were repulsively decadent. When Ludwig leaned towards his ideal, Lohengrin, he was unconsciously reaching out for a purity which he himself yearned to attain. As he put it to the understanding Elisabeth, "Lohengrin needs a woman who believes in him, who asks neither who he is nor whence he came, but will love him as he is; he seeks the woman to whom he will have no need to explain or justify himself, but one who will love him without reservation. What he is seeking is the one thing which can free him from his loneliness: love. To be understood through love."

The woman Ludwig had in mind was undoubtedly Elisabeth herself, but she was unattainable, a married woman with a husband and family, an Empress whose life, although she often shunned it, was ostensibly one of eternal obligation. She was the one woman he could not have and if he sought to find similar qualities as she possessed among his male acquaintances, it may to some extent have been because he knew no female intimately, apart from Sisi, who was capable of measuring up to his standards.

At the same time, Ludwig's eternal longing for untarnished glory was an acknowledgement of the fault deep within himself for which he felt an overwhelming sense of shame: his latent homosexuality or, more properly, his bi-sexuality. He obviously loved Elisabeth deeply and whenever he heard of her arrival at Possenhofen he would immediately abandon any plan in order to go to Berg to be near her. As pleased to see him as he was to see her, if Elisabeth heard of his arrival in the area, she too would cancel all her plans with alacrity to ride out to meet him, and they would spend hours alone together in perfect accord. From the moment of their meeting at Kissingen when she saw the adult Ludwig with new eyes, Elisabeth on her side became devoted to him and was clearly equally aware of his deep feeling for her. Yet, possibly as a defence mechanism or as a camouflage, she would sometimes give way to an almost cruel humour, unable to resist regaling her family with laughter.

Ludwig's eccentricities as, for example, the waxing and waning clockwork moon in his bedroom, were widely discussed throughout the family, as was his personal vanity. Yet beneath the jokes and brittle gaiety of Elisabeth's comments about her cousin lay a true feeling of concern and it is worth noting that while she permitted herself to laugh at him occasionally, she never allowed others the same liberty and would spring angrily to his defence at any misplaced word about him. On one occasion, however, she was unable to restrain her own mirth when she caught sight of Ludwig arriving on a visit to Possenhofen in heavy rain in full Austrian military uniform, and walked the gangplank to the shore carrying his helmet in one hand and a large umbrella in other. When Elisabeth teased him about the comic figure he cut, his wounded explanation was that his hairdresser had taken so much trouble that he was reluctant to spoil his coiffeur. This may indicate personal vanity, but does it not also demonstrate his consciousness of the feelings of others? Despite reports that Elisabeth found his reply hilarious, she would probably not have thought it as funny as all that, since her own reaction in a similar situation would probably have been the same. Ludwig's resplendent uniform was on this occasion worn primarily as a compliment to the Austrian Empress, but at the same time, he certainly looked more impressive than in his civilian clothes which always looked as if they had been tailored to fit an even larger man.

It was at about this time that he first caught the eye of Elisabeth's younger sister Sophie. He had naturally known her all his life and corresponded with her occasionally on family and cultural matters but since he avoided Possenhofen except when he knew that the Empress was there, he did not often meet her face to face. Recounting the visit to Possi already mentioned, Elisabeth wrote to her nine year old daughter Gisela, "Yesterday the King paid a long visit, and if Grandmama had not come in at last, he would still be here (...) We are completely reconciled. I was very charming and he kissed my hand so many times that Aunt Sophie, who was watching through the door, asked me afterwards if I had any hand left. He was again wearing Austrian uniform and was covered with Chypre perfume." If this letter tells us nothing else, it indicates that, even then, Sophie was jealous of her sister's relationship with Ludwig. The reconciliation to which she referred followed a quarrel which they had had at Kissingen, probably sparked off by Ludwig's attentions to the Tzaritza or, indeed, Elisabeth's own occasional disappearances to read poetry with a mortally sick Englishman, John Collett and the elderly, sightless Duke of Mecklenburg for whom Elisabeth had a very soft spot. Knowing that her family in Vienna would receive blow-by-blow reports of Ludwig's visit, Elisabeth made light of it, but she pointedly failed to mention her long unaccompanied excursions with the King, omissions which were made up for by her staff.

* * * * *

CURRENTLY full of Wagner's plans for the theatre, Ludwig wanted to adopt it as his own, and having commissioned Semper to design it, hoped that it would be finished in 1867 to coincide with the completion and first production of *Der Ring des Nibelungen**. Characteristically, having once set the wheels in motion, the King put the matter from his mind to concentrate on other things.

Despite the sour comment in the *Allgemeine Zeitung* that "...public opinion would be grateful for any sign that the music of Mozart and Beethoven arouses any interest in the Bavarian capital", Ludwig's cultural aspirations had a far wider scope than mere patronage of Wagner's works. Although still eager at that time for his "large stone theatre", he wanted also to open a music academy and other schools of the arts. Earlier he had confided to Wagner, "My aim is to bring the Munich people into a more thoughtful and lofty frame of mind by the production of more serious and important works such as those of Shakespeare, Caldéron, Goethe, Schiller, Mozart, Gluck and Weber, to help it gradually to free itself from a taste for cheap and frivolous entertainment and to prepare it for the marvels of your own works or those of other great men; for everyone ought to be made conscious of the seriousness of art."

Beyond the youthful intensity and vague air of priggishness, Ludwig's judgment and understanding were impeccable for so young a man. He knew better than Wagner himself that the Munich public was not quite ready for Wagner's *avant garde* works, and his intention to prepare them gradually for the astonishing revelations of the Master was an astute piece of business acumen as well as being an expert artistic pronouncement. No theatre can flourish if its seats remain empty, nor can performers give of their best if what they do is not understood by the audience or, indeed, by themselves.

To open his ambitious programme was a work for which he considered at least some of the operagoing public was ready: *Tristan und Isolde*, which had been offered in Vienna some years previously but abandoned in mid-rehearsal as "impossible to perform". Ludwig, who already knew both score and libretto by heart, was impatient to see the

---

* This was Ludwig's estimate, not Wagner's.

work brought to life by the finest cast of singers the composer could muster and Wagner did not disappoint him. For the title roles he chose Ludwig and Malwina Schnorr von Carolsfeld, a highly successful married couple who held a good long-term contract with the Royal Court Theatre in Dresden, where they were justifiably held in high regard. Mutual admiration existed between the Schnorrs and Wagner and he had no difficulty in persuading them and their patron, the King of Saxony, that they were the only possible singers for his opera.

Physically, they appeared to be almost laughably unsuited to their parts. At 29, Schnorr was dangerously obese but in addition to high intelligence and a wonderfully good natured and generous temperament, he possessed a superb tenor voice which could not be bettered anywhere in Germany. Ten years her husband's senior, Malwina was built on the same heroic scale and with her glorious soprano voice was a perfect match for him. She too had an unusually sweet and charming personality for one of her calling and she shared her husband's high intellect. The pair were universally adored and their services were always in great demand.

Rehearsals for *Tristan und Isolde* began on April 15th, 1865, and although the King was delighted with the Schnorrs, he was less pleased with some of the other artistes who had been engaged. Hans von Bülow was to conduct the orchestra and, with the exception of Wagner himself, was quickly to become the most detested man in Munich owing to his ill-concealed contempt for the Bavarians. When he wanted to enlarge the orchestra by means of removing some of the front stalls, for example, his tasteless assertion that it was "immaterial whether there were a dozen or more less of the *Schweinehünde* in the stalls", widely reported in the press, provoked great indignation.

Wagner himself was no less objectionable and was apparently determined that everyone should be aware of his supposed power over the King. He repeatedly ignored the request that he should conduct himself with decorum and seemed to go out of his way to inflame public anger. His behaviour both in public and in private was abominable, his attitude towards his benefactor less than respectful. With his acid-spiked pen, Count Blome reported to Vienna: "What can one say (...) when Wagner produces letters from the King in which he addresses him as '*Du*'* and praises him verbally and in the most effusive manner too? That the musician, during His Majesty's illness, was summoned to the King's bedside while the most pressing Government business remained untouched and no Minister could be granted an audience? That two days ago on his birthday Wagner was invited to Schloss Berg to be received personally by the King with a bouquet (...) More and more people are calling Wagner "Lolus"** and King Ludwig I is said

---

* Thou.   ** The masculine equivalent of Lola; a reference to Lola Montez.

to have told somebody yesterday, 'Very sad, that my grandson is going astray, but it will not last long – the people will put an end to it'."

The scandal hovering over the Wagnerian clique had earlier broken into a storm when, on April 10th, Cosima gave birth to a daughter. With the possible exception of Ludwig, who was ever magnanimous in giving even his worst enemy the benefit of the doubt, not a soul believed Bülow to be the father. When the child was defiantly called Isolde, even Ludwig could not ignore the implications. Convinced still of the impossibility of allowing Wagner's genius to be lost to the world, and especially not for so sordid a reason, Ludwig swallowed his pride and reconciled himself to the fact that he was not the only person in Wagner's life. In the event, it did not prove to be difficult. As a lasting proof of his generosity of spirit, he carried out his earlier plan to rename his steamship the *Tristan*,* and after a long silence, again granted audiences to the composer. Encouraged by a few more crafty effusions from Wagner, Ludwig at last capitulated and began once more to haunt the Briennerstrasse for news of *Die Meistersinger*.

Making the most of his chances, Wagner ingratiated himself back into Royal favour, whispering compliments into one ear and demands for money into the other. To the less perceptive, who refused to accept that Ludwig was not, and never had been infatuated in the accepted sense with Wagner, his passion for the composer seemed more rabid than ever. Wagner believed himself to be firmly reinstated in the King's esteem. So confident was he that the time was ripe to impose his political will upon the King that he even he boasted to Elise Wille that his power over the King was now so great that he planned to overthrow the Government and, in particular, his arch-enemy, Baron von der Pfordten, simply by pointing out his defects to the seemingly impressionable King. Nothing was ever enough for Wagner: having, as he thought, made a satisfactory beginning, he next launched an attack on Pfistermeister, whom he quite justifiably did not trust. Prince Taxis was quick to warn the Cabinet Secretary of the composer's vengeful plans, although for the moment his anxiety was misplaced for at that point in time it suited Ludwig to leave things as they were and dispense with the services of both Pfordten and Pfistermeister only when it was convenient to himself.

Wagner had greatly overestimated his own importance, but it was a mistake he shared with most of Munich. His arrogance, quickly emulated by his friends, was the talk of the town. He treated every Bavarian with contempt and freely criticised the Government and the administration. The press naturally retaliated and launched on him a bitter

* Formerly called The Maxmilian after his father.

campaign which could have ruined him but for the fact that the Munich theatregoing fraternity shared Ludwig's own level-headed opinion that a man's art was not to be confused with the man himself, and his work at least was becoming increasingly successful.

The composer himself was a different matter. One by one, those members of the cabinet who had previously merely disliked him now showed an active hatred for his arrogance, for his interference in things which did not concern him and, above all, for his hopeless extrvagance with the King's money. Blind to the intensity of the feeling against him, Wagner refused to moderate his behaviour and inevitably began grad-ually to destroy his own unique position. He was incapable of accept-ing the fact that the King only tolerated him for his talent; as one of the King's more astute contemporaries observed, "It quickly became ap-parent that, whilst the King undoubtedly enjoyed Wagner's company occasionally, he was by no means excessively influenced by him. In this connection, his constantly changing moods were completely sincere. The King was often angry with Wagner and possessed a character which did not believe in self denial."

Unfortunately, this enlightened view was not universal and Pfordten himself was deeply anxious about both the friendship and the scandal by which it was surrounded. When he tried to express his concern to the King, Ludwig merely raised his eyes heavenwards and began to whistle, an irritating and somewhat childish means of conveying his indifference and one which, ironically, had also driven Wagner frantic when the ruse was tried on him. Frustrated, Pfordten reported to Pfistermeister, ".... and so I keep quiet as I have neither the right nor the presumption to stand judgment on anybody. I only feel it is my duty to caution him on the dangers which I believe that HM in his idyllic seclusion from his real work, is unaware." He was grumbling to the wrong person, however, since Pfistermeister's interests and those of the King did not always coincide and his own loyalty is open to speculation.

Meanwhile, in a torrid atmosphere of quarrels and disturbances, the rehearsals for *Tristan und Isolde* continued. Bülow complained about the orchestra, the orchestra complained about Bülow, Wagner com-plained about the theatre and the King complained about the delay. Far from trying to placate his patron, Wagner raised his voice even more loudly against the very people who supported him, including Ludwig himself.

Anxious to ensure that as many people as possible should enjoy the new production and determined that the spectacular work should be shown to the best advantage, the King wanted it to be produced in the Court Theatre while Wagner was adamant in his preference for what he termed the "intimate" atmosphere of the Residenztheater. The dispute continued until Ludwig, worn down by Wagner's persistent railing, conceded. It was not long before the composer, struggling to achieve the desired effect on the tiny stage of the Residenztheater, was forced to agree to Ludwig's flawless judgement in matters theatrical and the whole production was transferred back to the more accommodating Court Theatre in mid-rehearsal. Wagner's confidence in his leading singers at least was justified and he was moved to write triumphantly to Frau Wille, "You can have no idea of the splendours of both Schnorrs. All their life's strength is concentrated upon this one performance which they master now with full artistic dignity." This pronouncement was to prove sadly prophetic.

The dress rehearsal took place on May 10th, 1865, and predictably, Ludwig was spellbound. Six hundred guests were present but while this performance of *Tristan und Isolde* was an artistic triumph it was not, as Ludwig had hoped, fully understood by subsequent audiences who were accustomed to the precise rhythms and tuneful melodies of French and Italian masters. Unfortunately, Malwina von Schnorr caught a chill and the first public performance, originally scheduled for May 15th, was postponed. Non-adherents to Wagner's work were quick to assert that the composer's "barbaric, unsingable" music had ruined her voice, which was nonsense. She was genuinely ill and sent her apologies with the greatest expressions of regret, as indeed she might after the ovation she received at the dress rehearsal. In a state of near-dementia at this sudden reversal of his fortunes, Wagner behaved like a spoiled child, raving like a madman and making all kinds of absurd threats. Expecting the King to be similarly affected, he was greatly put out when, upon hearing the news, the unpredictable but eminently sensible Ludwig merely offered the mild hazard "Perhaps tomorrow?" before retiring to Berg.

May 15th was, in fact, likely to be engraved on Wagner's memory for many years, for the cancelled performance was not his only disaster. Bailiffs had most embarrassingly arrived at the imposing villa on the Briennerstrasse and were demanding 3,000 French Francs or goods to that value. During a visit to Paris some years previously, Wagner had imprudently borrowed - and conveniently forgotten - this sum from yet another cast off mistress, an English Jewess, one Julie Schwalbe. When Madame Schwalbe heard of Wagner's improved circumstances, she saw no reason why she should not recoup her losses. Wagner considered her very reasonable request as an affront, but realising that he would have to pay despatched Cosima to the Royal Treasury to beg for assistance, confident that help would be forthcoming. Sick to death of Wagner and his wants, the Treasury officials took their revenge by

giving Cosima the sum she demanded in small coin, leaving her no
alternative but to drive through the streets of Munich with the sacks
heaped inside her carriage. Belatedly conscious of his social position,
Wagner was outraged but having got precisely what he had demanded,
he could scarcely complain.

Malwina von Schnorr's indisposition lasted for some time and the
première of *Tristan und Isolde* did not take place until June 15th.
Greatly looking forward to seeing it again, Ludwig sent an enthusiastic
note to Wagner enthusing "Day of rapture! Tristan! Oh, how I long for
this evening! If only it would come!"

More to be seen and to see each other than to hear the new opera,
the Wittelsbach family, including the frail but frenetic Ludwig I, arrived
in force for the occasion. The King shunned them all, sitting well away
from the inattentive element, a solitary, regal figure in the Royal box,
his eyes fixed upon the stage with almost fanatical joy. It may have been
true that he had no great technical knowledge of music, but he was
highly susceptible to its emotive power. Few of his contemporaries
appreciated this and even his priest, friend and tutor, Ignaz von Döllinger, had written of Ludwig when he was still in his impressionable
teens, "Don't imagine it was the music which excited the feelings of the
Prince for Wagner. Certainly it had a truly demoniac effect on him,
and it was not a pleasant one. It got painfully on his nerves and on some
occasions made him feel really ill. For example, his whole body appeared to be affected by a kind of convulsion every time *Tannhäuser*
returns to the Venusberg (it comes in the Overture also). On one
occasion it was so bad that I feared an epileptic fit. The composer
never conquered him; it was the poet who held the dreamy spirit of the
young Prince in bondage."

Döllinger was right to some extent but it was far more than poetry
which held Ludwig and the rest of the audience spellbound by the *avant
garde* work which was so totally different from anything previously seen
or heard. Each Act met with tumultuous applause and when at last
Wagner's triumphant singers led him on to the stage to share in the
accolade, the bitter quarrels of the past were forgotten. Still full of hate
for "Lolus", the public was unsparing in its praise for the genius who
had shown to what heights he could aspire when he troubled himself
to work. Ludwig himself, emotionally overcome and deeply imbued in
the romantic atmosphere of the legend, wrote to Wagner, "How wonderful! Completely! I am consumed with enchantment! Drowning,
sinking, greatest pleasure – an immortal work!"

Five days later, he attended the second performance, but was
conspicuously absent when, on June 29th, his uncle and godfather, King
Otto of Greece, arrived to hear the much-discussed work. Ludwig was

so enthralled by *Tristan* that he could not bear to sit through it in the company of such a philistine and predictably, the now familiar bulletin appeared to the effect that the King was too ill to attend the performance. Ludwig compensated for his loss by attending the next performance on July 1st and this time the experience was so shattering that he left for Berg the moment the opera ended and, stopping the train *en route*, went the rest of the way on foot, striding through the forest like one possessed.

The King shared Wagner's admiration for the Schnorrs and commanded several concerts in which they were to sing Wagnerian excerpts, but the huge and habitually genial tenor seemed tired and listless, complaining of a cough and pains in various parts of his body. Because of his indisposition, the singers returned to Dresden without fulfilling their commitments and three weeks later, the King was shocked to learn that after what was termed "a general rheumatism", the tenor had died. Wagner also was deeply upset by Schnorr's death, the more so because the griefstricken Malwina refused to perform without him.

Ludwig meantime remained at Berg where he isolated himself, making excursions into the forests and mountains accompanied only by his favourite groom, Voelck. He also paid regular visits to the Roseninsel, a heavily wooded island set in the midst of Lake Starnberg where he kept many a rendezvous with Elisabeth. Here in the privacy of the wooden villa built by King Max, they could enjoy each other's company engulfed by the perfume of the 30,000 rose trees which grew there. They continued to meet privately here until a few months before the King's death, after which Elisabeth never went there again.

At the end of the summer of 1865, Elisabeth returned to Vienna and Ludwig reluctantly went back to Munich. Far from being refreshed from his holiday, he still suffered from a surprising number of ailments for a man of his physique, enduring violent headaches and toothaches which tortured him to the extent where he began to seek relief in chloralhdyrate. Although in the 19th century such drugs as chloralhydrate, opium and the very popular laudenum were in common use both as painkillers and soporifics, it was less common for a man of Ludwig's age and type to resort to them and since he never did things by halves, on occasions he undoubtedly went too far. Pfistermeister later averred that he greatly disapproved of this and attempted unsuccessfully to dissuade him from the habit, but if this was the case, others in his suite were less scrupulous and actively encouraged him.

Whoever was responsible for introducing him to these "cures", the effects of the substances in which Ludwig indulged were evidently sometimes worse than the ailments he sought to alleviate, as his staff soon discovered to their cost. Frequent use of chloralhydrate could lead to hallucinations, outbursts of uncontrollable rage and sudden euphoria which, though quickly subdued, forgotten and repented, were not appreciated by anyone who got in his way. Throughout the King's life, references were made to these "character traits" but it is likely that, far from stemming from eccentricity or from some inherent defect, his aberrations were merely the result of too much chloral. There is no suggestion that he wilfully became a drug addict: he was simply a man who, with his dislike and distrust of medical men, resorted to somewhat drastic self-help in order to alleviate his pain. Sadly, this was quickly seized upon by those who sought to ruin him.

Not all of Ludwig's headaches stemmed from physical pain for Wagner might well be described as Ludwig's permanent headache. Having already paid a fortune to the composer, the King was justifiably frustrated by his failure to come up with the goods and, indeed, by his general attitude. Despite his frequent enquiries as to the progress of *Die Meistersinger von Nürnberg*, Wagner remained obstinately vague. In an attempt to spur him into action, Ludwig bombarded him with effusive letters full of flattery and fulsome encouragement, but all to no avail. Pleasantly occupied with Cosima, Wagner had quickly tired of what had appeared to be the lovesick outpourings of the adolescent King, complaining arrogantly to an ex-mistress, Mathilde Maier, in September: "I work; I have said to the King that no other construction can be placed on my words: I want absolute peace, quiet, seclusion." All this sounded very noble on paper when addressed to a doting woman, but it was of course, not what Wagner really wanted at all.

His work, in fact, lay untouched while he enjoyed stolen hours with his friend's wife. Fed by Ludwig on what Wagner assumed to be blind adoration, his arrogant self-esteem grew to even greater proportions and his letters to the King now began to take on a different tone. Satisfied that he had totally imposed his artistic will on Ludwig, he decided that the time was now ripe to put a few political suggestions to his "lad". At first, the democratic King was responsive, interested to know what the people were thinking. He asked the composer for detailed reports, although he was soon to regret ever having swallowed Wagner's bait.

Wagner's own friends also disapproved of his attempts to interfere in politics; Peter Cornelius, for example, wrote to his fiancée: "There is one thing that I have never mentioned to you until now, and that is that Wagner has begun to touch upon political questions in his inter-course with the King, that he has become a kind of Marquis de Posa. It seems that the King has requested him to give his views on German affairs in general and ever since Wagner has expounded his opinions

In long letters which are forwarded regularly. When Bülow told me this I felt a shudder run down my spine because I saw that it would be the beginning of the end."

Virtually submerged under the weight of Wagner's outpourings, Ludwig's enthusiasm waned; the flood of letters to Wagner was immediately reduced to a trickle and personal contact ceased. Far from being the pursued, Wagner found himself after all to be the pursuer and it was some time before he managed to track down the elusive King who, like an eagle, soared ever higher into the mountains, staying at remote huts, restless, timid and full of distrust for almost everybody. He had every reason to be apprehensive about Wagner for, whenever he did make contact, the composer would barely give himself time to greet the King before launching into an impassioned demand for money or an equally demented plea for a change of government.

In the main, Ludwig's financial arrangements were dealt with by Pfistermeister, but it was so long since Wagner had been granted a personal interview that he was determined not to waste it on pleasantries. The crafty composer well knew that, if he asked Ludwig personally for something instead of going to the secretary as arranged, the young King would give in out of sheer embarrassment because he had not yet learned how to say no. On this occasion, what Wagner wanted was something like 200,000 Gulden, 40,000 of which was required immediately in order to discharge some of his enormous debts. To soften the blow, he magnanimously offered to leave the balance of 160,000 Gulden under Government control on the understanding that by doing so he could expect a yield of five per cent interest on his quarterly payments!

There was no end to Wagner's audacity and even the open-handed Ludwig was unable to comply with his incredible demands; 200,000 Gulden in fact comprised two-thirds of what was annually available to Ludwig himelf from the Civil List and to have conceded would have left him almost penniless until the following year. With barely a word of thanks, Wagner had accepted the luxurious villa, a splendid carriage and horses and endless personal gifts and monetary rewards, aside from the giant sums to be spent on the operatic productions which were still to be produced "as he wanted them"- and, indeed, when he had deigned to write them. At no time did it occur to him that he might one day ask too much of the King.

Undaunted by his unexpected failure, Wagner persevered; he was ever a man to wait if he thought there was something to wait for, but the eagle had wisely flown and weeks passed without a sign from the King. Obliged to resort once more to the pen, some of the suggestions put to Ludwig by the composer in this way included the possibility of establishing an official, politically orientated newspaper, that he should have a trained military militia, that he should remove his most experienced Ministers (namely, those in opposition to Wagner himself) and that the inexperienced 20 year old should place himself at the head of the Government. It went without saying that he was also prepared to give the King any amount of advice on how to run his country.

All this was to no avail. Ludwig still remained out of sight in his eyrie where he knew the composer would never venture. Like everyone else, Pfordten misconstrued Ludwig's motives and again wrote sourly to one of his colleagues in October complaining of Ludwig's "long absences". Even the Tzaritza Marie Alexandrowna, who looked on him with an almost maternal eye, was moved to advise him, "I am worried about this inclination of yours towards solitude, towards seclusion from the world and its people. I can understand it because it is in my nature also, but I believe we must struggle alone with it. So, as God willed us to do, we have no right to it."

After Ludwig's refusal to give up such a large sum to Wagner's frivolities, the composer had begun for the first time to feel anxious. When he heard at last that Ludwig had returned to Munich, he soaked himself in Chypre and presented himself at the Residenz, but while he was granted an audience he was disconcerted to find that the gullible boy of yesterday had disappeared and in his place was a mature, considerably more philosophic man who conceded nothing. Stunned, Wagner returned home with his tail between his legs and wrote peevishly to his unco-operative patron, "Whatever else you choose to grant me, I receive in my capacity as an artist, but what I ask now is on my value as a man and as a friend. For this purpose I am asking a sum as trifling as possible, scarcely sufficient for my needs." Somewhat rashly, he concluded, "Give royally and leave my conscience to remind me that I might one day reciprocate this Royal trust."

Worn down, Ludwig granted Wagner 40,000 Gulden but when the composer reappeared at the Residenz to express his thanks, he was again refused admittance. Bored with the sordid scandals and unremitting demands of his genius, the King pleaded illness and adroitly avoided further personal confrontation: well wishers were not slow in telling the outraged Wagner that on that particular day Ludwig, in perfect health, had been seen at the theatre. So inspired was the King by Emile Rohde's performance as Schiller's *Wilhelm Tell* that he immediately set off on a jaunt to Switzerland to explore the region connected with the Swiss hero.

After some idyllic days at Rütli, he returned to the capital to find the scandal surrounding the curious menage in the Briennerstrasse raging like a forest fire. The affaire between Wagner and Frau von

Bülow was now so notorious that even Cosima's father, Franz Liszt*, hitherto one of the composer's closest friends and himself no angel, refused to have anything further to do with either of them. Ludwig for once found himself in accord with the masses but remained courteous towards Cosima to further his own ends. Having found her to be an effective go-between he had carried on a correspondence with Cosima for some time and found her especially useful when he had something of importance to impart to Wagner, but was nevertheless to say of her, "She does not ring true; I prefer cowbells." Unaware of his true opinion of her, Cosima made the most of the King's favour.

In November, Ludwig relented and invited Wagner to Schloss Hohenschwangau. Starved for culture, he was glad to see the "Great Friend" and, for less laudable reasons, Wagner was glad to see him. Between fragments of *Tristan, Lohengrin* and works as yet incomplete, the composer sandwiched small but pungent fillips of advice which again were mostly concerned with getting rid of Pfistermeister, Pfordten and Hoffmann, another court secretary with whom he was at loggerheads. This trinity of officials formed a united front against Wagner; the composer on his side harboured a particularly strong hatred for Hoffmann whom he found especially obstructive. More or less tête-à-tête with the King for the first time for many weeks, he made the most of the opportunity to air his opinions, but each time he tried to offer suggestions concerning his advisers, Ludwig would gaze at the ceiling and begin to whistle or, even more irritatingly, would send for the object of Wagner's venom and proceed to show special favour to that surprised individual simply in order to annoy the interfering composer. The childish trick had become a diplomatic necessity and it clearly expressed his reaction. Yet Wagner remained convinced that he had a captive audience; he was later to write to his friend, Dr. Schwarzenbach in Munich, "During my visit to Hohenschwangau (...) the secretary, Lutz, explained to me the policy of HM's Government at that time (with the undisguised object of getting my co-operation). This policy was governed by the fact that, while it was impossible to rely on Austria and still less was it desired to stand for a German Parliament, an agreement was in train with Bismarck and the new Prussian policy, in pursuance of which it was proposed to restore the Bavarian constitution as it was in 1848. Since this involved a restoration of the absolute power of the Crown, I, so Herr Lutz supposed, as a particular friend of the King, would no doubt be glad to support the Government in being." Unbeknown to them both, Ludwig was perfectly well aware of all these political manoeuvres but chose to keep a low profile.

* Cosima was the fruit of Liszt's liaison with the Comtesse Marie d'Agoult.

Despite his thirst for culture, he always found it hard to tear himself away from the mountains. In letters to his many correspondants, he made frequent references to his surroundings, as if setting the scene for his reader:

"Because of the intolerable heat of the sun riding was, to be honest, a torture instead of a pleasure, and I left Berg just after midnight and travelled on a faithful horse to my beloved mountains. Shining stars lit the path, the moonlight shone magically through the venerable trees..."

"As I stood on the shores of the picturesque Walchensee, I was greeted by the golden rays of the majestic sun which made the tips of the mountains glow in rosy light..."

"I am writing this letter on a mountain in the high Alpine region far from the bustle of the crowd..."

"Slowly, the light of the day sinks and disappears behind the high chain of mountains; peace reigns in the deep valleys; the sound of cowbells, the song of a herdsman insinuate their way into my blissful solitude; the evening star sends its soft light from afar..."

"In the distance, at the end of the valley, the church at Ettal looms out of the dark green of the fir trees..."

Ludwig loved nature with every fibre of his poetic soul and would have been happy to live permanently on a mountain top or in the heart of a forest. Most of his more prosaic relatives frittered away their time hunting and slaughtering everything that moved, but with a characteristic explanation which confounded his fellows, Ludwig never killed a living thing in the whole of his adult life. "What harm have they done me?" he would say. If he accompanied his family on a hunting trip, he would shoot only into the air. On one occasion, as a practical joke Otto, who shared the family view that Ludwig's attitude was quaint, turned up for the hunt wearing full mourning "In advance, out of respect for the animals." Ludwig was not amused.

Although Wagner claimed to be a poet, he was basically a realist, with as little patience with Ludwig as his own family and certainly no time for his compassion. He was frequently rude and unpleasant while obligingly accepting the many totally undeserved gifts which continued to arrive from the King. Among other things, the King had given him an exquisite blue enamelled watch which opened to reveal a picture of Lohengrin in his swan boat, a variety of cufflinks and several rings. Still

Wagner gave nothing in return but unwanted homily, and when verbal entreaty failed, he continued to pursue the King by letter: "Summon the new secretary!" he advised, "Nowhere, nowhere at all is there anyone who understands you! You cannot expect to hear a 'Hail!' from anywhere until you drive the 'new man' like an arrowhead into these alien opposing interests!" He was nothing if not persistent and had it not been for Ludwig's aesthetic need of Wagner, whose ideas and talent surpassed all others at least in the musical field, then the King might have concerned himself with finding a new composer rather than a new secretary. Yet for all his determination to ignore Wagner's hysterical suggestions, there was the constant danger that, as in other matters, he would eventually be persuaded by sheer force of repetition.

November was so unseasonably fine and mild in the Allgäu that Ludwig could not bring himself to leave it and of course, Wagner stayed too. Unable to stomach the proximity of his *bête noir* any longer, on the pretext of acting as a go-between for the King and his cabinet, Pfistermeister returned to Munich, thereby perhaps unwittingly unleashing on Wagner another potential enemy in the shape of Minister Lutz, an ambitious and unscrupulous man who hoped ultimately to become Prime Minister. Prince Hohenlohe described him most graphically as "unwholesome". Despite the presence of this stocky, malevolent figure, Ludwig enjoyed his holiday and the time spent with Wagner helped him to recapture the essence of *Lohengrin*. This was not particularly difficult at Schloss Hohenschwangau, with its breathtaking surroundings of mountains, lakes and rich highlands. Swans were very much in evidence, not only on the lakes but also in various art forms inside the castle, and a huge stone swan was even poised on the roof.

The castle had been built between 1832 and 1856 by Ludwig's father on the ruins of a medieval stronghold, employing among others Moritz von Schwind and Dominik Quaglio to embellish its interior. Hohenschwangau was used extensively by the family, all of whom were deeply attached to it, possibly because it was so totally different from all the other chill and lifeless Royal residences.

It stood on a height overlooking on the one side the Alpsee and on the other the tiny, jewel-like Schwansee. Built in yellow limestone, it contrasted sharply with the dense foliage of the surrounding forest. In its walled garden bloomed roses in profusion and from Schwanthaler's large stone fountain guarded by a quartet of stone lions flowed clear mountain water. Inside, the glowing tempera frescoes, especially those depicting the Arthurian legend of *Lohengrin*, were a source of eternal fascination to Ludwig.

Unfortunately, most of the rooms in the castle bore the unmistakeable stamp of the provincial housewife; valuable *objets d'art* and pieces of sentimental *bric-à-brac* of no monetary or artistic value were scattered about or crammed together in cabinets in such disarray that nothing could be seen to the best advantage. Queen Marie had somehow managed to lower the standards of beauty and charm imposed by the architect to mere bourgeoiserie, and only the glorious natural beauty of its surroundings rescued it from aesthetic obscurity.

Predictably, Ludwig's own alterations caused much comment. With relish, Count Blome had reported to Vienna, "I don't know if Your Excellency has heard that His Majesty's bedroom at Hohenschwangau has been embellished with an artificial lamp in the shape of a moon which, according to whim, can represent the waxing and waning of the quarters, half and full moon and that the dull glow of this moon is accompanied by the continual splashing of a miniature fountain. Orange trees were to have completed the scenery but when Dr. Gietl, the physician, advised against the installation of these vegetable elements, the exotic growths were at least only to be painted ones. Fortunately, only the scenery from the Royal Court Theatre has thus been brought to decorate the Royal bedroom." With his total lack of interest in the feminine sex, Ludwig must have been a bitter disappointment to Count Blome, whose joy would have known no bounds had a ballet girl been installed to match the scenery.

After Wagner left Hohenschwangau, Ludwig and Taxis remained, holding firework displays over the lake and re-enacting scenes from Lohengrin with Taxis, in full costume, playing the title role. Ludwig's inexplicable pleasure in these childish games and, indeed, others less childish, were somewhat dimmed by reports to the effect that his behaviour was causing gossip. On his return to Munich, he wrote to Sybille Leonrod, "I hear that there are still the most curious rumours in the country about my relations with Wagner; do not lend your ears to such gossip, I entreat you. People must always have something to talk about but they exaggerate everything."

It is possible that the "gossip" was being perpetrated because Wagner continued to plague the King with political advice which he was now presenting to Ludwig in the form of a kind of journal. For reasons of his own, Ludwig duly presented copies to the ministers, who were not amused. The simple truth was that Ludwig frequently asked advice on the understanding that he did not feel obligated to take it, but Wagner failed to appreciate this and, assuming the King's interest to be greater than it was, began to press hard for the reinstatement of Maximilian von Neumayr not merely as a cabinet minister but as Prime Minister*. Inevitably, Ludwig now became increasingly irritated be-

---

* This gentleman had been forced to resign his post as Minister for the interior some time before because Ludwig and his grandfather, with justification, did not trust him.

cause Wagner would not leave him alone, but was understandably unwilling to alienate him totally until he had fulfilled his contractual obligations.

Prudently, the King wrote to his interfering friend, "I have considered your advice very carefully. Rest assured, my dear friend, that what I now write in answer is not the result of hasty and superficial consideration - I had the best of reasons for letting Neumayr go, and for withdrawing the confidence I had in him - so it would be fully inconsistent for me to entrust this man with whom (I repeat) I have every reason to be dissatisifed, with the formation of a new Cabinet. There is no doubt that Pfistermeister is stupid and second rate; I shall not keep him for much longer in the cabinet, but to dismiss him and the other members of the cabinet at this moment does not seem advisable; the time is not ripe." This shows remarkably level-headed judgement on the part of the new and "inexperienced" monarch.

When eventually Ludwig did replace both Pfordten and Pfistermeister, he did so for his own reasons. In the same letter to Wagner, he acknowledged a newspaper article from the Volksbote of the previous day which the composer had thoughtfully enclosed. It was the second such article. The first, a vitriolic attack on Pfistermeister, which had appeared some two weeks earlier in the *Nürnberger Anzeige*, was entitled "Plain words to the King of Bavaria and his People on the Subject of the Cabinet Secretariat". The latest piece pointed out that Richard Wagner had cost the country a fortune and that another small fortune was about to slip into his greedy hands. In a vein highly uncomplimentary to Wagner, it even hinted that the composer himself might have written the first article as a means of furthering his own nefarious ends, which was probably true.

Ludwig's reaction to all this was disappointingly cool and Wagner, determined to have his own way, now sent to the *Neueste Nachrichten* an "anonymous" article in which the King's devotion to Wagner was emphasised in a manner so blatant and personal that it deceived nobody, least of all Ludwig, who calmly observed to Pfordten, "I hear that the mood is somewhat agitated and that the public seems very occupied with R. Wagner. I urge you earnestly however, not to believe the exaggerations which the people are spreading about my relationship with him. People even say - and it is out of the question - that he draws me away from Government business and seems to gain influence himself. I follow him solely for artistic purposes and request you to deny every rumour at every available opportunity and to refute them in every way."

Sadly for Ludwig, Pfordten did not see fit to do as he was asked but instead, in a lengthy reply, poured out his rancour towards Wagner.

As he read it, the King can only have seen confirmation of his own conclusion: Wagner was becoming an embarrassment and whether or not he completed the operas, would have to go. He knew that he must find a way of dispatching the composer from Munich without losing face and remaining on good terms with him. This was no simple task, but Wagner himself had unwittingly provided him with the ammunition he needed. Meticulously, he consulted his mother, his more level-headed relations, his doctor and his Archbishop. It was Dr.Gietl whose voice carried the most weight and Ludwig gave all appearance of listening when the doctor reminded him how the whole of Bavaria condemned Wagner's influence over him as "doubtful", how their faith in him had been eroded and that "deep shadows" lay between King and people. Ludwig was deeply wounded. "Feel my pulse," he offered, "You can feel how upset I am." Admitting that he had, perhaps, permitted Wagner to "encroach", he agreed: Wagner must go. But did he really allow others to pursuade him? It is clear from his letter to Pfordten that he was already aware of the answer before he had asked the question. Ludwig did not dismiss Wagner for his Ministers but for himself.

On December 3rd, 1865, from the safety of Hohenschwangau he produced as fine a piece of diplomatic prose as he could muster: "Oh, my beloved Friend, my agony has been great over the past few days! My first days in Munich were therefore strenuous and dreary for me; it will be a long time before I can find the peace which is so important to me. That article in the *Neueste Nachrichten* contributed not a little to embitter my stay. It is, without doubt, written by one of your friends who hopes to do you a service. Unfortunately, however, instead of helping you he has done you an injury. Oh, my friend, how frightfully difficult people make things for us! However, I will not complain. I have at least the Friend, the Only One. Let me not complain, in spite of everything. Don't let us lose our way; let me draw back from the outside world that does not understand us!"

Another article in the *Neue Bayerische Kurier* pronounced "The least evil that this foreigner brings to our country is in connection with his insatiable appetite which can only be compared with a swarm of locusts which darken the sun for months on end. This terrible picture of a plague like those of the Pharoahs, however, amounts to nothing compared with the disaster which this one, excessively overestimated man wreaks when, instead of the '*Art of the Future*'* he puts in motion the politics of the future. The paid music maker, the man of the barricades from Dresden who once marched at the head of a band of arsonists with the idea of burning down the Royal Palace in Dresden,

---

* Wagner's lengthy prose work.

intends at this stage to gradually separate the King from his faithful followers, replace them with his political supporters in order to isolate the King and exploit the treasonable actions of a ruthless revolutionary party."

Strong stuff, this, but no stronger than what the King's own Ministerium was mumbling to itself. Not realising even now how acutely Ludwig was aware of the present and potential dangers or indeed, how tiresome he himself found the composer, the Cabinet continued to criticise the King. They had already decided amongst themselves that extreme measures must be taken to rid the country of Wagner, mistakenly attributing Ludwig's gradual but definite withdrawal from his official obligations as being due solely to the composer's influence. They had not grasped the fact that Ludwig's basically hermetic nature was the result of his upbringing and the misguided methods and ideas which had been employed without thought for the boy on whom they had been inflicted.

Summoning his Ministerium, the King at last gave Lutz, who was at that time the Minister of the Upper Court of Appeal, the welcome task of giving Wagner his marching orders "for patriotic reasons." Lutz could hardly wait. He was accompanied to the Briennerstrasse by Pfistermeister and both men were full of contempt for Wagner's histrionic reaction to the news. In vain he protested, unleashing a stream of invective against his tormenters, mostly against Pfistermeister until Lutz felt moved to remind him contemptuously, "Control yourself! I am here in my official capacity!" Wagner would have found little comfort in the knowledge that, while this real life drama was in progress, the King was at the theatre, calmly enjoying a performance of *Ifegenia* with one of his favourite tragediennes, Frau Janaschek, in the title role. Only the following day did he spare a thought for his discarded friend: "My dear friend, It grieves me that I must ask you to carry out the wishes which I expressed yesterday through my secretary. Believe me, I must act in this way. My love for you will last forever; therefore, I ask you always to preserve your friendship for me. With a clear conscience I dare to say that I am grateful to you - who dares to part us? I know that you feel with me and can gauge exactly the deep pain I feel; rest assured I had no other course, otherwise, never doubt the fidelity of your best friend - it is certainly not forever. Until death, your faithful Ludwig."

Simultaneously, "faithful Ludwig" informed Pfordten, "My decision stands firm. R. Wagner must leave Bavaria. I want to show my faithful people that his trust, his love for me, can surmount everything. You will be able to judge that it was not easy for me; however, I have overcome my feelings." Clearly, he wanted to appear as the martyred young King deprived of his only friend, but in actuality, he managed very well without Wagner and approached him only when he needed artistic stimulation.

When less demanding company came his way, Wagner was invariably forgotten. At other times he wrote to the composer fulsomely, flatteringly, cloyingly even, because he knew the way to get the best response from him, but never was he blind to Wagner's many fault as has so often been suggested, nor was he as sorry to see him leave Munich as he would have everyone think. For after all, Ludwig ruled over an autonomous land where the Monarch's word was still law; if he had really wanted the composer to remain in the capital, all the Ministers in the world could not have prevented him from keeping him there, and public opinion would not have mattered one iota. It was his own decision and it is obvious that fundmanentally, Ludwig was relieved to be rid of him.

And so, on a cold and misty November dawn, Richard Wagner departed for Switzerland a shocked and temporarily chastened man. His "young lad" over whom he had thought he held such sway, did not see him off and only his friends Cornelius and Heinrich, together with the distraught Cosima, came to bid him farewell. Cosima at least was genuinely griefstricken for as she was still officially the wife of the court musician, she could not go with her lover into exile. Perhaps the love which Wagner in turn bore for her was the only truly constant thing in his life,* for even his devotion to his work was often outweighed and forgotten in his eternal quest for pleasure with her.

The train thus left Munich watched only by sleepy-eyed officials who were sent to ensure that the composer was on the train. To date, Wagner had cost the King an amount equal to a year's Civil List and it is small wonder that his departure received better notices in the newspapers than had some of his operatic works.

---

* Even so, there is evidence of his infidelity after their marriage in 1867.

CHAPTER FIVE

THE WAR OF 1866

IF Wagner, languishing in Switzerland, imagined that Ludwig was grieving over their separation, he was mistaken. On the contrary, events show that once the composer was out of the King's sight he was usually out of mind, and at this particular time Ludwig's days were totally occupied with Elisabeth of Austria.

The Empress had found a reason to visit Bavaria in the recurrence of one of her many illnesses for which she preferred to seek treatment from her family physician, Dr. Fischer, rather than from a Viennese specialist. Both her illness and her visit to Munich provoked much speculation but she was determined to go. Franz Josef, who was not in Vienna, was much annoyed when, out of the blue she telegraphed asking his permission to travel to her homeland. He agreed only reluctantly and telegraphed Ludwig forbidding him to meet the Empress at the railway station as was customary. For whatever reason, the Emperor wanted the visit kept as quiet as possible, either because he felt an element of responsibility for his wife's illness or because he suspected that her friendship with her handsome young cousin was warmer than it should have been.

Undeterred, Ludwig ignored the Emperor's request and rose eagerly from his own sickbed to meet her. Nothing would have kept him away and his presence with a large bouquet provided a feast for Court gossips in both capitals. It did not go unremarked that once on Bavarian soil, Elisabeth's health took an immediate turn for the better or that during her stay in Munich, she spent most of the time with the King.

Elisabeth's sudden departure from Vienna caused endless speculation: many people thought that Ludwig was her sole reason for leaving her family immediately before the Christmas festivities while others were busy guessing whether there was something nefarious or even shocking about her ailment. Yet another school of thought was that Sisi was not ill at all but had merely quarrelled with the Emperor. On the whole, opinion swayed towards the theory that she was using the visit to Dr. Fischer as an excuse to be with Ludwig. Their devotion to each other was no secret but in view of their age discrepancy it had earlier been assumed that their closeness was merely that of cousins with similar interests.

To escape the flutter of gossip and because they both disliked the city, the pair fled to Starnberg where, in defiance of Sisi's allegedly poor health, they met frequently in continued driving rain and biting winter winds at Schloss Berg, Possenhofen and deep in the forests of the Ammerland. An even more frequent rendezvous was the Roseninsel. Its secluded, zig-zagged paths were denuded at this time of year of the breathtaking summer display of heavily scented roses, but it still had a beauty of its own and even on the days when the waters of the lake were swollen with rain, the waves tossing as wildly as those of the open sea, Ludwig and Sisi would brave the elements to spend hours together in the wooden summerhouse which had long been regarded as their private domain. Only a very few of Ludwig's friends were taken to the Roseninsel while Elisabeth on her side invited only her daughters to share its charms.

Despite her initial promise to Franz Josef to return home after a few days, Sisi remained in Bavaria to spend Christmas and her birthday with Ludwig and only made her way back to her family in Vienna on December 30th. She offered further proof of her deep feeling for Ludwig in a note written to him just before her arrival in his capital: "Whatever circumstances should arise, remain convinced of the deep love with which I cling to my homeland and of the true and loving friendship which I hold for you especially."

The circumstances to which she referred did arise shortly after her return to Vienna, when the situation between Austria and Prussia deteriorated sharply. Placed both geographically and politically speaking between the two, Bavaria could no longer avoid the necessity of siding with one or the other. Already equipped with a draft agreement with Prussia, Pfordten now presented his views to the horrified King. War against Austria meant war against Sisi. It was unthinkable. A pacifist to the core, he could not bring himself even to think about war yet the Empress, considered by most to have little interest in politics, had evidently recognised the trend some weeks earlier and had already accepted the inevitable.

Ludwig still refused even to discuss the matter with his Ministerium and Pfordten was forced to lapse into a frustrated silence until given leave to withdraw. Even the persuasive Taxis could not induce Ludwig to involve himself. The Ministers' reaction to all this nevertheless seems ambiguous, for while in one breath they were complaining about the King's seeming indifference to his duty, they were in the next congratulating themselves on having a more or less free hand. For the decisions had still to be made even if the King refused to have anything to do with the matter.

Ludwig was never a fighter; when things went wrong, his instinct was to withdraw into his shell rather than enter into an undignified dispute and this is what he now did. More than that, he avoided signing State documents concerning the war by leaving the city and the situation was thus becoming more desperate by the hour. When he heard of his grandson's defection into the mountains, the deposed Ludwig I was filled with foreboding. Attempting to avert a catastrophe, he sent a peace bid directly to the King of Prussia: "An unjustifiable war is rather dreadful in this world; dreadful also is the answering to posterity. A war between Prussia and Austria could have the most unfortunate consequences. Your Majesty would not wish it to be said that King Wilhelm's aspirations to enlargement [of territory] threw the Fatherland into ruin."

But despite this reasonable letter Wilhelm, easily manipulated by Bismarck, did not apparently care what posterity thought. Everywhere, preparations for war were being made, but few countries possessed the military might and high standards of training of the Prussian forces and the outcome of a conflict was obvious. The Bavarian Government had decided upon "immediate mobilisation" and proposed a recall of the Landtag on May 22nd, which was not only Wagner's birthday but also a day far more important to Ludwig because of a scheduled gala performance of *Lohengrin* than for any more bellicose reason and he would not agree. This is inevitably presented as an indication of his total irresponsibility but in fact, his apparent obsession with unreality cloaked a very real desire to prevent war. And what better way could he have chosen than to put himself out of reach of the mobilisation order which only he, as the reigning monarch, could sign? He was eventually persuaded to append his signature to the document, but having done so, retired to his apartments with an excruciating headache and the conviction that he had done the wrong thing.

To alleviate the headache he took a large dose of chloral, convinced of its beneficial properties despite Pfistermeister's [alleged] entreaties for circumspection. As Ludwig's reliance on this substance increased, there were days when he was undoubtedly not his own master and he would become either violent or morose. Sometimes the violence would erupt in the form of unreasonable anger while on other occasions it found its outlet in passionate longings for the unattainable. He was also subject to hallucinations and following such manifestations, would summon his secretary and announce, "I am ill. I am going mad." Pfistermeister's suggestion that all he needed was less chloral and a visit to the family doctor to find a different cure for the headaches invariably led to a lengthy monologue on the possibility of abdication in favour of his brother were the histrionics of a young man totally out of his depth in the current climate and high on the drug, he cannot have expected to be taken seriously, especially since Otto, although admit-tedly fonder of war games, was even younger and more inexperienced than Ludwig himself. When not under the influence of his "medicine" Ludwig would have been the first to see this.

His headaches did not abate with the aid of the chloral, but Pfistermeister, struggling to reason with the King when he was under the influence, might well have succumbed to the same ailment. He was never allowed to send for Dr. Gietl since the very mention of a physician struck fear into Ludwig's heart and throughout his life, he dreaded consultations of any kind; he even suffered severe myopia and agonies of toothache rather than seek the services of an optician or a dentist.

When Pfordten sought out the King to discuss the war with him, he could not be found. Still disgusted with himself for signing the mobilisation he wanted only to get away from the scene of what he saw as his crime. He had set off with Taxis and a groom, Voelck, ostensibly for his morning ride but actually to take the ferry to Konstanz in Switzerland to visit Wagner, who now lived at Tribschen.

Wrapped in a cape and hat which concealed most of his person if not his identity, he announced himself as "Walther von Stolzing" knowing that the composer, who discussed his work only with his closest associates, would immediately guess his identity. Doubtless in the expectation of a renewed stream of presents, Wagner accorded his Royal friend a warm welcome although involved as he was with Cosima it is unlikely that he was truly pleased to see him. The King at any rate was in his seventh heaven. All he wanted was to get away from Bavaria for a few hours to enjoy some erudite conversation instead of the gloomy talk of war, knowing well enough that his Ministers, who had arranged everything between themselves, could get along perfectly well without him. His lack of surprise at finding Cosima in residence would confirm that he was perfectly well aware of the true situation in that quarter. Wagner made good use of the opportunity to bend Ludwig's ear. Still angry with his cabinet, he was more than usually gullible and on his return to Munich after two days of blissful release at Tribschen, sent the ominous telegram to his host, "Safely arrived in Munich. Deeply moved by the parting. Tempered by the time of ecstasy while I was with you. Firmly decided to tear out the weeds by the roots. Proud and sure of victory."

His spirits were soon to be deflated for when he entered the capital he found that news of his weekend in Switzerland had leaked out and had spread like wildfire. The people of Munich were not given to concealing their feelings and indignant in their assumption that he had abandoned them, were quick to show their disapproval, hurling abuse as his carriage moved through the streets. Dolefully he informed Cosima, "How empty and dull all the people now seem to me with their miserable, insect-like souls, in comparison with you and HIM!! [Wagner]. Wherever I look I find mediocrity and narrowmindedness. The people are good, their innermost core is healthy, but they are without ideas of their own and are easily led."

The Cabinet had advised him to show himself and this was the result. Hurt and mortified, he crept back into his shell but after some lengthy persuasion was prevailed upon to open the Landtag. This time he was not greeted with jeers but with an equally upsetting resentful silence. There is no doubt that public reaction at this time effectively served to strengthen his resolve to carry out some of the revolutionary ideas which had been put to him in Switzerland. Again, he telegraphed to Cosima, "The opening of the Landtag took place today. Reception icy cold. Press disgraceful! Does the *Freundin* believe that a moment of trepidation and repentence shakes me? Oh no! The great goal in sight remains unshakeably firm (...) I am filled with courage and confidence."

He proved it by demoting the Chief of Police to a post in Augsburg following that gentleman's report concerning his safety when he appeared in public. Having thus tried out his wings, he fled again to the Roseninsel, and sending for three beds for himself, Taxis and Voelck remained sulking, out of reach of the Ministers who dared not follow and, indeed, had no means of doing so. Prince Hohenlohe noted in his diary on June 16th, 1866, "The King sees no one. He is staying with Taxis and Voelck on the Rosen-Insel and lets off fireworks. Even the members of the Upper House who were to deliver the address to him were not received - a case unparallelled in the history of the constitutional life of Bavaria." Count Blome, who could always be relied upon for some ascerbic comment, merely quoted the tongue-in-cheek reply which he had received when he asked one of Ludwig's more loyal subjects what he was doing: "A prosaic sailor whom I questioned when he rowed me and my family past the island gave me the information, 'He is doing his exercises.' In all probability, it was a costumed performance of *Lohengrin* on which he was engaged."

Blome was being somewhat hard on Ludwig. To open the Chamber had been a great ordeal for the young man who deeply resented this sudden public hostility. Predictably, he reverted to thoughts of abdication, pointing out repeatedly to the scandalised secretary that, with his easy, outgoing nature, his aptitude for the military and his willingness to marry, Otto would make a better King. Pfistermeister's only defence was that the people's anger was only momentary and that they loved him enough to feel they had the right to criticise him when he incurred their displeasure. To abandon them totally now that war was imminent would not only break their hearts but would undoubtedly weaken their morale, he told the doubtful Ludwig.

Other considerations aside, Pfistermeister was clearly convinced that Ludwig's threat to give up his throne and go to live with Wagner in Switzerland was spoken with the voice of chloralhydrate, although he must have speculated privately as to how the King would have fitted into Wagner's love nest and how pleased the composer would have been to have found him on the doorstep with all his possessions as opposed to a romantic incognito arrival for a weekend visit.

The argument continued for some time, Pfistermeister remaining calm and continuing to plead quietly with Ludwig, the latter becoming increasingly excited until at last the exhausted secretary agreed to set in motion the wheels to arrange for Wagner's return to Munich. "Otherwise", Ludwig asserted, "all will be at an end." As usual, Pfistermeister did as he was bid, but when sending the official request to the Privy Counsellor concerned (Dr. Gietl), he took the precaution of adding "I do so herewith according to instructions, but naturally on the firm assumption that you, esteemed Privy Counsellor, will not even consider complying with such a request.(...) After he [Ludwig] spent 1 1/2 hours with me discussing such things, he rode off at 3 in the afternoon, via Seeshaupt, to dine on the Island and came back immediately afterwards, as he has done for the last couple of days, in a heavy shower of rain. That should certainly cool him down, but it will be of little benefit to his health. Therefore, don't change anything!"

Some months earlier, Count Blome had made the contemptuous observation that Pfistermeister had "only been in such high favour for so long because he never openly opposes but either tries to carry out the command or finds a way of paralysing it during its execution." While this is fair comment and whatever motive lay behind it, Pfistermeister's system certainly averted many a crisis during his years of service with the King. There is, however, some ground for believing that towards the end of his appointment, he had already joined Ludwig's growing band of enemies.

While Pfistermeister wrestled with the current problem, Ludwig again ordered his horse and rode to Seeshaupt undeterred by the continued bad weather, to keep a rendezvous with Elisabeth. It is a curious fact that rain seemed always to dog their meetings but they were oblivious to the elements when they were together. Elisabeth undoubtedly had a calming influence on the King and, after seeing her, he returned to his duties cheered and refreshed, all thoughts of abdication dispelled by the combination of Sisi's company and abstension from Chloral. In a moment of depression a few days earlier, he had telegraphed to Tribschen, "If it is your will, then I shall gladly relinquish the Crown and its dreary glamour, and come to him, never more to be parted." By the time he received Wagner's horrified reply, he had come to his senses and saw his views in a more rational light.

For once, the composer and Ludwig's family were in accord, if for different reasons. The last thing that Wagner wanted was a King without a Throne or, more to the point, a King unequal to bestowing kingly gifts. His advice to Ludwig was that he should remain on the Throne and do his duty, not forgetting that his artistic dreams would never come to fruition if he was not in a position of power. The counsel itself was good, but as with all of Wagner's advice, it was inspired by the wrong motives and counted as a black mark against him in the eyes of the disappointed recipient. Like most people who constantly pester their friends for advice, Ludwig would have been appalled by the idea of acting upon it.

Battle was now imminent and, one by one, Ludwig's male relatives made futile attempts to arouse his interest. Even the septugenarian Prince Karl, who was at that time in command of the Army, visited him to try to persuade him to return to his capital and review the troops. Unwillingly and with obvious distaste he agreed, but he did not receive the same warmth of welcome as that accorded to his deposed grandfather who, in the continued absence of the younger Ludwig, had appeared in public as often as possible to try to boost the morale of the dispirited public. Old Ludwig had long since been forgiven his indiscretions and was not only seen as a staunch patriot but also as a man who still loved the people who had destroyed him. In a bid to regain his own lost prestige, the King ultimately responded to his family's wishes and participated in the Corpus Christi procession in Munich. But it was no longer enough. The Bavarians were not ready to forgive their young Adonis for his feet of clay.

Another scurrilous article now appeared in the *Volksbote*. Written by the editor himself, it contained the damaging words "It is scarcely a year since Madame Hans von Bülow got away in the famous carriage with 10,000 Gulden from the Treasury for her 'Friend' (or what?)(...). For the moment she is staying with her 'Friend' (or what?) in Lucerne where she was also to be found during the visit of an exalted person." There were no prizes for guessing the identity of the "exalted person" and a fresh eruption of public fury ensued. In a feeble attempt to salvage his honour, Bülow challenged the editor to a duel. He was all too well aware of his wife's infidelity and, indeed, as part of the much discussed ménage-à-trois, appeared to condone it. But the fact that all Germany knew of it was another matter. Presumably in his anguish he thought erroneously that his action would protect his good name and Cosima's also. In the event, he pleased nobody; his puny efforts were not enough for Cosima, who had no more scruples than Wagner when it came to appealing to the King for assistance. "On my knees," she wrote, "I humbly beg my King to write the letter for my husband so that we may not be forced to leave the country in disgrace and shame. Only your Royal word can re-establish our insulted honour (...) How would it be possible for my husband to work in a town where the honour of his wife has been doubted? My Royal Lord, I have three children to whom I must transfer the honourable name of their father without a stain."

Surely Cosima did not believe that Ludwig was ignorant of sordid reality? She had asked the King to perjure himself and extraordinarily, he complied, gallant if disbelieving. The letter was, of course, addressed to Bülow himself and the recipient was pleased to read "As I have been in a position to obtain the best intimate knowledge of the character of your honourable wife, it remains only for me to discover the inexplicable reasons for these criminal insults." A noble gesture indeed since, having just returned from Tribschen, Ludwig of all people knew the extent of Cosima's guilt and the nature of her relationship with Wagner. Shortly afterwards she not only again betrayed her husband but the King as well, for at the very time when Bülow's letter appeared in print, Cosima announced that she was pregnant again and this time not even Ludwig could have doubted that Wagner was to blame.

The country had been involved in a more serious dispute than this when, on June 8th, in company with Saxony, Bavaria had at last pledged herself to assist Austria. War had been declared on June 15th and on the 16th Prussia marched on Hannover. Totally out of his depth, Ludwig could only repeat from his lakeside retreat "I want no war! All I want is peace and quiet" before immersing himself again in his more aesthetic activities. Count Blome, who seemed to spend his life in the unworthy pursuit of gossip, continued his usual acrimonious stream of complaints to Vienna: "Since the 10th, the King has been on the Roseninsel letting off fireworks. No one has been able to speak to him for days, and this at a time when it is a matter of war and peace. People are beginning to take him for mad."

Nevertheless, on the 26th and 27th, Ludwig was prevailed upon to visit the army headquarters at Bamberg, an act which, despite Blome's uncomplimentary remarks, won him much approval. He was accorded a rapturous welcome by troops and civilians alike: he was their darling again, loved and admired by all. With his good looks and enigmatic, slightly unworldly air, even rough and hardened men gazing on him for the first time were speechless with admiration. Striding in his silver-blue uniform through the ranks of men, taller by some six inches or so than any man present, he awoke in every soldier's breast the most fervent loyalty.

A famous and oft-quoted anecdote describing his effect upon people stemmed from the first-hand impression of the famous charisma on a non-Bavarian: "At a regimental officers' dinner of the participating States of the German Union, the double doors flew open to admit a youth so handsome and of such unearthly beauty that my heart almost stopped beating. He wore a silver-blue service tunic and a hanging riding mantle with rich folds. With the brilliance of his wonderful dark eyes he was like a living Knight of the Grail. So enraptured was I that I even experienced a feeling of anxiety: this Godlike youth was almost too beautiful for this world. I whispered to my Bavarian comrades who were my table companions, and who, like all the Bavarian gentlemen present, had risen at the entry of the fine figure, 'Who is that?' and the reply came in an almost hallowed voice, 'That is our young king'." Something about Ludwig invariably inspired such emotions in all who met him and it was clearly not merely on account of his physical appearance for the reaction to his personality remained long after the famous good looks had disappeared.

Ludwig was delighted, if surprised, by his reception but while he enjoyed the adulation for a short while, he could not sustain this kind of thing for very long and only days later he returned to the Roseninsel to mend his shattered nerves and to re-live happier days spent there with Taxis and with Elisabeth, who had loyally hurried to her husband's side on the outbreak of war.

Inspired for the moment in the same way as Ludwig himself, the Empress had thrown herself wholeheartedly into the self-imposed task of caring for the casualties and nursing the more severely injured men with her own hands. Momentarily in favour, she fully justified the title "Angel of the wounded" gratefully conferred by those who had received help from hands which were more accustomed to holding the reins of her hunter than the dressings of the wounded.

Meanwhile, the war advanced and Ludwig put on a good front for the sake of morale. Whether or not he was sincere, he was even moved to write to Wagner; "Germany will not - cannot - go to ruin; this will never happen. My belief in its durability, its greatness, is unshaken. God will protect it. The dear one has already heard about my journey to the Headquarters; unfortunately, I could not visit the entire Army because a part of it had already crossed the Bavarian border. Also, because of many pressing duties I could not leave the capital earlier. I was greeted everywhere by my brave troops with storms of joy; they march against the enemy full of courage and enthusiasm. Justice will conquer!"

His confidence and enthusiasm were as short-lived as the war itself. Prince Karl was universally held to be too old to command and, despite his highly critical remarks about Ludwig, somewhat incompetent. Karl had complained bitterly to Ludwig's grandfather that when he had sent his adjutant to the King with important orders "he did not ask a single question concerning the Army or what it was doing", but in fact Ludwig, who kept himself informed, had no need to do so. His absence provoked further criticism, although it made little difference whether he was there or not, for there was nothing he could have done to change the inevitable outcome. Tireless and powerful, the Prussians forged towards Aschaffenburg and old Ludwig I was obliged to beat an undignified retreat from the Johannisburg. Little Saxony had been quickly overpowered and the Hannoverians brought to heel. Then, on July 3rd, the Austrians suffered a terrible defeat at Königgrätz [Sadowa] and Bavaria tasted the bitterness of defeat a week later when Bad Kissingen was the scene of another bloody battle. Only a year before, Ludwig had strolled in the Spa Gardens in the sunshine with Elisabeth on his arm and every female under 90 at his feet, intoxicated by the gaiety, the music, the champagne and the fascinating Empress whom he adored. Now there existed only blood, death and horror. Corpses and broken bodies lay strewn across the countryside and the stench of decaying flesh was strong in the heat of the Bavarian summer. Every day, Ludwig's army was forced to retreat, weary and humiliated but willing to fight to the last.

The Prussians had always been a militaristic people and now they seemed all too eager to prove that they had lost neither the taste nor the ability for fighting. It was even rumoured that both Munich and Vienna were about to be overrun by these titans. In fact, the battle of Königgrätz heralded the end of the hostilities.

Ludwig's overwhelming humiliation in defeat was overshadowed by his shame at having signed the mobilisation order for in his view, had he not done so there would have been no war. He felt increasingly guilty of causing the deaths of Bavaria's sons who had given their lives for a lost cause. He was never to forgive himself. The fact that it had been a case of German killing German had made it that much worse and with his trust in his Cabinet totally dissipated, the 21 year old King despairingly to Wagner "Everywhere is gloom and betrayal; sacred oaths mean nothing; agreements are broken; however, I do not give up hope. God will see that the Bavarians will keep their independence; if we must endure Prussian supremacy, I will not continue as a shadow King without power."

With an anxiety stemming from less noble motives than Ludwig's, Wagner replied forthwith, "On my knees I beg you to appoint Prince

Hohenlohe immediately. The dissatisfaction is so general that your decision would be totally justified." But Ludwig was in no mood to listen to advice of this sort and turned again to Prince Taxis. For some three years their relationship had waxed and waned with monotonous frequency. When they were on good terms, they were inseparable and created for themselves a private world in which Ludwig became "Heinrich" while Paul was known as "Friedrich"; these pseudonyms not only provided a convenient cover for their private correspondence but also carried a deeper psychological meaning for Ludwig, who felt that he could do things as "Heinrich" which he could never attempt as the King.

Taxis was deeply fond of Ludwig although he could not always anticipate his mercurial moods. Following the many altercations with his Cabinet, the King was becoming increasingly sensitive and an ill-timed or badly phrased remark would send him, like Elisabeth, into an impenetrable shell. In spite of their closeness, Taxis was constantly falling from favour because of some hasty remark or, more frequently, when Ludwig had discovered him to be "faithless". Paul was unable to control his sexual appetite and rumours of his off duty amorous pursuits in the brothels and taverns of Munich as well as with girls nearer his own station in life were constantly being whispered into Ludwig's ear.

Nevertheless, Paul's supportive attitude had been a great comfort in in his postwar despair. Defeat by the Prussians was harder to bear than merely being blatantly deceived and used by Richard Wagner. In his present mood, Ludwig could not even bring himself to visit his defeated and humiliated army, mistakenly believing that they in turn would not want to see him. Instead, he rather unforgivably laid this unpleasant task on Paul's shoulders. Prince Taxis was too well trained and probably, if the truth were known, too afraid of Ludwig's unpredictable temper, to express disapproval when he was asked to do something from which his Sovereign shrank. He decided that it was better to go as Ludwig's emissary rather than have the men believe that they had been abandoned altogether and set out with a willing if not entirely happy heart to look into the accusing eyes of the humiliated and exhausted men who were disappointed to see a proxy in place of their handsome young monarch.

After agreeing to do this, Ludwig had dropped another bombshell and told Taxis of his intention to abdicate. The aide was appalled and before setting off to visit the troops, sent the King a note telling him "...I am very much disturbed by your resolution and by the ease, indeed the equanimity, with which you agreed to take that TERRIBLY SERIOUS STEP by which you may destroy your and the Friend's great plan, and by which you may destroy us all. A stream of tears for you and your young life has at last relieved me. Oh, Ludwig, you are destined to do great things, and only in your present position can you realise them - and achieve the great aim. Unless I receive a counter-order tonight I shall go tomorrow morning at five o'clock to Miesbach! The day after that to the hospitals." Nobly, Taxis faced the injured and defeated men, an unenviable and depressing task which he carried out with great diligence.

A few days later, the anguished King wrote again to Tribschen renewing his threat to abdicate. Not realising that the King was a classic exponent of the art of "cry wolf", Wagner's reply came swiftly, "Oh Heaven, my Ludwig, you are so young, still so new to the world! Apart from some of the castles in your country you almost only know Bavaria and the people who inhabit the Residenz in Munich. Will the world always seem to you the way you imagine it? Certainly not! As you ripen to maturity, you will find the world wider and your demands also. You shall discover yourself." As a spur to the King's continuing support of Wagnerian art, he concluded with a flourish, "Being King, believe me, is like a religion. A King believes in himself or he is not a King."

It was all too easy for the dogmatic composer to advise his Sovereign from the comforting arms of the redoutable Cosima. Despite frequent assertions that exile caused him great hardship, Wagner had actually fared somewhat better of late than his patron. Emerging unscathed from his banishment after a brief sojourn in Bern, Vevey and Geneva he took a villa, Les Artichauts, where for some weeks he attempted in an alien atmosphere of faded gentility to resume his long-neglected work, but the place dampened his spirits and he missed his noisy clique. Most of all he missed Cosima and abandoning his work yet again, he set out to seek a permanent home so that she and her brood might join him.

It was while he was thus engaged that he heard of the death in Dresden of his wife. He received the news more calmly than when his favourite tenor had died. After Schnorr's untimely demise he had been genuinely griefstricken. His only feeling when Minna died was the joyful realisation that he was free. He did not even attend her funeral. Theirs had never been a happy marriage and from the earliest days of their union, Minna had been no more faithful to him than he was to her. The best one can say is that they deserved each other.

With Minna out of the way, Wagner pursued his househunting with even greater vigour and he had found the ideal home in the Landhaus Tribschen at Vierwaldstätter on Lake Lucerne. It was a large, secluded villa built on an incline but screened from curious eyes by the heavy elms which surrounded it. After the usual orgiastic decorative attack on the interior, Wagner found himself without the means to pay for the extravagant embellishments without which, he assured the King he found it impossible to evoke the right working atmosphere. Easily swayed by this argument Ludwig increased his stipend by 2,000 Gulden a year, payable in advance as usual. In return for this generosity, Ludwig thought it reasonable to request a piano recital by the composer, including fragments from the long-promised but strangely elusive *Meistersinger von Nürnberg*. When he suggested a meeting at his hunting lodge in the Riss to this end, Wagner prevaricated. Enjoying the novelty of domesticity with Bülow's wife, the composer had no time for the benefactor who had again rescued him from ruin.

Having left the war to progress without him, Ludwig now left the cabinet to attend to the peace negotiations although he was far from pleased with the results. Peace had been officially declared on August 22nd after only seven weeks. As well as costing Bavaria her honour, the defeat had also meant 30 million Gulden in war damages. The Treaty of Prague, signed on August 23rd, embraced the annexation of Schleswig-Holstein to Prussia and Austria's surrender of Venice to Italy. It also imposed an obligation on Bavaria to close a secret defence treaty with Prussia, one of its conditions being, to Ludwig's chagrin, that in the event of any future attack on Prussia Bavaria must also take up arms. This clause was to have disastrous consequences in the future and, realising this immediately, the King was deeply upset by it. His critics were quick to say that he had only himself to blame but in fact, it had been brought about by his Cabinet which contained various pro-Prussian elements who always found a way to make the King comply with their wishes. Ludwig himself was penalised in Bismarck's carefully thought out Treaty: he was to cede various territories to Prussia, including certain residences, castles and all the works of art to be found in them, including the greatly prized Johann Wilhelm Collection of paintings in Düsseldorf upon which Ludwig placed great value. The final blow to his pride was his cousin Wilhelm's personal demand that he should relinquish the old Hohenzollern castle which also lay in the ceded territory. Heartbroken, Ludwig could not bring himself to do this but suggested in a letter to Wilhelm that they might compromise and own it jointly. Romantically, he added, "When from the towers of the castle which belonged to our common ancestors shall float the banners of Hohenzollern and Wittelsbach, may this be seen as a symbol that Prussia and Bavaria are joint guardians of the future of Germany, to which the providence of Your Gracious Majesty has given new life."

It says much for Ludwig that he could write such a letter to the Hohenzollern he detested. The ungracious Wilhelm had no option but to accept and the man accused of being an inexperienced dreamer thus proved that, of the two, he possessed not only the greater integrity and dignity but also an innate diplomacy.

These sacrifices and the circumstances which had brought them about nevertheless cost Ludwig dearly in many ways and he saw in them the end of the Bavarian autocracy. He became deeply depressed.

With Wagner thus too occupied at Tribschen to provide him with cultural relief and Elisabeth in Hungary where she was now involving herself in Austro-Hungarian politics, Ludwig's loneliness deepened. In desperation, he turned again to Prince Taxis, allowing their relationship to become as intense as it had been three years earlier in 1863 when they had spent the summer together at Berchtesgaden. Since Taxis was the King's right hand he saw him every day in his official capacity but he enjoyed the element of conspiracy attaching to their personal relationship, wrote effusive letters to him addressed him as "Friedrich" and visited him at his lodgings in the Türkenstrasse where he also met a number of people of whom his strait-laced advisers would never have approved. He also frequently invited Paul to supper in the Wintergarden, that precarious edifice so dear to his heart built on the floor above the Hofgartenzimmer in the Residenz. The underflooring had been inlaid with lead so as to accommodate the full-sized pond full of water on which floated the now almost obligatory swan shaped canoe. An exotic Indian backdrop showing painted palms and a temple completed the scene. A folly, perhaps, but no worse than some of the grandiose "ruins" which had mushroomed all over Europe as playthings for the rich. Ludwig's own particular toy was harmless except for one occasion when the Queen mother, seated in her apartments below, was "surprised by a sudden shower of rain" after the lead lining proved inefficient.

The only access to Ludwig's paradise was through a panel in his private suite and here he would entertain the privileged few to lunch or supper to the accompaniment of music supplied either by Bülow or by the little band of permanent Court musicians. Here too he was able to savour his clandestine friendship with his aide. He fondly supposed that their relationship was unsuspected but in fact it was widely discussed in court circles. His attempts at discretion are understandable since he had endured more than enough scandal during the Wagner episode. Tongues had been stilled only by the composer's departure from Munich and, sadder and wiser and with distressing memories of the unpleasant gossip he was determined that there would be no repetition.

Inevitably, as his friendship with Paul reached fever pitch, he became tormented by guilt. Part of his complex self refused to accept that hc, thc King of Bavaria, was indulging himself in a relationship with his aide which he knew to be wrong. Taxis seems to have been happy to go along with the idea of becoming "Friedrich" and "Heinrich" as a kind of absolution, even though fundamentally he was a far more prosaic type than Ludwig. The latter suffered painful remorse for the acts he performed and no latent homosexual ever tried harder to suppress his own deepest instincts than Ludwig; despite the occasional "fall", to the end of his life he never relented in his fight against them.

Paul of Taxis was also bi-sexual, for he certainly never objected to the King's advances and his own correspondence proves that his feelings towards the King were unnaturally warm. He cared deeply for Ludwig personally and it must be remembered that in Ludwig's life this was something of a novelty. Up until now, his only other close friend other than Elisabeth was Richard Wagner, and he had repeatedly given Ludwig cause to wonder if he was really a friend. The man who professed, albeit insincerely, to live only for his art, had actually advised him at the end of the war to live for six months without poetry, music or the plastic arts and to lead instead a prosaic and politically-orientated existence with no spiritual distractions. To do so was quite beyond Ludwig; he was aching to hear some of Wagner's divine works, preferably the one which remained tantalisingly incomplete and, tired of waiting for it to appear, despatched Prince Taxis to Tribchen to find out what was going on there. He was also disappointed by Wagner's unexpected reaction to his *cri de coeur* concerning his abdication and wanted to hear what he had to say on the subject to Taxis. Paul obediently departed on his curious errand but easily bedazzled by Wagner's carefully mustered charm he proved to be no less impressionable than the King himself. The moment Taxis came into contact with the ebullient sybarite, he too fell under Wagner's nefarious spell. "The miracle triumphs! The tears flow!" Paul telegraphed enthusiastically to Ludwig and, bored to death with Munich and the eternal peace treaties in which he himself had so little say. Ludwig avidly read the rest of Paul's telegraph, which continued at length in the same vein. The ecstatic words conjured up enticing memories of past joys without reminding him of the horrors of Wagner's peccadilloes. He began to brood about what he was missing, especially when he read Paul's account of his reception, which duly arrived on August 7th: "I have just left the intimate circle of our dear friends and have retired to the cosy little room which we shared when we were here together. Yesterday, directly after arrival in Zurich, I telegraphed to the dear friend asking whether I cold stay with him, and was received with the kindest hospitality. Hans has kindly left so that I might have the room which you know so well (...) I prefer to write - according to the advice of the friends - as being safer than telegraphing. The precious one is very excited and needs rest (...) May God protect AND KEEP YOU ON THE THRONE. This is their wish and my own because only then can we achieve our high ideal (...) Wagner is working, is willing to go on, and only begs to be left in peace so that he may finish the work he has promised. He will leave politics alone."

Poor Hans, it seems, was always obliged to cede everything to the needs of the master, even his wife, for this letter makes it clear that Wagner had totally usurped Bülow's place in Cosima's bed, although it is known that they actually shared her affections for a while. It has often been asserted that Ludwig was still ignorant as to the affaire between Wagner and Cosima at this time but Paul's statement about Bülow's giving up his room leaves no doubt that the King was perfectly well aware of the situation and was apparently unconcerned by it.

Pressurised by his Ministers, Ludwig was at last persuaded to make a tour of war-ravaged Franconia. To Wagner he confided in November: "It is not easy for me to make this journey and (I must confess it, dear friend), to emerge from the pleasant solitude which I find so comforting and which makes my separation from the beloved easier to bear."

Four days later, he set out with a huge retinue on the first and only progress he was ever to make. Bayreuth was the first stop and there was an almost Medieval quality to his entry. The city was brilliantly illuminated for the occasion as much to raise public morale as to welcome the King, and from the balcony of the Margrave's Residence, Ludwig made a sincere speech which evoked cheers of the kind he had not heard for months. While he found this agreeable, he was understandably confused: first they had cheered him for going to war; now they cheered him because the war had ended, albeit ignominiously. It is not surprising that he began to wonder if their demonstrations truly meant anything at all and if their homage was genuine. The first seeds of doubt and distrust formed in his mind and from these seeds gradually sprang a dense forest of sceptical disbelief, the tendrils of which were to entwine in the years to come to the extent where they would hamper his otherwise excellent judgement.

For the time being, however, he decided to accept their fervent welcome as something to be taken when it was offered but never taken too seriously. No one can ever say of Ludwig that he did not learn from experience in this particular regard.

Leaving Bayreuth, he continued on to Bamberg where he was received by his uncle, King Otto of Greece and his Queen, Ludwig's Aunt Amalie, an amiable if slightly dotty lady known irreverently as "that fat noodle". Another exile, poor Otto spent his days in this sleepy provincial city trying to maintain a splendid court on a pittance. Bamberg was also illuminated and the venerable buildings gleamed romantically in the blaze of the Bengal lights, lending a little enchantment to help Ludwig's visit.

The King endured a constant round of engagements ranging from parades and receptions to balls and theatre parties; few of the functions were really his métier but he tried to do his duty and unexpectedly found himself enjoying it all. His next destination was Kissingen, where he took to his bed, physically and mentally exhausted. He could not accustom himself to being fêted and stared at so unremittingly but he was so charming and handsome that inevitably every eye was riveted on him. Apart from the mental agony that this constant appraisal caused him, he had a genuinely weak constitution and, like many a man of considerably sterner stuff would also have done, he found it all too much for him. Nervous and overwrought, he cancelled the proposed visit to Schweinefurt and stayed in bed until the time came for his projected tour of the battlefields and a visit to his grandfather who had now returned to Aschaffenburg.

Like a robot, he again set out to behave as people expected their King to behave. Never had he received so many declarations of loyalty, shaken so many hands or smiled his shy but dazzling smile so often. He was in private torment yet he somehow summoned the will to continue to Würzburg where, caught up in the whirl of festivities, he stupefied everyone by playing scenes from one of his favourite plays, Schiller's *Maria Stuart* with the actor-manager Ernst Possart who had himself taken the part of Mortimer. Illness again overtook him and the functions which were anathema to him even when he was well became even more of a trial.

After the visit to the graves of the fallen at Uttingen, he was so deeply affected by the horror of it all that he cancelled his projected visit to the theatre that evening; this sacrifice proves conclusively the sincerity of his sentiments.

Throughout the tour it had snowed heavily and the weather had been bitterly cold. When he reached the ancient and beautiful city of Nürnberg, however, the skies cleared magically and the sun shone brilliantly. Always sensitive to things Medieval and cheered by the sight of the better weather, Ludwig recovered his equilibrium and fell under the spell of the old city. He moved into the Kaiserburg and felt so happy there that he prolonged his visit from three days to a whole month. With renewed energy he threw himself into the general festivities.

As in the other cities he had to endure a round of obligatory social functions but even this chore was lightened by a visit to one of Nürn-

berg's industrial establishments which fascinated him, and he created
a sensation by arriving unannounced in nearby Fürth. This was a new
kind of King and the public liked what they saw. At the Nürnberg
Citizens' Ball, he further enhanced his reputation by dancing with
almost every lady present, paying special attention to those of less lofty
rank. So charming and extrovert did he seem that no-one suspected
how much he disliked dancing and socialising. At last he appeared to
have found a way of pleasing everybody, including himself, and his
advisers breathed a sigh of relief, supposing their worries at last to be
at an end.

In Nürnberg he was joined by his brother Otto and when eventually
they returned to Munich together the burghers who had heard about
the tour were as quick to show their approval as only months earlier
they had hastened to demonstrate their displeasure. For the second
time, Ludwig tasted the joys of the rapturous love of his people and his
future seemed assured.

Sadly, this was no more than an pleasurable interlude. What went
wrong? Why was it that such a potentially popular King could suddenly
have brought storms of critical dislike upon himself from a people who
had been prepared to love him unreservedly if only he on his side was
prepared to go on as he had begun?

Dissatisfied with the Government which had persuaded him to go
to war and especially with those who were most deeply opposed to
Wagner's return to Munich even for a short while. Ludwig began to
complain about everything they did and predictably they reciprocated.
The King's appetite for Wagner's work had been whetted by his earlier
visit to Tribchen and in a series of written effusions to the composer,
he now continued to bemoan his friend's continued absence from the
Bavarian capital.

Yet despite the high flown phraseology and the passionately avowed
enthusiasm and longing contained in those letters, Ludwig was actually
far from desolated by Wagner's continued banishment; this important
fact cannot be stressed strongly enough. Ludwig the innocent was in
fact a deft dissembler. The real "awful truth" as opposed to the "awful
truth" expressed in a fervent letter to the effect that he could not live
without his genius, the "beloved and only one" was that, like so many
introverts, Ludwig enjoyed pouring out sentiments which were not
necessarily meant to be taken literally. It was his misfortune that he
chose as his confidant the one person who was vain enough to believe
everything he said and wrote. For Richard Wagner the meglamaniac
could never resist being told that he was loved "unto death".

Bored to distraction by the continued wave of political talks which
were still in progress four months after the war had ended, Ludwig

made tentative approaches to his cabinet on the subject of a short visit by Wagner, if not his permanent reinstatement, but needless to say he received a cool response. It was not really Wagner whom he wanted but merely an escape from reality and he was thus reduced to conjuring up the aesthetic atmosphere he craved by making endless enquiries to the composer as to his progress on *Die Meistersinger*, and indeed, who could blame him when he had paid such an enormous price for it? Despite Wagner's perpetual assertions that he was making excellent progress, there seemed to be little concrete evidence to back up his statement. Ludwig's efforts to spur him into action by writing extravagant prose and giving him endless presents were totally wasted and he was forced to accept ruefully that, without constant badgering, Wagner would never finish anything except the money he had been given. Nevertheless, Ludwig's attempts continued. In desperation, he wrote of his "life of unrelieved misery" wrought by their separation; he wrote of despair, suicide and abdication - and he could well afford to wave the latter threat over Wagner's head, having discovered it to be one of the things to which the composer invariably responded with alacrity.

His averred wretchedness did not prevent him from continuing to enjoy almost nightly visits to the theatre. When he was not in the capital, he spent his leisure time walking and riding in the mountains without a second thought for Wagner, but the moment he looked at the frescoes at Hohenschwangau he was reminded of the composer. Presumably he was equally conscious of the fact that Wagner's luxurious home in the Briennerstrasse was still standing expensively empty. With a view to getting Wagner reinstated in time to supervise the première of *Die Meistersinger von Nürnberg*, which after his recent visit there had assumed an even greater importance than before, renewed overtures were made to Pfordten. This elicited the angry reply "I regard Wagner as the most evil person under the sun who will ruin the young King body and soul. For this reason, I can only remain [ie, in office] if His Majesty promises definitely and completely to keep away from Wagner. This man and I cannot exist side by side."

This was enough for Ludwig who had been awaiting his chance to rid himself of the man who was increasingly becoming a thorn in his side. With all Wagner's shortcomings, Ludwig sincerely felt that in the long term he was of greater value to posterity than the ageing and irascible politician. His grandfather Ludwig I was less convinced. Sadly, he wrote to the King, "In our time, monarchistically minded Ministers are precious; do not be persuaded by flattery; don't disregard the experience of your grandfather who wants to do his best. Take care that history does not say 'Ludwig II dug the grave of the Bavarian monarchy'." The old man's advice was based on his own bitter experi-

ence but it fell on deaf ears. In view of all his ensuing troubles, it is a
great pity that Ludwig refused to listen to the grandfather who tried so
hard to save him from himself. Ludwig often did take his advice as is
evidenced by the original dismissal of Max von Neumayr whom the
older Ludwig considered to be a danger to the State. Wagner, in one
of his interfering moods had argued for Neumayr's reinstatement but
on that occasion Ludwig had followed his grandfather's instincts. Now,
he was too piqued, too proud, to accept advice even if he knew in his
heart that the old man was right.

Only weeks before, Hohenlohe, a contender for the vacant post, had
written prophetically in his journal concerning these constant rumours
of a change in Government: "The truth seems to be that the King has
not abandoned his plan, but that intrigues are being made against it
from all sides (...). In any case, these intrigues will continue for some
months longer. The provisional Cabinet will continue until December
1st, so Von der Tann tells me. But if Pfistermeister is definitely
deposed, it will be impossible for Pfordten and Bomhard to remain."
Hohenlohe proved to be correct on all of these points.

Another diary note of Hohenlohe's stated, "On November 21st,
Holnstein arrived. He began by offering me, in the name of the King,
the Ministry of Domestic and Foreign affairs, and the post of Prime
Minister (...). My entry to the Ministerium would be generally approved, but there is no great anxiety for my appointment. Parties are
not yet organised, and the anti-Prussian feeling not yet sufficiently
pacified. At the same time I cannot conceal from myself that the King's
desire to have me as Minister in accordance with Holnstein's communication stems from his passion for Wagner. The King remembers that
I formerly deemed the removal of Wagner to be an unnecessary
measure and hopes that I will be able to secure his return. I have no
desire to form a Wagner-Ministerium, though I also consider that
Wagner's return *later* would by no means be a misfortune (...). Meanwhile, Holnstein will attempt to retain the King's favour and to represent my interests."

A new Ministry was formed on December 31st, 1866, with Hohenlohe as Prime Minister. A man of some renown in diplomatic circles,
he came of a noble family, one of the oldest in Germany, was cultivated
and superficially charming and could converse with the King on his own
intellectual level, which was a great point in his favour where Ludwig
was concerned. Unfortunately, he was extremely pro-Prussian; he had
already served Prussia directly in 1848 and in his early youth had been
open in his favour of a German Federation under Prussian leadership.
Naturally he was also an ardent admirer of Bismarck.

With the exception of Wagner and the open minded Ludwig,

everyone in Bavaria from the nobility to the peasants hated him, referring contemptuously to him as "the Prussian". Needless to say, Ludwig I was strongly opposed to him. Even though he was no longer on the throne old Ludwig was still deeply concerned with the fate of the country and visited the King at Berg to remonstrate with him on the subject of his seeming indifference to the current trend, but to no avail. Fundamentally, Ludwig had washed his hands of all politicians and their intrigues and could not find that one party was any better than the other. When Pfordten, pushed beyond endurance by the Wagnerian circus, had avowed that either he or Wagner must go, Ludwig had no hesitation in choosing Wagner, although he was later bitterly to regret this. Pfordten's eternal complaint was that he "often had no personal conference with the King for six weeks at a time". No such complaint ever issued from Hohenlohe's lips, for Ludwig's indifference to political matters suited him all too well. Inevitably, people said that, contrary to his insistence that he would never tolerate political interference from Wagner, Hohenlohe had got his post purely on the composer's direct instruction. It was certainly true that Wagner had put Hohenlohe's name forward on several occasions but at the same time, it must be remembered that Hohenlohe was no ambitious upstart but an erudite and politically experienced man well qualified for the post he now filled and was, at least at the time of his appointment, reasonably acceptable to the other ministers if not to the general public.

Nevertheless, Wagner understandably thought that Ludwig had been ruled by him and now renewed his efforts to influence the King. His euphoria can be imagined when, on December 20th, Ludwig wrote to Cosima, "Yesterday I approved Pfordten's resignation. The wretch who behaved so badly has gone. Therefore, *Pfi[stermeister]* and *Pfo[rdten]* are powerless and I am listening to the plea of the friend on the concession of which, I may say, depends my life's happiness."

Ludwig's reasons for writing such a foolhardy letter are inexplicable, since he must have known that Wagner would take it literally. Of course he was merely dissembling again to suit his own purposes and to flatter Wagner into creative action. Whether the ploy worked or not is another matter. To the dismay of the recipients of this letter, Ludwig concluded, "I beseech you, dear *Freundin,* to tell the dear one that, after the completion of *Meistersinger,* that is to say in the Spring, he shall come here. The prejudice shall disappear; he shall make the attempt to love me. Oh, confirm it dear *Freundin,* confirm that I must not endure this separation! I have no one here who understands me!" That, at least, was the truth.

CHAPTER SIX

SOPHIE

AT the beginning of 1867, Ludwig evidently resolved to make a fresh start. Life in Bavaria may have virtually returned to normal after the brief but crippling war, but Ludwig himself had changed. He had quickly learned the value of dissembling with his staff. His days of being totally straightforward with everyone were over and it is evident from Hohenlohe's comments that Ludwig knew them to be less than straightforward with him. Doing his best to conform to convention, he presided over dinners and suppers and granted audiences to the important and influential instead of inviting only those who attracted him personally. He now received the daily reports of his cabinet with apparent interest although in fact his thoughts were frequently on a much more agreeable plane. However occupied he was, he endeavoured to spend most of his weekends at Berg in the eternal hope of seeing the Empress, but Elisabeth had become intoxicated with Hungary and even hoped to buy an estate there, the beautiful Gödöllö, some 25 kilometers from Budapest. In vain, Ludwig haunted the Roseninsel and was left with the inconvenient alternative of visiting Schloss Possenhofen, the family home of the Dukes in Bavaria, willing to submit even to the critical gaze of his Aunt Ludovika, whom he disliked intensely, in order to quench his thirst for news of the Empress.

But Elisabeth did not appear and the face constantly before his eyes now was that of Elisabeth's sister Sophie. With one daughter on the Throne of Austro-Hungary and a second the Queen of Naples, Ludovika had every expectation of finding a suitable Monarch to take her youngest daughter off her hands. Although she heartily reciprocated Ludwig's ill feeling, she was not blind to the fact that for all his fanciful ideas and what she considered to be unmanly activities, he was a King. He was also a Bavarian and, with all his faults, more presentable than most of the other eligibles within Sophie's reach. Finding a husband for Sophie had nevertheless not been easy: the Princess had already been hawked unsuccessfully around Europe for some time and her mother was becoming desperate. There is no doubt that Ludovika saw the answer to her prayers in the impressionable Ludwig who was thus earmarked for Sophie long before the idea occurred to him. Sophie herself would have had little say in the matter, although in fact, the 17 year old was cool headed and ambitious enough to see the advantages of such a marriage and was all too ready to comply with her mother's instruction to make herself agreeable to the King.

Born on February 22nd, 1847, Sophie Charlotte appeared at first sight to be the ideal partner for the King. Her red gold hair was rather less beautiful and luxuriant than that of Elisabeth and although she had the same lovely features and tall figure as her four elder sisters, the resemblance ended here. A somewhat self-willed girl, she was born as far out of her time as Ludwig himself. Clever and superficially pretty, she was considerably more mannered and self-possessed than her Imperial sister and totally lacked the poetic mystery in Sisi which so captivated Ludwig; Elisabeth's incomparable physical beauty and inner loveliness tinged with a bittersweet sadness appealed irresistibly to his romantic soul and her elusive charm so fascinated him that he found it hard to think of anyone else when he was with her. Sophie's conversation also fell short of Elisabeth's deep and intellectual scope. She possessed some musical talent and had made a point of learning some of Wagner's piano pieces and transcriptions of his operatic themes; she was even able to warble some of the arias in order to make Ludwig notice her but it is probable that her enthusiasm was fostered purely for his benefit. For all her forceful display of charm and virtuosity, she found her pursuit of Ludwig to be hard going. When he presented himself for tea at Possi, having ascertained that Elisabeth was not there, he would sit staring dolefully into his cup until he found an excuse to escape.

Sophie's wiles were thus totally wasted on him and his Wittelsbach cousins, all of whom were in favour of the match, found his irritating resistance difficult to understand. It soon became obvious that, after all their careful preparations, the only real deterrent to the marriage was the prospective groom, who made it clear that Sophie could never in any way compare with her sister Elisabeth.

Her only hope of capturing Ludwig's attention was to display her appreciation of the arts and in particular her interest in Richard Wagner. Only after she had cornered the King on several occasions and pestered him with questions about Wagner did he become aware of her existence. As soon as she hit upon the idea of rendering a few piano fragments from *Lohengrin*, his fate was sealed. With such armoury she could not fail to capture his interest if not his heart and although he still made no effort to meet her more frequently, they began an almost daily correspondence. For years they had corresponded from time to time but now they both diligently attempted to turn their wisps of family gossip into passionate love letters.

When Ludwig left Berg for Hohenschwangau, her childish, artificial missives followed him there. Pleased by her sudden interest in Wagner,

Ludwig told her everything he could of the composer without initially including too many details of his own personal relationship with him, although to some extent the omission may have been based on his failure to totally understand it himself. There is strong evidence that after the initial flush of enthusiasm had faded there were occasions when he actively disliked the man. His feeling undoubtedly fluctuated between hatred and adoration, tolerance and revulsion, irritation and the kind of affection which one feels for a wayward child. Aristically, however, he regarded Wagner as a god. At his best, the composer was the greatest musical genius that Germany had ever produced; at his worst he was a megalomaniac, a spendthrift and coarse womaniser who all too frequently found difficulty in concentrating on his life's work if feminine distractions were too pressing, and excused himself by twisting the facts into shapes which were acceptable both to himself and his ego.

Sophie, who had no imagination, would never have understood the King's very complex relationship with the composer and he wisely gave her no insight into it apart from announcing that Wagner was his "only one unto death". Even this discouraging confession failed to dampen Sophie's ambitions and she continued to pursue the King with admirable determination. Thereafter - and one can only think that he was deliberately trying to put her off - he sent her a selected misellany of Wagner's letters to read, together with the libretto of *Der Ring des Nibelungen*. He knew from the beginning that Sophie was not for him. It is clear that he relegated her early on in their relationship to the imaginary plane which he already shared with Paul where she would not exist as a future wife but only a shadowy figure whom he could discard at will. Informing her that he was to be known as "Heinrich" and Taxis as "Friedrich", he added that both held Wagner "in an esteem unrivalled by any other living soul," but could not resist adding somewhat histrionically that when his genius died, he too would perish, just as he was later to say "If I cannot build, I cannot go on living."

Throughout his life, Ludwig was curiously obsessed with the idea that he would not be blessed with longevity and repeated this sentiment to Sophie so many times that she must have longed for the more prosaic companionship of the young men whose attentions she had scorned since setting her cap at Ludwig, who seemed only to want to indulge in games of make-believe and imbue himself constantly in the charged atmosphere of the old Germanic and Arthurian legends. However, if she was disappointed to find the King lacking in the rough masculinity of her brothers, she evidently decided not to make too much of it for Ludwig was, after all, a King and little else truly mattered but that she should become his Queen.

By the end of October the two were, at least on paper, on familiar terms and growing confident, Sophie began to try to put ideas into his head in much the same way as Richard Wagner had done. Sophie's plans did not include the gradual appropriation of the Civil List but centred around the gradual but relentless eradication from Ludwig's affections of Prince Paul. As her sister Hélène had just married Paul's brother, she knew Paul quite well and appears to have detested him with a jealous spite which prompted her constantly to try to set the King against him. Paul in fact was quite capable of engineering his own disgrace and very frequently did, but Sophie may have been unaware of this for she slyly began to pass on to the King rumours she had heard concerning Ludwig and his adored genius as well as some of Paul's indiscretions, evidently hoping to surprise and shock him. What, for instance, could she have told Ludwig to elicit from him the plaintive reply, "Would you have the goodness to explain to me the sort of rumours with which you say you have been plagued lately? Wagner's letters are with Friedrich. There is no doubt of his loyalty and discretion, although lately he has given me some reason to be discontent with him in some respects. Friedrich is now with his parents in Regensburg."

Ludwig was strangely foolhardy in ridding himself of those who, for one reason or another, had become *de trop*, and it is easy to speculate that some years after the event he may have realised his mistake in dismissing Paul who had been invaluable in many ways as well as having been unquestionably loyal. Despite his very human faults, Prince Taxis had much to commend him. Fond of music and poetry and an ardent devotee of Wagner, he also liked riding and mountaineering but unlike the King, also enjoyed the court functions which Ludwig found so very tedious. With equal enthusiasm, Paul would accompany him to a Court ball or a solitary ride into the mountains which might well last for several days. Ideal companion as he was, he was unfortunately too highly sexed for Ludwig's taste and it was his liking for women which finally destroyed the King's love for him more effectively than any of Sophie's efforts.

It was unquestionably she who first put the idea into Ludwig's head that he was in need of a new aide, and she clearly found it all too easy to poison his mind. Possessive and jealous where his friends were concerned, Ludwig could not bear to think that someone else, and particularly a woman, could have usurped his place in Paul's affections and a number of people besides Sophie knew it. Word reached Ludwig frequently from his body servants and advisers as well as from Sophie, of Paul's "frivolous" activities. Previously he had been lonely enough to tolerate Paul's misdemeanours, but now he had a new friend to whom he could unburden himself on paper and with whom he could discuss the arts and decided that Taxis must go.

Having discovered that he could rid himself of anyone who did not please him, Ludwig used Paul's latest escapade with "a young lady from Munich" as a convenient reason for dispensing with his services. At their next meeting, Taxis was given an icy reception which upset him so much that he wrote an indignant note enquiring "What in the name of all the saints has your poor Friedrich done to you? What did he say that no hand, no goodnight, no 'Auf Wiedersehen' favoured him? I cannot say how I feel. My trembling hand may *show* you my inner disquiet. I did not mean to hurt you. Forgive me; be nice to me again. I fear the worst - I cannot stand this. May my notes climb to you reconcilingly. Amen. Forgive your unhappy Friedrich."

Somewhat fulsome perhaps, from one grown man to another, but taking into account the customs of the age and the contemporary German prose style it can be accepted as no more than a sincere plea from one who knew he had lost a friend, for this time Ludwig remained unforgiving. His feeling for Taxis were almost dead, exhausted perhaps as much by over-exposure as destroyed by Sophie's interference, he confided to the latter "Friedrich became too haughty so I had to remove him; a better one is now in his place. Künsberg is faithful, reliable, loyal and open." But very, very dull. Ludwig soon realised that he had lost more than an able adjutant when he relieved Paul of his duties and allowed him to marry his inamorata. The sentiment may have been mutual for Paul himself fared no better. After his morganatic marriage he was obliged to renounce his name, titles, estate and all his possessions and was totally disowned by his family for marrying beneath him. All of this must have been a bitter blow. He took up as a theatre director, failed in the venture and died shortly afterwards. Taxis was the only one of Ludwig's discarded friends and staff for whom he made no attempt to provide, from which we may assume that this particular wound went far deeper than the others.

Bereft of his witty and erudite Paul, Ludwig suddenly found himself beseiged by the ubiquitous Sophie. Worn down by the constant hints from his mother and from his Ministerium who wanted him out of mischief, he was easily persuaded to propose to her on New Year's Eve 1867. Everyone was delighted, especially Sophie who already saw herself on the Throne of Bavaria and obviously hoped also to supplant her sister Elisabeth in the King's heart.

Even aside from Ludwig's constant enquiries as to Sisi's whereabouts, Sophie could never have been in any doubt as to the affinity which existed between the King and the Empress. It was likely that she also knew of their various trysts and assignations on the Roseninsel.

Sophie herself had hinted that she too would be pleased to accept an invitation to visit the island but the King dismissed the idea as "unsuitable". Interestingly, the same did not apply to the actress Lila von Bulykowsky, nor to Wagner. Enraged as she might have been, Sophie had no option but to hide her jealous humiliation at the obvious rebuff. She assumed that marriage would soon change his attitude towards her but she was wrong, for Ludwig did not love her and did not intend to conform to her standards when they were married. Even at this early stage, he was having second thoughts about marrying her and to Wagner he revealed the true level of his feeling for Sophie when he telegraphed news of the engagement to Tribschen: "Walther confides to the dear Sachs that he has found his faithful Eva! Siegfried his Brünnhilde!" But not, it would seem, Ludwig his Sophie. To Cosima he wrote coolly, "Sophie is a sympathetic soul whose destiny has a certain similarity to my own. We both live on an oasis on a sea of sand in the desert."

But he made little effort to visit his fiancée in the customary manner. Ludwig liked Sophie best when she was elsewhere, properly occupied as a pen friend and no more. His passion for corresponding with almost anyone who might answer never abated, and as he became increasingly lonely, he amused himself by creating a love affair from a string of rather artificial notes to his bride. As a courier for these outpourings, he employed the overwilling Max Holnstein, an unfortunate choice of messenger for many reasons, not the least of which was the fact that, although he was a married man and she was promised to the King, all Bavaria was whispering about Sophie's amorous entanglement with him.

Holnstein, a childhood companion of Ludwig's, held the position of Oberstallmeister which gave him every opportunity for close contact with the King and being an opportunist, he took ready advantage of his office. Heavily built with somewhat brutish features, he had small eyes set close together and a thick beard which obscured the lower part of his face. He was an expert horseman and was also well known for his expertise in the handling of weapons. Ambitious and totally unscrupulous, he was adept in the art of ingratiating himself with the influential, and styled himself "Count Holnstein von Bayern"; it was said that in his signet ring he bore the Bavarian coat of arms with the bar sinister, indicating that he was the acknowledged illegitimate son of a Duke of Bavaria. By his marriage to a granddaughter of Prince Karl and the latter's morganatic wife, the Countess Bayersdorff, he had a tenuous connection with the Ducal family at Possenhofen but this did not deter him from pursuing his clandestine romance with Sophie.

Ludwig did not get on particularly well with Holnstein but shared with him a strange love-hate relationship based and fostered on the fact that he knew all of Ludwig's secrets including details of his friendship with Elisabeth and with Prince Taxis. If his tongue were to be loosened by wine, money or spite, Holnstein was a potentially dangerous man. It was therefore in the King's best interests to remain on friendly terms with the sly-witted *Rossober** as the peasants called him. To compensate for his less attractive traits, however, Holnstein was always willing to undertake commissions, always ready to ride to Munich, Hohenschwangau or Possenhofen at any hour of the day or night as an escort or messenger. For a while, he became the King's right hand.

Sophie's family were to be disappointed if they expected Ludwig to marry her immediately, for only weeks after his rash proposal, he was already looking for a means of extricating hmself from her clutches. Her parents were anxious for a short engagement one suspects because they were finding it difficult to control the girl, and when Ludwig emitted only a loud silence on the subject, Ludovika became first waspish and then openly hostile. To Pfistermeister's successor, the patient and kindly Lorenz von Düfflipp, Ludwig admitted to feeling trapped. "Must I marry her?" he pleaded, "I would rather drown myself in the Alpsee." Like everyone else, the secretary was perfectly well aware that Ludwig preferred the company of Sophie's elder sister and even that of his adjutant to that of the somewhat brittle Princess but was apparently shy of pointing out that the young King would have to accept second best, if only to please his subjects who were greatly looking forward to celebrating the forthcoming nuptuals in the typical Bavarian manner.

As time passed and Ludwig continued to prevaricate, however, Ludovika eventually sent Karl Theodor to Berg to enquire as to his precise intentions. In view of the King's earlier hero worship of his cousin Gackl, as he was known, he was not perhaps the ideal messenger, but the Duchess had never been noted for her finesse.

Karl Theodor was the brainy member of the family and was later to become an internationally famous oculist, an extremely rare departure for a member of a Royal family in the days when Royalty's role was considered to be one of idleness. Like his father, the King had a deep and enthusiastic interest in science and his admiration for his cousin may possibly have had its root in the fact that he was so brilliantly clever. Before Taxis had become his adjutant, Ludwig and Gackl had spent a good deal of time swimming and riding in the Ammerland and they were to remain friends until the King's death.

Nevertheless, their meeting to discuss Sophie was far from friendly. He had come to tax the King on the unpleasant rumours which were

---

* Horsemaster – Literally, Master of Horse, but meant in a derogatory sense.

circulating to the effect that he was playing with Sophie's feelings at the expense of her good name. This was a somewhat unfair accusation in view of the fact that Sophie's "good name" had already been linked both with the unsavoury Holnstein and with that of Edgar Hanfstaengl, one of the Court photographers. Greatly insensed, Ludwig childishly denied ever having proposed to Sophie. Any illusions he may have had about her had been dispelled by his discoveries concerning her weakness for men, but apart from a natural reluctance to accept damaged goods, he was also undoubtedly terrified of the whole concept of marriage. At any rate, Karl Theodor was despatched back to his mother bearing the indignant King's negative response to her demands. Following his interview with Ludwig, Gackl wrote stiffly to him: "After I gave my mother the news, any further discussion on the subject is superfluous: at least she knows sufficient of your intentions to deduce a definite conclusion from them. There is no question of continued correspondence."

Sorry at least to have lost a useful contact to keep him informed of Elisabeth's movements, Ludwig wrote direct to Sophie on January 19th:

"My dear Sophie,

"It is very difficult for me to write these lines to you but I regard it as my duty to write to you now. It is very painful for me if we really have to break off our written friendship because, as I have repeatedly assured you in my letters, you will never cease to be dear to me and all my life I shall preserve for you a sincere feeling of true friendship. Oh, keep no bitterness in your heart; be kind to me and do not deprive me of your friendship. You know what my destiny is; I wrote you once from Berg about my mission on this earth. You know that I have not many more years to live; when my star shines no more, when the truly beloved one goes, then my time will also be spent. And then I may no longer live. The main content of our meetings was always R. Wagner's extraordinary, stirring destiny; you can bear witness to that. Oh! Don't be angry; send me some friendly lines to let me know that you can still have some kindly thoughts remaining for me. Your friend has perhaps only a few more years to live. Shall his remaining time be embittered by painful thoughts that one of the few beings who understood him and who was still dear to him, still hates him? No, I dare to say it boldly, it cannot be! Farewell, my dear Sophie, and if you want to, don't write to me again, but live happily and think of me.

"In sincere friendship, Your truly faithful cousin Ludwig."

The Master had taught his pupil well. While playing heavily on her sympathy, Ludwig managed at the same time to make it clear that he did not want her. Ludovika was furious at having her plans ruined, as indeed was Sophie herself. Considerably more worldly than any of her sisters, she had looked forward to becoming Queen of Bavaria as much for the elevated social position and importance it would bring her as for the acquisition of a handsome husband which would in itself have made her the envy of every eligible girl who had been pushed hopefully in Ludwig's direction.

Determined to win him back, she put on a good display of heart-break, allowing rumours to circulate freely to the effect that she was dying of grief. She knew the King's character well enough to calculate the effect that such reports would have on him and her plan worked to perfection. When the incurably romantic Ludwig heard how badly she appeared to have taken his rejection, he wrote to their go-between "Elsa [Sophie] is not completely out of my mind and I now almost think that it will not be long before the feeling of sincere and honest friend-ship that I carry in my heart will turn to love and I will try to see her as my wife. For I do not hold it as impossible. She must remain calm and comforted, and say to her that you believe my liking turns to love. If it should come to marriage, it shall be on condition that she must be faithful right through to the death to my dearest one, my everything!"

Somewhat ominously, he added, "If it is in any way possible for a woman to make me happy, it would be she and no other." With a letter full of ambiguity and half-promises, Ludwig was carried away and totally forgot that sooner or later he would be called upon to honour any vows he was foolish enough to make now, if not to explain the ambiguity. By the time the message had been conveyed to Sophie, the family tension had relaxed and with an air of resignation and indif-ference which did not go unremarked, Ludwig resumed his languid pursuit of his prospective Queen.

* * * * *

PRESUMABLY following another lecture from his mother, Lud-wig at last approached Sophie again. He wrote a letter to her which culminated with the fatal words, "Will you be my wife? Companion of my Throne? Queen of Bavaria?" Having committed himself irretrievably, he punished his nonplussed mother as well by insisting that she should be his courier, and she found herself driving to Possenhofen in the early hours of the morning to put the fatal note into Ludovika's eager hands. The flamboyant and theatrical tone to his proposal put the whole thing in perspective. Everyone in Lud-wig's circle knew that he did not love Sophie and had no desire to tie himself to her for life, but gave in only under pressure from his mother and from his well-meaning if misguided advisers*. Sophie and Ludovika were all too ready to accept Ludwig's offer, however reluctantly it was made, and although Sophie was no more in love with him than he was with her, she did not trouble herself unduly as to the likely consequences of so disastrously incompatible a union.

On January 2nd, 1867, a Court ball took place at the Munich Residenz. The occasion was a brilliant one, the floor a glittering swirl of jewels, silks and colourful gala uniforms. Princess Sophie, the guest of honour, appeared dressed in the obligatory white with touches of Bavarian blue presumably calculated to catch the King's eye, although at the same time she was determined to paint a picture of the hurt and rejected bride. Robert von Mohl, the Baden Ambassador in Munich, observed: "They were a fine bridal pair: the King, a very tall, slim young man with dark, dreamy eyes, carried the uniform of his cavalry regiment very well. The bride, also a tall, slim figure, was attractive to look at in her white and blue ballgown. And yet there hung over the festivities an uncomfortable atmosphere which was neither bridal nor festive (...) I could not avoid the impression that the Princess did not show any signs of a kindly or devoted nature. There was a hard coldness in her pretty face which did not disappear when the King went over to talk to her."

Although they danced together several times, Ludwig took care to avoid any deep discussion with her, and later that evening, clearly demonstrated that his interest in her remained minimal. Seeing Bomhard, he strolled over to him and asked the time. Surprised, Bomhard confessed that he was not wearing a watch and pointed out that, as the clock was immediately behind him, etiquette forbade him from turning his back on the King in order to look at it. Undaunted, the myopic Ludwig laughingly suggested that they should both turn a little so that no one would notice him diligently looking at the clock while conversing with his Sovereign. Torn between outrage and amusement, Bomhard complied; when he told Ludwig that it was nearly ten o'clock, the King speculated whether if he left immediately, he might reach the Court Theatre in time for the last act of the play. When Bomhard said that the guests would be deeply shocked by such a sudden departure from his own ball, he was unwise enough to add, "And what will the noble bride think if Majesty should leave the ball so soon after arriving? Will it be in order with Her Royal Highness?" Ludwig made a brief and pointed reply to the effect that Sophie's reaction disturbed him not at all. Bidding Bomhard goodnight, he turned on his heel and left the ballroom. Sophie's angelic face was reported to have worn a look of

---

* In particular the now out of office Bomhard, who had spent weeks trying to convince Ludwig that he would change his mind about marriage once he had tried it.

fury as she gazed after his retreating figure and in moments, the news had spread like wildfire that the King had deserted his fiancée in favour of Lila von Bulykowsky without even taking his leave of her. "Nothing will come of this marriage," was the common verdict.

On another occasion, the composer, Franz Liszt who had attended a dress rehearsal at which the King and Sophie were also present, observed that Ludwig sat alone in the Royal box and only "after the second act he [Ludwig] spent five minutes with his fiancée who was sitting in a box on the left. The wedding has been postponed until November. *Les ardeurs matrimonielles de Sa Majesté semblent fort tempérées* (His Majesty's matrimonial ardour seems very temperate). Some people say that the wedding will be postponed for ever."

Having done his duty by proposing at last, Ludwig disappeared smartly from view, ready to resume more enjoyable pursuits than wooing Sophie, but he was hunted down and made to behave like a bridegroom. Now that their engagement had been publicly announced, they were expected to appear everywhere together. The people were delighted and relieved to see that their handsome King was at last showing himself to have the normal appetites. Like the cabinet, they had long been shaking their heads over the King's expensive adventures with Wagner and Prince Taxis and evidently considered that Sophie would be a steadying influence.

For some reason, the King felt bound to explain himself to his friends at Tribschen and informed Cosima, "When I often wrote to my cousin Sophie last summer about the esteemed and beloved Master, about whom she was also enthusiastic, and sent her books, letters, etc, about him, her mother came to know of the correspondence which was taking place between me and her daughter and as is her way, she thought they were the usual love letters. She could not believe that the correspondence consisted of purely spiritual matters. That is the way people are and everything exalted takes their own narrow standard as a basis. Sophie, whose attachment for me was really love, felt indescribably unhappy when she heard that it was not the same on my part and from emotion and really sincere compassion for her unfortunate position, I was moved to take the unconsidered step of an engagement." This letter says it all, although at the same time, he could not resist the romantic suggestion that his capitulation was more to mend Sophie's broken heart than to put an end to his mother's nagging.

A whole series of gala balls and banquets were held in honour of the Royal couple and at first Ludwig did his best to put on a good show for the public but inevitably his politely suppressed boredom got the better of him. The public went wild at the dazzling sight of the the handsome King and his well turned out fiancée, but those closer to the Royal pair wore no such blinkers and were not slow in sizing up the situation as it really was.

To Sophie's chagrin, she discovered that at the precise moment of their engagement Ludwig suddenly embarked upon a new friendship with the actress Lila von Bulykowsky. Although he had adamantly refused to take his fiancée to the Roseninsel he had no hesitation in inviting Lila who, in the event, was a disappointment to him. She complained bitterly that the muddy paths soiled her dress and when he placed a freshly plucked rose into her hand, the unromantic Lila threw it down in disgust: *"So ein Dreckzeug!"* (dirty thing) she shrilled, looking at her ruined glove. Undaunted, possibly to spite Sophie, he also took Lila to Hohenschwangau and, greatly flattered, the lady totally misinterpreted his intentions.

Basically, Ludwig wanted her to continue to play offstage the part for which she was famous, namely, Schiller's *Maria Stuart*. The worldly Lila failed to grasp this and decking herself out in her most seductive attire, joined the King on a tour of the castle, which she evidently assumed was to culminate with a bedroom seduction scene. Since he insisted upon showing her his bedroom she could not be blamed for this assumption, although his motives were not what she supposed.* The actress was surprised to find the appointments of the tiny Schloss to be so homely, but was shattered by the sight of Ludwig's bedroom. The ceiling was dark blue with silver stars painted on it and his artificial moon made its clockwork way across the heavens at the touch of a switch. The murals here were full bodied nudes depicting the legend of *Rinaldo and Armide* and Lila became very coy when she caught sight of them (She afterwards claimed to have been shocked by them). Her reaction greatly diverted Ludwig who, despite his reputation for melancholy, was certainly not without a sense of humour.

When he asked her for a scene from *Maria Stuart* she was happy to oblige; she was used to being asked to recite from her current hit, regarding the request both as a compliment to her art and as an anticipated means of singing for her supper. It was a customary chore for any performer who was invited to suppers and soirées. Unfortunately, the down-to-earth Hungarian had no conception of Ludwig's intellect and failed to appreciate that he regarded her more as the personification of the Scottish heroine than the well-worn woman of the world. In his romantic vision, she was simply a vessel. As an encore she did a scene from Goethe's *Egmont* which she took to be the prelude to a profitable amorous dalliance or, even more to her taste, open horseplay. They began sedately enough, but as the script called for her,

---

* Ludwig was inordinately proud of his murals and his clockwork moon and dragged everyone he knew on this particular pilgrimage.

as Klara, to move ever closer to Ludwig/Egmont and offer him a kiss, Lila became too bold and he was brought back to shattering reality by the implantation of a kiss from her painted mouth. This was too much for Ludwig and, disengaging himself he fled, calling loudly for his secretary to come and rescue him.

Aware that Dufflipp would greatly relish telling the tale of her rejection, Lila lost no time in circulating a story to the effect that it had been Ludwig who, taking advantage of a poor defenceless woman and his own exalted position, had tried to make love to her against her will under the painted gaze of *Rinaldo and Armide*. A gentleman to the core, Ludwig never denied it but the actress fell from favour immediately: she was granted no further privileges, the generous gifts ceased and there were no more excursions. Doubtless her days would have been numbered in any case since Ludwig tired easily of ladies of her type. He enjoyed Lila's company in small doses although he was frequently irritated by her temperamental behaviour and constant coompplainnts.. He tolerated her tantrums and sullen moods for a while because, when the time and surroundings were right, he found her to be a witty and informative conversationalist with a low, fascinating voice which enthralled him. Full of pithy anecdotes about her theatrical colleagues as well as being a talented actress she might have lasted a little longer had she not ruined her chances by trying – and failing – to take advantage of him.

An interesting postscript to this episode is the fact that the scene chosen by Ludwig included some lines spoken by Egmont which might have been written with him in mind: "...That Egmont is an irritating, stiff, cold Egmont who forced himself to assume now this, now that expression... who is tormented, misunderstood, confused because people take him to be happy and gay - loved by a people who do not know what he wants, esteemed and held on high by the masses with whom he has no link, surrounded by friends whom he does not trust, watched by people who would like to get the better of him at all costs, working and putting himself out often without purpose, mostly without reward..." Obviously, Ludwig identified himself closely with Egmont, but it is doubtful if Lila noticed the parallel.

A year after the incident at Hohenschwangau, Lila was still unsuccessfully pestering Ludwig's staff for private audiences but Ludwig resisted. When her contract expired he instructed his secretary, "I wish her to leave Munich for a short time only, not for good. I am perfectly happy to treat her as before, provided she does not forget the respect due to a King. Try to put her in a good humour and calm her down, because women who have been scorned in love are like hyenas." His comment in itself leads one to speculate on Sophie's private reaction at being jilted.

Whatever Sophie thought about Ludwig's interlude with his actress, she was obliged to swallow the pill uncomplainingly, possibly because he appeared to be trying to compensate by visiting Possenhofen slightly more often, although it is likely that he did so more in the hope of seeing the Empress than his fiancée. On these visits the task of chaperoning the happy pair was frequently undertaken by the Baroness von Mensi-Klarbach, who reported that she would sit in the next room with the adjoining doors open, but never heard anything more lurid than Ludwig's occasional dutiful compliments, delivered in an acutely bored voice, "Ah, Elsa, you have such beautiful eyes," "How pretty you are, dearest," and similar chilly endearments.

Sophie herself was dismally aware that he was never going to change and that unlike so many young men he had no interest in her whatever. The wedding preparations on the other hand provided him with hours of entertainment. Enthusiastic over one aspect of their nuptials at least, he wrote to Sophie, "Tomorrow I shall come to you (...) I will (...) bring the crown and see it placed upon your head. If it is too heavy and broad, then I shall have another made ready that you would rather see upon your head at the wedding because a head as beautiful and dear to me as yours is can only be worthy of the highest earthly jewel, the sign of earthly Majesty and Sovereign power."

True to his word, he duly appeared accompanied by Herr Merk, the Court jeweller and custodian of the Royal goods. Ludwig placed the crown upon Sophie's head like an artist perfecting his masterwork, but paid scant attention to the bride herself and indeed, remained with her only long enough to ascertain that the crown fitted. Sophie was afterwards heard to complain to Baroness Sternbach "He doesn't love me, he is only playing with me," which can scarcely have come as a revelation to anyone.

Enjoying himself immensely, Ludwig next set about preparing the Royal apartments on the first floor of the Residenz to receive their new occupant. Included was a boudoir for Sophie, the decorations and furnishings for which he supervised personally. A narrow staircase was built to provide a link with the King's study above but although he enjoyed the romantic idea of so intimate an access, it is unlikely that he would ever have thought of using it; undue haste to reach Sophie had never been a feature of the relationship. All these frenzied preparations seemed to be the end rather than the means to Ludwig since he applied himself with the same fervour to the design and building of the ornate gilt State Coach which was ostensibly to carry them from their wedding. Ironically, its panels bore delicately painted scenes depicting a theatre interior with a rapt audience intent upon the performance. This was evidently how Ludwig saw his forthcoming marriage and we can imagine the skittish Sophie's fury when, after a few more weeks of somewhat indifferent passion on Ludwig's part, she received a note from him which read "My dearest Elsa! Albert* has just sent the enclosed photograph of Us Two; will you please have the goodness to give it to the Empress in my name? Perhaps she will like it. Hearty greetings! Your faithful Ludwig."

Ludwig's thoughts were still only with Elisabeth who was due to spend a few days at Possenhofen. When she arrived, although he was suffering from the usual feverish cold, he willingly left his bed as on a previous occasion in order to greet her at Munich station. A number of people observed Sophie's unmistakeable sourness as the King bent over Elisabeth's hand, holding it for much longer than was necessary. Sophie must have found it hard to retain her composure when he replied to Elisabeth's dutiful congratulations on his engagement for all to hear "How could I help wanting to marry her when she is your sister? How could I find her anything but attractive when she bears so close a resemblance to you, dearest Sisi, who will always represent for me the ideal of womanhood?"

Totally forgetting his fiancée, he did his best to capture Elisabeth for himself during her visit, making tentative plans for her entertainment and enquiring of Sophie like a lovesick schoolboy, "Do you think the Empress will accept anything for tomorrow or not? To the astonishment of the audience, I appeared in Austrian uniform during the third act at the theatre! How are you? What did you do in the evening? What did the Empress say?"

Elisabeth evidently deemed it unwise to remain too long in such an atmosphere and in any case she was anxious to continue her journey to Switzerland where she was to visit her other sister Mathilde, the Countess Trani, who had just given birth to another child in Zurich. The opportunity of comparing the sisters together had apparently provoked Ludwig into a new wave of second thoughts about marrying Sophie and his prevarications began again as soon as the Empress left Possenhofen. It is possible that he might have got over his aversion to her but he became so irritated by the detested family functions to which he was constantly subjected that her very name became anathema to him. To his credit, Ludwig did make some effort to breathe life into his artificially created and quietly dying romance by sending Sophie flowers and books, and writing increasingly flippant notes whose forced heartiness cannot have escaped her: "Tomorrow the whole family will be fed by my mother, then to Meyerbeer's nonsense in the

---

* Another of the Court photographers.

hot Africa where someone dies romantically in the shadows of the trees while a real *brouhaha* is going on. *Quelle fête!* So I shall see you only tomorrow and not today (my heart is longing for you) amidst the hurly-burly of the family feeding!"

Unsurprisingly, as the days passed and his misery increased, the blinding headaches returned. Like many of the Wittelsbachs he was constantly plagued with migraine; the pain would begin at the back of his neck, make its way across his forehead, behind his eyes and even, as he sometimes complained, along his spine. His agony was to continue for the duration of his engagement but the "noble bride" had little sympathy with Ludwig's troubles.

Ironically, eager as Sophie was for a speedy settlement, the greatest obstacle to the courtship was her mother. On the rare occasions when, in a romantic mood, Ludwig would ride to Possi at dead of night armed with one of his huge bouquets, the Duchess would see to it that every lamp and candle in the Schloss was lit and every lackey standing at his post. Whether this was because she did not trust Ludwig (or indeed, her daughter!) or whether she fancied she was honouring her Sovereign with this ill-timed display of respect we shall never know, but the fact remains that she was slowly widening the already gaping chasm between her daughter and the King.

With arrangements at last in hand for Wagner's visit to Munich, Ludwig was determined to arrange a meeting between his fiancée and the composer – a sure indication that he did not regard Sophie as a chaste young girl. In the age in which they lived, such an introduction would have been unthinkable; as it was, he took care not to set his scene at the Residenz. Instead, he conspired with Sophie's broadminded brother, Duke Ludwig in Bavaria* for the unprecedented encounter to take place in his Munich house, an establishment where Court etiquette was barely observed. The Duke had married an actress, Henriette Mendel and like the King enjoyed anything which smacked of the theatre. He took great pleasure in indulging in Ludwig's whim but his willingness suggests that even Sophie's own brother set little store by her virtue or he would never have agreed.

On that great occasion, the servants were dismissed and the Duke's wife herself admitted the Sovereign and his fiancée. Wagner was less than overcome with admiration for the cold and mannered Sophie but predictably offered Ludwig suitable praise on his choice of bride. Like the others, he was well aware that Ludwig had little regard for her if he introduced her to a notorious womaniser of doubtful background and scant moral reputation. Nor, indeed, would she have been permitted to meet Cosima, the mistress with whom Wagner now quite

* Usually known as Louis to distinguish him from several other Ludwigs in the family.

openly lived. Ludwig's action states clearly that his knowledge of Sophie's sidesprings contributed largely to his reluctance to marry her and he proved it by placing her on the same level as Cosima.

The political atmosphere was no less imperfect. On Ludwig's own admission his confidence in Hohenlohe was already on the wane and by March 1867 was already describing him to ex-minister Bomhard as *"un Filou"* [A swindler or double dealer]. It is a tragedy that Ludwig did not involve himself more deeply in politics for, in August 1867, Hohenlohe announced to the astounded Landtag that an alliance had been concluded with Prussia, a move which caused a great outcry throughout Bavaria. To a man the Bavarians hated the Prussians and objected strongly to being subjected to what was being freely described as "bonds of slavery" to their North German neighbours.

Hohenlohe's unpopularity did nothing to deter his activities; he had also re-organised the Bavarian army on the same pattern as the Prussian army which had recently created such havoc throughout Bavaria. After the fiasco of the civil war of 1866, it was obvious that the dishonoured and decimated force needed something to revitalise its potential and its morale, and to dispel the feeling that Bavaria was now no more than a satellite of Prussia which was widespread. The measures for the army were therefore loudly decried simply because they were Prussian. Adding the finishing touches to his renovations, Hohenlohe set about making the schools independent of the Church – again, not a bad thing in itself but resented by those who felt that only a Bavarian should settle Bavaria's affairs, especially since the church in Rome was likely to be upset by the move, which in the event it was.

The populace was again up in arms and as usual it was the King who was hissed and booed in the streets rather than the Ministerium who had mismanaged matters. Ludwig felt his people's reaction just as keenly as he had previously felt their goodwill and their attitude did much to turn him against appearing in public. One suspects that he was already wishing he had never rid himself of the loyal, old fashioned solidity of Von der Pfordten which he had so recklessly squandered for the sake of keeping Wagner close enough to be supervised. However, unless Pfordten himself had asked to return there was nothing that Ludwig could do to correct his error without losing face, although in any case he had no reasonable ground for dismissing Hohenlohe so soon after his appointment. His only course was to wait for fate to take a hand.

CHAPTER SEVEN

THE JILTED BRIDE

LUDWIG's painfully forced romance still dragged on with the aid of his continued stream of artificial love letters, but he was bored with every aspect of his future bride. This miserable situation might have pertained for some time had he not found an exciting new friend who for some years was to wield great influence over him. A new *Stallmeister** had been appointed who wore his Bavarian blue uniform elegantly enough to catch the King's eye.

Richard Hornig was 27 years old at this time, blond, handsome and of athletic build. Ludwig capitulated totally when he discovered that in addition to his military bearing and general élan, the former army officer was well educated, intelligent, diplomatic, practical and amusing with a strong interest in the arts. The two quickly became firm friends and over the ensuing years, Hornig's capability was to prove invaluable to the King.

The Hornigs were Silesians, Richard, the eldest son, being born in Mecklenburg on September 10th, 1840. He was accomplished in the usual sporting pursuits of the country gentleman and although moderately interested in politics he had no aspirations to embroil himself in State affairs. He never took advantage of his position although he was frequently accused of doing so, and indeed did not lack for opportunity. He had recently left the army after a brief and successful career in the artillery, and now proposed to serve his Sovereign with the same passionate application.

The post of *Stallmeister* called for a man of integrity and was as important as it was exacting. The work entailed the provision of transport for the Royal family and staff and he was also responsible for the equipment and stable stock. Additionally, he had to work out the itineraries and had the thankless task of accompanying the King and the inevitable mountain of luggage on his interminable sorties. Since Ludwig had a restless nature and was constantly moving between Munich, Berg and Hohenschwangau, Hornig was always kept busy. Once Ludwig had claimed him for a friend as well, he can have had little time for himself and his family.

The King found it most convenient to have another man like Paul von Thurn und Taxis on his staff, a man whom he could engage in erudite conversation and since most of his staff were on a totally different plane, he began to ignore them altogether in favour of Hornig. His fiancée was neglected even more than before and like others before

---

* Master of Horse. Not to be confused with Holnstein's post of Oberstallmeister, which was equivalent to the post of the Lord Great Chamberlain in England.

it, the new friendship ripened in the hot spring sunshine of the Allgäu and Ammerland.

Outraged because Ludwig openly preferred the warmth and bright intelligence of the Stallmeister to the cold superficiality of his intended, Sophie had no one but herself to blame; since she herself had various friendships of her own simmering towards boiling point, however, it is possible that she did not care what Ludwig did, so long as she wore the crown at the end of the game. Neverthless, when Hornig began to appear in public with Ludwig her attitude changed, for to be publicly abandoned in favour of an army officer was more humiliating even than to be neglected for the sake of an actress.

If Sophie was upset by his behaviour she was not alone. In his euphoria, Ludwig completely forgot about Wagner, to whom he continued to sign his letters "until death" and the composer was extremely put out to find that he was not the only star in Ludwig's firmament. The supreme egotist who considered he had the right to pick people up and put them down again at will was outraged if others did the same to him. His outrage turned to fright when Ludwig, otherwise occupied, allowed the friend's birthday to pass unnoticed. The King had cooled considerably towards the spendthrift and idle Wagner and no longer cared what he did so long as he honoured his commitments to produce the promised operas.

Recovering quickly from the initial shock, the composer soon convinced himself that his disfavour was not permanent and continued to make impossible demands on a King who had lost interest. Even Cosima tried to warn her lover that if he did not make himself more agreeable to the King now, he would probably lose his friendship for ever; if this were to happen he was unlikely to find another patron as generous as Ludwig, since by this time all Europe knew the true cost of offering him a helping hand. Although up until now the King had discreetly ignored the blatant affaire between Wagner and Cosima von Bülow, the pair now flaunted themselves so openly that he could no longer do so without appearing to be a complete fool. Even when he had earlier acceded to Cosima's impassioned plea for a testimonial to clear her good name, he must have known that the accusations were true and that he was merely being used to extract them from their sordid difficulties.

Ludwig was much looking forward to the new production of *Lohengrin* in June, but from the first rehearsal there was a bad atmosphere in the theatre tempered with quarrels and ill feeling on all sides. This was a situation which invariably developed when Wagner produced one of his own works, but this time the offstage scenes were more horrendous than usual. Albert Niemann, a great personal favourite of the King's, refused to sing the part of Lohengrin unless certain cuts were made and this led to violent altercations. Ageing tenors do not relish attention being drawn to their failing powers and Niemann, past his best, was no exception. But the King, who knew every word of the text, wanted to hear it in its entirety and since he was footing the bill, this was not unreasonable.

Unprepared for temperamental outbursts by his patron, Wagner suggested that Niemann should be replaced by Josef Tichatchek, who was even older than Niemann and whose talents were known to have deteriorated beyond repair. Outraged, Ludwig refused: the thought of Lohengrin, the being on whom he based his whole philosophy and outlook, being sung by a man who could hardly walk upright let alone with dignified nobility was quite untenable. Not daring to upset Wagner too deeply in case he walked out in a tantrum, Ludwig at last gave in but later, at the dress rehearsal, he was so appalled by the the dismal offering that he again demanded that Tichatschek be replaced by a tenor in better vocal and physical condition. His own suggestion was Heinrich Vogl, a young man who was just making a name for himself.

Having overridden Wagner's ideas over one singer, Ludwig developed a taste for it and began to scrutinise the rest of the cast in a more criticial light, complaining that the "unsuitable" Ortrud should also be replaced. The outraged Wagner threw down his baton and set off in high dudgeon for Tribschen. Unperturbed by this and determined not to abandon the production at this late stage, Ludwig leaned heavily on Bülow who somehow bullied the cast of *Lohengrin* into shape.

By the time the first performance took place on June 16th, King and composer had both calmed down somewhat although as usual it was Ludwig who first put pen to paper in reconciliation, pronouncing that he was "tolerably pleased" with *Lohengrin*. "I believe that if you knew how awful the punishment of separation was, you would never have decided upon this step (...) However, I will not weary the friend with complaints. I will not grumble. I kiss the hand that strikes me."

What he really meant was that he was afraid he would never see *Die Meistersinger* if he failed to lure Wagner back to Munich. A number of florid effusions were exchanged before Wagner allowed himself to be persuaded but in the meantime, despite the plaintive longings expressed in his correspondence, Ludwig found himself able to continue his duties with equanimity and indeed, gave all appearances of having forgotten Wagner altogether.

Among the official functions at which he participated was the installation of the newly-created Knights of St. George, an annual engagement which he found very much to his taste. Paradoxically, although the King shunned public appearances and official ceremony wherever possible, the historical mysticism of this and similar ancient rituals invariably captured his imagination and helped to boost his flagging spirits as well as reviving his sense of autonomy. It is likely that, while he officiated in his blue and silver robes, he imagined himself to be transported back into the age of chivalry to which he spiritually belonged.

To Sophie's annoyance, the Empress arrived at the end of June and Ludwig changed all his plans in order to spend every possible moment with her. He even neglected his new friend Richard Hornig for the first time since their meeting. Together the King and the Empress rode to their favourite haunts, spending long hours together deep in the forests and mountains, released from the scrutiny of a thousand eyes, and forgetting everything, apparently, but each other.

Ludwig had now matured considerably while Elisabeth was so perfectly preserved owing to her fanatical care of her beautiful body that the seven year disparity in their ages was not discernable. Interestingly, none of their contemporaries found anything bizarre in their friendship. If anything about them aroused comment, it was that same rare affinity which bound them together separated them totally from their fellows.

When the Empress at last left Starnberg, Ludwig accompanied her on the Royal train for part of the journey and for a short time they were completely alone again. In a euphoric letter to her [one of the few to survive from their reportedly copious correspondence] the following day, he wrote, "You have no idea, dear cousin, how happy you have made me. The recent hours spent in the railway carriage with you I count among the happiest in my life. The memory will never fade. You gave me permission to visit you at Ischl; if the time comes for this ardent hope to be fulfilled, I shall be the happiest man on earth. The feeling of sincere love and devotion that I carried for you in my heart even in my boyhood years makes me imagine that I am in heaven here on earth and the feeling will only be extinguished with death."

Shortly afterwards, Ludwig encountered Elisabeth's husband, who put a stop to any such meeting and to console himself, he set off instead on a visit to France with Otto, Hornig and his aide, Baron Sauer, to see the much-discussed Paris Exhibition of 1867. Even Wagner, whose own visit to the French capital had, as with all his expeditions, ended in disaster, pressed him to go, little realising that the King's chosen companion was to oust him finally from his own unique position in Ludwig's private world.

En route, the party visited the Wartberg in Thüringia where the famous Medieval castle offered superb views of the rolling Thüringian hills and surrounding forests. But it was the Minstrels' gallery which set Ludwig's pulses racing and decided him that he must have a similar one of his own to provide a setting for Wagner's immortal works if not for Wagner himself. The composer had, in fact, used this ancient place as the setting for his opera *Tannhäuser*, thus linking forever in Ludwig's mind the composer and the venue. Contrary to popular supposition, he decided to dedicate his castle not to Wagner the man but to his genius and his art.

Since his early childhood, the King had fostered secret hopes to build like his grandfather and indeed, his own father, and for his first project he looked towards a peak which soared up towards the Säuling, almost immediately opposite Schloss Hohenschwangau. A Medieval fortress had once stood here and Ludwig longed to see it rise again, dwarfing his father's castle. By the time the party had reached Paris, Ludwig's agile brain was already busy considering the merits of various possible architects; his ultimate choice fell on the celebrated Christian Jank. Unfortunately, what he failed to see in his imagination was the cost.

On July 10th, the party led by the "Count von Berg" arrived at the Hotel du Rhin in Paris, where he was, although ostensibly incognito, easily recognised from the many postcard portraits which now flooded the market. The Empress Eugénie, whom Ludwig liked and admired as he liked and admired all the cultured and elegant women he met, was not at this time in Paris and in her absence, her husband Napoleon III was obliged to act as Ludwig's guide, a task which cannot have been particularly pleasing to either party. Napoleon took Ludwig to Pierrefonds, knowing that the beautifully restored château would be infinitely more appealing to the aesthetic young man than the more carnal entertainments which he was in the habit of offering to his male guests in whose number was included Ludwig's own grandfather, who had also come to Paris for the Exhibition.

The younger Ludwig also visited Compiègne, the Louvre, the Tuileries and, of course, as a *pièce de resistance*, Versailles, where he saw enough to set his heart aflame for the second time during his holiday. This time, he burned with admiration for the Bourbons and, in particular, for his boyhood hero, Louis XV and the tragic Austrian, Marie Antoinette. He also spent two days at the exhibition itself where, to Hornig's horror, he insisted upon purchasing a Moorish kiosk which he threatened to install in his Wintergarden* at the Residenz. Fortunately, it proved to be too heavy for imposition on the existing structure which was already overburdened with a number of other things includ-

---

* The Wintergarden was destroyed together with some of the State apartments during the bombing raids of World War II.

ing the notorious pond, and the Kiosk ended its days at Linderhof, where he used it as a tea and coffee pavilion.

In the intoxicating company of Hornig, Ludwig was caught up in the rich and colourful history of the French capital as well as its excellent theatre but took a violent dislike to contemporary Paris with its "barren, inartistic bearing" and found it to be a "modern Babylon, the seat of materialistic people with common ideals and ungodly frivolity."

His holiday was interrupted by the death of his uncle Otto, the exiled King of Greece. The poor old man had been mentally unbalanced and Ludwig had made a point of avoiding him, perhaps wondering if his own blood was similarly tainted. Owing to the excessive degree of intermarriage in the House of Hesse, this would scarcely have been surprising. Intermarriage was still regarded as being the best way of avoiding the cardinal sin of a morganatic marriage or the inconvenience or political undesirabilty of marrying into some distant foreign House. One might almost say it was an occupational hazard of Royalty in the 19th Century. Ludwig himself had evidently given considerable thought to this problem and it is clear that he was constantly haunted by the fear that he might follow some of his more deeply distressed relatives to an early grave. With his highly coloured sense of the histrionic, he was fond of reminding his friends of his fears, both verbally and in his many letters: "You know that I have not long to live," for example, appeared with monotonous frequency every time he failed to get his own way with somebody. But taking his fixation more seriously, he probably found it preferable to assert that destiny would not permit him to go on living after "the Friend" had gone, rather than to state baldly that he was afraid he might go mad and die, perhaps during some horrendous fit. Quite aside from his latent homosexuality it is logical to suppose that this same fear was at the root of his aversion to marriage. Ironically, with the exception of his over-prosaic mother, Ludwig was undoubtedly the most sane and rational member of the family.

Protocol obliged him to abandon his pleasurable tour and pay his respects to his bereaved Aunt Amalie, an obligation which he dreaded and although he felt sorry for the "fat noodle", he was glad to leave the gloomy and oppressive atmosphere of the impoverished little court at Bamberg and escape to the Alpine tranquillity of Hohenschwangau. Even here his pleasure was to be marred as he complained in a letter to Wagner in August, "... since my birthday, I have been at Hohensch- wangau where I am at the moment with the Queen, my mother, and find little time for myself. It is often enough to drive me mad; my dear Hohenschwangau, otherwise (when I am alone) is for me the very heart of my wellbeing, separated from the world and in peace as well as the highest and truest poetry, but which under these conditions becomes comparable to a place of suffering. The Queen loves me truly and sincerely and so I could, as a good son, do nothing more than fulfil her wishes and spend more time here together with her, although I must confess to the Dear One that it costs me a great sacrifice because my mother does not understand me at all and life here is highly prosaic. I respect my mother, the Queen, and I love her as I should, but I can do nothing about the fact that an intimate friendship is impossible because of her nature which is so different from yours."

To Sophie he confided, "the present stay is completely spoiled by my mother, who tortures me with her endless love. She has no idea of rest and every spark of poetry vanishes in her company." It is difficult not to sympathise with Ludwig's frustration, and sadly, he was just as much out of his element in Sophie's company. She was certainly well aware of this and can scarcely have been overjoyed to read his complaint on the very day scheduled for their wedding, when she might have hoped his mind would be on another plane.

Sophie's demands for a new wedding date had also become a source of deep irritation to the King and even when a decision was wrung from him it was far from final and he had now procured a postponement until October 12th. This at least appeased his mother, since he had cunningly chosen the date of both his parents' and King Ludwig I's marriages. Marie might have been less pleased had she discovered the real reason for Ludwig's prevarication.

While Ludwig was in Paris enjoying the Exhibition, Sophie had been engaged with diversions of her own, making secret rendezvous with one of the court photographers, Edgar Hanfstaengl. In a strangely similar vein to what Ludwig himself had written about her, on July 23rd, she told her "Dearly beloved friend" Edgar, "I look into the future with horror; my wedding day stands like a black shadow. I would like to flee before my remorseless fate. Why did I have to meet you now when my freedom lies bound in chains? I love you so deeply, my Edgar, when you are with me I cannot tell you how deeply the sight of you stirs my heart, so deeply that I shamefully forget my duty to the poor King. Please rest assured that your letters will be carefully guarded; the world shall never have any idea of what is between us, and shall never pass cold judgment on you. Can you come to me at the Palais around 1/2 6 o'clock, but please don't come earlier because up until this time we shall have people with us..."

But Hanfstaengl was not Sophie's only secret love for only three weeks later she was writing similar notes to Max Holnstein, who had apparently some cause of his own to wonder about her activities, "In what circumstances I arrived here at Canal Street [Edgar's home] I cannot tell you, it is a wretched business, so dreary and hopeless. Please let me know immediately if you were lucky enough to leave the Palais unobserved – our people did, it appears, notice and I made myself look as sad as possible and swallowed down yet another cup of Camomile Tea, at which Nathalie [her companion] fell about. We cannot see each other for four weeks. It must be although it breaks my heart – I dare not even imagine how I shall endure this eternity. I kiss you a thousand times. Don't forget me ...."

The reason for the separation was the visit of Napoleon III and Eugénie of France to Austria. En route for Salzburg they were to spend a few days with Ludwig in Munich, where he would present her to them as his future wife. Even the flighty Sophie realised that she would have to behave with decorum for a while. She was clearly still determined to be Queen of Bavaria even if her opinion of Ludwig was no warmer than his feeling for her, but with a vanity typical of the cold-hearted flirt, and despite her own avowal that he was "only playing with her", she did not believe, even now, that she could not make him love her.

All thoughts of matrimony had in any case been erased from Ludwig's mind by his anxiety over the deterioration in Empress Elisabeth's health. Following fresh altercations with her husband and her malevolent mother-in-law, she was close to a nervous breakdown and was recouperating with her family at Possenhofen. In the present climate and with Elisabeth's indisposition, it would be difficult for them to arrange a rendezvous; if he wanted to see her he would have to endure his fiancée and her mother as well. Since he was in bad odour with both ladies, this was an uninviting prospect.

Ludwig continued to walk his narrow fence of bachelorhood until the beginning of October when, getting cold feet following his inevitable discovery of Sophie's amorous adventures, he suddenly asked for yet another postponement of the wedding. Losing patience her father, Duke Max, habitually a benign and patient if somewhat eccentric man, presented the King with an ultimatum and his wife followed it with a stiff note to Ludwig's mother in which she complained: "These continually repeated postponements of the wedding have seemed an unfavourable omen to us and have given rise to unpleasant gossip. Therefore Max considers it necessary to write to the King that he is trifling with Sophie's honour. He must beg the King as a subject either to keep the agreement at the end of November or regard the engagement which has pertained for more than eight months as something which never happened and we will certainly not insist upon the union continuing, as it has never been our intention to force our daughter upon him."

This was not strictly true and however much at fault Ludwig himself was, the rightous hypocrisy of the letter infuriated him. He was so angry with the Duke and Duchess that he picked up the plaster bust of Sophie which had simpered at him from his desk for the past few months and to the great delight of the domestics hurled it out of the window where it shattered in the courtyard. With it shattered the last remains of any feeling he might have had for his bride.

When Ludwig later commented to his secretary on the Duke's impertinence, the philosophical Düflipp pointed out that he had written more as a father than a subject, adding somewhat rashly that had he himself been in the Duke's position, he would probably have done the same. The King took his point but made up his mind that nothing would now persuade him to marry Sophie. The Ducal family's pressurisation had merely provided him with the opportunity to break off the engagement. They had made the same mistake as Wagner in believing that the King needed only to be pushed whereas in fact, he was one of those people who react by moving firmly in the opposite direction, as he did now. On October 7th he composed another of his literary masterpieces to Sophie:

"My beloved Elsa!

"As like our engagement the wedding day has been forced through like a hothouse plant, I consider it my sacred duty now, while there is still time, to tell you something before it is too late. You have always been precious and dear to me in my heart and I cling to you with true and sincere affection. I love you like a dear sister and this feeling which is deeply rooted in my heart shall never leave me, and I would like to beg for the continuance of your precious and amiable affection. Should you remember me with sorrow and bitterness, it would cause me deep grief.

"When we wrote to each other in the summer before last, when I told you of my friendship and gave you my trust, your mother pressed me for a decision; she believed I had wronged you because she did not believe in the existence of friendship without real love. You must remember the answer which I gave your mother through Gackl. It was with deep sorrow that I learned how unhappy this had made you and that you would have to go away and we would never see each other again; I was deeply touched by this sign of true love which you gave me; my affection for you was so increased that I was carried away and asked for your hand. As I had now put all the preparations for the wedding in motion, I wrote and spoke to you about a postponement, but did not wish to give you up entirely, nor was it in order to deceive you. I would never want to do that. That was out of the question. I asked in the firm belief that everything would come to a satisfactory conclusion and I have now had time to test myself, to counsel with myself and see that, although it is true that a sincere, brotherly love for you is rooted in my soul, it is not the love which is so necessary to a matrimonial union.

"I owe you this honest admission, dear Elsa, and beg you for the continuance of our friendship if you agree to let me take back my promise and we part from each other. I beg you most sincerely to let us do so without bitterness and resentment; please keep all the mementos which you have had from me and permit me to keep yours. They will remind me of a dear friend and relation who lies close to my heart. I shall pray to God every day.

"Should you, in about a year's time, not have found somebody else with whom you could be happy, and if I should find the same applies to me, which I do not think is altogether impossible, then we could still be united forever on the assumption, of course, that you still wish it. But it is better now that we part and do not bind ourselves to a specific promise for the future. I must repeat that the sudden interference of your mother in our affairs last winter remains very disagreeable to me.

"May the Father who watches over us – and this is my dearest wish – help you to find the way to true happiness which you, my beloved Elsa, so richly deserve. And now farewell, and do not forget to keep in your heart your faithful Heinrich."

"Will you be so good as to inform your parents of the main content of this letter."

Was he justified or was he behaving like a cad? Aside from the inevitable public outrage, Ludwig was wise in avoiding an ill-advised union with a girl who had apparently loved everyone in Munich except himself. He himself was convinced that he had made the right decision. Having finished his letter, he noted somewhat callously in his diary, "Sophie written off; the gloomy picture fades. I clamoured for freedom; now I feel reawakened after a terrible nightmare." To his cabinet secretary he wrote, "By the time you read this letter you will have received Captain Sauer who will have informed you of the whole history of our engagement. Please arrange for any sensation to be avoided; people should learn that the decision was made with the understanding of both parties that the relationship was on the decline. In fact, it was better to have averted a great catastrophe which would not have been very long in coming."

Already after the first postponement he had written to Baroness Leonrod, "The happy feeling which inspires me now I have shaken off the burdensome bonds which I knew would turn out unfortunately for me can only be compared with the rapturous sensations of a convalescent who at last breathes fresh air again after a dangerous illness. Sophie was always dear and precious to me as a friend and as a dear sister, *but she would not have done for my wife.* [Author's italics] The nearer the date of the wedding came, the more I dreaded my intended step. I felt so unhappy that I resolved to free myself from the self-imposed bonds and chains: for Sophie also it was not difficult to take back her word because she saw for herself that we did not suit each other. So we have avoided misfortune and now we both have the opportunity of making an agreement which promises to make us both happy. I am sure that she will pick a suitable *parti* in the near future and as far as I myself am concerned, I am not in any hurry. I am still young and marriage would have been premature anyway."

Explaining himself to Cosima, he wrote, "I have known her from my youth, always liked her as a true relation, faithfully and sincerely as a sister; I gave her my trust and my friendship but not my love! She must have seen how dreadful to me was the thought of the wedding as it drew closer and closer and must have recognised that this union could never bring happiness, either for her or for me (...) Why should I be forced into unhappiness, to run blindly into it when I am still so young and there is still time to take the way decreed by God? (...) The thought of the future swirled around me, black and gloomy (...) It is true that the storm which broke around my head was one which I myself had evoked. I thought it better to displease Sophie now and explain everything to her in a detailed letter." Behind all his florid words was hidden more common sense than his advisers ever showed, and as there was no political advantage in the match, who can blame Ludwig for not wanting to be chained to a woman he did not love and who was already liberally dispensing her favours throughout Munich?

Although he may well have been tormented by the thought that his own mother could have tainted him with bad blood and by the guilt of his latent homosexuality, basically he had been put off by Sophie's flighty behaviour. Ludwig's domestic spy network and his cabinet staff were always ready to carry tales; he had certainly been made aware that with her various affaires of the heart she was not the wronged innocent so often pictured. "To marry her would never have done," he had told Leonrod. At the same time, if Sophie had been Elisabeth, there is no doubt that he would have married her without a second thought for her peccadilloes. Elisabeth was the one woman who could have made him happy and she was the one woman he could not have.

Having made up his mind, Ludwig wrote to Hohenlohe, who was Minister of the Royal Household and Foreign Affairs at the time, telling him to arrange for a public announcement. "This," pronounced

Hohenlohe, "is evidently a fixed determination. At any rate it is better than setting me, a year hence, to bring about a separation." "But there is absolutely no reason for the King's step," remarked the unworldly Düfflipp. "For that very reason matters can be arranged in such a manner that she may find a pretext for withdrawing. Go at once to the Mint and order them to stop striking the medal," was Hohenlohe's practical rejoinder.

When Ludwig jilted Sophie it can hardly have come as a surprise to anyone but whatever his motives, his behaviour was universally condemned as being "without precedent." Enthusiastically, the gossips put forward a variety of "real reasons" for the broken engagement, the most popular being that Ludwig's intention to abandon Sophie was cemented when, arriving unexpectedly at Possenhofen one morning, he was greeted by the spectacle of a lady's maid running from Sophie's room at top speed followed a moment later by a basin of water energetically hurled by his betrothed. This brief glimpse of a totally different Sophie from the well-behaved young lady he usually saw was enough to convince him that she was no substitute for the moody but comparatively passive Elisabeth who would resort to tears rather than violence when she was upset. Whether or not there is any truth in this story it tells us that both Sophie's volatile temperament and Ludwig's preference for Elisabeth were well known.

Whatever the basis for Ludwig's action, he was understandably touchy on the subject and clearly felt the need to justify himself with those he loved, particularly his understanding grandfather to whom he confessed, "I have held it as my sacred duty to break off the engagement with Sophie, who will at least remain a dear and precious cousin to me," and to Wagner, "That which has occupied me during the course of the past months, which was like a burdensome nightmare to me, kept me on awful tenterhooks as you must have noticed from my letters to the *Freundin*. Now I have awoken as if from a gloomy dream and now the inner peace which has for so long deserted me has again recovered in my soul (...) I have only to add that I would have been unhappy with Sophie; she is not the one decreed from above to be the woman whom God entrusts to me! She understood my character only superficially, only enough to criticise, and she did not possess the depths which I would expect in my future wife, but I was temporarily dazzled by her superficial charm."

The Austrian Chargé d'Affaires, Count Zwiering, obviously as ghoulishly fascinated by Ludwig's love life as everyone else, wrote posthaste to Vienna that, since the early morning when the announcement was made, "The news has been spreading like wildfire around the City and has evoked unusual excitement; it is obvious that the like is unheard of in Bavarian history; the King's behaviour, already strictly censured, is being interpreted in the most regrettable way, while the position of the Princess meets with general deep sympathy."

To appease the family, Elisabeth was also expected to express her displeasure at Ludwig's seemingly offhand treatment of her sister although she knew that they were totally incompatible, and as one who was similarly placed with her own husband, cannot have been truly critical of Ludwig when he avoided a similar fate. Dutifully, she wrote to her mother from Schönnbrunn, "You can well imagine how angry I was with the King, as is also the Emperor. There is no expression for such behaviour. I don't know how he can bring himself to show his face in Munich after all that has happened and I am only glad that Sophie takes it as she does. God knows, she could never have been happy with such a man. I only wish twice as much now that she may at least find a good man - who will it be?" Yet long after Ludwig and Sophie had announced their engagement, Elisabeth had continued to meet Ludwig alone and they still spent hours together on the Roseninsel attended only by a local boatman. She could scarcely have been as "angry" as all that.

Apart from Julius Andrássy, the Hungarian patriot with whom she enjoyed a close and much-discussed friendship, Ludwig was the only man with whom Elisabeth felt a true rapport. She had become increasingly obsessed by the Magyars, her suite was now exclusively Hungarian and she had learned to speak the language fluently. To the great joy of the Hungarians, in August 1867 she had been crowned Queen of Hungary and as a token of their love - a love which they did not extend to the Emperor - they presented her with the beautiful Gödöllö, an estate some 26 kilometers from Budapest. When she had first laid eyes on it some time before, she had begged Franz Josef to buy it for her and had been inconsolable when she received a curt refusal. The gesture of the Hungarian people thus inspired in her an inextinguishable love which was considerably stronger than the feelings of hatred shown her by the Viennese who had done much to assist Archduchess Sophie in her campaign to make Elisabeth's life unbearable. How different was the attitude of the warmhearted, hospitable Magyars who took her to their hearts and shared her love of horses. Elisabeth showed her gratitude by spending much of her time in Hungary and in championing the Hungarians' political cause.

She therefore neglected not only Ludwig but also the Viennese, who then began to hate her more than ever. Elisabeth is not generally credited with her obvious attempts to do the right thing, but after the fiasco between Ludwig and Sophie, it seems likely that the distance which she placed between herself and the King was deliberate for reasons which later became transparent. They now met only rarely but she never ceased to love him and when her family criticised him, which they did with some frequency, she would leap to his defence in a way which must have betrayed her innermost feelings for him a hundred times.

This was of little practical use to Ludwig who was in dire need of an understanding friend. Above all, he needed the warmth and depth of a woman's love such as his woolly-headed and insensitive mother had denied him. He had enjoyed such a love for a few short years in his childhood when his beloved governess had cared for him, but with the exception of Elisabeth and, for a short time, the Tzaritza Marie Alexandrowna, he had not encountered it since. He did at least know himself better than those around him seemed to, and had the wisdom to see that marriage to Sophie would have been an unqalified disaster for them both. Deeply perceptive, he foresaw that, after the initial novelty of wearing the crown had worn off, Sophie would have become bored, discontent, indiscreet and, above all, distracted by his love of fantasy which she did not share, not to mention his habit of disappearing into the mountains when things went wrong.

He on his side would have been constantly wounded by Sophie's total lack of understanding. There is one final hint, however, that his rejection of Sophie had its main root in her infidelity. He had once commented sagely to Von der Pfordten concerning his relations with the opposite sex: "With most young people, sensuality is mixed with their affection for the opposite sex. I condemn this."

Dismayed by the wave of public disapproval Ludwig retired to Hohenschwangau where he remained throughout November in the familiar surroundings of his childhood. He made daily excursions on to the Alm, into the forests and to the crest of the Säuling, re-living happier days spent there in the company of Meilhaus and Otto, if not perhaps his tougher treks in the wake of his mother. After a few days spent thus, he felt calmer and revitalised, confiding to Wagner, "Thank God I am alone here at last. My mother, who really became a burden to me last summer because of her depressing prosaicness and spoiled my idyllic stay, is far away. Far away also is my former bride, because of whom I became so wretched and unspeakably unhappy."

Enjoying his long-awaited freedom, Ludwig had no further contact with the Ducal family for some months and his first encounter with Sophie did nothing for his dignity. In May 1868, while out riding at Starnberg, he was thrown from his horse and, having been abandoned by the creature, he set off home on foot but encountering a farm cart, begged a lift from the delighted peasant. As they rode amicably along together, an equipage of the Ducal house approached and the peasant politely pulled his cart to one side to allow it to pass. Sophie and her mother were inside, surprised to see the King comfortably installed in a nest of straw, his clothes muddied from his fall and his whole appearance somewhat less elegant than they were accustomed to see.

With the approach of Spring 1868, Ludwig's desire to be imbued again in the magical works of Wagner gained in momentum, but he must by this time have been asking himself if he was ever to hear any of the promised works and in particular, if the *Ring des Nibelungen* cycle would ever be produced in its entirety. He also longed to hear again the composer's earlier works conducted by their creator, and it was for this reason that Wagner was to be permitted to visit Munich. The composer, having learned his lesson and, indeed, having found greener pastures, had no intention of spending too much time in the city where he had almost as many enemies as he had debts but greedy as ever, he hoped for large rewards in exchange for his brief sojourn.

Having learned his lesson Ludwig had misgivings about becoming involved with Wagner again. Strangely, the composer did not realise this and with his almost paranoid vanity, still saw himself as the King and Ludwig as his vassal to be manipulated as he saw fit. He was about to discover how far from the truth this was.

Nothing further had been said about the Munich theatre project and Wagner now expressed his fear that Ludwig had lost interest, as indeed he had. In January 1868, the King had written to Wagner "How pleased I am with Semper's work (...) In my imagination I see our longed-for building before me in all its splendour. I see the towering arcs across the seats, I see the rows of pillars, I see the people, full of anticipation, in front of the inner sanctum, pervaded by the thrill of delight; the mystical tones resounding, the curtain rises and now the splendid drama is spun out before our souls and eyes. I see the Gods and heroes before me, the curse of the Ring is fulfilled!" And, months later when the project was no further ahead, "I see the streets crowned with the splendid building of the future; the people flock to the performance of the *Nibelungen* and *Parsifal*. The prejudices have vanished; they have all been touched with admiration, dearest friend (...) Oh, how blind they all are, who do not see the importance of these works!"

This was probably the extent of Ludwig's admiration and despite his early enthusiasm his attitude raises doubts as to whether he ever seriously intended to finance this ambitious project. The King's enthusiasm for Wagner and his clique had also long since evaporated although he took care to avoid giving this impression to the composer. He still enjoyed the occasional uplifting conversation on the arts with Wagner, and there is no doubt that in this sphere his every anticipation was fulfilled, but as he was to confess to a less volatile friend years later,

Wagner's voice gave him a headache after a few minutes and he never ceased to be shocked by the bad language which the composer did not see fit to curb in the presence of his Sovereign. Wagner was to the sensitive King like a foul-tasting but beneficial tonic: small doses could bring great relief but an overdose was likely to make the patient worse.

Like Wagner, Gottfried Semper waited impatiently for some monetary reward from the King, and had taken to appearing at the Residenz hoping to seduce the young man with his startling theatre plans, but he fared no better with Düfflipp than he had with Pfistermeister and no audience was granted. Semper's letters received no reply and he therefore no longer had any idea whether or not the theatre would actually be built. Urged on by Wagner, he had rashly declined all other commissions in the hope of finding fortune and glory in Munich, but by the end of 1867 he had become tired of waiting and had filed a suit against the King in a Court of Law, thereby killing all possible hope for the future. To be taken to court by a commoner was too much for Ludwig's Wittelsbach pride. His reaction came as an unpleasant surprise to Wagner, who hastily scribbled a note to the King asking for an audience. While his request was granted very little came of it and on his departure he left behind him an angry King who quite rightly blamed him for Semper's unprecedented action.

Ludwig was saved from any further visits by Wagner by the sudden death of Karl Theodor's wife which meant that all audiences were halted by Court mourning. Typically, Ludwig himself regarded this as a personal slight on the part of the Almighty but he could not offend his family by flouting convention. While he was still annoyed with Wagner, he was anxious to extract a final completion date for *Die Meistersinger* and as soon as he decently could, he arranged for Wagner to spend some time at Starnberg. Putting the more unpleasant aspects of the man from his mind, he thought only of the forthcoming revivals of *Lohengrin* and *Tannhäuser*; after the miseries of the past months, Wagner's masterworks were his only salvation.

One of his many disappointments had been that, despite his repeated efforts towards reconciliation following their angry altercations over Sophie, Karl Theodor's attitude towards him had remained cool. His wife's death had provided Ludwig with a suitable opportunity to make amends and by the time Gackl had departed for Rome to recover his equilibrium they were friends again.

Following his example, Ludwig turned again to thoughts of Wagner's visit; the Villa Prestele near Starnberg had been rented for the composer, but ungrateful as ever he prevaricated and announced that he would not arrive until May 30th. Perhaps he would have been more eager had he known that the King had specially commissioned from

Bechstein a combined piano and desk. Offended, the King decided not to give it to him and it stands to this day at Schloss Hohenschwangau.

It was about this time that Wagner also found himself in difficulties with the opposite sex. While enjoying to the full his liaison with Cosima, which by this time had become an established domestic partnership, he had uninentionally become involved with Malwina Schnorr von Carolsfeld. Following the death of her adored husband, Malwina had become almost deranged with grief. In her confused mental state she was easily convinced by one of her singing pupils that she could still reach her husband in the spirit world. With a little prompting from Wagner, who saw a profitable future in it, Malwina announced that she was receiving messages from her husband on the other side which closely concerned both the King and Wagner.

Contrary to the expectations of the conspirators, however, Ludwig would have none of it, nor would he listen when Malwina, turning sour in the face of what she considered to be competition from Cosima for Wagner's favours, suddenly began to make public accusations against Cosima and Wagner which, though true, were highly embarrassing to the parties concerned. None of Malwina's tidbits came as news to Ludwig who, aside from his own observations, had already heard them *ad nauseum* from a variety of wellwishers. Bored and disgusted by the whole Wagnerian clique, he removed himself even further from their reach. Somehow, he managed to retain his natural tact and loyalty when, faced with the latest piece of news concerning the trio, wrote back tongue-in-cheek to his informant, "I am astonished that the affaire between Wagner, Frau von Bülow and Frau von Schnorr may not be quite *'kosher'*. Should that rumour be true, which I cannot make up my mind to believe, should there indeed be 'adultery in the play – love'!" And having quoted from a favourite play, he prudently held himself aloof from this latest series of scandals and intrigues. Although he was still longing to hear *Die Meistersinger von Nürnberg*, when Wagner reappeared in Munich he was not granted an audience, nor did he receive the usual shower of gifts. Ludwig's pen remained still for twelve weeks while Wagner waited vainly for a response to his letter.

At last Ludwig had learned to play a waiting game.

CHAPTER EIGHT

LUDWIG AND THE OPERA

KING Ludwig I died at his residence the Villa Diesbach in Nice on February 24th, 1868. The old man's death came as a great shock to Ludwig, who had been deeply attached to the grandfather to whom he had so often turned in the past for guidance and comfort of a quality he had never found elsewhere and was never to find again.

He was not alone in his grief, for despite the life he had led and the criticism heaped upon him during his lifetime, old Ludwig had been greatly loved by everyone who knew him, whatever their opinion of his morals. His demeanour both before and during the war of 1866 had also brought him great respect and gratitude; now that he was dead, his sins and errors were forgotten and only his brilliance, his gaiety and his fine architectural legacy to Bavaria were remembered.

Well trained by this time to present a stoic composure to the world Ludwig successfully hid his grief although his grandfather's death undoubtedly affected him far more deeply than that of his own father, with whom he had enjoyed no such rapport. While he recovered from the misery of losing his most helpful and understanding relative, the young King drew comfort at least from the realisation that he would now receive that portion of the Civil List, a quite considerable sum of money, previously allotted to his grandfather. Thus financially liberated, as soon as the additional funds became available to him, he would be able to fulfil his great ambition and erect at Hohenschwangau the Medieval castle on which he had set his heart. He planned to build near the existing family home, either consciously or unconsciously visualising something which would dwarf his father's existing castle.

He showed little interest in the marriage of his cousin, Prince Ludwig, to the Grand Duchess Maria-Theresia of Austria-Este, unmoved when his absence from the festivities caused a mild sensation. Although he had sent word that he was too ill to travel no one believed it, although he was certainly still confined to his apartments some time later when the couple moved into their apartments at the Residenz.

By this time everyone in the capital was appalled by the King's continual absences but he was no longer affected by what they thought; his shell was gradually thickening and as far as he was concerned, the court and its gossip no longer existed. All he cared about now was his new castle. To Wagner he wrote enthusiastically, "I am proposing to have the old castle ruin near the Pöllat Gorge rebuilt in the genuine style of the old German Knights' castles and must confide to you that

I am delighted to think that in three years' time there will be a house to live in. Several quiet, comfortable and homely rooms shall be built from where one can enjoy a splendid view of the noble Säuling, the mountains of the Tirol and, further off in the distance, the plains, and you must know who is the revered guest I would like to hide away there. The place is one of the most beautiful to be found, healthy and inaccessible, a dignified temple for the immortal friend, through whom will flower the only salvation and true peace of the world. It will be reminiscent of Tannhäuser's Minstrel's gallery, with a view of the castle in the background and of Lohengrin (castle courtyard) outside approach to the chapel. You will find the castle to be more beautiful and comfortable in all respects from Hohenschwangau below, which is annually desecrated by my prosaic mother. They will take their revenge, these desecrated Gods!" Wagner saw little in all this to his own advantage and failed to make the required response.

With his heightened passion for bricks and mortar and his determinaton to commission artistic works of lasting value to embellish his castle when it was built, Ludwig's interest in human beings waned accordingly. He had once remarked bitterly that animals made better friends than humans because they were more trustworthy. He had apparently now made the discovery that inanimate objects were the most faithful and enduring friends of all.

Desperate for a little Wagnerian culture if not for the man himself, Ludwig broke the silence in early March: "I cannot go on any longer without news of you" and, as a sop to the composer's vanity, "If you want me to be fit and well again I implore you to hesitate no longer, dearest of men, and let me have a long letter without delay." Although purporting to be engaged on *Siegfried*, Wagner, with intoxicating memories of past favours flooding back, condescended to reply, "Why do you do this to me? Why do you re-awaken the old hopeful music in my soul which should by now have died away?" Encouraged, Ludwig obliged with the reason, appeasing the somewhat waspish response of the composer who took perverse joy in making people feel guilty.

At the end of March, the composer arrived triumphantly in Munich with his circus in his wake, full of high hopes of the revival of the old custom of receiving lavish gifts and money. To his chagrin, after having written specifically asking him to come, Ludwig did not even grant him an audience and he returned to Tribschen in a pique although shortly afterwards he was persuaded back for a gala performance of *Lohengrin* which was to be given in honour of Crown Prince Friedrich of Prussia. Ludwig, who detested his Hohenzollern cousin, had no intention of being present, even at his favourite opera, and immediately feigned illness. When he refused for the second time to see Wagner, the composer at last felt stirrings of unease. He had no alternative but to swallow whole the hint conveyed by these recent displays of a Royal will which he had not even known existed or at least which had not manifested itself noticeably in the early days of their relationship. Wagner had so long seen himself as a god in Ludwig's eyes that he had failed to notice the King had a mind of his own. The unexpected discovery came as an unpleasant shock. For Ludwig to miss a performance of *Lohengrin*, the situation must be serious.

In actuality, the King had more pressing matters than Wagner on his mind at this time for on April 22nd, Empress Elisabeth's fourth child, Marie Valerie, was born. She was to love this strange, excessively shy little girl more than all her other children and so publicly that the Viennese, who were always quick to criticise their Empress, christened her "the little Divinity". Valerie was the only one of her children whom she was allowed to keep by her. Rudolf, Gisela and the first born, Sophie, who had died in infancy, had all been wrenched from her almost at birth by her mother-in-law. Strangely, the Archduchess made no attempt to kidnap Valerie and indeed, virtually ignored her, and this curiously uncharacteristic attitude lends weight to the widely-held theory that Franz Josef was not the father.

Elisabeth's poor relationship with her husband was widely known and the Hofburg seethed with speculation as to where Valerie's parentage lay. Many of her enemies in Vienna asserted that the child's father was Count Julius Andrássy, the fiery Hungarian political leader with whom Elisabeth had formed a close alliance during 1865 and 1866. But even stronger and more persistent rumours had it that Valerie's father was Ludwig of Bavaria and it is certainly an indisputable fact that he and Elisabeth had spent a very great deal of time together in inaccessible places at the time when the child would have been conceived. Valerie's close resemblance to Ludwig also cannot pass unnoticed, although it is true that many members of this handsome family had similar features.*

Was there any truth in any of these stories? We shall never know. Most of Ludwig's more prominent and lasting friendships were with members of his own sex, but if anything, he was bi-sexual. He certainly liked women, however spiritual he insisted that liking was. It is difficult to believe that all the ladies with whom his name has been linked were content with a totally platonic liaison; the fact that he "never even kissed his fiancée, except on the forehead" is hardly proof of his total indifference towards the fair sex; quite aside from the fact that he did not love Sophie, it was not the custom for Royal persons to demonstrate their affections or indeed, any other emotions, in public.

---

* It was later rumoured that they actually had two children and pretenders sprang up all over the world.

Elisabeth, on the other hand, was on his own admission the lady who eternally filled his thoughts and in this respect she may inadvertently have ruined his life, for she was wise enough to keep away from him as much as possible, and he was never to find another woman who affected him as deeply as she did. He adored her and would never have done anything to hurt her; he would certainly never have stooped to discussing her with other persons. On one occasion, he dismissed one of his Aides on the spot for making some innocent remark about Elisabeth. Always gallant towards members of the opposite sex even when he disliked them, discretion would have been of the essence. His treatment of Cosima von Bülow is a good example of this.

On his birthday, probably still in the hope of prodding Wagner into doing some work, he relented and invited the composer to the Roseninsel. The excursion was an even greater disaster than when he was accompanied there by Lila von Bulykowsky and it resulted in a renewal of his earlier resolution, broken only in moments of desperation, to confine future meetings with his genius to the ambit of the theatre.

Whatever the difficulties of their personal relationship, however, Ludwig was greatly looking forward to the projected collaboration with Wagner on the first production of *Die Meistersinger von Nürnberg* which had suffered so many interruptions to its completion. As a birthday gift, Wagner had sent him a copy of the libretto and score, although he was already familiar with every aspect of it. For the production, Franz Nachbaur had been engaged, together with Ernst Betz and Mathilde Mallinger. In Ludwig's very expert opinion the opera could not fail but inevitably there were the usual tantrums and traumas during the rehearsals. In spite of this, after watching the first rehearsal, Ludwig was moved to write to the composer that he was "too moved to applaud lest he break the spell", although in fact, he was never to feel the same way about this opera as about Wagner's other works.

At the première on June 2nd, 1868, with Hans von Bülow conducting, Wagner was given the unprecedented honour of sharing the Royal Box in the centre of the auditorium. Ludwig was soon to regret his gesture which had been intended as a tribute to Wagner's art, for the egotistical and ill-mannered composer behaved as if he himself was the King, his bows and acknowledgements to the audience showing the unmistakable stamp of megalomania.

From the moment the curtain rose the audience was enthralled, applauding even between scenes which, although common nowadays, was virtually unheard of in the 19th Century. Inevitably, Wagner marred his finest moment by incurring the displeasure of King and public alike. While magnanimously adding his own applause to that of the enraptured audience who appreciated the quality of Wagner's work if not his unlovable personality, the King found himself for the first time at one with his subjects in his disapproval. Despite the unpalatable antics of its creator the new work was hailed as a masterpiece and given the unbridled praise it deserved.

Wagner's triumph provided him with the necessary inspiration to continue his flagging work on *Der Ring des Nibelungen* and Ludwig took the opportunity to sever relations with the composer. Having imbued himself in the revitalising ambiance of the work of his evil genius, he hastily left the capital before Wagner had the opportunity to approach him for money. He drifted towards Kissingen, where he spent a week in the company of the Tzaritza of Russia, but he could not relax and while he enjoyed the company of the charming Marie, the artificial atmosphere of the Spa soon began to irritate him. To Baroness Leonrod he complained "The place itself, the surroundings and monotonous life, go altogether against the grain." The reason for his restlessness was his longing to return to Hohenschwangau to watch progress on the new castle. With his dream at last becoming a reality, his already dormant interest in the Isar theatre project also took another downward turn and Wagner was obliged to accept finally the unpleasant truth that it would never now materialise. An even bitterer pill was the realisation that he was unlikely to regain his lost power over the King which in any case was never as great as he had imagined. The composer admitted as much in a letter to a friend, "I must tell you quite honestly that I shall one day see myself deprived of any protection and without any benefit from there." He had no one to blame but himself.

By September, Bavaria was again looking forward to a Royal wedding and again the bride was Sophie. The groom was the Duc d'Alençon, grandson of Louis Philippe of France and apparently more gullible than Ludwig. The wedding took place on the 28th in the great hall at Possenhofen and lending a certain irony to the proceedings, Wagner's wedding chorus from *Lohengrin* was played during the banquet.

On the whole, the wedding celebrations were a great success, the only apparent blight on the proceedings being Sophie herself. It was observed by many that, far from being heartbroken after Ludwig's rejection of her Sophie, with the help of her mother, had lost no time in finding another man of almost as exalted rank as Ludwig himself if of a less decided personality and one cannot but suspect that this suited the wilful Sophie admirably.

From the way in which she already publicly dominated the poor little blond duke and her curiously offhand manner during the ceremony, Ludwig's worst enemies were bound to admit that he had, after all, shown sound judgement in jilting her. Prince Hohenlohe in his diary commented "Nobody cried but Duke Max looked rather like it once or twice. The bride appeared extremely self-possessed (...). The Duchess's "Yes" sounded very much as if she meant "Yes, for my own part" or "Yes, for ought I care". I don't wish to be spiteful but it sounded like that to me. After the wedding I kissed the Duchess's hand and congratulated her. She seemed very gratified and pleased." Acutely aware of the piquancy of the situation, Hohenlohe was not slow in commenting on Ludwig's firework display.

Although the rest of the Wittelsbachs turned up in force, etiquette and lack of interest prevented the King from attending the ceremony, although during the celebrations he arranged a special dinner and firework display on the Roseninsel - another piquant touch in view of his earlier refusal to allow Sophie to set foot on his island. The bride and groom were naturally not invited to this. The official reason given for Ludwig's festivities was to honour the Tzaritza of Russia, but Ludwig was probably privately celebrating his own lucky escape from Sophie. The fireworks and illuminations, the music and the elegance of all the festivities combined to produce a spectacle of fantastic beauty and it went without saying was wildly expensive. When the Tzaritza's reaction touched disappointingly on this aspect of the display, Ludwig's warmth towards her cooled noticeably. Elisabeth on the other hand was enchanted by the King's fireworks and did not hesitate to say so.

The closeness of their family ties made it inevitable that Ludwig and Sophie would meet from time to time; after the first of their trying "official" meetings, Ludwig asserted that he was "bored to death"; Sophie's reaction is not recorded. In the long term Ludwig's judgment proved to be faultless for Sophie was continually unfaithful to her husband and some years later when she was 42 with a brood of four, she created a great scandal with her blatant affaire with a prominent Munich doctor which only came to an end when her embarrassed family put her into a mental home officially for a "nervous breakdown" but actually to cure her nymphomania. She eventually vindicated herself by a display of great bravery in an horrific situation: while working at a charity bazaar in Paris in the 1880s, she was burned to death while trying to save some of her young helpers when the booth was suddenly engulfed in flames.

As Autumn 1868 turned to Winter, the King remained quietly in the mountains. Now that the construction of his castle was well under way his thoughts were already turning ambitiously towards a second which was to be a palais in the French style. All his life Ludwig had felt a special regard for the Graswangtal with its secluded beauty and heady mountain air. At the end of this valley stood the ancient monastery of

Ettal and close by was the village of Oberammergau, whose dicenniel penance since 1634 was the performance by the inhabitants of a Passion Play to celebrate their deliverance from the plague with which the village had been struck two years earlier.

At the other end of the same valley stood a small hunting lodge known as the Linderhof which had been built by Ludwig's father some years before. Here, on the site of this modest place, Ludwig proposed to build his new residence. The designs were produced by a group of distinguished architects but the plans adopted were mainly those of Dominik Quaglio and Eugen Drollinger, although most of the original ideas were Ludwig's own. The Palais was to be dedicated to the Bourbons and in particular to the Sun King, Louis XVI. Ludwig himself described it as being a "unique jewel" and he had a deep affection for it but his feeling was quite different from that inspired by Neuschwanstein. Linderhof was to be the only one of his creations to be completed.

Simultaneously, alterations and additions had been made to the Wintergarden in the Munich Residenz. It now boasted a grotto similar to the one at Neuschwanstein, smaller than the huge, theatrically lit grotto at Linderhof but nevertheless unique. In the Wintergarden was also housed a collection of exotic birds which had reached such proportions that the domestics had good ground for complaint. One or two of Ludwig's ferocious but entertaining parrots would take their revenge by terrorising such unfriendly servants.

Birds had always fascinated Ludwig and throughout his life the swan, the peacock, the eagle and the dove had a special significance for him. Aside from the living creatures in his collection, his residences were filled with ceramic, metal and wooden representations of these varieties while in his Moorish kiosk at Linderhof his gorgeously coloured enamelled peacocks displayed their plumage by means of clockwork.

He was also apt to use his avian friends as allegorical parallels with humans, referring to Elisabeth as his "Dove" (later his "Seagull") while he himself was appropriately enough, the "Eagle"; this was a game which appealed to Elisabeth's sense of fantasy as much as to his own. He explained his follies and the living creatures which often inhabited them to Baroness Leonrod with the heartcry "Oh, how necessary it is to create for oneself such pretty places of refuge where one can forget for a little while the times in which we live."

Able now to combine his love of the Graswang with his admiration for the autocratic Bourbons, Ludwig spent an increasing amount of time in the area in the company of Richard Hornig, watching the progress of the new building. So engrossed was he in this pursuit that for the first time Wagner's birthday passed unnoticed and when, in August, the composer hurried in a panic to Schloss Berg to greet the King on his birthday, he waited in vain for two days before he realised with horror that Ludwig did not even propose to grant him a birthday audience.

Evidently, Wagner had been listening to the rumours which circulated for, erroneously, he believed that he had been ousted by a well-known sculptress. Born in 1835, Elisabeth Ney was related to the famous Napoleonic general, and was said to be even more emancipated than Cosima von Bülow. She had gone to great lengths in her determination to capture the King's interest and had accomplished this difficult feat by literally slipping into the clothes and character of one of his literary favourites, *Ifegenia*, quoting from the play while dressed alluringly as the lady in question. How could Ludwig resist? Ney understood perfectly what Lila von Bulykowsky had failed to comprehend. As a result she was granted several sittings for a portrait bust which was later extended to a full length statue in which the King is portrayed in the robes of a Knight of St.George. It stands today, an excellent likeness and a tribute to her great talent, at the foot of the unfinished staircase at Herrenchiemsee.

Witty and intelligent, Ney's conversation was a lively and pungent mix of gossip, the arts and political matters and her views on these diverse topics amused Ludwig greatly until she committed the inevitable folly of seeking to advise him on matters which did not concern her. Ludwig had already endured enough interference in that direction from Wagner and did not propose to put up with similar meddling from a woman, however attractive and entertaining she might be. His interest cooled immediately and she was never granted another audience. Reticent about her private affairs, Ney never told Ludwig or indeed anyone else in Munich, of her marriage to a Scottish physician, a Dr. Montgomery, and was also the soul of discretion where Ludwig was concerned. She possessed other sterling qualities: apart from a house in Munich which she allowed the King to buy for her (before they met) for use as a studio, she would never accept any gift from him except flowers.

Delightful as Ludwig found her, she was not his only female friend and certainly not his only confidante. In addition to Empress Elisabeth, who always held first place in his heart, Baroness Leonrod, his cousin Princess Anna of Hesse and the Tzaritza of Russia, he was on close terms with several eminent ladies of the theatre. For a while he was diverted by a singer, Josefina Scheffsky, a large, bovine woman who, though pretty in an overripe way, possessed none of the ethereal grace which he so admired in his Elisabeth. Poor Josefina, who had a glorious voice, was obliged to sing to him from behind a screen because he could not bear to watch her facial contortions. He had no objection, however, to the occasional tête-à-tête supper with her when she would regale him with the scandals of the opera house. She too fell from favour when she tried to charge to the Treasury the sum of 1,500 Marks for a carpet which she had "presented" to the King on the general understanding that she could get a refund via the King's secretary. This was common practice and one which Ludwig, who well knew the limitations of an artist's salary, was fully aware. But he would not tolerate abuse of the system and he was so disgusted when it transpired that she had bought the carpet for 300 Marks from her brother-in-law, that he would have nothing further to do with her, and even her much-envied title of *Kammersangerin** was stripped from her.

An amusing anecdote concerning Josefina was lovingly told by her friends to the effect that, on one occasion during a visit to the Wintergarten in the Residenz, she jumped fully clothed into Ludwig's pond in a desperate attempt to reclaim his wandering attention. Bored by this unseemly display as much as by the singer herself, Ludwig merely rang for a servant to fish her out and left abruptly without even waiting to find out if the lady had caught a cold.

Marie Dahn-Haussmann was of a totally different type who filled a special niche in Ludwig's life over a period of many years. An ageing but brilliant tragedienne whose most famous role was that of Thekla in Wallenstein's Lager, she came of a good background and, having been a family friend of Ludwig I, was socially acceptable. She was a lady in all senses of the word and never took advantage of the King's friendship. She was often the one to hold out a hand when Ludwig was in need of sympathy and well understood his need for mature feminine companionship. Although beset by personal problems including an invalid husband and a difficult daughter, she was always charming, cheerful and interesting. Ludwig never forgot her kindness of heart and when he heard that her daughter had suffered a mental breakdown he was especially considerate towards her for by that time he himself had an all-too-personal experience of such illnesses.

None of these ladies could totally allay the boredom and apathy which shrouded his spirit. Since the memorable production *of Die Meistersinger* Wagner had been unusually quiet and, as always, it was the King who broke the silence between them with the heartcry "In the summer *Tristan und Isolde* as well as *Rheingold* are to be produced. I beseech you, dear friend, to bring yourself to help make the production possible. Oh, how I need such pleasures if I am not to become lost in the maelstrom of everyday life."

---

* Official Court singer.

After the initial production difficulties with Tristan had been resolved in 1865, apart from the difficulty in finding suitable singers it was
unproblemmatical; but *Das Rheingold,* the prologue to the *Ring* cycle
was another matter. Although like *Tristan* it had been completed some
years previously it had yet to be performed publicly and owing to the
almost insurmountable difficulties now encountered it looked is if it
would have to be abandoned in mid-production. Bülow, his health and
his private life in ruins, had resigned as musical director and in his place
came Hans Richter, one of Wagner's own protégés. Unfortunately, he
was an insolent and arrogant acolyte of the Master and looked like not
only emulating but actually surpassing Wagner's audacity. Ludwig
took an instant dislike to him. In Wagner's eyes the King was still no
more than the holder of the purse strings and saw no reason why his
own wishes should be ignored when it came to the hiring and firing of
theatrical staff. King and composer had had public altercations in the
past on the same subject and while in most cases Ludwig, who had
impeccable judgement in artistic matters, was right, Wagner could
never bear to admit that a mere King knew better than he.

Added to all the personal acrimony there were technical difficulties
with the special effects and in particular the floating Rheinmaidens
who made their watery way across the stage in a state of panic.
Suspended high above the other singers on weirdly constructed ambu-
lant pedestals behind the flats and wheeled at speed across it, they were
in real physical danger and their screams were not always in Wagner's
libretto. Richter, puffed up by his own sudden elevation to conductor,
continually upset the theatre staff and quickly became as detested as
Wagner already was. Ludwig disliked displays of temperament and was
particularly irritated by this brash and as yet unproved youth. He had
also taken a dislike to the tenor, Ernst Betz but the moment he
informed Wagner that the singer was to be replaced forthwith Richter,
with great temerity, refused to direct. Furious, the King sent a note to
Düfflipp, "If Richter – or any of the theatre people – continues to
immediately oppose orders given to them, the weeds must be rooted
out without compassion. I charge you to intervene sharply against such
infamy."

But the overconfident 26 year old, sure that Wagner would protect
him in any serious contretemps with the King, continued to ignore
Ludwig's wishes. Angrily, the King wrote to Düfflipp again "I am firmly
convinced that you summoned everything you could to carry out my
wishes and I want to make you my special acknowledgement of all your
trouble. The behaviour of Wagner and the theatre riffraff is truly
criminal and shameless; this is an open revolt against my commands
and is not to be endured. In no case is Richter to be allowed to direct

any more and is instantly dismissed. That is settled. The theatre people must observe my commands and not the whims of Wagner. It has already been stated in several pages of instructions that the performance will otherwise be cancelled. I can see this coming." After grumbling further, he continued, "If these abominable intrigues of Wagner are allowed to pass the whole pack will become more audacious and shameless and eventually they will no longer be able to be retained. Therefore, the evil must be torn out by the roots. Richter must go and Betz and the others brought to submission. Such insolence is not to be credited. I repeat, I am satisfied with your efforts in the affair and expect you to return the reluctant workers to submission. *Vivat Düfflipp! Pereat Theaterpack!*" If he had only applied the same forthrightness towards his politicians, the course of Germany's history might have been changed. In another note to his secretary Ludwig optimistically specified the date of the first performance, together with the unprecedented instruction that Wagner's stipend was to be withdrawn immediately because of his obstructive attitude, and this at a time when he still addressed letters to "The only beloved" and "dearest friend".

Somehow, *Das Rheingold* was finally produced to the general satisfaction in September 1869, but with a different director and when Wagner discovered that Ludwig had gone behind his back in the matter, he was as furious as if he still owned the production rights. The rift between the two men widened still further, although Ludwig sent the inevitable placatory letter to Wagner with the usual plaintive cry "Ach, God, the craving to hear your immortal works was so powerful, so all conquering, as it was in the years of my first youth, that I seemed to sink into the spirit itself and would die after drinking in its heavenly bliss. Now I have damned myself!" Having thus committed himself, he continued unrestrainedly and, as it transpired, most unwisely, "Oh write to me and forgive your friend who is at fault. What is even the dazzling ownership of the crown compared with a friendly letter from you! It is like the short, earthly happiness compared with the eternal bliss of paradise! Yes, Parsifal knows his duty, goes forth purified, believe me, from all his trials!"

But it was not lost on Wagner that Ludwig asked only for a letter and not for a personal confrontation. In his reply he complained "It is not the difficulties of the thing itself, nor yet our position which so often seems to separate us so completely, but it must sometimes occur to me, as you wander in quite a different direction from that in which you might hope to meet me, that you would meet someone quite different from me. When you hold yourself aloof from me, avoid me – yet with all the difficulties which together we could easily surmount, you barricade yourself against me, so that I now seem to be totally alien to you and I have to ask myself whether, up to now, I only dreamed I had a King for a friend."

This did nothing to mend matters; the old warmth and enthusiasm had cooled beyond rekindling, and only Ludwig's admiration for the work of this dreadful man remained. It was a bad mistake on Wagner's part to have underestimated Ludwig's ability where the theatre was concerned for the King was genuinely greatly talented and knowledgeable in all matters relating to the arts with the kind of instinct which, in other spheres, would have bred a brilliant impresario.

With painful memories of *Das Rheingold* still vivid in his mind, Ludwig had no intention of enduring a similar struggle with *Die Walküre* and astutely arranged the production of this second part of *Der Ring des Nibelungen* without consulting the composer. He had a perfect right to do this, having paid handsomely for the privilege some years before. When Wagner eventually made the discovery at the beginning of 1870, however, that *Die Walküre* was in course of production he flew into an uncontrollable rage declaiming loudly on the fickleness of royalty, conveniently forgetting his own treacheries and duplicities and the vast sums of money which he had extorted from the King in exchange for the publishing rights which Ludwig now chose to exercise.

Wagner had, in fact, some years before he met Ludwig "given" these same rights to two other friends in exchange for financial assistance, although both had graciously conceded to King Ludwig. It was Wagner's own fault entirely that the King had decided to go ahead without him, for had he not left Munich in a temper he would undoubtedly have been invited to supervise the remaining sections of the cycle despite the fact that productions always went more smoothly in his absence. Nevertheless, both Wagner and Cosima remained unforgiving and Ludwig on his side made no further overtures of reconciliation. Where Wagner was concerned the last wall of illusion had fallen from the King's eyes.

Now that he had Hornig for company he had no immediate need of the volatile and double-dealing Wagner; now that he had his building he had a better spiritual release even than that of the music and poetry which invariably arrived from the Master wrapped boa-like around a hardcore of political homily and financial demand. Now that he had hit upon the idea of keeping a secret diary, commenced in December 1869, he had no need to confide his deepest torments to friends whom, like Egmont's, he could never really trust. His greatest problem was his latent homosexuality, which was made worse because he had no one with whom he could discuss it. He could never have poured out such things to the genteel and kindly Leonrod or the unworldly Elisabeth (although both may possibly have been instinctively aware of his secret anguish). His more "normal" relationship with Elisabeth led, in any case, to "normal" letters. Curiously, although their respective staffs complained eternally about their interminable correspondence, very few of their letters to each other have survived. If Ludwig did write love letters to Elisabeth, they were either destroyed or remain under lock and key in the Wittelsbach Archives.

Poor Ludwig had much to suffer on account of his mixed emotions. Because of his abnormally warm feeling toward Richard Hornig which he repeatedly but unsuccessfully tried to stifle, he quickly developed a guilt complex. A devout Catholic, he knew that what he felt for Hornig was wrong. Had circumstances been different, he would have been ideally happy with Elisabeth but since she was unattainable he tried to content himself with the charming and intellectual Stallmeister rather than with someone of the opposite sex who could, in any case, only have been second best. Having reached the stage where he was desperate for any kind of human love, instead of suppressing his baser desires as his conscience frequently dictated, he spurned instead his church, to the sorrow of his friend and tutor, the great theologian, Ignaz von Döllinger with whom he had earlier enjoyed a warm and rewarding friendship. Bitterly disappointed at receiving no word of comfort when he called upon his God to deliver him from the dreaded "falls" which he experienced, Ludwig finally lost faith and turned instead to his secret diary for absolution. Over the ensuing years he was to fill the luxuriously bound volumes with references to the Bourbons, who had become an obsession, and his guilty love, his shame and horror of what he did, his longing for redemption and his determination to overcome his weakness.

Ludwig's reckless behaviour was beginning to cause such comment within the family that finally his mother persuaded him to visit the family physician; this was no small achievement on her part since Ludwig disliked doctors intensely and could not bear physical examination despite the fact that he had known Dr. Gietl from childhood. Having thus submitted himself for inspection by Gietl and his colleagues, the worthy gentlemen found themselves somewhat out of their depth and were able only to prescribe cold baths and douches to alleviate his headaches and insomnia - a cure which La Rosée had also employed years before to little effect. Unfortunately, Ludwig found recourse to chloralhydrate and laudenum to be more effective than the water torture, at least in the short term. Although he did not realise it, the drugs only aggravated the headaches and adversely affected both his temper and his metabolism.

Less harmful were his excursions into the fresh air with Richard
Hornig although strangely, they produced more growls of disapproval
than the drug taking. Among their favourite haunts were the beautiful
region between Hohenschwangau and Linderhof, the Ammerland and
the brilliantly coloured Plansee, whose waters were reminiscent in
colour to the plumage of Ludwig's beloved peacocks. The two would
ride to Reutte in Tirol and to the little town of Pfrondten. Depending
on the season, they would travel on horseback, by carriage or by sleigh.
To avoid prying eyes, the increasingly sensitive and neurotic King
preferred to travel by night although he evidently found this to be
somewhat hazardous. He very sensibly began to confine these outings
to moonlit nights when Diana would light his way along the steep and
rocky paths. If the weather was too inclement for the horses, he would
have his favourite mount saddled and would ride around the *manège*
in the Royal stables for the equivalent distance to one of his usual
excursion places and then annouce to the amazement of his staff that
he had "Just ridden to Innsbruck and back" or "to the Riss."

Needless to say, all of this was grossly misinterpreted and only added
to his reputation for eccentricity for few people were open minded
enough to see the logic of what he did: despite his occasional threat of
suicide which was never seriously meant, the still-youthful Ludwig had
no true desire to lose his life and still less to maim or disfigure his regal
and handsome person. To his great chagrin his very practical means
of avoiding such mishaps by travelling only when there was a full moon
to light the way gave rise to such malicious gossip that he began to lose
faith even in some of the villagers whom he had always loved almost as
members of his own family.

All this, together with his growing mania for building, did much to
alter public opinion of him; the man who could once do nothing wrong
could now do nothing right, and those who thought that Ludwig's
troubles would end now that Wagner was no longer hanging over him
were proved to be sadly mistaken.

CHAPTER NINE

THE FRANCO PRUSSIAN WAR AND THE FORMATION OF THE REICH

IN 1869, the question of the Prussian alliance and the new school laws instituted by Ludwig under the tutelage of Prince Hohenlohe led to bitter opposition between the Particularists and the Ultramontanes on the one hand and the National Liberals on the other. The opposing parties put every possible obstacle in the way of the Government and as the King's failure to get rid of Hohenlohe was construed as open support, his popularity waned sharply with the Munich burghers. At the same time the Pope was in process of publishing his inhibiting Dogma of Papal Infallibility to which Ludwig himself was opposed.

The Ultramontanes gained a majority in the consequent elections and the current Ministerium resigned. Ludwig refused to accept Hohenlohe's resignation and there ensued further battles between the two factions; this resulted in the majority opposition taking a vote of censure against Hohenlohe, who promptly turned tail and far from resigning, now clung stubbornly to office.

With so much going on in the capital, Hohenlohe viewed Ludwig's excursions with the same rancour as had Von der Pfordten since quite aside from all the internal convolutions he had been at pains to warn the King of the rapidly deteriorating relations between France and Prussia. Inevitably Ludwig's feelings underwent a change and he began to distrust Hohenlohe; he refused to listen to him not because he lacked interest in these important issues, but because he no longer felt a rapport with the man who offered the advice. Regal to the core, Ludwig nevertheless, remained kind and courteous towards him.

On July 8th Hohenlohe recorded, "Yesterday at half past twelve, I received a telegram from Lipowsky informing me that the King wished to see me at Schloss Berg between two and three, and would send a carriage. At first I thought this last sentence must be a mistake, but a carriage actually came and took us to Berg through the Fürstenrieder Park. We arrived at three. The King received me first. He gave me his hand, which he seldom does, and was very amiable. I spoke to him first of my report of the discussion with Bismarck and enlarged on the reasons why a further threat to Bavaria through Prussia was now to be thought of. The King is always distrustful, which is due to his extremely sceptical nature. We could give up the Treaty of Alliance at any moment, he maintains, as there is a passage in it which makes this possible for us. I, of course, disputed this, but on the other hand I conceded that one can give notice to withdraw from any Treaty if one finds it in one's interest to do so. This, however, is not the case here. I pointed out the danger into which this could bring us. It would be better to conclude the alliance with Prussia on the lines of the old Germanic Confederation. Those Ministers who maintained that such an alliance would be too little for the Progressives and too much for the Ultramontanes would certainly be against this. The King answered very pertinently that it would be all the same, and that too much must not be left to public opinion (...). The King was, as usual, very sharp in his questions and answers. It is a pity that he confines himself more and more to the bad company of that horsebreaker, Hornig. Yesterday he intended driving to the Riss, probably to escape the arrival of the Emperor of Austria."

A few days later Hohenlohe submitted his report to the King, stating, "The Governments concerned all agree that the fullest freedom of division must be firmly assured to the Council in the religious domain but that, on the other hand, every intrusion of this spiritual assembly in the domain of the State must be averted equally firmly, and that resolutions of the Council of the character which the undersigned foresees will bring with them the gravest dangers for religious peace and for the tranquillity of social life (...). It now becomes desirable that, by the medium of a reliable plenipotentiary of German States, suited for that mission by personality as well as by his social position, the necessary steps should be taken at home to gain a closer view of the proposed resolutions and to draw attention once more to the dangers which would certainly threaten religious peace and the church itself from such resolutions of the Council which should intrude upon the sphere of State rights."

Digesting this at Hohenschwangau, Ludwig added in the margin [on July 31st, 1869], "The negotiations up to the present have shown the difficulty of persuading the Governments to take joint preventative action in the matter of the Council, but have served to awake more vigilant attention and so partly fulfilled the end in view.

"To despatch an agent without credentials, yet intended to speak in the name of the collective German Governments seems to me, in view of their having hitherto declined joint action and of the varying positions of the different Governments, not quite practicable and unlikely to succeed. If, however, you consider that the constitution and the law do not arm you with a ready means of defence, and that therefore your care for the full security of my Royal supremacy and for the interests of the State compels you to take this course, I shall not prevent you from resorting to it. In that case, however, be sure to send me a report here, and be careful about the person you propose to send as an envoy."

Such was the "indifferent" King who was accused of allowing his talents for ruling to lie fallow. He was, on the contrary, deeply aware of Bavaria's unhappy position. In a personal letter he wrote miserably, "That I stand in the wretched, comfortless world so completely and utterly alone with my ideals uncomprehended and mistrusted is no mere trifle to me. When I first ascended the Throne there was, in a manner of speaking, the charm of novelty by which I pleased the people. Oh, what pain to those who have had to deal with the masses, and happiness to individuals like you who are able to manage it! Believe me, I have grown to know the people; I came to them with a true heart. But now I feel sickened, and such wounds heal slowly, very slowly."

One of the most curious paradoxes in the King's nature was that, despite his belief in absolute Monarchy, he did not embroil himself in the running of the country, although this may have been due in part to the fact that, in his formative years, his father had decimated both his confidence and his interest by keeping him in ignorance of State affairs. At this crucial time, therefore, he was rarely to be found when his presence was required. Ministers were rarely given the opportunity to tackle him at social gatherings for Ludwig assiduously avoided all the usual court functions and no longer invited them to dine privately with him as when he first came to the Throne. The luckless gentlemen whose duty it was to pursue him to his various retreats to present their reports were rarely even honoured with his personal presence. Depending upon their time of arrival, they would be given some cold collation to be eaten in spartan conditions and would be kept waiting for hours in unheated anterooms presumably with the idea of encouraging them not to linger where they were not wanted. Did Ludwig deliberately torment them to ensure that they did not outstay their welcome, or was he merely absent-minded? His copious memoranda to his staff suggest that he may have behaved as he did in order to annoy them to the point where, if they began to argue with him during the conference, he could more easily put them out of countenance. It was a favourite ruse of his. Alternatively, when he received them cordially and gave them his full attention, he was quite probably merely "lathering them up" [einseifen], or pulling the wool over their eyes, in order to get rid of them more quickly. Undeniably, he played with people whom he disliked as if they were animated toys.

Even more horrendous to visitors than going to the Residenz or Berg was the necessity to visit the King at Hohenschwangau since in view of its remoteness, they would have to stay the night there in the

expectation of receiving little or no hospitality from their Royal host.
Ludwig himself detested these overnight invasions quite as much as
they disliked spending the night under the roof of a host who refused
to dine with them and who was, in all probability, not even there. If
Ludwig knew in advance that they were coming, he would set off
immediately for one of his less accessible hunting lodges, leaving his
aide to explain his absence as best he could. The game of cat and mouse
could not go on indefinitely, for by early 1870 it was obvious that
Bavaria was dangerously near to war.

Following the continued political skirmishes over the Dogma of
Papal Infallibility which had caused enormous dissention among the
various political factions, Hohenlohe was obliged to give up. On
February 14th, 1870, he tendered his resignation and received the
King's very fairminded reply:

"My dear Prince!

"You have repeatedly petitioned me to relieve you of your duties as
Minister of the Royal House and of Foreign Affairs. After a careful
investigation of the circumstances I have assented to your request today
as a consequence of the *personal* motives you have adduced. In offering you this explanation I feel bound to express from the bottom of my
heart my appreciation of the self-sacrificing devotion and unfailing
loyalty which have marked your tenure of office. To give tangible
expression to this appreciation, I have included you, my dear Prince,
in the Roll of Capitalaries of my Knightly Order of St. Hubertus. In
the renewed assurance of my good wishes, I remain,

"Ever your affectionate King, Ludwig."

Hohenlohe's successor was Otto, Count de Bray-Steinberg, whose
political persuasions were the same as those of Hohenlohe, if less
obtrusive. He at least refrained from constantly reminding his colleagues of Prussian supremacy as Hohenlohe had persisted in doing,
but it made no difference to Ludwig, who knew all too well that war
was inevitable, and he also knew that Bismarck, whom he admired but
did not trust, had tricked him. Further, it was painfully obvious that
this current political crisis was a long-expected development and he
felt deeply humiliated because he had walked into Bismarck's obvious
trap like an innocent child, betraying his people for the second time by
following the advice of his Cabinet.

The crux of the problem was that Leopold von Hohenzollern had
been selected for the candidacy of the Spanish Throne upon which no
King had sat since 1866. The choice was an unpopular one with the
French, who were naturally nervous of being hemmed in on all sides by

the powerful and arrogant Hohenzollern family. The Continent-wide protest led inevitably back to the discussions concerning a unified Germany and the only man likely to be gratified by this was Bismarck, whose vision of a united Germany was now far more than a vague dream for the future and, indeed, more than a wish that the States of Germany would become one consolidated Nation: behind Bismarck's scheming was the determination that any such union would only exist with Prussia as the dominant and decisive power.

Napoleon III of France found himself forced into a situation where he must go to war or lose face in the eyes of the world. To avoid this humiliation, he arranged that Prince Leopold should withdraw from the candidacy on the advice of King Wilhelm of Prussia, but Bismarck would have none of this pacific and reasonable stance. He wanted war and to assist him to this end the French Ambassador, Count Franz Benedetti, visited King Wilhelm at Bad Ems and extracted from him a "binding promise" to refrain from making any further bids for the Spanish Throne. The crafty Bismarck, who was even more adept at getting his own way than Richard Wagner, then carefully "doctored" the famous Ems Telegram so that it appeared to have a totally different meaning from the one intended by the writer.

When it first reached Bismarck's hands it read, "As His Majesty has told Count Benedetti that he was waiting for news of the Prince, His Majesty decided, in respect of the above request, on the advice of Count Eulenburg and myself, not to receive Count Benedetti again but to inform him through an adjutant that His Majesty has now received from the Prince confirmation of the news which Benedetti had already had from Paris, and that he had nothing to say to the Ambassador."

By the time it left his hands the message, carefully pruned, read "His Majesty the King thereupon refused to receive the French Ambassador again and had him communicate through the Ambassador." As it appeared to refer directly and tauntingly to France's unfortunate position, Bismarck was well aware that, unprepared for war as she was, France must be provoked into defending her honour in such a way that Prussia appeared to be the wronged party. He was equally cognisant of the fact that Prussia, with her formidable array of brand new weapons and an alarmingly well-trained army, had been prepared for such an eventuality for some time and could only win such a confrontation.

Less eager than his Chancellor for further bloodshed so soon after the Schleswig-Holstein affair of 1866, Wilhelm attempted to find a suitable compromise, but Bismarck refused to be cheated of a war which he hoped would pave the way to fulfilling his dream of a united Germany and ultimately, the United States of Europe. While Wilhelm was still plodding through diplomatic channels to avert the tragedy, Bismarck deftly thwarted his efforts by having published in the press the craftily altered version of the Prussian King's private account of his dealings with Benedetti. With no one to stop him, he was manipulating several heads of State and their ministers as if they were marionettes.

Knowing exactly how Ludwig would react to the Ems Despatch, he sent a copy of it to the Prussian Embassy in Munich, confident that it would be shown to the King. But unfortunately, he did not know Ludwig quite as well as he thought. If there was anything the King abhorred more than a scheming politician it was a scheming diplomat. He disliked Benedetti intensely and sensing the importance of the obvious intrigue, let it be known through his adjutant that "HM the King of Bavaria had the feeling that Benedetti spoke provokingly to him during the promenade, against his will" and to tell him that he was "obliged never to give his consent should the Hohenzollerns return to the question of the candidacy." Behind his autocratic words Ludwig was sadly aware that, while Bismarck wanted his support and goodwill he could, if necessary, manage very well without it.

In the negotiations Bavaria was represented by his new Prime Minister, Bray-Steinberg, under whose auspices a variety of pertinent, if unwelcome questions were discussed. Benedetti's visit to Ems had resulted in so strong a possibility of war that the Bavarian cabinet had decided after all that the time had come to summon the King. As usual, he could not be found and was reported to have departed with Hornig to some remote hunting lodge where he was "not to be disturbed unless it was absolutely necessary," but was later discovered watching the builders' progress at Linderhof. Aware that this time he must appear in his capital, Ludwig arrived at Berg in the late evening of July 13th and, despite the hour, August von Eisenhart*, the new cabinet secretary was asked to present his report.

Eisenhart had been briefed to expect total indifference from the King and was agreeably surprised to find him well informed and ready to discuss the matter fully. Bringing into the conversation newspaper reports as well as the official ministerial and diplomatic outpourings, he interrupted frequently with the most probing of questions and, as he often did, offered some remarkably astute observations for one who was reputed to spend his entire existence staring into the proscenium of a theatre or at the panoramic views from his mountain eyries. He nevertheless became "very nervous and excited", pacing the room and expounding his theories on the *casus foerderus* and its import in the case of war, but was still reluctant to give any binding instruction to his Cabinet.

Curiously, while stressing the urgency of the matter in one breath,

---

* Eisenhart's wife was a close friend of Queen Marie and a leading personality at Court.

Eisenhart suggested in the next that it might be prudent for the King to postpone his final decision until Count Berchem arrived from Munich with Bray's proposals. This could have been an expression of his famous tact to disguise his awareness that Bray had actually already concluded the necessary arrangements without even consulting the King, but at the same time it was obvious to him that Ludwig had no "final decision" to give when it came to declaring war. One cannot help wondering if, had Ludwig been left to struggle alone with the problem, he would have found a solution more beneficial to Bavaria and, indeed, one which might have changed the course of history.

*   *   *   *   *

THE heavy grey skies over Starnberg presaged rain when Count Berchem arrived with his Pandora's box, and the weather thus fittingly set the scene. In addition to Bray's report, Berchem carried a mobilisation order signed by Von Pranckh, the Minister for War. It contained the ominous words "The tension which has existed for a week between Prussia and France because of the determination of the Prussian Leopold von Hohenzollern to become King of Spain, and who has not removed himself completely from the Spanish Throne (...), the political conflict between the mighty countries has now become very much more abrasive over the past two days and a war between France and Prussia seems inevitable.(...) In view of the most important factors of this subject, the most obedient under-signed feels himself to be in complete agreement with the other Ministers of State to make the most respectful plea to the All Highest that Your Majesty will be pleased to discharge immediately that directive which will place him in a position to be able to keep the policy of Bavaria well in mind, which the All Highest promises and declares. The truly obedient undersigned would be very pleased if Majesty would permit him personally to approve and, in this respect, personally administer, all instructions in all submissive-ness, the demands of the All Highest. It is absolutely necessary for this to be settled by tomorrow morning when it will not be too late to arrange for the protection of the country. As things are, it is scarcely possible that Bavaria will remain neutral and, if active participation in the war is not to be avoided, the choice will offer fewer difficulties because a war between France and Prussia can only be an offensive war and will be a struggle for the integration of German territories and, in this case, under Article I of the Treaty of Alliance of August 2nd, 1866, the obligation of Bavaria remains unequivocally laid down as well as that already agreed in the old German Federal Law."

From the moment Count Bray presented Pranckh's report, Bavaria's fate was sealed. In the capital there was great excitement based on the fear of procrastination on the part of the Ultramontanes and the Ministers in Munich were impatient for news from Berg. Those who were present spent some time persuading Ludwig to agree to their proposals. Quite apart from the fact that he disapproved fundamentally of war, he disliked being given orders by his cabinet; the decision must always at least appear to be his own. Resigning himself at last to the realisation that he had no alternative, he pronounced *"Bis dat qui dito dat!!* (he who gives rashly, gives double), You may order the mobilisation and call the Ministers to conference."

The Ministers omitted to tell him that they had already done so without waiting for his official declaration and this omission provides us with the only reasonable explanation for Eisenhart's curious advice for the King to wait for Berchem's arrival before deciding, presumably in case he awkwardly decided the opposite of his Cabinet's intention. When the talks ended, Ludwig was pressed to return to Munich with his cabinet to present the declaration personally but, tormented with the inevitable headache and the feeling that he had made a dreadful mistake by agreeing to his Government's proposals, he found the calm solitude of Berg infinitely more attractive than the tumult of the city. He refused to go and swallowing their indignation, they left without him. Only the level headed Hornig (who, incidentally, was invariably subjected to unjustified verbal abuse by a number of Ludwig's Cabinet Ministers) could persuade him to change his mind. To do this, Hornig had only to remind him that public opinion would be set even more firmly against him if he failed to appear.

Meantime, rumour and speculation had become rife in the capital and crowds had gathered outside the Residenz. They had scarcely expected to see Ludwig and went completely wild when he appeared. Astonished and unprepared for such an ovation and overcome with an emotion which matched their own, he appeared repeatedly at the window to please the enraptured crowd. He was again their darling. Repeatedly he asked Pranckh, who had accompanied him, "Should I go to the window again?" Despite his fundamental dislike of public appearances of any kind on this occasion he was only too happy to do whatever they wanted; clearly this unexpected demonstration alleviated his depression, even if he knew that the current climate could not last. Warned by his cabinet to expect the worst, he had been truly surprised to find that, despite prolonged ill-feeling over Wagner and the disasters brought about by the war of 1866, and the new educational and governmental measures which had certainly not pleased everybody, they loved him still.

At that moment, Ludwig held them in the palm of his hand, yet he made no attempt to manipulate them as many a lesser being would have done. It seems likely that, knowing from earlier experience how bitterly quickly he could fall from their good graces, he thought it prudent to avoid involving himself too completely. Whatever his innermost trepidations were, he now informed Bray "I have confirmation of the note currently sent by the Prussian Envoy on July 18th of this year, have examined it and now empower you to inform the representatives of the Prussian Government immediately that I have given consideration to the *casus foerderus*, after which the further measures we have arranged are to be carried out immediately."

The following day, Ludwig telegraphed to Wilhelm of Prussia, "My troops shall take up the fight with enthusiasm on the side of your glory-crowned confederation for German right and German honour. May it be to the good of Germany and to Holy Bavaria." It must have cost Ludwig a great deal to send such a message to the detested Wilhelm and no one could accuse him of failing to do the best he could to appear to be riding on the wave of enthusiasm for the forthcoming hostilities, but his heart was certainly not in it. To a favoured few he had already confided his fear that, whatever benefits war might bring to Prussia, it might very well bring Bavaria to ruin. Far from being a wealthy country, Bavaria had not yet recovered from the wounds inflicted in 1866, a war which had lasted only seven weeks. The King was therefore justifiably concerned as to what might happen if this new war should last somewhat longer. Unfortunately, he appeared to be completely alone in his bitter resentment and forebodings of further bloodshed but with Bismarck waving his treaty aloft and, like the perfect salesman, convincing almost everyone who mattered that it could only be advantageous, Ludwig had no option but to submit.

To celebrate the arrival of the war lords and the commencement of hostilities, a gala theatrical event took place at which Schiller's masterpiece, *Wallensteins Lager*, was given with one of Ludwig's favourite actors, Ernst Possart, in the leading role. In an inflammatory curtain speech, the experienced player whipped the audience into an even greater state of bellicose euphoria than when they watched Ludwig and his cousin Crown Prince Friedrich Wilhelm of Prussia make their entrance together.

No two men could have been so totally different as they stood side by side in the Royal box. Friedrich Wilhelm, blond, haughty and arrogant, his cold grey blue eyes and militaristic bearing contrasting strongly with the darkly romantic Ludwig whose whole bearing seemed wrapped in dreams and whose thoughts, all too obviously, were more concerned with the aesthetics of the play than with the noisy demonstration around him. Unfortunately, in the prevailing climate, the crowd admired the Prussian more than they admired their own pacific Sovereign and Ludwig knew it. His dislike of his cousin now turned to a hatred which was never to mellow.

Friedrich Wilhelm on his side was scarcely better impressed with the Wittelsbach and afterwards observed, "I find him strikingly changed; his beauty has very much diminished, he has lost his front teeth, looks very pale and has a certain tension in his manner of speaking so that he does not wait for an answer to his question but while the person to whom he was speaking was answering, he was already posing questions concerning other things." His criticism concerning Ludwig's "diminished beauty" was no mere spiteful comment from a rival, for owing to his increasingly eccentric lifestyle, irregular meals and unhealthy intake of drugs, his physique had suffered while his predilection for *Naschwerk* (sweets) had resulted in hopeless tooth decay. Nevertheless, from a distance he was still a handsome, regal figure admired by all except those who disapproved of his way of life and surprisingly democratic ideas.

When Friedrich Wilhelm left Munich the following day he wore the air of having conquered the Bavarian capital before he conquered the enemy. Bitterly aware of his cousin's unexpected popularity, Ludwig was left, sulky and furious, with the prospect of having the love of his subjects stolen from under his nose. His own feelings of patriotic fervour quickly dissolved, leaving him with a punishing headache for which, hoping to dim both the pain and the memory of his humiliation, he prescribed for himself a hearty dose of chloralhydrate.

He then disappeared into the mountains without saying goodbye to his guests. When Eisenhart arrived at Linderhof from Berg on August 7th with the first half of an incomplete telegram which he thought the King should see, he found Ludwig about to depart for an even more remote place of refuge. It was easy to discern that the King's feelings had undergone a sharp reversal and that he had put the war from his mind as if it did not exist. Eisenhart was nevertheless determined to deliver his news and called out "A telegram has just arrived of the greatest importance regarding a great and, it appears, victorious battle. The end with the outcome has yet to arrive. Majesty must wait a little longer before leaving on his journey." Ludwig turned cold eyes upon his tormentor and retorted angrily, "Majesty must do no such thing!" before instructing the coachman to drive on. Sensitive to the fact that, following Prussia's example, even his own staff had taken to giving him orders, he perversely extended his excursion on this occasion simply to annoy Eisenhart.

The King had enjoyed the war only as long as he himself had been the hero of the hour and no blood had been shed. But now, in every report and despatch he was confronted with the name of Friedrich Wilhelm, his valour in the field, his tactical brilliance and his undisputed popularity with officers and men alike. Driven to a jealous, frustrated fury which he found impossible to control Ludwig could no longer bring himself even to read the reports and despatches. Stung on one occasion some time later, into commenting on the events leading up to the Franco-Prussian war and Bavarian involvement in it, he was moved to say of his cousin, "I never want to see him again."

Eisenhart was well aware of Ludwig's animosity towards the Hohenzollern but apparently hoped that in time the King would have learned to master his feelings in the interests of protocol. Ludwig did make some effort in that direction: on Friedrich Wilhelm's departure from Munich with the troops, for example, he sent him a note in which he expressed the wish "to see Bavaria in possession of happy, autonomous freedom" together with his good wishes for the success of the campaign, but thereafter his efforts came to an end. From the seclusion of Berg, he wrote to Baroness Leonrod on August 28th, "How I long for the mountains! In the mountains there is freedom and there men never bring their pain. Woe to those who began this awful war in that irresponsible way! The terrible judgement is already beginning!" Later in the same letter he added in puzzling contradiction, as if trying to correct an earlier impression, "You can imagine how pleased I am at the brilliant victories of my brave troops: who would have dreamed of such extraordinarily rapid results! Those quick and decisive victories of the Germans over the indefatigable French army! All the same, I yearn with all my strength for an early, lasting peace which will be victorious for Germany but especially good for my beloved Bavaria!"

He was clearly still playing with words and the phrase about the "infamous, indefatigable French army" carries a distinct ring of insincerity when one recalls that no greater Francophile than Ludwig walked the earth. Doubtless the Baroness knew exactly what was meant by his ambiguous comment, "You can guess how pleased I am at the brilliant victories of my brave troops" for she of all people knew him well enough to realise that he could never be in favour of sending men to certain death, and was of the opinion that the outcome of battles were more likely to be decided at the conference table than in the field.

The war dragged on through the sweltering heat of August until the French suffered a disastrous defeat at Sedan. On September 3rd, his men routed, his supplies gone and his pride crushed, Napoleon III was obliged to surrender. With this capitulation, the Second Empire came to an ignominious end and Bismarck made another giant stride towards his goal. Even victory could not lure Ludwig back to Munich, and he felt no need for celebration. As he had bitterly informed one of his Ministers, "As there is neither a German Empire nor a German Republic, as hitherto there has been no German Confederation, it is my wish that only Bavarian flags shall be hoisted on public buildings, or better still, no flags at all."

Ludwig's birthday had fallen in the midst of the war and this year it proved to be a double celebration. Cosima's long-foundering marriage had been dissolved in a Berlin court and she was at last legally united with her Richard. As a sop to the King's vanity and doubtless with a view to the restoration of the stipend, the pair had carefully chosen Ludwig's birthday on which to tie the knot. Appeased, if not perhaps particularly flattered, by this somewhat belated gesture, Ludwig graciously hid his disappointment in Wagner and expressed the mild hope that the union would revive Wagner's apparently comatose creative powers.

Coincidentally, on this same day the Vatican Council, summoned by Pope Pius IX, had defined the Dogma of Papal Infallibilty, a Dogma which was bitterly resented and opposed by many a Bavarian churchman, including Ignaz von Döllinger. As a former pupil of the theologian, Ludwig was extremely well-informed on ecclesiastical matters despite his recent personal disappointment in the church and strongly supported Döllinger, thus inevitably arousing the hostility of the Bavarian Ultramontane Party which was composed principally of Jesuits loyal to the Pope. The Ultramontanes felt so strongly on the matter that they began to intrigue to force the King to abdicate. The sceptical and deeply suspicious Ludwig was, indeed, surrounded by enemies. On this particular occasion, it was the King who triumphed and a year later the Jesuits were expelled from Bavaria. For a time, however, Ludwig's future had been uncertain, even precarious, and everyone at court knew it. Hohenlohe had recognised Ludwig's difficulties some time earlier and later events were only to prove the accuracy of his assessment of the situation as it really was.

Wagner, who also kept himself informed on such matters, saw an even more powerful reason why he could expect no further monetary favours from Ludwig. It was now, when the King was in danger of losing his throne, that the composer's vision of Munich as the site of his theatre faded. He cast his eye instead on the little Lower Bavarian town of Bayreuth. The Bavarians meantime had momentarily forgotten Wagner's very existence. Their thoughts were totally occupied with the war and its consequences, namely, the revival of the talks concerning the German Confederation.

Writing of those endless discussions in his journal, Prince Hohenlohe observed, "The idea of the 'wider confederation' is thoroughly impractical since Baden, at any rate, and Württemberg probably, will enter the North German Confederation. Bismarck counts on our isolation and reasons very shrewdly that he will be able to force us in without any concessions. In the meantime, our impractical schemes, which he will finally refuse especially if, as heretofore, no persons with definite mandates and instructions are sent to headquarters". And further, on the 18th, "The dynasty will be left in the lurch by the bureaucracy merely to stand well with Prussia, by the army in order to have a good position with their North German comrades, and by the people, whom the King in his idleness ignores. Bavaria will therefore be drawn easily in to the German Empire which, under the overwhelming circumstances, is not to be deplored. At all events, nothing else can be done, so it might be done with dignity."

Again, Ludwig went through the motions of expressing a joy he did not feel over the victory over France. He wrote a series of over-patriotic and blatantly insincere letters to those who expected him to do so, but escaped at the first moment he decently could from the capital which now seethed with intrigues as well as with disapproval.

Unwilling to face his Hohenzollern cousin again, Ludwig provoked fresh comment by refusing to appear at the Munich victory celebrations at which, of course, the conquering hero would be Friedrich Wilhelm. It was now patently obvious to all that he nursed a deep and unforgiving hatred of the Crown Prince and no one was in any doubt as to the reason for his sudden flight. From his refuge in the isolated Saierhütte high in the mountains, he put his true feelings in a letter to Baroness Leonrod: "The generation of strong-willed men with courage, energy and strong convictions such as I want and am in need of has died out. One hears only of vagueness and indifference and that is why I feel so forsaken and lonely on this earth, like a left-over from better times, blown into the present which I hate and where I shall always feel like a stranger."

So much a stranger that he not only refused to relent and show himself to the public but also continued obstinately to avoid contact with his Cabinet because he knew that the moment he appeared he would be besieged by questions as to whether or not Bavaria would participate in the German Union if it was formed. This time, however, he was not allowed to escape and, pushed headlong into action by his determined cabinet, was obliged in mid-September to authorise them to "negotiate proposals for a constitutional union with the North German Union."

It was not his own decision. Now totally embittered and lacking in trust or confidence where those in his immediate circle were concerned, Ludwig washed his hands of the whole affair, aware that they had in any case already settled the matter between themselves, and that no objections on his part would have made any difference. Following the peace talks had come the endless proposals for the formation of the Union to which Ludwig, in his heart, remained bitterly opposed. At the end of December, Baron Delbrück, the President of the North German Federal Chancellor's Office and Minister von Mittnach, Minister for Württemberg, had already arrived for discussions. Indeed, negotiations between the Ministers for Württemberg, Hesse and Baden had already begun but no agreement had yet been reached with Bavaria, since no Bavarian representative had been present at the time.

Paradoxically, this also annoyed Ludwig, who enquired peevishly, "Why do they conclude agreements with Württemberg, Baden and Hesse and not until later with my Government?" although the fault was his own. Resigned to the fact that the talks must go forward, he had no wish or intention to be part of them and his attitude of total non-participation was now regarded by his cabinet not only with irritation but with open contempt. Ludwig himself, of course, was hopeful that no firm agreement would ever emerge. After he had been received by the King at Schloss Berg, Baron von Söglen was later informed, "HM the King of Bavaria is very much against such restriction of rights of Sovereignty as has been mentioned on several occasions by opposing ministers."

But Ludwig's personal objections did nothing in the long run to hinder negotiations and within a few weeks plans were laid for a conference proper to take place at Versailles. Weaving his customary web of intrigue, Bismarck did his utmost to arrange for Ludwig and his *bête-noir*, the King of Prussia, to meet at Fontainbleu beforehand in order to come to some kind of agreement on the more important facets of the ambitious plans ahead for the German Empire but torn between hatred of the Hohenzollerns and the deep-rooted fear or losing his autonomy, Ludwig could not make up his mind to attend.

Knowing of the King's predilection for the Bourbons, Delbrück even made the crafty suggestion worthy of Bismarck himself, "Let us give him one of the famous historical suites, possibly the bedroom of Louis XIV and he will be so enraptured that he will not notice the absence of all the usual conveniences." What Delbrück really meant was that if Ludwig was sent into a trance by surroundings which held deep connotations with the Bourbons, he would fail to notice that Bavaria was being brought to heel by Prussia. They underestimated him, however: Ludwig saw through the ruse immediately, realising that Bismarck's intentions had in no way altered; the Iron Chancellor was determined that, however much opposition and resentment he encountered from individual States, the smaller corners of Germany were to be gathered together into one large Empire, or Reich, under an Emperor's crown. It went without saying that the crown in question would be worn by a Hohenzollern. The *pièce de resistance* would be for Ludwig of Bavaria to offer it personally to King Wilhelm with the whole world watching as proud little Bavaria with her ancient Wittelsbach heritage openly acknowledged Prussia's supremacy in Europe. The pride of the other newcomers would also be crushed since it was not anticipated that they would be equal partners with Prussia.

Enraged, Prince Hohenlohe wrote in his diary, "The wish is said to have been expressed at Headquarters that he [Ludwig] should come as the head of the German princes in order to offer the Imperial Crown to King Wilhelm, but that is not certain. I would dissuade him from doing so, and I have sent the same advice to Eisenhart. That would make him the laughing stock of Europe unless in exchange for this demonstration he could get some real gain. For example, some positive concession or other. As a return for this, he might finally consent to play this comedy."

Ludwig was naturally of the same opinion. With an astuteness with which Bismarck did not credit him, Ludwig steadfastly refused to travel to France and his fears were well founded. Much as he admired Bismarck's statesmanship and eloquence and, indeed, his prose style, which he had for some years enjoyed in the form of a personal correspondence, he no longer trusted Bismarck and was far from blinded or misled by the camouflaged motives of the Iron Chancellor. No amount of articulate prose could now convince Ludwig that what he was being forced to do was for Bavaria's benefit.

Prince Otto was also firmly against the idea; from Versailles, where he had been despatched by Ludwig as a special envoy, he wrote "The German Kaiser, the German Reich, Bismarck, the noisy Prussian enthusiasm, the boots ... all of this makes me inexpressibly sad (...). Hear my voice again. I beg you not to do this dreadful thing. How can it be possible for a gentleman and a King to give up his independence to a 'compelling authority' and recognise, apart from God himself, one who is still higher than he? How will the name of Bavaria still be known and respected abroad? Let us therefore attain for the present moment advantages and chances which are, perhaps, from the great periphery, able to counter-balance, though they certainly cannot outweigh by a hundredth part the disadvantages we must suffer to our independence."

Otto's concern for his brother and for the future of Bavaria was totally sincere. As early as 1870, Hohenlohe had written to him requesting him to refute a newspaper report which had laid his [Hohenlohe's] loyalties firmly with Prussia: *"The Kölnische Volkszeitung* reports: The story is told of Prince Otto that he came into the Chamber prepared to vote against the address, but that before the beginning of the sitting another Prince of the Royal House requested him to examine in an adjoining room documents which were intended to prove that Prince Hohenlohe, the Premier, had pledged himself to Count Bismarck to act in a way which entailed danger to the independence of Bavaria.

"Your Royal Highness will agree with me that this article contains the gravest charges which could be brought against a Bavarian Minister, and that I am bound to contradict such reports. I take the liberty, therefore, respectfully to beg Your Royal Highess to tell me whether any actual occurrence could have given rise to the above report, or whether the whole matter is mere invention." Otto denied the charge, but since he was only one of many who suspected Hohenlohe's professed loyalty to Bavaria to be mere camouflage, he probably did so only to avoid embarrassing his brother. At the same time, he persistently warned Ludwig not to ally himself with Prussia, the more so now that he had seen for himself exactly what was going on at Versailles, but unfortunately his newly-volatile disposition had become too well known. Some asserted that, like Ludwig, he was overfond of chloral as a sleeping draught but if Otto had vices at this time they inclined towards alcohol and women rather than soporifics or narcotics; in any case, since he spent most of his time in the officers' Mess, he would have had little opportunity to indulge himself in anything other than the usual pastimes. Nevertheless, shortly after his return from Versailles he began to act in an erratic and excitable manner and on occasions was apt to sink into incomprehensibility. The change in Otto's nature is dramatic although for years, perhaps because he had been highly-strung as a child, it was passed off as another example of the Wittelsbach legacy. In view of other strange occurrences within the Court, it is possible that he was also the victim of an intrigue and unknowingly given drugs in his food or drink, which could account for his devastatingly altered condition. It was some time before Ludwig would accept that there was anything wrong with him, and when he did he blamed himself.

As a result of all this, the Prince's advice to his brother was not accorded the serious consideration it deserved in Ministerial quarters and although Ludwig agreed with his boldly-expressed opinions there was little he could do to change the course of events. Bismarck had done his work well. Interestingly, Hohenlohe had not observed anything strange about Otto apart from his aversion to attaching Bavaria to Prussia: while they were both in Versailles the Minister had noted in his diary "Otto has rushed here agitating against the Kaiser idea, against travel and against everything (...) When the Queen wanted to speak to the King he said to her, 'I am not in the mood to talk to a Prussian princess.' So they vacillate between will and won't, between submission and old family pride, and will finally give in out of fear." This was partly true since in the face of so much opposition Ludwig was obliged to accept defeat without battle. He was nevertheless astute enough to see that he must obtain something to Bavaria's advantage.

On October 1st, Eisenhart sent a long report to Bray-Steinberg stating "His Majesty the King has repeatedly charged me to inform Your Excellency that the All Highest lives in the pleasant hope that Your Excellency will succeed in obtaining two million for His Majesty. Furthermore, I am instructed by my most Gracious Majesty to repeat most emphatically to Your Excellency the question of a 'moderate enlargement of territories' in the name of the All Highest, and would like you to discuss the matter immediately with Count Bismarck."

On the same day, Ludwig sent a message to Düfflipp to the effect that "with every passing day His Majesty becomes more convinced as to how impossible it is for him to undertake the projected visit to France. Majesty therefore believes it is necessary to plead some illness, for example 'a pulled tendon' and would the Herr Hofrat have the goodness to see that this was made known to the public and the troops." The embarrassed Düflipp had no option but to comply and convey the message, as requested, to the officials, saying that the King was "indisposed".

The Bavarian contingent set off for Versailles without him and on October 20th the discussions began. The preliminaries went smoothly enough; the claims, rights and demands of Bavaria were discussed at length and Ludwig got his two million from Bismarck, a sum which was taken from the Welffenfonds* but predictably, the request for enlargement of territories was refused. It was now clear to everyone that Bismarck had more power than all the Kings in Europe put together.

Versailles was swarming with Royal and political figures from all quarters of Europe but among those present, one personage seemed unusually prominent both at the business meetings and the inevitable social functions: Max Holnstein, who had a special reason for being there although his presence, like the ghost at the wedding, was far from welcome. As there was no pressing need for him to attend in his official capacity, it is likely that he had blackmailed Ludwig into allowing him to go as another "special envoy" possibly by threatening to expose certain aspects of the King's private life. His relationship with Richard

* See page 155.

Hornig, for instance, would have created a great scandal in 1870, and would undoubtedly have resulted in the King being ostracised by all "respectable" people.

Holnstein was an unpopular man in his own country, and was heartily detested at Court where his audacious ambition to become Prime Minister was widely known if not so widely approved. Swaggering through the salons of Versailles he boasted openly to the Grand Duke of Baden that it was he who had persuaded Ludwig to offer King Wilhelm the Kaiser's crown, and it was of course this fundamental insult which had led to Ludwig's ultimate refusal to attend the talks. In the first instance he had naturally assumed that the wearer of the Imperial Crown would stem from Germany's oldest ruling house. To find that Bismarck had engineered the proceedings so that the ultimate choice fell on a Hohenzollern was a bitter blow. The ultimate humiliation was for the proud Wittelsbach to be asked to formally offer the crown in public. This was too much for the hypersensitive Ludwig who withdrew so far into his shell that he did not even know that Bray had openly joined Holnstein in Bismarck's coterie. It was perhaps as well that he was also unaware that, after the Reich was officially formed, Bismarck was openly to admit, "It was Holnstein who did most in this matter. He played his part very cleverly. (...) What Order can we give him?" As is later to be revealed, Bismarck's ultimate reward to Holnstein was immense.

Knowing that he must eventually give in, through various intermediaries Ludwig halfheartedly pursued his request for an enlargement of territories but Bismarck, in the stronger position, would have none of it and finally silenced the King by pronouncing crisply that Baden was *noti ne tangere* and adding, unsurprisingly, that neither King Wilhelm nor the Grand Duke of Baden was likely to agree to such a request. Ludwig could only counter with the final suggestion that perhaps he and Wilhelm might share an Imperial crown, wearing it alternately, this idea having been put into his head intially by his cousin, Prince Adalbert. Bismarck dismissed this idea with ill-concealed contempt: "The King of Bavaria lives in a world of dreams. He is little more than a boy who does not know his own mind."

Ludwig now telegraphed Bray to tell Bismarck that he could expect Holnstein to present himself at Versailles to discuss the matter - but since Holnstein was already in constant direct contact with Bismarck, this was a somewhat hollow threat. It was probably only now that the King realised how totally Holnstein had betrayed him, for the Oberstallmeister had shown unusual willingness to act as a courier between France and Bavaria and it soon became apparent that it was not for love of his Royal master. In the final stages, Holnstein was only too

Ludwig II of Bavaria:
(top left) in 1867, (top right) in 1875,
(bottom left) in 1879 and (bottom right) in 1885

Maximilian II, Queen Marie and Princes Ludwig (left) and Otto (right) in 1861

Ludwig I, from a painting by Franz von Lenbach. Brilliant and charming, the King's affaire with Lola Montez cost him a throne.

(Above) The Official engagement photograph of Ludwig II and Princess Sophie-Charlotte in Bavaria taken in 1867. He jilted her after several months of prevarication

(Opposite) Empress Elisabeth of Austria. She wears the robes created by Worth of Paris for her Coronation as Queen of Hungary in 1867.

Richard Wagner. Under Ludwig II's tutelage, the penniless anarchist became the founder of the art of the future

Richard Wagner with Cosima von Bülow, the wife of his best friend whom he later married. After Wagner's death, Cosima continued the work of the Bayreuth Festival Theatre.

(Top left) Otto, Prince of Bavaria, the King's brother whose army career was cut short when he was certified as mad.
(Top right) Stallmeister Richard Hornig, a close friend of Ludwig's for many years.
(Bottom left) Alfred, Count Dürkheim-Montmartin, the adjutant who remained loyal to the end.
(Bottom right) Josef Kainz, the Hungarian actor; with Ludwig's assistance he became one of Germany's great classical actors.

(Top left) Prince Luitpold of Bavaria, the King' uncle, who became Prince Regent when Ludwig was deposed and his brother incarcerated.

(Top right) Max, Count Holnstein, Ludwig's former aide, was a traitor who worked towards his downfall.

(Bottom left) Senior Medical Adviser, Dr. Bernhard Gudden, who declared Ludwig insane without a personal examination.

(Bottom right) Otto, Count (later Prince) Bismark; he schemed for a United States of Europe under Prussian leadership.

Schloss Nymphenburg, the Wittelsbach summer residence near Munich; Ludwig's birthplace was built between 1664 and the late 1770s.

Schloss Hohenschwangau in the Allgäu, 4 kms from Füssen. To the right is the Schwansee; on the left out of the picture is the Alpsee. The castle was restored from a ruin by Maximilian II between 1832 and 1836.

Schloss Neuschwanstein, which stands almost opposite Schloss Hohenschwangau; building commenced in 1869, but it was still incomplete at Ludwig's death.

Schloss Herrenchiemsee. The most inaccessible of Ludwig' castles is set in woodlands on the Herreninsel on Lake Chiemsee. Almost a replica of Versailles, it was commenced in 1878 but was never finished

Schloss Linderhof in the Graswangtal near Oberammergau. Built between 1874 and 1878, it is the only one of Ludwig's castles to be completed

The summerhouse on the Roseninsel on Lake Starnberg, a favourite trysting place of Ludwig and Elisabeth over many years

(Top) Schloss Berg. Ludwig loved this place and spent much of his time here. Sadly, it was also the scene of his untimely end.

(Bottom) The cross in the water marks the spot at Lake Starnberg where Ludwig's body was found.

happy to undertake the long journey between Versailles and Hohenschwangau to plunge in the knife personally, as it were, and in such
a way that he could enjoy boasting of it afterwards.

Holnstein carried with him a letter from Bismarck and also the
suggested draft of the *Kaiserbrief* which, as the King had refused to offer
the crown personally, was to be presented to Wilhelm by proxy. All
Ludwig's plans for suggested compromise had failed and he was
obliged to cede and agree to "voluntarily" offer the crown to his
Hohenzollern relation because, it was put to him, "if he did not, the
other Princes or even the Reichstag would do it".

The resultant draft was Holnstein's personal contribution in the
affair. Standing at Bismarck's elbow while the chancellor penned his
letter to the King, the unscrupulous Holnstein was heard to remark,
"You know, Excellency, you should write a letter yourself right away
as it should be done; otherwise things will be all upside down again."
Bismarck saw the point and, anxious to get the matter signed and
settled, lost no time in complying with Holnstein's suggestion. On his
return to Bavaria, Holnstein had travelled with a party of other negotiators, namely Bray, Lutz, Von Pranckh and Lerchenfeld. As soon as
they were settled in their railway compartment, they naturally began to
discuss the *Kaiser* question. Deeply conscious of his own importance
in the affair and lacking any shred of discretion, Holnstein could not
resist boasting of it. He even went so far as to show his companions
the draft of Bismarck's letter - an action which did nothing for his
honour or that of his fellow travellers.

When Holnstein eventually made his way up the steep carriageway
to the castle, he demanded to see the King immediately but was refused
admittance and was left to wait, fuming, from ten in the morning until
just after three-thirty when, in desperation, he sent another message to
the effect that if he did not conduct his business and leave soon, he
would miss the Paris connection. Ludwig relented only when he heard
that Holnstein carried a letter from Bismarck.

The Oberstallmeister found Ludwig "propped up in bed wrapped
in blankets, his face muffled in a scarf". The King's decaying teeth were
notorious and his toothache genuine enough. According to his valet,
he had taken a good deal of chloral to ease a pain of some kind, mental
or physical, and was in no condition to attend to affairs of State. Any
reasonable, loyal official would have appreciated this immediately and
taken his leave without attempting to settle so vital an issue, but to
Holnstein, Ludwig's indisposition was a gift from Heaven and he took
ready advantage of it. Ludwig's petulant objection that he wanted
"only to be left in peace" fell on deaf ears. Relentlessly, Holnstein
stated his business, handed over Bismarck's letter and demanded a

reply forthwith. Playing for time, Ludwig pleaded that he had no pen or paper to hand, but Holnstein was not to be fobbed off with feeble excuses; he had writing materials brought and Bismarck's draft was re-written in Ludwig's large, flowing hand. For decades thereafter, many Bavarians who hated Holnstein insisted that Ludwig had never put pen to paper at all, but that Holnstein himself had forged the letter which read:

"All Serene Highness, High and Mighty Prince! Brother, Cousin and Friend!

"After the entry of South Germany to the German Constitutional Union, the Praesidial law ceded to Your Majesty stretches of land throughout German territories.

"I have already declared myself wholeheartedly to the Union, that through it, the combined interests of the German Fatherland and all the Princes are united in the belief that they will be true to the vested rights of the General Praesidium, according to the formation of which Your Majesty works towards unified agreement between the Princes.

"I have therefore turned to the German Princes with the suggestion that the Praesidial Rights of the Union should be bound together under the leadership of one who holds the title of German Emperor. As soon as Your Majesty states his intention to all the Princes, I shall instruct my Government to carry through the further details of the attainment of the same in accordance with this.

"With the assurance of deep respect and friendship, I remain Your Majesty's friendly Cousin, Brother and Nephew, Ludwig.

"Hohenschwangau, November 30th, 1870."

And so it was achieved, with Ludwig in despair and Holnstein ostentatiously consulting his watch. Ludwig now began a letter to Eisenhart. It read "In all haste these lines; read the enclosed letter to the King of Prussia. Meanwhile, you will have heard the latest about the German constitution from my Ministers and for this reason will be in a better position correctly to assess the situation. Should a differently worded letter be considered better or more appropriate, well then I authorise you to tear up the letter to the King of Prussia". After adding a few more lines in the same vein, he concluded, "I leave the matter in your hands." For the third time, Ludwig gave up because he knew that the result of the fight had already been decided.

Eisenhart had indeed already discussed the matter at length with Bray and apart from considering Bismarck's original to be "too starkly businesslike" could find nothing to complain of and so, in the small hours of the morning of December 1st, the letter was sealed and

returned to Holnstein, who went first to the North German Envoy and
then back to Versailles, where the official presentation of the document
was ultimately made with all ceremony by Ludwig's pro-Prussian uncle
Luitpold who, like Holnstein, was more than happy to assist in Ludwig's
destruction.

Holnstein's week-long journey to Hohenschwangau and back was
regarded with great satisfaction by Bismarck; the Oberstallmeister's
expediency in carrying out his mission resulted in the gift in 1871 of
300,000 Marks - some 10% of the total war damages resulting from the
hostilities themselves, a not inconsiderable reward for what was tantamount to treason. When the news of the "gift" leaked out, Holnstein
denied receiving the money and claimed that it went towards Ludwig's
building costs, but it created a great scandal and was afterwards
referred to as the "Welffenfonds Affair."

The Welffenfonds was a large trust fund which stemmed from the
former Braunschweiger Welffen, an ancient family who, in Medieval
times, had lived in Hohenschwangau. The King of Prussia was the
custodian of these funds to dispose of as he saw fit, but as Bismarck
had control over everything which would normally receive the King's
attention (indeed, he had control over the King of Prussia as well by
this time), he was empowered to do exactly as he pleased with the
money without having to answer either to Parliament or to his Sovereign for his actions. As some sort of redress for his "co-operation" over
the *Kaiserbrief*, Ludwig was to receive 300,000 Marks annually from
the Funds which was less than generous when one considers that he
was actually being given his own money.

The much-vaunted 2 million Marks which Ludwig himself had
claimed from the Welffenfonds never reached him but also disappeared into Holnstein's pocket. The Treasury noted meticulously that
the money had been withdrawn by Holnstein on the King's behalf, but
did not trouble themselves to check whether or not it reached its
legitimate destination. Whether Ludwig himself knew the finer points
of the whole sordid transaction and Holnstein's involvement in it is not
known, but he was no fool and from this moment, would have nothing
further to do with the unsavoury Oberstallmeister.

Resignedly, the King was now obliged to write to his Ministers, "I
had wished it might have been possible to have the Foederative principle brought to reality in the Federal state. I will nevertheless not deny
the Union my approval." While Ludwig's already low opinion of the
new Emperor changed from a discreetly hidden dislike and resentment
to the open hatred he already showed for Friedrich Wilhelm, curiously,
he retained respect, if not trust, for Bismarck. In view of his political
astuteness this seems strange, for since 1866 and the signing of the fatal

Trotz und Schütz Treaty which had been the original cause of all his troubles, he had recognised the fox like duplicity of the Iron Chancellor and one wonders why, when he was usually so quick to detect double dealers, he appeared to remain blind to Bismarck's shortcomings until it was too late. Fond of allowing people to think he knew far less than he actually did on various matters, it is possible that this was merely another ploy, played out to the end in the hope that Bismarck might ultimately betray himself, but which had unfortunately backfired.

In Versailles, meantime, there had reigned a pregnant hush while Ludwig's response was awaited. "The King is irresolute; he does not want to be seen in public and has decided to be ill, has toothache, lies in bed where even the Ministers cannot reach him. Or he takes himself off to an inaccessible hunting lodge in the mountains where there is not even a proper road," Bismarck pronounced contemptuously. Some of his comments were justified but Ludwig was certainly not "irresolute". He simply did not agree with what was happening to his beloved Bavaria and hoped that procrastination might save the situation at least in the short term. He was also deeply and justifiably offended and in fact his Wittelsbach pride was never to recover from the blow.

Still trying desperately to behave like a King and with some dignity despite his deep outrage and disapproval, he wrote to Bismarck, "What you have done for the German Nation is great and immortal and I may without flattery say that you must take the most prominent place among the great men of our century." But his last iota of trust in his fellow men had evaporated. He now disassociated himself totally from the world of the 19th century and that everyday life which he so despised and dedicated himself to his books and his building.

Seeking solace in culture, he swallowed his pride and approached Wagner after a long silence: "The building of the new castle at Hohenschwangau is going forward with ease, even though one must wait for some time yet for its glittering completion. On the walls of my suite shine a wonderfully successful series of pictures taken from the sagas which, through my exalted, best beloved friend, have grown very dear to my heart. *Tannhäuser, Lohengrin,* a cycle from *Tristan und Isolde,* Walther von der Vogelweide, scenes from the life of Hans Sachs, are all to be seen. Pictures from the old, yet through you newly-inspired *Nibelung* will follow. The fourth floor of the high-placed castle, on which will be a Minstrels' Gallery and great hall, shall proceed, with a cycle of the life of *Parsifal*, and will be completed in '85."

Ludwig may have been carried away by all this but Wagner, as usual, was unmoved. Doubtless he had heard that, although Ludwig still occupied the Bavarian Throne, he was now a King of the shadows.

CHAPTER TEN

OTTO

PRINCE Otto's participation at the Versailles negotiations was his last official engagement. Of late he had been experiencing fits and frightening voids of reason when he would become a totally different person from the "Merry Otto" so beloved of the Munich burghers. With his inbuilt fear of bad Hessian blood, Ludwig found it all too easy to think the worst of his brother's sudden illness. In January he confided to Baroness Leonrod who of course had known Otto intimately since his babyhood, "It is really painful to see Otto in such a suffering state which seems to become worse and worse daily. In some respects he is more exciteable and nervous than Aunt Alexandra, and that is saying a great deal. He has not taken off his boots for eight weeks, behaves like a madman, makes terrible faces, barks like a dog and at times says the most indecorous things and then again, *he is quite normal for a while* [author's italics]. Gietl and Solbrig have examined him but if he doesn't take their advice SOON it will be too late."

In confirmation of these suspicions, two months later, on March 9th, Dr. Gietl wrote Ludwig a letter which must have struck a chill into his heart. Between the sycophantic lines of polite introduction and the elaborate, formalised ending was sandwiched the information, "The four doctors unanimously consider it necessary that the seriousness of the situation as well as the various consequences of his behaviour should be explained to His Royal Highness. Unless Your Majesty orders otherwise, I think I shall myself have to undertake the task because I have known His Royal Highness since he was born and because I have observed him for longer than anyone else."

But what exactly was wrong with Otto? Until the war of 1870, although highly strung as a child he had been regarded as a perfectly normal young man with normal appetites and a promising military career ahead of him, charming and easy going with a reputation among his friends as being something of "a card". The account of his sudden descent into madness has been accepted for years, but was he really insane or was his "madness" a drug-induced state designed to stop him from making political waves? For Otto had firm political opinions and a deep personal loyalty towards his brother. Interestingly, it was not until after Ludwig, surrounded by untrustworthy men, began to use him as a "special representative" that his fits and wild behaviour began.

Final judgement on Otto was passed without any real proof that he was mad.

The shattering blow of Bavaria's lost autonomy and the news that Otto's illness, whatever it was, was incurable, combined to make Ludwig desperately unhappy. Although they had little in common, the King loved his younger brother and was extremely distressed by his sudden illness. Ludwig himself had been deeply depressed since the formation of the Reich, as is evidenced by a letter to one of his mother's ladies-in-waiting, to whom he confided "Since the signing of those wretched agreements, I have had few happy hours, am sad and out of humour because of everything I have endured through political incidents and cannot be otherwise." In mid-July 1871, at the end of the horrifying siege of Paris which had lasted throughout the winter, had come the inevitable treaties to which he referred so dolefully, binding Bavaria to the Federal Union of German States. The ensuing troop celebrations, for which he was obligated to return to Munich, brought him neither joy nor satisfaction. As he put it in a letter to his "insane" brother, "Just imagine, Otto; pressed on all sides by political matters, I am now invited by the Crown Prince to see the procession of my own troops, which brings me almost to despair; is it any wonder that over the past years (campaign, conclusion, agreements, etc.) the Government and the people have become hateful to me, even though the position and the office of ruler is the most beautiful in the world. It saddens me that I am rent in two at a time when everything makes me feel embittered." Not the least of which was Otto's own puzzling mental decline which he could hardly discuss with the sufferer himself.

On July 16th, 1871, the City of Munich was gay with decorations for the triumphal entry of the troops and thousands flocked into the capital from all quarters to enjoy the spectacle. Ludwig rode at the head of the column with Friedrich Wilhelm, detesting the noisy ceremony only slightly less than he detested his cousin. Their destination was the Oberwiesenfeld near Nymphenburg, which was used as a rifle range as well as a parade ground. On this occasion, the review of the troops was to be held there together with a short memorial service for the fallen. The moment Ludwig took his departure, the Crown Prince began to distribute Iron Crosses in the name of his father, the newly-crowned Emperor Wilhelm, an obvious act of ingratiation which Ludwig understandably found acutely distasteful.

Instead of watching this, he rode along the Ludwigstrasse built by his grandfather, at the end of which waited his mother and scores of officials on a series of decorated platforms. The crowd was now so dense and noisy that Ludwig would probably have given his soul to have been able to gallop away into the mountains. He saw little point in this kind of demonstration, but his Prussian cousin took a very different view and presided over the proceedings exhuding a brash insincerity which Ludwig cannot have been alone in finding untenable or at the very least, extremely irritating. There followed endless speeches and a parade of the troops led by the veterans, Generals Von der Tann and Hartmann.

The diffident King summoned the will to attend the ensuing military dinner but his toast "My brave Army and its victorious leaders" was as brief as protocol would allow and the approval of all present fell instead on Friedrich Wilhelm, whose lengthy response provoked the cheers which Ludwig was denied. With renewed bitterness he realised that hardly a man present in the huge salon agreed with his own pacific views and he quickly excused himself, leaving his mother and Friedrich Wilhelm to preside in his place. Later at the theatre, it was generally observed that he could scarcely bring himself to speak to the Crown Prince or even look at him.

The worst was still to come and the following day proved to be the last straw. With the continuation of the troop celebrations, Ludwig was again expected to be affable towards his cousin and he was far from pleased with his insensitive mother's plan to take the boastful and condescending Friedrich Wilhelm to dine on the Roseninsel. Making a supreme effort, Ludwig paid him the compliment of offering him a commission in the Ulans, Bavaria's crack regiment of lancers. Blind to the honour and to the cost of Ludwig's self esteem in extending it, the thick-skinned Prussian laughingly quizzed the whole party as to "whether the slim cut of the Bavarian uniform would suit" him, which the King regarded as a veiled reference to the unhappy position of Bavaria where Prussia was concerned. Ludwig was so annoyed that he refused to attend the state banquet at the Glaspalast that night. All his secretary's pleading could not induce him to change his mind and he left the capital in a fury the following morning without taking his leave of the Prussian visitors.

His attempts to hide his true feelings about the German Union were short lived and it was not long before he gave up the pretence entirely; the Prussian envoy reported, "From little bits of scandal I become convinced that the correct bearing and docility of King Ludwig is in conflict with his Wittelsbach pride and they originate less in trust than in a feeling of bewilderment and fear." This was an astute assessment but hardly one which Ludwig himself would have appreciated; his attitude was understandable especially since 1871 found Holnstein the willing slave of his Prussian masters, informing Bismarck, "Before every audience and court ceremony, the King drinks large quantities of strong wine and then says the most extraordinary things. He wishes

to abdicate in favour of Prince Otto, who does not wish it." In view of
the reported disintegrating health of the younger Wittelsbach Otto's
lack of desire to become King is scarcely surprising but Holnstein's
poison continued: "The Ultramontanes know this; they have chosen
their candidate for the National Assembly: Prince Luitpold. He is also
the candidate for the Throne. *Perhaps they will succeed in spite of
Prince Otto's claim.* [author's italics]

Holnstein was well informed indeed! Small wonder that Ludwig's
companions were chosen increasingly from more modest walks of life,
those, for instance, who could assist him in his building objectives but
who would refrain from making mischief or abusing his friendship.
Doubtless Ludwig knew very well what Holnstein was doing behind his
back and also of the generally hostile attitude of his people towards
him. Friedrich Wilhelm's boorish behaviour had upset him deeply.
From the safety of his eyrie he wrote in his diary, "Feasts, theatre,
drives, the presence of the Crown Prince very disturbing and disagreeable." Miserably, he repeated the complaint in a letter to his Aunt
Amalie on July 23rd, "Very disturbing to me was the presence of the
Crown Prince of Prussia who rather pushed himself into the limelight.
Of course I had to invite him, *bon gré, mal gré.*"

He remained at Linderhof for some days, visited Garmisch and the
Zugspitze, travelling restlessly in the high mountain region which he
loved so deeply. Only here could his spirit find some solace; he
commanded a separate performance of the Passion Play at Oberammergau and in company with Empress Elisabeth he took the opportunity of supervising the renovations to the mountain lodge at
Schachen. On the inside of the prosaic looking wooden hunting lodge
was now installed an exotic Turkish salon; he loved Oriental and
Middle-Eastern decorations which appeared to satisfy some erotic
need. Wherever possible, he now avoided the capital and had, to all
intents and purposes, totally thrown off the whole tiresome business of
Kingship. The Envoy to Baden, Robert von Mohl, complained, "The
tendency of the young King to isolate himself has reached the point of
morbidity (...). The only opportunities one has to meet the King (...)
are at the gala concert on New Year's Eve, the two grand balls and the
bourgeoise *Oktoberfest* (...) and even these infrequent meetings have
now been virtually abolished by the young King. The New Year's
Concert has gone completely, the State Balls are now limited to one
and occasionally, under some pretext, does not take place at all, and
now, finally, the King as a rule no longer attends the *Oktoberfest* or, still
more typically, he comes but refuses to receive the Diplomatic Corps."

But Ludwig's time was occupied with other problems. Building was
expensive and he was spending money with the same reckless abandon

as that for which he had earlier reproved Wagner. At least he did not fritter away the Privy Purse on useless baubles as Wagner had done, but lavished it on bricks and mortar, on marble, gilt and porcelain, on paintings and *objets d'art* and on wages, fees and salaries for those who had contributed their talents and their muscles to his building projects.

Queen Marie, apparently in a sudden surge of remorse for the lack of understanding which she had shown her elder son in the past now attempted, somewhat belatedly, to make amends and offered to loan him money until his next Civil List became available. Touched, he wrote back gently refusing her offer "because last year I had the impression that you said in a somewhat regretful tone that you would not be able to go to the mountains for financial reasons. That is why I made a certain sum available to you." He may not have loved his mother, but no one can deny that he always did his best to be a dutiful son and despite unpleasant gossip to the contrary, was invariably kind and considerate towards her, showing a patience and compassion which may well have resulted from his observations of her reaction to Otto's difficulties. It is obvious that as time went on he began to feel sorry for her. He himself seems to have been reluctant to have personal contact with his brother if he could avoid it and looking anxiously in the mirror, he would now enquire of Hornig or Dürflipp "Am I going mad?"

Fortunately he still had a kind, practical and understanding friend in Richard Hornig who would comfort him in the only way he knew how, thereby unintentionally hindering Ludwig more than he helped him. As had been their custom for many years, they would ride together through the countryside, meeting only the occasional peasant for whom the King always had a friendly word and, more often than not, the gift of a jewel or money. On impulse, he would call unannounced at the hut of a herdsman or farmer and ask if he might join him in a meal or a glass of ale, finding some relief in chatting with men who would not afterwards twist his words and spread unpleasant gossip. The secret of Ludwig's popularity, aside from his natural charm, was his ability to exchange with them knowledgeable views on the subjects nearest their hearts, namely the herd, the harvest and the weather.

By no means without humour, Ludwig was always ready to enjoy a joke, even and he especially liked the broad humour of the peasants; they on their side would love to hear his high-pitched laugh ringing out above everyone else's. Laughter was rarely heard within the walls of the Residenz where Ludwig himself had little to laugh about. With Hornig as his only companion, he found not happiness perhaps but relief from misery and loneliness. Amid the peasants who adored him he had no need to be constantly on the defensive and in fact, while his

Cabinet accused him of wasting his time he was mingling with his people in an even more democratic manner than the Royalty of today. Sometimes the expensive gift which inevitably followed a visit to a peasant's home would not always be appropriate to the recipient, but was nevertheless greatly esteemed and many a peasant was the proud owner of a ruby ring, a silver watch or the eternal cufflinks presented by the beloved *"Kini"*.

A typical anecdote concerns the cowherd who met the King on the Alm and called out,

"Most fine one, what time is it? I want to bring the cows in."

"Haven't you a watch, then?"

"How should I have a watch?"

The King smilingly told him the time and went on his way. Shortly afterwards the astounded herdsman received a silver watch, one of hundreds which Ludwig was in the habit of giving away. On another occasion, he gave a trio of labourers three hundred Marks between them so that they "might share a little of what I have". The people who lived near Schloss Hohenschwangau or Berg did even better. He never forgot a name, a birthday or some small service performed out of love for him. Births and weddings were also marked by gifts of money and smallholders in difficulties could always be sure of assistance.

Between rustic encounters, Ludwig and Hornig continued their close personal relationship but despite the dire need for love of any kind, illicit or otherwise, Ludwig was constantly tormented by his guilt and found expiation only in his diary entries and in the time spent with the Empress. On his return to Berg after an extended mountain holiday, he wrote in his diary "On the 17th at half past ten o'clock with the adored one after a long separation. Blissful embrace! Happy hours! Sat in grotto; faithful unto death. Oath in thought, projected before the balastrade of the Royal bed of lilies, July 18th. Take it to heart!" The "adored one" was not Hornig, for they had been together constantly over a period of several weeks. Was it then Elisabeth, who was certainly in the area at the time?

Although the ill feeling which had pertained on both sides had gradually subsided, Ludwig was no longer in contact with Richard Wagner. The latter had undergone a metamorphosis and become a paragon of domesticity now that he had made an honest woman of Cosima. Remembering the unsavoury affair with Malwina von Schnorr and the untenable tantrums which had accompanied the production of *Das Rheingold*, Ludwig had for some time studiously avoided the composer.

Now, deeply depressed and in need of aesthetic stimulation, he longed to hear Wagner's uplifting work and at last he approached the composer. It was probably mainly in an attempt to regain Ludwig's financial support that the composer at last made a grudging acknowledgement of all the King had done for him in the past, and how much he had contributed to his success. "Above all," the composer conceded craftily, "Without you my *Nibelungen* work would have remained uncompleted. Because I had been so completely carried away by the struggle for existence I could never have attempted to carry out such a plan again. Still less could I ever have thought about the production. In order to carry out such an undertaking, my personal interest and advantages for my personal life were mixed in with his requirements. My entire strength had been paralysed and I had not been able to contribute all my strength to it. To care for me, that creator, so that I could carry out my life's work, free from all troubles, could only be undertaken by a great and gracious king!" The style is markedly more like Cosima's than that of Wagner himself and probably Ludwig recognised the fact but decided nevertheless to take up the correspondence once more, making the inevitable enquiry as to the progress of the final part of *Der Ring des Nibelungen* and also *Parsifal* which was allegedly on its way to completion but which had, in fact, been cast aside for some years.

Growing wiser as well as older, Wagner did not want to commit himself too far. Now intent on producing the whole of the *Ring* cycle himself without Ludwig's "interference" and preferably in the dreamed-of theatre of his own, he began to prevaricate and again their delicate relationship toppled.

Somewhat rashly, Ludwig had opened his heart to the composer by writing "I also want to withdraw from the pain of hell which draws me constantly away from your vaporous atmosphere in order to be blessed in the twilight of the Gods, the exalted moutains, in solitude, far from the affairs of the hated enemy. Far from the daily glare of the scorching sun, far from the profane, everyday world, the unhealthy politics which want to entangle me in their octupus arms and completely shake the poetry from me.(...). Soon the day will come when I return to my capital and because of doing so, shall become dreadfully unhappy again. This will always be the case when I have to go into the bustle of bright day, and the Throne and the jubilation of the crowd which makes me feel quite ill and unhappy. The thought that *Götterdämmerung* is going forward is very much on my mind. Oh, when shall we receive the enthusiastic news of the beginning of *Parsifal*? Oh, what a day of celebration that will be! Just the kind I like! How different from the current political ovations from which the spirit can glean no nourishment. The heart grows cold, the unmelodic tones tear the unaccustomed ear and torment the nerves."

True to form, Wagner failed him in his hour of need and his verbose reply betrayed only greed, ambition and the arrogant, egotistical pomposity which even the tolerant Ludwig could only digest in small doses. He was bitterly disappointed. Turning instead to a more sympathetic soul, he wrote to Baroness Leonrod in an outpouring of grief at the beginning of September, "That this war, which in so many respects ended so gloriously for Bavaria should have forced me myself and my country into the iron clutches of that damned German Reich with its Prussian colouring, that this unfortunate war which is so enthusiastically enjoyed by so many people, should have done it, is a most deplorable dispensation of providence. The popularity which, thanks to the speed of my resolution and my political sacrifice, I enjoy especially in North Germany, does not make up for what I have lost."

Hand in hand with his wounded pride at becoming little more than one of Bismarck's pawns went his concern for Otto. In September Ludwig informed his mother "I told Gietl to go to see Otto at Hohenschwangau because it is absolutely essential that he should begin to lead a different life, and that he should follow the advice of the doctors; already it is almost too late because he won't follow their advice." This again leads to speculation that Otto had recently acquired a specific vice, known to his family and which from Ludwig's own comments about him, could well be construed as drugtaking. As we know, Ludwig himself was inclined to turn to dangerous substances as soporifics and headache cures, but there is no suggestion that he indulged in drugs for pleasure. Otto, on the other hand, heavily involved with the fast military set, and perhaps encouraged by a Prussian sympathiser, could well have been experimenting with such drugs in much the same way as his second cousin, Archduke Rudolf of Austria, was wont to do and with very similar results. The alternative is that, as has already been suggested, he had unknowingly been introduced to drugs. Otto's own behaviour suggests the latter. Otto usually spent considerable time at Hohenschwangau for which, like his brother, he had a deep affection, but he was indignant when Ludwig suggested that he should stay there quietly under doctor's orders for an indefinite period. His refusal upset the King even more.

Discontent with everything, he began to quarrel even with Hornig. This was nothing new since their friendship, although close, was not without its difficulties. They disagreed frequently on many things and whatever else he was, Hornig was no sycophant. He had never been afraid to speak his mind, especially when the King's welfare was at stake. This was a more serious rift, however, and they were reconciled only after nine days of torture. It is possible that the incurably romantic Ludwig enjoyed the reconciliations more than the interludes of peace. The erotic pleasure which he found in the company of "Richard, beloved of my soul" was exquisite torture to him and he turned more and more to his diary as a confessional: "Symbolically and allegorically the last sin. Sanctified by this expiatory oath, washed of all sins, pure vessel for Richard's love and friendship." What he meant by all this, only he knew.

The entire diary was disjointed, written in strange codes and cyphers, polyglot and ungrammatical, it is clear that he now regarded it as his only safe outlet. Occasionally he allowed the current favourite to write in it, in particular Richard Hornig, with whom, despite their differences, he still spent most of his time. Together they rode to Schluxen, to the Riss, to Garmisch and to Ettal, to Burg Trausnitz near Landshut where, in the late 1860s, he had a suite decorated in the neo-German Renaissance style. They also travelled frequently to Linderhof where the new palais was now taking shape.

In December 1868, he had written to Düfflipp, "Louis XIV built for himself, in order to be able to endure the burden of eternal monotony of Court ceremonial, his pleasure Palace, Trianon, by which he was inhibited by the splendid rooms of Versailles. As this became enlarged to palacial proportions, he had the more modest Marly built in order that he might relax there for a short time after the cares of his representational life. I would like to erect close to Linderhof, in any case a little chapel and a pavilion and to have a garden, not too large, laid out in the Renaissance style and everything to be of modest dimensions. For myself I need only three rather rich and elegantly decorated rooms; the necessary service should naturally be very simple. The whole will be undertaken by Majesty himself; the plan is ready and as Minerva sprang from the hand of Jupiter, so I can give you right away everything concerning the outline of the plans. Then the preparations can be put in hand right away and at first will employ many people. Because I would like this plan to be carried out in such a way that a jewel, unique of its type, shall result from it ...." He told another correspondant "To a certain extent it shall be a temple of glory in which I can pay homage to the memory of King Louis XIV."

His exquisite miniature was hidden deep in the Graswangtal near Oberammergau. Anxious that everything should be authentic aesthetically as well as historically, he spent vast sums on this project as well as on the Neues Schloss Hohenschwangau* which was also proving to be more costly than anticipated. Alarmed by the expenditure, Hornig and Düfflipp tried to reason with him but remaining deaf and blind to the warnings of those who foretold disaster, he continued at fever pitch

---

* Later called Neuschwanstein.

with the building work, with his visits to the theatre and with the restless wanderings from one mountain eyrie to another, as if constantly searching for something which he never found.

Of Elisabeth he saw little; she now spent her time at Gödöllö or in England where her riding was much admired, in particular by Captain George ('Bay') Middleton, an English gentleman who quickly changed his initially unfavourable attitude towards the Austrian Empress once he had been riding with her. Elisabeth was a frequent visitor to Northampton, Leicester and to Ireland, and Ludwig was left alone with his frustrations and his longings.

Yet despite the complaints of his staff he was not truly indolent and did his best to carry out the tiresome public duties which he so disliked and resented, although his behaviour at these official funtions was causing comment. At State banquets and dinners he would now conceal himself behind mountainous displays of flowers so that he could eat in peace without being watched. Another favourite ruse was to have very loud music played so that he might avoid inane small talk with his table companions. His shyness and dislike of being looked at stemmed largely from the fact that his teeth had now decayed beyond repair and, vanity aside, he found eating so difficult that he was inclined to bolt his food without chewing it. Besides provoking whispers and glances from the other diners, this unfortunate habit also gave him indigestion which in turn affected his temper and probably added to his head and toothaches. Then he would seek the soothing agent of chloralhydrate which produced hallucinations, foul temper and the longing for sweets which had originally ruined his teeth. It was a vicious circle which, in its way, caused him quite as much grief as did Wagner's *Ring* cycle. And so he slipped gradually into a way of life from which even those closest to him were unable to shake him.

Fluctuations in his general behaviour, obviously due to the influence of the many drugs and potions which he took, evidently bewildered many people unfamiliar with his habits, but the Wittelsbachs had always been regarded as an eccentric family and the peasants at least thought none the worse of him when they listened to the strange tales which circulated about him. Not all of the stories were true by any means; some were mere spiteful gossip while others had a more fairytale quality about them. But never was it suggested that the King was "strange" because he resorted to drugs as painkillers. Yet this is the most obvious and rational explanation for his behaviour which swung violently from absolute normality to wild eccentricity: his insistence on seeing things which were not there and the urge for bright colours which was never noticeable when he had not been taking the "cure" for a headache.

Ludwig's protagonists regarded him as an endearing, slightly way-ward child while those who loved him less merely shook their heads and counted on their fingers the number of his family who had either died insane or were so ill that they were locked away from public view. Even at the rather sketchy "enquiry" which followed his untimely death when so many detrimental things were said, no such suggestion was made in his defence although all his staff knew of his penchant for chloral. Since he began to use these substances only after he came to the Throne, it is interesting to speculate as to who introduced him to chloral as a painkiller – it could even have been Pfistermeister who purported to deplore the habit.

One of the more unpleasant anecdotes which weighed heavily against him stemmed from the assertion of a servant that Ludwig always bowed to a certain tree as he passed it and how, in later life, he would refer to the presence at his dinner table of certain objects such as cutlery which were simply not there – baffling to a simple-minded lackey but easily understood by anyone who cared to stop to consider the strange effects of drugs taken in the quantities to which Ludwig occasionally resorted. He was not a pleasure-seeking degenerate, but merely a desperate man in search of pain relief. Otto, on the other hand, may have taken the same road for more sybaritic reasons before finding himself unable to change course, although in Otto's case also it is possible that he was deliberately introduced to drugs for political reasons.

In the 19th Century, little was known about the more dangerous properties of what we now know to be quite lethal drugs and medical men habitually prescribed opium, laudenum, morphia and even arsenic for various ailments. No-one appears to have connected Ludwig's hallucinations and moodiness with his intake of chloral, and it is interesting to compare the definitions* of this particular drug with a description of the mental illness from which Ludwig was later told that he was suffering: Chloralhydrate is described as depressing or event-ually paralysing the nervous system and resulting, among other things, in lassitude, weakness and hallucination. Schizophrenia sufferers are described as being "subject to hallucinations and delusions, frequently becoming illogical and rambling. The patient may develop a state of stupor (...) and resists all attempts to arouse him to do the most ordinary things."

In Ludwig's case, might not the one be mistaken for the other?

Over the years, King Ludwig has been dismissed as a "madman" simply because his ministers told the world that he was. Is it not possible, even likely, that he was neither schizoid nor paranoid but simply an acutely shy, hypersensitive man deeply unhappy with a

* Taber's Cyclopedic Medical Dictionary, 10th Edition (1965).

predilection for taking dangerous substances as a means of self help? Like the rest of us, Ludwig was a product of his own upbringing and environment. In his painful shyness he shared a common bond with Elisabeth, who would often hide behind her fan or disappear from view on one of her fast moving hunters, heavily veiled or hidden in the back of her carriage with the blinds drawn. For many years, the people of Vienna had gossiped about Sisi in much the same way as the Munich burghers talked about Ludwig, yet she too was as sane and normal as any one of them, if somewhat more neurotic.

Ludwig's shyness and misanthropy became more acute after Bavaria joined the German Union, and he never lost the feeling of guilt which soured his whole existence because he considered that he had betrayed his people and his crown. Much as he loved the theatre, his greatest pleasure was rapidly becoming an unbearable ordeal since protocol demanded that he sit with the house brilliantly lit and therefore under the close scrutiny of the audience who were all too often more interested in him than in the performance. Additionally, as a devotee of the arts, the constant coughing and chattering of the audience drove him to distraction.

When, in the autumn of 1871, he had attended a special rehearsal at which no audience was present, he had been pleasantly struck by the blissful silence in the auditorium, as also by the agreeable relief from the army of opera glasses which were invariably trained unremittingly upon him. Years before, in 1869, he had recounted in a letter to Cosima a dream in which he had attended a private performance of an opera which had seemed to him to be "Heaven on earth". He now aspired to bring his dream to reality by commanding a private or "separate" performance. Contrary to legend, however, he never forced the players to perform before an audience of one: greatly in sympathy with the artistic intellect, he well knew the value of audience response. It was his custom to invite favoured guests whom he could trust to keep quiet and whom he knew would appreciate the play or opera being performed. His guests would be seated in the back stalls directly under his box out of their view. His enjoyment was thus unimpaired and the players had the benefit of a most appreciative audience.

Besides this expensive relaxation, he continued to read avidly and had gradually built up a large and excellent collection of books specialising in the main on the lives and times of the Bourbons. Apart from his faithful Hornig, he had few friends who were near enough for personal contact and most of his acquaintances were now drawn from theatrical or military circles. Franz Nachbaur, Josefina Scheffsky from the opera, and the actresses Marie Dahn-Haussmann and Lila von Bulykowsky had been regular visitors to the Munich Residenz over a period of years and after the performance the King greatly enjoyed entertaining them to supper in his fantastic and beautiful wintergarten, usually pressing upon them some costly gift in exchange for an aria or recitation. He had a special affection for the tenor, Franz Nachbaur and considered him to be "one of the most amusing and amiable" of his acquaintances; he could never have applied this description to "the Great Friend", who had apparently forgotten all that Ludwig had done for him in the past and now wrote long letters to him only concerning the cost of his new project at Bayreuth.

On Wagner's birthday, the foundation stone for the new theatre was to be laid by the composer, thus frustrating for ever the idea of a National Theatre in Munich, dedicated to Wagner's genius. Offended beyond words by Wagner's ingratitude, Ludwig declined to attend the ceremony. He considered that Wagner had treated him badly, as indeed he had. Over the years, Ludwig had given him thousands of Taler and Gulden [later Marks], which he had recklessly squandered. Most important of all, Wagner had received recognition and an official artistic standing which he was unlikely to have found elsewhere. Surely at the very least, he could have allowed Ludwig his dream of a theatre in Munich, even if the King himself was not paying for it? But Bayreuth it was to be. Wagner had always hated Munich and its people, probably because he himself was so heartily detested there, but he had only himself to blame for that. Ludwig had wanted Munich to be the musical and theatrical centre of the world and that he would be termed co-creator of *Der Ring des Nibelungen,* as had long ago been the understanding, but even this joy was to be denied him. This time, Wagner had gone too far.

Nevertheless, Ludwig still wanted *Parisfal* and, aware of Wagner's temperament, he knew that if he berated him now, he would never see the work at all. The magnanimous telegram which he sent on the occasion of the laying of the foundation stone was typically effusive, despite his general annoyance with the composer. "I speak to you from the bottom of my soul, my dearest friend, to send you very earnest and innermost good wishes on this day of such importance to Germany. Hail and blessings to the great undertaking next year. Today, I am more than ever united with you in spirit." But Wagner had also cooled, if for different reasons, and nothing came of Ludwig's friendly greetings. Wagner was no longer interested in Ludwig's spirit if he was not also able to receive some more tangible sign of the King's appreciation.

It is also doubtful that King Ludwig's spirit was truly with Wagner, for he was occupied with something of even greater importance. In June 1872, he had confided to his Aunt Amalie "Poor Otto's state of health is really deplorable. Unfortunately, he is still no better; he is

much worse than Aunt Alexandra. His nerves are in a state of irrita-
bility which is difficult to imagine. He very seldom dresses, hardly ever
goes out in the open air, often suffers from the most horrible hallucinations; it really is a terrible fate." And one which Ludwig quite
obviously feared might be his own.

The King himself was becoming increasingly withdrawn, his demeanour sad and serious and his body gross now that the famous good
looks were fast disappearing. Despair was deeply and clearly etched
in every feature and it also showed in his letters. To Baroness Leonrod
he admitted, "You understand me so well as only a few people do. By
most of them I am misunderstood so that, naturally, I feel rebuked by
the world and retire more and more; it does me so much good to talk
to you to whom my heart clings in true and innermost love since the
happy and blessed days of my childhood." Almost simultaneously, he
wrote to his mother from Berg, "Fortunately, I found Otto less exciteable than I expected. He still does not like to go out and still pretends
to have boils on his feet. As we drove along, he continually buried his
head in his hands - did not always look at me and always saluted much
too late when the people had passed by."

Obviously, poor Otto was not the best of company and it says much
for Ludwig that he tried so hard to help his brother even though
personal contact was so distressing to him. In a desperate search for
congenial companionship, he allowed himself to become emotionally
involved with Count Hirschberg, one of the many aides de camp to
succeed Paul of Taxis. Hirschberg was scarcely in the same category
as his erudite predecessor but was a compliant, somewhat colourless
man whose main attractions appear to have been militaristic good looks
and unquestioning obedience. Inevitably, when Ludwig's interest in
Hirschberg palled he sought consolation with Hornig.

By the end of 1872, Otto's condition had allegedly so far deteriorated that his medical advisers again suggested that he should retire to
Schloss Nymphenburg where he would be out of the public eye and less
likely to embarrass his family. This idea was accepted by everyone
except Otto himself who harboured a deep dislike for the place,
possibly because he had already twice been temporarily banished
there. Beautiful in its way, it was scarcely a comfortable home for a
young man and no one could blame him for not wanting to spend the
whole of his time within its ornate walls. In his more lucid moments,
he bitterly resented what he considered to be his family's abandonment
of him and when Queen Marie tried to visit him, he would frequently
refuse to see her or would keep her waiting for hours. Worse, if she
was admitted, he would greet her with a vacant stare before wandering
away without a smile of greeting. This of course was no more than she

deserved following her offhand treatment of him in his childhood and her loudly proclaimed "love" was not held in high regard by either of her sons. Even in his depleted state Otto undoubtedly remembered this.

Previously, the shallow and obtuse Marie had found something comic in the antics and generally sad behaviour of lunatics in the mental hospitals of Munich. On one occasion, when making an official visit to one of these institutions in the company of the Empress Elisabeth, she had laughed uncontrollably at the poor demented creatures, pointing and gesticulating at them as if enjoying the performance of professional entertainers. Scandalised, the sensitive and compassionate Elisabeth never forgave her. Since so many members of her family suffered from mental disorders, it seems strange that she should have found the plight of the mentally sick to be so amusing, but when her "favourite" son appeared also to be afflicted, she took a more sober view. In her bewilderment she turned for the first time to Ludwig but she reaped only what she had sown in this quarter and while he was unfailingly polite and solicitous he had no spiritual comfort to give her; indeed, he had little time for her at all. Interestingly, when she died in 1889, three years after Ludwig himself met his end, ostensibly from a "death wish", it was with the hope on her lips that she would be forgiven "by all those whom I have hurt" and with a word of thanks for "those who have been able to love me"- a curious deathbed statement from one who to all intents and purposes had been a good woman.

Ludwig himself now inhabited a world of theatre, music and literature, and a world of bricks and mortar which gave him the same joys and sorrows which others drew from their offspring. Ludwig's castles were his children, and he now gave to his official duties only the most superficial attention.

Unfortunately for Otto, Dr.Solbrig died suddenly and he had been placed in the care of a certain Dr. Bernhard Gudden, a sober, hardlooking man in his fifties whose generally unsympathetic mien terrified Otto into even more erratic behaviour. The fact that they disliked each other on sight was hardly conducive to a good doctor-patient relationship and when one considers that Gudden was one of the first European practitioners to employ the newly-propounded theories of psychiatry, he seems to have been curiously lacking in the basic essentials of human understanding.

Gudden, in fact, seemed to go out of his way to upset his patient. As early as 1872, before Solbrig's death, the public was being gradually conditioned to the idea that all was not entirely well with their beloved "Merry Otto", but because he still appeared in public in Munich, the people naturally found it impossible to believe there was anything wrong with him. As his conduct became more erratic, however, it became apparent to those who knew him that Otto was not himself. "Otto von Bayern," wrote Friedrich Wilhelm, "Came to take his leave of me before his return to Munich (on his recall from the army). He was looking pale and wretched. He sat in front of me *apparently suffering from cold shivering fits* [author's italics] while I expounded to him the necessity of making common cause in military and diplomatic affairs. I could not make out whether or not he understood or only heard what I said." Cold shivering fits? This would seem more appropriate to a drugged man's withdrawal symptoms than a symptom of inherited madness; Otto's behaviour pattern was nothing like that of his Hessian relatives and Friedrich-Wilhelm's comment gives us an interesting alternative to the usual "raving madman" descriptions.

The King had not yet met Dr. Gudden but carefully read his monthly report on Otto; he soon learned from his brother's anxious friends of the unfortunate effect which Gudden appeared to have on his patient. It is an indisputable fact that Otto's condition worsened dramatically after Gudden appeared on the scene. Gripped anew by the fear that he might end his days like his brother, Ludwig now kept away from him, seeking instead the company of the reassuring Hornig. The Stallmeister was a happily married man who lived with his family at Seeleiten on Lake Starnberg in a villa which Ludwig himself had presented to him. Here the King would visit him at least once a week; he would play with Hornig's children, never forgetting to take with him presents of sweets and toys, and would spend happy hours in their ingenuous company like an ordinary man with everyday problems.

Even the joys of Seeleiten were forgotten when Empress Elisabeth arrived in Possenhofen and as usual Ludwig lost no time in seeking her out. He told a lackey to inform the Empress that he wanted to see her alone, but Elisabeth, for reasons of her own, refused to comply with his request and insisted that Marie Festetics, her Hungarian lady-in-waiting, was to remain and that Nopsca, her Master of Household, was to wait on him. Her instruction was that he should be treated like a King even if he refused to behave like one. This report, recorded by Marie Festetics, is puzzling, if indeed she was telling the truth, for Elisabeth herself was prone to make exactly the same request, and felt the same apprehensions as Ludwig did when confronted by the masses and understood his problems perfectly; she is unlikely to have deliberately subjected him to such an ordeal.

On this occasion Ludwig had appeared wearing Austrian uniform as a compliment to her and if he was no longer slender and handsome, he was regal and imposing and still wore the dreamy, romantic air which enthralled all who met him. Although he was still quite young, he had already developed the ponderous quality of an older man and emanated a deep unhappiness. According to Festetics, Elisabeth was determined to present her ladies to him but he immediately retreated into his shell with a wounded expression so that she was obliged to take his arm and lead him into the Schloss without achieving her aim.

Despite the unfortunate beginning to the visit (if there was any truth in Festetics' story), Ludwig and Elisabeth met frequently therafter during her stay, by appointment on the Roseninsel or in the dense Ammerwald, where it is worth noting that she did not insist upon his being "treated like a King" by being surrounded by people. It was a custom of Elisabeth's to arrive unexpectedly on horseback at Berg or Neuschwanstein, when she would spend long hours alone with Ludwig without apparent care for the conventions. There is no doubt that she was a steadying and cheering influence on the King but when she left Bavaria, as his staff were quick to complain, Ludwig immediately became noticeably restless and unhappy.

Paying brief visits to his two new creations at Garmisch (the hunting lodge at Schachen) and Linderhof, he returned at last to Hohenschwangau where his loneliness became so acute that he was even prepared to suffer the company of his unbearable mother. Otto was also present, arriving with the King at 11.30 at night and while the journey was uneventful it was something of an ordeal for Ludwig, who told Marie that he was uneasy with his unpredictable brother. The atmosphere of family reunion was spoiled by the arrival of the sinister Dr. Gudden, who appeared to derive some perverse pleasure by choosing Ludwig's birthday on which to present his monthly report on Otto. Ludwig never forgave him and this was to be their only meeting until they came face to face in very different circumstances in 1886.

Although Otto was only 26 years old, his appearance, like his brother's, had diminished with his mental condition; his pale hair, already sparse and dull, fell in untidy strands over a prematurely lined forehead and the once sparkling eyes were opaque and indifferent to his surroundings. Ludwig can hardly be blamed for seeking companionship elsewhere. Taking his friends where he could find them, they were all too often of the type unlikely to enhance his reputation, nor did they help his peace of mind or even satisfy his craving for love. At the end of the year we find him writing in his diary, "An oath, holy and never to be broken, on New Year's Eve, 1873. I swear and solemnly vow by the pure and holy sign of the Royal lilies inside the impassable, inviolable balustrade enclosing the Royal bed. During the year just begun as much as ever possible bravely to resist every temptation and never to yield, if at all possible, in acts, words or thoughts. In this way to purify myself more and more from the dross which unfortunately clings to human nature and to make myself more worthy of the Crown which God has given me. *Donné dans la chambre du roi, dans la balustrade sacre et unfranchisable, agnoille sur l'estrade la tête protegé par la dai du lit royale. Deo ceccable neo errato Dieu m'aidéra!"*

Disjointed and childish though these entries may seem, Ludwig undoubtedly intended to keep the very real vows contained in them, but as his loneliness increased, abstention clearly became more difficult.

After spending one last harrowing Christmas at Hohenschwangau with his mother and his brother, Otto was despatched to Fürstenried, a chilling, scarcely used residence on the outskirts of Munich where he remained for many years under guard with very occasional outings. He had not yet been officially certified, mainly because Ludwig could not bring himself to take the necessary action. Although the King spent hours ruminating on Otto's condition and describing it to various members of the family, he clearly had some difficulty convincing himself that Otto was incurably insane and with hindsight it seems very probable that Otto was not mad at all, but like Ludwig himself, the victim of a political plot. In Bavaria nowadays, it is increasingly believed that Otto's fate was similar to Ludwig's own. In print also the belief in Otto's madness has been considerably eroded in statements to the effect that, "in the secret Archives exists a letter from distinguished relatives who visited the invalid Otto in Fürstenried in 1913/1914 and conversed for hours with him about art and literature".*
For a man who spent years locked in a cell, frequently in a straitjacket to be wrongfully incarcerated would have been torture for a man of high intellect unless he was kept too heavily sedated to know what was going on. The puzzle in this impeccably documented statement is that, at least during his youth Otto had no interest in the arts but enjoyed only "drinking, hunting and visiting the musichall." Was the prisoner of Fürstenried sane enough to develop interests similar to his brother's, if only to pass the time, as he grew older? Coincidentally or otherwise, Dr. Gudden was as adamant about Otto's madness as he was about Ludwig's. Was he, together with Prince Luitpold, part of a conspiracy to clear the path to the Throne?

Following Otto's removal to Fürstenried only the unexpected return of Elisabeth could rouse Ludwig from his melancholy. This time the Empress stayed in the Residenz with the King while her daughter Gisela, who was married to Ludwig's favourite cousin Leopold, awaited the birth of her first child. Many people found it incredible that Sisi, who looked scarcely older than Gisela herself, should have become a grandmother. At 35, despite her many illnesses and, indeed,

---

* George Lohmeier – see Bibliography, and page 328.

the mental sufferings brought on by her unhappy marriage and eternal disagreements with her mother in law, no line or blemish marred her beauty.

Like Ludwig, Elisabeth had remained shy and hypersensitive and like him she was temperamentally unsuited to Court ceremonial and the rigours of public life. Nervous and highly strung as ever, she now spent her time pacing restlessly from one end of the Residenz to the other, apparently searching for something in the same way as Ludwig himself and like him, she rarely sat down; this must have been exhausting for their attendants who were not permitted to sit until they did. Ludwig saw as much as possible of Elisabeth during her stay, fearful that each time might be the last and that she would vanish as suddenly as she had arrived. Sadly, shortly after Gisela's daughter Augusta was born, this was exactly what happened.

In March 1877 Ludwig noticed a newcomer on the fringes of his entourage. The handsome face of Lambert, Baron von Varicourt was proud, his bearing stiff and formal. Being attracted to this particular type, Ludwig found him pleasing, delighted to find that he had served in both the recent wars in the same regiment to which Prince Otto and the Count de la Rosée had been attached. All of this paled before an even happier discovery: although Varicourt himself was Bavarian, his family had come originally from France and since Ludwig's interest in the Bourbons had by now become an obsession, Varicourt's ancestry alone was a passport to success. He was officially presented to the King and notified of Ludwig's intention to appoint him as his personal aide. Determined this time not to be on the losing side in any ensuing relationship, Ludwig at first kept a formal distance. Since the misfortunes of the early seventies, he was understandably less inclined to trust even his dearest friends. He began with great determination not to lavish his all on this new acquaintance but inevitably, he weakened after two weeks and sent a note to the Baron inviting him to a separate performance at the theatre. It was a piece about the Bourbons which he thought Varicourt might enjoy. Experience had taught him a bitter lesson, however, and while he openly offered his friendship, he did so with a firm request for "absolute discretion."

Eager to learn all he could about the Bourbons, Ludwig expected Varicourt to produce some personal family reminiscences. Enclosed with notes requesting such information were the usual gifts, as if he still felt the need to pay for his friendship; the vow to desist from giving expensive presents had been shortlived: "I enclose a pair of *Fleur de Lys* cufflinks with diamonds which I originally ordered for myself. I give them to you because you are much worthier to wear them inasmuch as two of your ancestors suffered heroically for this noble emblem of

Royal France. The photograph is in remembrance of our meeting on
Thursday last." The remainder of the letter was devoted to assurances
of the warmth he felt towards his new friend but again, sandwiched
between the compliments, was the renewed warning that if Varicourt
stepped out of line their friendship would end immediately.

Caught up in what he thought to be a meaningful friendship because
of Varicourt's supposed family connections, Ludwig took his new Aide
to Schloss Linderhof. He was doomed to disappointment for away
from the messroom atmosphere and separated from his comrades who
were cast in a very different mould from the King, Varicourt seemed
bored and listless. In an attempt to inject some spark of life into him,
the King arranged for supper to be served in the Grotto. So engrossed
was he in the thrill of entertaining his guest in this fantastic retreat that
he failed to notice that Varicourt's interest was centred only on the
food. The only crumb the Baron could offer in return for the King's
lavish hospitality was the confession that his lineage was not nearly as
noble as Ludwig had thought. He went on to describe his prosaic
childhood but to such good effect that Ludwig, reminded of his own
happy times with Otto, pressed for more. He was impressed anew by
Varicourt but this time by the man's honesty.

Their ill-matched friendship continued for a short time, but Ludwig
discovered all too soon that there was no poetry in the military soul of
the Baron. While Varicourt was flattered by the King's attentions, he
soon became bored by Ludwig's lengthy dissertations on the arts and
by his interminable questions. One evening at the grotto, he was foolish
enough to doze off in the middle of one of Ludwig's discourses and
while the King permitted every informality when he was in the company
of a friend, he was not prepared to tolerate this. "Freiherr von Varicourt!" he thundered, "Do you dare to sleep in the presence of your
Sovereign?" He left without waiting for an answer.

Magnanimously, he afterwards let the offender off with a caution
but the Baron, very full of himself, soon forgot both his manners and
his initial promise to the King. He was overfond of making observations about members of Ludwig's suite, evidently in the hope of amusing him but in a moment of stupidity Varicourt revealed that he was in
the habit of discussing his Royal friend with Max Holnstein. This was
too much for Ludwig who, since 1871 made a point of avoiding the
"*Ross-Ober*" at all costs. It was, of course, the end of Varicourt. He
dismissed him forthwith, wrote him a polite note of farewell and
disappeared into the mountains to lick his wounds, leaving the Baron
to wonder what he had done wrong. Varicourt had actually got off
lightly but he never saw the King again.

CHAPTER ELEVEN

BAYREUTH

SHORTLY after Ludwig's brief sojourn with Elisabeth came another figure from the past. In dire need of financial assistance, Wagner suddenly remembered his old friend and appealed to the King as if the rift between them had never existed. The new theatre under construction at Bayreuth could not be completed owing to the fact that Wagner, like Ludwig himself, had both overspent and underestimated the cost of the building. Recalling their sordid quarrels over money and the earlier theatrical productions, Ludwig refused at first to help him.

His excuse, by no means unjustified, was that he now needed all his money for his own building projects but as the days wore on with their sad uniformity, he began to brood about *Der Ring des Nibelungen* and the enticing prospect of seeing all four sections of the work in sequence produced by their creator. Unable to resist any longer, he wrote at last to Wagner, "I must come to your rescue." His gift was of 300,000 Marks which he could ill afford; optimistic as ever, he clearly hoped it would be regarded as a down-payment on a few hours' happiness when he finally saw Wagner's magical *Ring* in all its splendour. Nevertheless, he had still not forgiven the composer for his dishonourable behaviour in the Malwina Schnorr affair and for his decision to build in Bayreuth instead of Munich. His capitulation stemmed solely from his desire to hear the ultimate fruits of Wagner's labours, and this yearning proved stronger than the grievances which he had undoubtedly harboured against the Great Friend for some time. The much-vaunted "love unto death" never really existed.

Restless and disinterested in everything except his building projects, the King showed neither surprise nor pleasure when he heard of the projected second marriage of Karl Theodor to the 16 year old Infanta Maria Josepha of Portugal which, in happier times, he might have marked with a firework display or a festive dîner in the open air. When he did eventually meet the petite and pretty Infanta he was greatly attracted to her and when the wedding took place in April 1874 he took great pains to show the warmth of his feelings towards her.

Eighteen years older than his bride, Karl Theodor treated her more like a daughter than a wife. When the King placed her gallantly at his side at a gala performance of the inevitable *Lohengrin*, the Duke admonished her for failing to talk to the King who, he said, would be "deeply offended" if she did not. Her childlike confession that it was her first visit to the theatre and that she had been so entranced with the opera that she had totally forgotten her surroundings so endeared her to the theatre-loving Ludwig that he afterwards rewarded her enthusiasm with a set of watercolours depicting scenes from the opera. This gift was accompanied by a large bouquet and a note thanking her for "*listening* to the opera, something which very few people do." The theatre party was the King's first public appearance for many months and it proved so successful that two months later he was persuaded to take part in the Corpus Christi procession. He walked through the streets of Munich on this occasion with his head held so high that few of his subjects were able to look directly into his eyes. His step was ponderous and heavy and, it must be said, somewhat mannered.

Quite a number of people are on record as saying that the presence and bearing of King Ludwig was "theatrical" rather than "regal" in manner, "like a stage King" said one man who met him unexpectedly on the Alm high above Garmisch-Partenkirchen. Many no longer recognised him since he had changed so radically in the past few years. So rarely did he appear in the city that the public had had no opportunity to accustom themselves gradually to his altered appearance. In country districts he was, on the other hand, as familiar to the peasants as members of their own families.

Like his mother, he could now take a solitary walk in the Englischer Garten or even along the streets near the Residenz without being recognised. In the 19th century, of course, the public was not swamped with media material and could only rely on carefully doctored postcard portraits. At the age of 29, only the dark blue mysteriously glowing eyes remained the same, still gazing towards the sky as if he could not bear the sight of the everyday world about him. Ludwig in fact rarely looked at his subjects for long enough to accept their homage or, indeed, their shocked expressions. Paradoxically, aware that they still loved him, he afterwards remarked to his valet upon their demonstrations of affection. The success of this second appearance encouraged him to emerge yet again, although this time it was less willingly since he was to greet the German Emperor who was to make a brief stop in Munich on his way to take the cure at Bad Gastein.

Because the visit was to be mercifully short, Ludwig invited Wilhelm to dine in the Royal Salon at the Munich Railway station. Despite the strange venue it was a gala affair and Ludwig made a suitably flamboyant entrance wearing the uniform of a colonel in the Chevauxlègers, indicating that an element of competition still existed between himself and the Hohenzollerns. He was accompanied by Elisabeth's daughters, Valerie and Gisela and the latter's husband, Prince Leopold together with some of the other Royal princes. Ludwig's highly thea-

trical performance created quite a stir as of course he had intended
that it should. He was, as the saying goes, "keeping his end up" and for
once he was adequately supported by his family.

Gisela was now a mature and happy woman while Valerie was still
only a child. The latter bore a strikingly close resemblance to Ludwig
himself and like him was acutely shy. She was, in fact, terrified of him
while he in turn seemed unusually timid of her although as a rule he
got on well with children. Valerie's shyness prompted her to hide from
company when she could, and sometime before, when her mother first
expressed the wish that she should meet the King, she ran away. When
she was retrieved and persuaded to hand him a posy of jasmine, it was
observed that it was "hard to tell which of the two was more shy and
inhibited – the King or Valerie." As their likeness grew more apparent, busy tongues persisted in placing Valerie's paternity at Ludwig's
door.

The railway station dinner party was scarcely a success with Ludwig
on his best behaviour and the new Emperor, very conscious of his
elevated position making little pretence of listening to what his host
was saying. It was, after all, a mere façade for the benefit of the public
and presumably, having got what he wanted from Ludwig in 1871,
Wilhelm saw no further need to put himself out for the man who had
put the crown upon his head. Doubtless Ludwig was more than
relieved to see the train steaming out of the station.

Despite this and other representational efforts, Ludwig could not
sustain this prosaic existence and, having the sense to realise thaat he
was not cut out for public life, escaped soon after his uncle's visit to his
refuge at Hohenschwangau from where, tortured by headaches and
insomnia, he complained to Baroness Leonrod, "You can imagine what
it cost me to have to see the King of Prussia again – to whom I have had
to give up so many rights and to whom Bavaria has given such essential
services and helped to gain many a victory. Instead of being grateful,
Prussia treats us as if we and not poor France had been the enemy
during the last war."

As Otto's condition worsened, Ludwig himself grew steadily more
moody and introspective. He would spend hours staring into a mirror
as if he expected to find a raving madman reflected there. Otto preyed
on his mind so much that he expressed the frequent opinion that he too
was going mad. Equally great was his fear that, even if he was perfectly
sane and normal, his people might decide otherwise and place him in
the same category with his brother. When he confided this particular
fear to his secretary, that gentleman's advice was that he should allay
any such suspicions by showing himself to his people more frequently.

When Elisabeth next visited Ludwig, she found him pale and ill, despite his long sojourn in the mountains. He was steeped in oil of cloves to soothe his toothache and half stupefied by the chloralhydrate with which he continued to try to alleviate his aches and pains. On this occasion he bore little resemblance to the "fine man with all the allure of a theatrical King or a Lohengrin in his wedding clothes" as he was once spitefully described by Marie Festetics. Because of his physical distress he looked so wild and tortured that an outsider might well have taken him to be as deranged as his brother, and the Empress was deeply shocked. She always understood his problems if not perhaps his self-prescribed remedies, and on this occasion suggested that a change of scenery might be beneficial. Interestingly, in the light of future events, he decided upon France where, probably on his recommendation, she herself was to spend the summer.

This idea seemed so attractive that in August, noticeably at the time of year when Paris is habitually deserted by natives and tourists alike, he set off for his holiday with Max Holnstein in attendance. Although Holnstein was theoretically the best choice of guide since he knew Paris well, his inclusion in the party seems strange for Ludwig now openly detested the Oberstallmeister and had made a point of avoiding him since the *Kaiserbrief* affair.

The only logical explanation for this curious holiday alliance is, in a word, blackmail. With the passing of the years, Holnstein's hold over Ludwig had become stronger. In his capacity as Oberstallmeister, he knew everything that Ludwig did, both officially and unofficially, and would have had intimate knowledge of Ludwig's friendship with the Empress of Austria as well as his more nefarious relationships. He was dangerously well informed about the King's mountaineering expeditions and picnics with small parties of Chevauxlègers which, while they wore a superficially Bacchanalian air, were fundamentally as innocuous as his other pursuits. Had they been observed at first hand by their critics it is doubtful that they would have raised so much as an eyebrow even among Ludwig's most narrow minded opponents.

Nevertheless such tales, if they persisted, could only prove damaging to the Royal reputation. It may be assumed that, being the man he was, Holnstein was not slow in making the King aware of his supreme position to blackmail him. In such circumstances, it would be all too easy to persuade the King to take him to France.

The moment Ludwig arrived in Paris his gloom disappeared and he was swept away by the cultural delights of the French capital. He pronounced himself "astonished" by the splendours of the Imperial German Embassy where he stayed and where Prince von Hohenlohe-Schillingfürst, formerly his Prime Minister, now ruled like a King in his own right. Ludwig enthused like any tourist over the glories of France's world famous art treasures and historic buildings but most of all he delighted in the Théatre Français, where he spent every possible moment. He greatly appreciated the grand declamatory style of the actors and as he understood their language as well as they understood it themselves, no nuance was lost on him. So great was his enjoyment that he appeared in public to a far greater extent than he would have done in his own capital and even went so far as to accept a number of invitations, including a small dinner party at which one of the guests, a German diplomat, Rudolf Lindau, appeared to be fascinated by him especially after he had managed to provoke the King into an unexpected personal statement concerning the Union.

Questioning Ludwig on Bavaria's entry and the fact that the King himself had not been present at the ceremony, the King replied that his absence was due to his indisposition, but that his "representatives carried out their duties in accordance with instructions and to the general good of all." Somewhat unwisely, Lindau said "And to the benefit of the German Emperor, you may be sure," This annoyed Ludwig who now favoured the diplomat with his famous haughty stare. "If your words are intended to carry some deeper meaning, sir, then you are to be disappointed if you expect some reaction on my part. The terms agreed were indeed to the common good. I stand on excellent terms with His Majesty the Emperor and with Count Bismarck."

"I would not presume to suggest otherwise, Your Majesty. Please accept my apologies if the All Highest thought my words carried any other suggestion." Ludwig continued to stare penetratingly at Lindau for a moment before retiring behind the inevitable bank of flowers. "It is a source of satisfaction to all Germans that our interests have at last become one." Lindau observed, anxious to make amends, but he was in for another surprise.

"Not entirely, my friend," Ludwig corrected him, "The interests of Bavaria, for example, will always remain uppermost in Bavarian hearts. And if Prussia's interest is in Germany as a complete whole, then one suspects that Prussia's real object is to take enforced leadership over the other member States."

There was a long silence. This was much stronger stuff and the rest of the party now hung on Ludwig's unexpected words which seemed in direct conflict with his earlier careful statement to Lindau. There could be no doubt as to his sincerity now.

"Can Majesty believe that this is in the Emperor's mind?"

"I did not say that. His Majesty's interests are akin to our own. But the Crown Prince of Prussia has other ideas. I only learned recently that he is pursuing yet another of his political campaigns."

"Indeed, Majesty? Can this really be so?"

"The little strutting peacock hopes to gain for himself a whole new Empire. His efforts are bound up in the endeavour to take away from the individual States their autonomy. It is this disquieting thought which troubles me above all others." And with this, the King rose abruptly from the table, leaving the astonished guests to make what they could of his words.

After Ludwig had left the room, Hohenlohe remarked to Holnstein, "His Majesty is quite marked in his dislike of His Royal Highness." Holnstein replied, "Lindau was unwise to speak as he did; the King's good humour cannot be relied upon where the German question is concerned." (And if anyone knew how true and, indeed, how justified this was, it was Holnstein.)

"So I have observed. It is true that the King feels strongly on the subject."

There was nothing wrong with Ludwig's "humour" in other respects during his stay in Paris and he was so enthusiastic that his euphoria began to irritate the openly contemptuous Holnstein, who made no secret of his longing to sample the more titillating diversions for which 19th Century Paris was as well known as for her historic monuments.

The French capital in August was sultry and prone to sudden storms; clouds were also gathering in the Imperial German Embassy also and this other storm broke into full fury when Holnstein suddenly refused to accompany his Sovereign to the theatre; all the old grievances of 1871 came boiling to the surface. Holnstein had long since sold his loyalties to Prussia and it is probable that he deliberately provoked Ludwig on this occasion as a means of engineering his release from the Bavarian King's service. Having supposed himself to be shackled permanently to this dangerous possible blackmailer, Ludwig may also have been glad of an opportunity to get rid of him. He gave Holnstein an ultimatum: if he did not do his duty that evening his service was at an end. Holnstein's adamant refusal to accompany him was couched in terms which no man should use to his Sovereign. Outraged, the King went to the theatre alone, leaving Holnstein to some more attractive pastime and continued his journey the next day without his adjutant, Holnstein, according to Hohenlohe, electing to spend the day in bed. They did not meet again until 1886.

Ludwig visited Fontainbleu and the cathedral at Rheims but the highlight of his journey to France was undoubtedly his visit to Versailles, where he imbued himself anew in the charisma of his Bourbon heroes; transported into an era more agreeable to him than the one in which he lived, his troubles were momentarily forgotten. At great cost the ornamental fountains were set into play for his pleasure and he was so impressed that he decided on the spot to embellish the gardens at

Linderhof with such a fountain as would send cascades of water high
into the air.

Surrounded by these French architectural splendours, the ultimate
plan for Linderhof was now crystallised in his mind, not the least of
which was to be the golden disc of the Sun King to remind him of the
autonomy that he had lost and to inspire him to find the means of
regaining that autonomy, although in view of all the recent events, one
cannot believe that he truly thought this might be possible. There was
something childlike in Ludwig's everlasting love of clockwork toys,
firework displays and playing waters, all symbols of a fantasy world far
removed from the German question. Only one incident marred the
enraptured Ludwig's visit to Versailles: as he watched the play of the
fountains, his reaction was not lost on a group of rowdy students who
went behind him imitating his now quite extraordinary walk; they were
apprehended and punished but his pleasure was spoiled. His momentary rage and embarrassment quickly melted to the philosophical
acceptance that it was a small price to pay for his memorable trip.

Versailles may not have been Ludwig's only moment of bliss: did he,
during this extremely rare visit to France, visit the Empress? Elisabeth
had taken the Château de Sassetôt de Mauconduits near Fécamps,
Normandy, where she had remained in total isolation for several
months despite taking an instant dislike to the place. The Empress had
discussed this with the King beforehand and, indeed, he seems almost
to have persuaded her to go there. "The most beautiful and civilised of
countries is not to be judged by its present rulers" he told her. Much
has been made of Elisabeth's sudden need of a doctor to attend to "a
riding accident" but it was widely believed that she had gone to Sassetôt
to await the birth of a child, her fifth* a theory which was later enlarged
upon by her niece, Marie Wallersee-Wittelsbach. During her stay, she
was also observed by the fascinated locals in a close embrace wth a
"very tall bearded stranger". It was not her husband, who was busy
with his usual manoevres and memoranda in Vienna, but it could very
well have been Ludwig.

When the King returned to Bavaria he appointed a new aide whose
duties encompassed those previously undertaken by the Oberstallmeister, who had already taken up a lucrative post on Bismarck's
personal staff. The new aide was totally different from Holnstein and
Ludwig's trust was such that he confided to him the details of his visit
to France, the memory of which, despite the sour note struck by his
contretemps with Holstein, continued to overwhelm him for some time
afterwards. To his new adjutant he wrote "I shall always look upon this

* In her book, The Secret of an Empress, Countess Karoline Zanardi-Landi claimed
to be the child in question, but invalidated her claim by insisting that she was born in
1883.

year as one which has made me happy and content as no other has. I think about my journey to France as a beautiful dream in which I saw at last the adored Versailles." In all probability. he saw also his adored Elisabeth and possibly even his child.

The new adjutant, Alfred, Count von Dürkheim-Montmartin, was 25 years old, an officer and a gentleman in every sense of the word. Handsome in the formal, reserved way which the King so admired, his eagerness to serve his Sovereign made a refreshing change for Ludwig after some of his recent experiences. He got on so well with Dürkheim that he took him to Hohenschwangau, confident that he would appreciate the glorious Alpine scenery and excellent riding possibilities of the region.

Ludwig's faith was not misplaced and shortly afterwards Dürkheim accompanied Ludwig to Linderhof. Deeply impressed, he expressed his admiration for the King's masterpiece, and on their return, he received an album of pictures of Linderhof, together with a covering note. Dürkheim immediately wrote a courteous note of thanks: "I have just received Your Majesty's most gracious letter and the wonderful album of Linderhof, which will be a precious souvenir for all time of those days which will live in my soul like a fairy dream." Their friendship was assured when he continued "Every palpitation of my heart belongs to the Monarchistic principle which for me is embodied in the person of Your Majesty. I am always prepared to shed the last drop of my blood for the triumph of Kingship and the person of my Sovereign." Fine words, but he meant what he said and was later to prove it. Dürkheim was one of Ludwig's truly loyal friends who left him just before the end only when he was forced to do so by the hostile Prince Luitpold and the rebels.

For a time Ludwig was thus content if not actually happy. Dürkheim was of a different intellect from other male friends who had all too often proved disastrous to the King; he did not appear to inspire in Ludwig those dark, impossible longings which clouded most of his relationships. His friendship with Dürkheim was of a platonic, idealistic nature. The man's loyalty was incorruptible and it says much for his integrity that Ludwig trusted him enough to send him to Fürstenried to report on his brother. Dürkheim, who already knew Otto well, duly reported "There are some favourable changes in the health of HRH Prince Otto - two days ago he gave up the strict fasting. He is now much happier, less self-centred and less absorbed by horrid dreams, and although he still only sees Baron Branca, HRH took more part in the conversation at dinner. Today he started with the warm baths."

Further observations in Dürkheim's report were less encouraging. "The strongly religious atmosphere seems to continue (...). Whether the improvements will last or whether it is only the calm before the storm it is impossible to say." Other members of the family were equally anxious about Otto's decline. In 1874, after a visit to Queen Marie, the Empress Elisabeth rose to leave and Otto, who was also present, immediately offered her his arm to escort her to her carriage. With some apprehension, Elisabeth is said to have whispered to Marie Festetics who was, as always, her companion, "Please watch him carefully; I have the feeling he is going to throw me down the stairs."

Even his mother was at last persuaded that there was no real hope for Otto's recovery or his ability to lead a reasonably normal life and when she joined Ludwig at Hohenschwangau he did his best to help her in her misery, welcoming her in his usual courteous manner even if his heart sank at the sight of her. Marie soon found an alternative source of comfort; having been brought up to be a Protestant, she had decided to enter the Catholic church. Although the King's own bond with his church had been more or less severed and his faith* had become somewhat eroded, her intention met with his full approval he genuinely hoped that Marie might derive some comfort from her new religion..

For many years, Ludwig perhaps justifiably, had openly blamed his mother for some of his own problems, and she would have been obtuse indeed if she was not aware of it. Now, in middle age, she appears to have experienced new fears of death and retribution. Whatever her reasons, her obvious need invoked in Ludwig's generous heart a deep pity for her, and his attitude mellowed noticeably towards her. He gave his wholehearted consent to her conversion and on October 12th, 1874, she was received into the Catholic faith in the tiny village church at Walthenhofen some three kilometers from Hohenschwangau.

*   *   *   *   *

AFTER much persuasion he agreed to appear at the much-heralded Troop Review of 1874, an event which attracted multitudes to the capital. In their thousands they swarmed expectantly to the Oberwiesenfeld to enjoy the colourful spectacle, the prospect of some serious drinking afterwards and even, if they were lucky, a rare glimpse of their King. He was accompanied by his brother and this offers us a further indication that Otto's illness was by no means regarded as being permanent. The puzzling acceptance of it again leads one to conclude that his family had assumed that his "madness" was either self-inflicted rather than artificially induced. Ludwig himself had as early as 1871 referred in a letter to Marie to the inadvisability of Otto's lifestyle: "I told Gietl to go to see Otto

* Both Ludwig and Otto were Catholic.

at Hohenschwangau, because it is absolutely essential that he should begin to lead a different life, and that he should follow the advice of the doctors". In fact, Otto showed no signs of mental disturbance at this spectacular parade.

It was a dazzling occasion. Ludwig rode from the Residenz to the Feldherrnhalle, an imposing Italianate edifice built, like so many of Munich's showpieces, by his grandfather Ludwig I. There he was greeted by his generals led by the ancient Von der Tann; Ludwig rode with them on his chestnut, an imposing figure in his colonel's uniform, the bright red Wittelsbach sash accentuating the pallor of his skin. If ever he showed an aptitude for acting it was now, when his heart was breaking.

The brothers enjoyed the same warm reception as they had been given on previous occasions and they were cheered unceasingly as they made their way through the broad avenues and narrow winding streets. After the display, Ludwig joined Princess Gisela in her carriage for the return journey. Elisabeth was absent as usual from this Wittelsbach family gathering, having gone to England where she was again tasting the joys of the hunt and renewing her acquaintance with Captain Middleton.

The success of the Review and the welcome Ludwig received encouraged him to show himself freely in the capital until the death of his aunt, Princess Alexandra of Hesse, sent him back to the solitude of the mountains. She had hovered for years on the brink of total madness and although her death was inevitable, it nevertheless cast a long shadow over her relatives. Ludwig's relapses into his old ways after the occasional attempt to lead a representational life can be directly attributable to these family tragedies. And who could blame him as he watched the Hesses lapsing one by one into insanity? He was a sensitive, deeply thoughtful man anxious to do the right thing. To abdicate had crossed his mind on many occasions; usually it was merely a question of "cry wolf" when something had upset him or when he could not get his own way, but at other times, when a member of the family died in a state of derangement, his thoughts undoubtedly ran along quite different lines.

He had now evidently decided against marriage although one wonders if he might have cast aside his principles had the Empress Elisabeth been free, for she was actually only his second cousin and as the Wittelsbachs had often intermarried, he would probably not have regarded this as a deterrent. In fact, Elisabeth's own marriage to Franz Josef was dangerously close for comfort, for theirs was the 22nd such union between the Wittelsbachs and the Habsburgs and a special dispensation from the Pope had been obtained before the Viennese clerics agreed to their union. Children of all such intermarriages were likely to be temperamental and highly strung, talented, eccentric and unstable. Ludwig's decision not to marry Sophie did not hang on this problem alone, however, and her pre-marital amorous involvements had given him the perfect excuse to jilt her.

It is easy to adduce that Ludwig stayed out of the public eye as much as possible not merely because of his shyness but because of the fear of being labelled "different". His salvation was his building and his hero-worship of the Bourbons. No wife and family for him but a series of sublime castles and palaces, each more breathtaking than the last.

Immediately before the news of his aunt's death he had commanded a private performance of a play about Louis XVI and, rather than spend his evening alone with his own morbid thoughts, insisted that the performance should still take place even though the public theatres were closed as a mark of respect. This provoked a fresh storm of disapproval. By no means as heartless as the people thought him, Ludwig wrote to his other Hessian aunt [Amalie] "Although it is always painful for the survivors when a member leaves one's family forever, it really is a good thing in the case of Aunt Alexandra. Her continuous sufferings from her nervous disease were seldom interrupted by moments of happiness."

Having got this off his chest, he fled from Munich the day before the funeral, evidently not wishing to be upset again, nor reminded that another sufferer waited at nearby Fürstenried, for Dr. Gudden had reported that despite his occasional lucid periods, Otto would never again lead a normal life. There had been some talk of his paying an official visit to England, but the new doctors who had been called in advised the King that as Otto could no longer be trusted unaccompanied in the streets of Munich, there was no question of his appearing before the formidable Queen Victoria. At the same time, there is something highly suspect about these regular reports on Otto's "madness" which were totally belied by his subsequent public and semi-public appearances apparently of perfectly sound mind. Only one embarrassing incident has been recorded and repeated endlessly as proof of his insanity. although here again, he could merely have been "high" on drugs on the day in question.

At the time of the Corpus Christi procession, Ludwig decided not to take part since he was in the midst of a dispute with the politically-orientated Jesuit clergy. He had also forbidden Otto to attend this important festival but when the time came the over-zealous Prince found his way to the cathedral and as the procession entered he flung himself on to the altar steps and began to confess hysterically to the Archbishop that he had "committed the unforgivable sin against the

Holy Ghost." His condition was said to be so wild that four strong men were required to remove him. In Otto's defence it must be said that public confession of this type was common at the time, and Otto's exhibition was only publicised because he was a prominent figure in society. Nevertheless, after this incident Ludwig took to reading the reports on Otto even more avidly, as if searching for the secret of his own destiny. There is no doubt that, however sane he actually was, Ludwig was increasingly tormented by the thought of madness. Sadly, malicious rumours were being circulated by some of his less scrupulous ministers and because his temper on occasions left something to be desired, he was to some extent digging his own grave.

Ludwig's own hypersensitivity was also increasing and a chance remark would now send him either into a fury or into a deep, cold silence. During the Ministerial conference, which he hated, he would pace the floor like a caged animal longing for freedom or, in the midst of the discussion, would suddenly embark on some totally different topiic which the prosaic officials found most disconcerting. Ludwig rarely sat during private interviews with cabinet ministers and this meant that the unlucky gentleman would also have to stand, perhaps for two or three hours. Another favourite ruse to gain advantage over someone was to deliberately place him in such a position that the sun would shine directly into his eyes, thus temporarily blinding him. His dislike and distrust of his Ministerium was strong and he made no secret of his feelings.

Occasionally, if there was something to be discussed and the King was away he would expect them to seek him out. It was not unknown for a cabinet meeting to be held in a meadow, a forest clearing or on the alm where the pompous ministerss were forced to convene to the accompaniment of birdsong and cowbells, their documents blowing in the wind and their voices, to Ludwig's great satisfaction, barely audible.

His spite was nevertheless directed only against those whom he knew to be his enemies; he treated people as they treated him and if he found them to be sympathetic he would shower kindnesses upon them, as for example, on his old friend the actress, Marie Dahn-Haussmann. He was very fond of this dignified lady who was also a friend of his grandfather, and honoured her with a visit to his new palais, Herrenwörth, his last project in the French style, which was being erected on the Herreninsel, the larger of the islands set on the Chiemsee.

Ludwig bought the Herreninsel in 1875, merely to rescue it from timber speculators not realising until five years later what a splendid site it would make for his Palais. The building of Schloss Herrenchiemsee commenced in 1878. Intended as a memorial to absolute monarchy, it was a copy of Versailles, its main focuses being the "paradise" bedroom with the huge, uncomfortable looking ceremonial bed, and the breathtaking mirror salon. Having spent years poring over his books on France, her monarchy, her culture and her history, Ludwig was able to plan his Palais with absolute accuracy. Buried deep in the forest of the island and approached only by his own ferryboat, Herrenchiemsee was perhaps the most secluded of all his castles being, at the time, even more difficult to reach than Neuschwanstein or Linderhof.

Enthusiastically awaiting its completion he would stay occasionally in the old Schloss (an abbey), so that he could watch it grow and to this end so far forgot his love of nature as to have the tops of the trees removed in a straight line from the building site to his window so that his view would be unimpeded. Elisabeth spent Christmas 1878 in Munich, accompanied by her son, Crown Prince Rudolf, an introspective, somewhat debauched intellectual who formed an instant rapport with the lonely King. Both men had been poorly treated by fate and were fundamentally misunderstood by all with whom they came in contact, but Rudolf had dangerous political interests which were to lead him quickly to disaster and death.

Ludwig was sublimely happy to be near Elisabeth but her lady-in-waiting, Marie Festetics was quite obviously jealous of the affinity between the King and the Empress and repeatedly asserted that Elisabeth did not reciprocate Ludwig's feelings. Since it was Elisabeth who frequently sought out the King, her protests do not carry the ring of truth.

Marie Festetics tells a story about an evening visit which Ludwig paid to the Empress who was "tired after a long day of family festivities" which she loathed. After the King had stayed for some time, Festetics reports that Elisabeth took her to one side and whispered that she must find a way of rescuing her. When Festetics later returned to the room where the King was being entertained by the Empress, she said "Your Majesty has ordered me to knock when it is 10.30 as Your Majesty has to get up early tomorrow. I did not dare to disturb you earlier but it has already gone eleven and I fear a migraine. Please forgive me for disturbing Your Majesty." According to Festetics, the King threw her "an angry glance" and said "When I am here I forget the time." After his departure, the Empress is reported to have remarked "Thank God it is over. It was awful. I feel very sorry for the poor King. I like him so much but I like my bed better." More unlikely still, "I think there is a certain similarity between him and me and among these similarities is a dash of melancholy and the love of solitude." Festetics tells us she replied "Heaven forbid that there is any real similarity. Your Majesty will forgive anything by presenting it as a family trait when it is something for which you cannot account ..." and went on to say that Elisabeth looked "first astonished, then she laughed: 'It is shameless to say that, even if there is something in it. I have endless sympathy with the poor King'."

"Yes, a King is certainly poor who is not mad enough to be locked up but is too abnormal to move in the world among ordinary people," was Festetics reportedly sage rejoinder.

It is inconceivable that she would really have dared to say such things to Elisabeth of all people who herself came into the same general category as Ludwig and who, in any case, would never hear a word said against the King by her own family, never mind a mere lady-in-waiting. Unless she was deliberately trying to paint a certain picture it seemed unnecessarily spiteful to repeat such a conversation, if it really took place. Her account ended with the assertion that when Ludwig asked Elisabeth if he could accompany her for part of her journey as he often did, she [Festetics] was told to inform the King that it was not possible because the Empress' dog *Shadow,* was "so unpleasant that she will tolerate no one she doesn't know". This can only be sheer fabrication since Ludwig was fond of all animals and was certainly not afraid of poor old *Shadow* who had followed Elisabeth about for long enough to have become very familiar with the King and who died of old age not long afterwards. Elisabeth, in fact, never went anywhere without at least two of her many canine companions and if Ludwig had waited for her to appear without her usual escort, he would never have seen her at all.

Immediately following this particular visit, Ludwig sent his aide at dead of night to present Festetics "personally" with a huge bouquet of two hundred roses in varigated colours ranging from dark red to white. The gift was divine, but could there have been just a spark of devilment in the King's insistence that she should be dragged from her bed to receive it?

With a heart still glowing from his interlude with the Empress, Ludwig returned to Hohenschwangau. Despite the warmth of his relationship with Elisabeth and her son, he found it increasingly difficult to communicate with others, in particular with his Ministers, and began to rely increasingly on Richard Hornig and on Alfons Welker, a 23 year old body servant. The trustworthy Dürkheim was involved elsewhere carrying out duties which gave him less opportunity for personal contact with the King.

With Richard Hornig also frequently away transacting business on his behalf, supervising the building work or spending time with his family at Seeshaupt, Ludwig thus had no companions except his body servants. Welcker unfortunately, was another opportunist eager to establish good relations with all around him. Quick witted and sly, he well knew how to ingratiate himself with members of Ludwig's entourage at all levels. As a body servant he knew a great deal about Ludwig's untidy business affairs as well as details of his personal relationships. The current secretary, Friedrich von Ziegler, was a better proposition. Eisenhart had served Ludwig throughout the troubles of the war and the entry into the Reich; he was dismissed in 1876 after six years' service with the comment from Ludwig "I cannot imagine how I could have endured that stupid face around me for so long."

He had no such complaint about Ziegler, but he often shocked his new secretary. Like his predecessors, Ziegler had a genuine liking for the King and was deeply disturbed when on January 25th, 1876, Ludwig commanded Welcker to write to the secretary on his behalf. Engrossed in putting the finishing touches to the newly-completed Schloss Linderhof and occupied still with the other two castles, Ludwig no longer had time for more prosaic matters and seemed indifferent to the struggle for power which was going on around him, engineered by Johannes von Lutz and his shadow cabinet who never slackened their efforts to gain power. If they succeeded, it would result in Bavaria having even closer links with Prussia.

Lutz, an ambitious, self-made man, had been making his presence felt since 1866 when he had shared Pfistermeister's task in ridding Bavaria of Richard Wagner. Ziegler was not anxious to see Bavaria tied closer to Bismarck but found it difficult to draw the King's attention to such things and all too often found himself sidetracked into topics more interesting to Ludwig personally or worse, left to make decisions himself. Fortunately, he was loyal and honest and never took advantage of his potential power. When he made State decisions on Ludwig's behalf he always did so with the King's interests in mind. Despite his indignation when Ludwig relegated the task of letter writing to a mere valet, the conscientious Ziegler soon forgot his anger and philosophically concluded that a letter from a servant was better than no letter at all; Welcker was at least no stammering idiot and could convey Ludwig's instructions either verbally or in writing. Doubtless Ziegler's basic worry was that it might only be a question of time before Welcker began to amend the messages or, indeed, even invent or withhold them, as it suited him.

Ludwig's needs were far from simple and if a message was not properly conveyed all sorts of complications could arise. He would become almost childishly peeved, for example, when the mechanical aids to his private world failed to function or when his building instructions were not carried out to the letter. Hornig was constantly charged with the correction of lighting faults*, mechanical breakdowns and

* A complex system of theatrical lighting was employed in the grotto at Linderhof, and Ludwig was to be one of the first to employ electricity, central heating and an early form of telephone at Neuschwanstein.

worse, the breakdown of good labour relations. Convinced with some justification that he was being cheated by some of the building contractors and suppliers, Ludwig gave up grumbling to Hornig and began to haunt the building sites not only to inspect the work but also to keep a check on the actual building materials used. His rage on discovering that some of the "marble" pillars ordered for one of his castles were only poryphry at a marble price was almost as monumental as the building itself. Avidly interested in the latest scientific inventions, Ludwig's brainchild, Neuschwanstein, was one of the first buildings in Germany to be equipped with electricity, central heating and an early form of telephone.

It was at about this time that he began to demand "brighter colours", "brighter lights", "stronger tones." Gradually, the colours specified in the original designs for Neuschwanstein were changed to more strident and dazzling hues. The sudden changes can be directly attributed to the twin factors of failing eyesight and too much chloralhydrate which undoubtedly excited in him the need for brilliant effects. Years of reading, mostly by artificial light, had damaged his sight; the same two factors may also have accounted for his excruciating headaches which grew worse as he became older and which were further exacerbated by constant brooding about Otto, whose tragic fate haunted him day and night.

In a desperate attempt to prove that he was not like his brother, Ludwig at last conceded to the pressure of his advisers and embarked once more on a more outgoing existence and although his financial position was far from good, he spared no expense to entertain a procession of visitors, Royal and otherwise. The whole charade was fundamentally distasteful to him and continued to place an impossible burden not only on the Civil List but also on his naturally retiring nature. His public appearance when he presided over the Festival of the Knights of St. George proved to be the final straw. Unnerved by the thousands who came to watch, he vowed that he would never make such an appearance again.

In the same year, he appointed Count Dürkheim as a Royal Chamberlain; among his duties was the selection of staff and willing and resourceful as he was, poor Dürkheim found this particular task impossibly hard. In desperation he reported, "The search for a new Chef de Cabinet continues unsuccessful. The chief whom Your Majesty needs must not only be devoted and faithful, he must be absolutely trustworthy, have more than the usual acumen and maturity of judgement, great skill, great energy and must be of an iron constitution. I must confess that, at the present moment, I do not know of anyone who could guarantee all that. I have often wondered whether such a man could be found among the present members of the Coalition*." This was a sad reflection on the general state of affairs in Bavaria.

It is evident from these impossible requirements that Ludwig had somehow held on to his high ideals; he had equally high expectations where his friends were concerned. He was frequently disappointed in them, although not in Marie Dahn-Haussmann to whom he gave an illuminating insight into his own view of himself when he wrote, "I believe there is an affinity of our souls to the point where we have hatred for the base, the wrong and unjust and all kindred things, and that pleases me. That I am seized by a true fever of anger and hatred against the outside world from which I wrathfully turn away because it offers me so little, is understandable. Perhaps I may one day make my peace with the earthy world, when all ideals whose holy fire I carefully nourish shall be destroyed! But I do not wish for that – I shall remain an enigma to myself and to others."

He continued to yearn for Elisabeth and was horrified to learn that she had been involved in a riding accident in the Bois du Boulogne during a visit to Paris. He contacted Rudolf immediately: "You fortunate, enviable man," he wrote, "who is permitted to be so much with the Empress! Please lay me at her feet and vow in my name that she must consider me as her devoted slave for ever. It moved me very deeply when Louis** assured me from Gödöllö in October that she would 'put the rein' on her impetuosity in riding. Nothing could ever be more painful for me than if she should have another accident. God protect me from such a thing! And protect you and me from having to experience such a dreadful thing. I will have your picture framed do that I may have it, together with that of the Empress, constantly before my eyes. Because no one on this earth is dearer to me than you and she. Please recommend me a thousand times to the Empress." This letter is revealing in more ways than one, for he makes no mention of the alleged accident at Sassetôt which was the only one of her many spills and falls from horseback ever to be reported so minutely, even though, from the description, it was one of the least serious. One possible explanation for the omission is that he was present at Sassetôt and knew the real reason for the doctor's visit, or he was aware that Elisabeth had "gone to earth" in France and her reason for doing so. He was certainly very concerned by the report of her accident in the Bois, which might also suggest that the Sassetôt "fall" had no real significance.

An event even more dreadful than for Elisabeth to have another riding accident shook him on June 25th, 1876, when a deputation of army officers, medical advisers and ministers virtually forced him to approve the plan to have Otto gazetted from the Army and certified

---

* Ludwig's secret militia   ** Elisabeth's elder brother Ludwig.

insane. In all this time, Otto had clung to his old life with intermittent spells of incarceration, but Ludwig was told that, little by little, the periods of normality had grown fewer. He had no option but to concede. It was a tragic fate for a young man whose future had seemed so promising. Ludwig was losing an ally as much as a brother for despite his shortcomings, Otto had done his best to serve his brother and his country and was one of the few people who agreed with the King that Bavaria should never have participated in the German union. Indeed, here may lie the key to Otto's sudden mental disintegration for a number of Ludwig's enemies were delighted to have him out of the way. Having signed the necessary documents, he left immediately for Schluxen, where he remaned in an isolated hunting lodge brooding for some days with only Hornig to console him. With a fast-dwindling circle of friends, he cherished anyone even vaguely sympathetic and was lucky at least in his relationship with his secretary, Friedrich von Ziegler.

Since Ziegler was well-informed in the arts and related matters which interested the King, the daily reports became less tiresome since he could simultaneously hear news of artistic events and political developments in Munich and Vienna. He revelled in the lively and stimulating company which he was able to enjoy with the new secretary; soon he was confiding to him "There is no person on earth whom I trust as steadfastly and boundlessly as I trust you."

He forebore from writing the same to Richard Wagner who at last approached him from Bayreuth with news of the première of the *Ring* cycle which was at last ready to be performed in sequence in the new theatre. Forgetting his earlier anger and disappointment, Ludwig was thrilled and excited by the prospect of hearing in its entirety the work which had so fired his imagination and which, over the years, had placed such a strain on the Privy Purse.

The cycle was to be performed on four consecutive evenings and Wagner made it clear that he expected Ludwig to be present. As always, it was the arrogant composer who issued the Royal command but Ludwig graciously overlooked his presumption. He had waited too long for this moment to allow anything to spoil it and wrote at once to the once Great Friend, "I am writing this letter on the top of a mountain surrounded by the aether in God's open, noble nature where I feel at home, far from the hated everyday world which has so revolted me that I feel eternally disconnected from it. First of all, a thousand thanks from a stirred soul for your wonderful letter which filled me with blissful pleasure and, if this was possible, with the enthusiasm which diffuses through your unrivalled person, even more inflamed me; how delighted I am over the sublime, heavenly pleasure-laden days in

August! I have just read Porges' extremely interesting paragraph about
the rehearsals of *Der Ring des Nibelungen* which held me spellbound.
I don't believe there is another writer who could grasp the spirit of your
immortal works, and have so fundamental an understanding as Porges
and Schure. In Bayreuth I will give myself up entirely to the pleasures
of the festival performances. Oh, how glad I am, after so long a parting,
to see you again at last, dearly beloved, truly esteemed friend. But I
want to avoid anything which entails a public ovation. I hope to be
spared dinners and audiences, visits of strangers - I hate everything like
this with all the power of my soul. I come in order to refresh my spirit
and heart, not in order to offer myself up as an ovational sacrifice to
inquisitive gapers."

Despite this adamant request, he knew perfectly well that, when he
arrived in Bayreuth, he would still find thousands waiting to see him as
well as Wagner's controversial music drama, since everyone in Bavaria
knew of his reverence for the composer's work, and the thought of
being confronted by so many of his subjects at once filled him with real
horror. His dislike of crowds had by this time become so intense that
he was thinking of retiring completely to some totally alien place, and
while to some extent one can sympathise with the Ministers who rightly
considered that he was hopeless as a ruler, despite his great enjoyment
and appreciation of being one, their attitude towards him had certainly
contributed to his growing misanthropy.

With a view to finding an even more remote retreat he had already
despatched Franz von Loher, the Court archivist, to various parts of
Europe to look for some suitable place, just as Elisabeth of Austria had
done some years before when a domestic crisis had driven her to take
refuge on Corfu. Predictably, when it came to actually laying aside the
crown he could not bring himself to do it. His immediate heir was Otto,
who was now effectively disbarred from ruling; the next in line was their
uncle Luitpold and knowing him to be blatantly pro-Prussian, Ludwig
certainly did not want the crown to pass to him during his own lifetime.
He had no option but to remain on the Throne and take solace where
he could find it. Happily there was always the work of Wagner.

Their meeting after seven years was almost as dramatic as the work
shortly to be performed. In order to avoid the dreaded confrontation
with the public, the Royal train came to a half in the middle of a field
at Rollwenzel, just outside Bayreuth, where he had arranged a rendezvous with Wagner. A carriage was then to take the King to the
Eremitage, the Royal residence at Bayreuth where he had stayed only
once before in his childhood.

Pale and nervous, Ludwig alighted from the train, shattered to find
the squat figure of an old man tottering unsteadily towards him. Burnt

out by too much living, Wagner showed every year of his age and Ludwig found that the most powerful and dominant figure in his life had dwindled to little more than a benevolent gnome.

What did Ludwig think when he saw the master? And what did Wagner think of him? Seven years is a long time and the shock on both sides must have been considerable. Ludwig's unearthly good looks which Wagner had praised over-effusively and with more sycophancy than he would care to admit, were now only a memory. The King was bloated and unhealthy looking, a haggard and suspicious man with a ponderous tread and an unhappy mien which had become his trademark. Nevertheless, their reunion was a moving experience for both of these highly emotional men and we can well imagine that the first embarrassed silence was soon followed by cascades of the stimulating conversation which had so thrilled the young Ludwig. In this respect at least, Wagner would not have disappointed him.

The King spent the ensuing days joyfully attending the final rehearsals for *Der Ring des Nibelungen*. Having learned a bitter lesson from the past he now made no attempt to interfere with Wagner's vision of the production but was content to sit watching and listening, completely absorbed and happy for the first time in months. Despite his intense enjoyment he could not bring himself to remain in Bayreuth for the first public performances of the *Ring* cycle.

Anxious to maintain his renewed good relations with Wagner, however, he afterwards wrote to his old friend, "It is impossible for me to describe to you the impressions I drew from my visit to the sublime State Festival at Bayreuth which surpassed all bounds, and the happy reunion with you, noble friend. I came with high expectations and, at the same time, slight apprehensions; these high expectations were exceeded. I was so deeply moved that I might well have appeared taciturn. Oh, please understand that I was stirred to my deepest soul, that the crust of ice which had begun to form around my heart and soul because of so many unhappy experiences has melted in your victorious light!"

He ended his eulogy, "Oh, fortunate century that saw such a spirit in its midst! How ensuing generations will envy the precious good fortune and happiness of being your contemporary. Oh, how proud I am to have your friendship, especially now, immediately after such an indescribably ecstatic experience. I swear to you that I will make possible for you three series of the production. I have a burning desire, like the feeling of searing thirst, to experience once more the wonderful drama and to bury myself enthusiastically once more in the fervour of those stirring sounds! I beg you to have me cordoned off with a screen from all the Princes and the nobility who will certainly be attending and

please arrange for the Gendarmes to stop anyone who tries to come
near me in the interval."

Having once heard the entire *Ring* cycle, Ludwig became obsessed
by it and a few weeks later even the prospect of appearing in public
again in a crowded and fully-lit auditorium could not deter him from
hearing it again. He arrived at Bayreuth in time for the third and final
presentation on August 27th and his pleasure was crowned by an
unexpected bonus. In his curtain speech Wagner most uncharacteris-
tically acknowledged his indebtedness to King Ludwig, publicly prais-
ing the "co-creator" of this and other works. The tribute was long
overdue but however belated, his words meant a great deal to the King
who returned to Hohenschwangau in an even greater state of euphoria.

The weeks crept by and Ziegler was growing impatient because
Ludwig still showed no signs of returning to Munich for the Winter. He
relented only when the secretary reminded him that, if he did not return
to his duties he would also miss the theatre season. When he did make
up his mind, he threw Ziegler into disarray by announcing out of the
blue that they would go "tomorrow". Ziegler did not dare to protest
at the short notice in case Ludwig changed his mind again. He hated
Munich so much that he would use any pretext to avoid going there and
was quite capable of changing his mind when they were actually en
route and ordering the carriage to reverse. The habitual stay in Hohenschwangau had already been officially extended by a month so that
he could remain longer in his beloved mountains. When he was at last
persuaded to return to the capital he would remain in his apartments
complaining of feeling ill and discoursing at length on the "burden of
life" to anyone who would listen.

In September Ludwig learned that all was not well in Bayreuth. The
festival which had inspired him and delighted the afficionados had won
considerable acclaim from the few who understood it but had been a
commercial disaster. Foundering once more in a sea of debts, Wagner
again implored Ludwig for help but this time the King had none to give
and informed the composer forthwith that he was also in a state of
pecuniary embarrassment. Wagner disbelieved him; he was determined that the King would settle his debts somehow, reasoning that
since Ludwig had not only had the pleasure of seeing *Der Ring des
Nibelungen* performed in its entirety as promised years before but had
also received long-overdue public recognition of his part in making the
production possible, he was committed to the privilege of paying all
over again for the pleasure. The composer wrote again, telling the King
that he was reduced to selling Wahnfried, his sumptuous new home in
Bayreuth, in order to accommodate his creditors and then proposed

to tour the United States as a further means of raising capital to avert the inevitable financial disaster.

But Wagner did not know Ludwig any better now than he had in 1865 when he had so cleverly given his Great Friend his marching orders for, unimpressed by Wagner's display of bathos, Ludwig responded, perhaps tongue-in-cheek, "In that obstinate American soil your roses cannot prosper, there where Mammon is lord of selfishness and lovelessness."

The moment he realised that Ludwig did not propose to accommodate him, Wagner predictably dropped his former patron like a hot brick and receded into the background ostensibly to work on *Parsifal* but in fact to approach Wilhelm of Prussia for patronage. *Parsifal*, which was to be Wagner's last work, had been commenced simultaneously with *Lohengrin* many years before but had been constantly cast aside in favour of other projects. Ludwig was certainly not ignorant of the reason for Wagner's renewed silence and, disappointed, acknowledged that the passage of time had not changed the composer's fundamentally greedy, mendacious and selfish nature.

Adding to his misery, Otto had forgotten his birthday for the first time. He regarded this as a sure sign that his brother's mind had gone completely since family birthdays, even in this curiously disunited family, had always been occasions for special celebration. From Berg, Ludwig wrote to Baroness Leonrod, "Poor Otto! For a long time I have had no news from him personally about his health; he seems to suffer more than we all imagined. He needs a better doctor very urgently. Brattler - as I have learned from Branco - is rather careless."

It was a gloomy year made gloomier by the final and perhaps heaviest blow of all: the assertion by his staff that his personal fortune had dwindled to the extent where the building projects had come almost to a half and he despaired of seeing the completion of either Herrenwörth or Neuschwanstein. Unpleasant rumours were being whispered throughout Europe and even the usually discreet members of the banking fraternity had begun to whisper about the pecuniary difficulties of the King of Bavaria.

In September Hohenlohe, the German Ambassador in Paris, had noted in his diary that the Parisian banker, Erlanger, who had apparently just left him, had said that the "rumour of the King of Bavaria's monetary diufficulties was a fabrication. If the King were in the need of money, he would apply to his [Erlanger's] father, who would never refuse him 500 thousand Florins." He dismissed as equally groundless the assertion that a syndicate had been formed to raise money for the King. But the rumours persisted and inevitably they began to reach Ludwig's own court. It was not easy for the King's proud spirit to bear reports of the gossip, faithfully transmitted by his body servants, and he spent the whole dismal Christmas alone worrying about the crushing debts which, despite the loud denials, his staff assured him were far from non-existent.

It was all too much for him. Unable to bear his loneliness any longer, he sought solace in the usual quarter and then, deeply repentant, turned to his secret diary for the first time in four years. On January 21st, 1877, consumed with guilt at the enormity of the crime he had committed against the crown, against himself and against his God, he sought expiation in the tormented confession: "In the King's name I swear today – the 21st January of terrible memory, the anniversary of the assassination of the King of France and Navarre, Louis XVI by name, that what took place yesterday was for the last time forever; atoned for by the Royal blood (The Holy Grail). Absolutely the last time under penalty of ceasing to be King. Sworn the 2lst January 1877 at Hohenschwangau (four years after the year so costly to so many rights.)"

Determined to stick to his resolve, he made yet another "fresh start" and buried his torment under what was now only an ephemeral pleasure: the theatre. He invited his old friend, the actor-manager Ernst Possart, to return to Munich to take part in some guest appearances. Possart was rewarded with a generous fee, a ring and cufflinks, a beautiful Renaissance goblet and other trinkets. Describing these gifts to a friend, Possart said that he was "overwhelmed" by the King's expressions of gratitude but unlike so many of Ludwig's theatrical guests, he was not motivated by avarice. He liked and respected the King and would have been happy to perform without any return at all, monetary or otherwise, regarding it as a great honour to serve the Monarch whose interest and knowledge in the arts was so profound. Much as Ludwig enjoyed Possart's acting, all the plays in the world could not blot out the fact that he was growing sere and withered with loneliness. Shrinking from the outside world, he realised finally that his life was to remain irrevocably empty and unfulfilled.

When Elisabeth arrived at Feldafing, near Berg, for her annual visit, his misery quickly changed to joy. Richard Hornig seemed less enchanted, possibly because he feared the deep depression which would inevitably follow her departure. To Ziegler he wrote on July 19th, 1877, "If he sticks to his intention, the King will write tomorrow to the Empress at Feldafing to ask her to permit him to see her once more on the 23rd or 24th, and then go for a walk alone with her on the Roseninsel and make a round trip of the lake by steamer. The King is longing for the Empress. What do you say to this? It is to be hoped that the

Empress will not allow him to come. Anyway, the letter is not yet written and his longing may cease."

But of course, Ludwig's longing did not cease and Elisabeth appears to have shared his sentiments for eventually it was she who sought him out rather than *vice versa* and they spent many happy hours together at Berg and in the solitude of the Roseninsel. Inevitably, Elisabeth's own restless spirit ultimately got the better of her and she returned to Gödöllö.

Having tasted perfect companionship, Ludwig began once more to shun the prosaic, refusing even to see his mother. Her quest for solace in the Catholic faith had apparently been a disappointment and seemingly nothing could erase the guilt which both her sons evidently inspired in her. Marie would now spend hours at Fürstenried waiting in vain to be admitted; when she appealed to her elder son to ensure that she saw Otto, Ludwig prudently replied that he thought such a visit "unlikely" as his brother was "said to be very excitable." Fed with all kinds of lurid reports concerning him, Ludwig could no longer bring himself to visit Otto personally and if his illness was induced by the same intriguers who eventually cost Ludwig his throne, then by his atttitude towards Otto, Ludwig innocently played directly into their hands.

He spent his birthday in the exotically appointed hunting lodge at Schachen, calling on the peasants and grooms who were now virtually his only companions to share his sad but harmless pretence that he was an oriental potentate who did not suffer the cares of Bavarian Kingship, unconsumed by loneliness and free of financial worry. If the men on whom he pressed unfamiliar dishes and costumes did not appreciate the entertainment and hospitality, they at least appreciated its purpose, namely, to please the beloved *Kini*.

His misanthropy, although not directed towards these simple people, nevertheless continued to accelerate. He scarcely went out in daylight now but preferred to make his carriage or sleigh excursions at night and while these nocturnal outings irritated his prosaic Ministerium, the sight of the proud and handsome man gliding through the night in his ornate equipages and depending upon the season, wrapped in furs and accompanied by liveried outriders bearing torches made an indelible impression on the romantically minded peasants who loved not only the colourful spectacle but also the man who gave it to them.

Accustomed to the eccentricities of the Wittelsbachs, they considered him to be no worse than the horse-mad Elisabeth or her zither-playing, poetry-writing father, Duke Max, who wore peasant costume and spent his time among the lower echelons of society. To these simple people Ludwig was a magical being from another world, an heroic figure whom they could love and admire and remember. More importantly, they knew that he reciprocated that love and regard.

Barred from any further large building projects, Ludwig tried to forget his unhappiness by building in the woods near Linderhof a hermit's hut "leaning on a rock like that of Gurnemanz" (in *Parsifal*) as he described it to Wagner. Ludwig was fascinated by Wagner's interpretation of the old legends and, indeed, by the symbolism behind them, his only dissention being the composer's blatant and ugly anti-semitism of which he deeply disapproved and about which they had frequently argued bitterly.

Towards the end of the year the long-awaited libretto of *Parsifal* arrived. Ludwig read it avidly and became imbued immediately in its mystic aura. Eager to identify with the unsullied Knight of the Grail, he re-read Wolfram von Eschenbach's version of the legend, recalling from memory whole passages of the work which he had known and loved since his childhood. It was the same old story: what he sought was oblivion from his life as King Ludwig by taking on the mantle of another person. But now there was no Friedrich, no Heinrich or Lohengrin. Now there was only Parsifal.

By this time he found it impossible to relate to his Cabinet and staff on an everyday level just as they found dealing with him increasingly difficult; he also felt totally remote from the sophisticated burghers with whom he had no such affinity as with his peasants. In an unworthy attempt to regain a little of his lost Wittelsbach honour he began for a while to emulate his Bourbon heroes by showing less consideration than that to which they had been long accustomed towards some of his more insolent staff who thought they could do as they pleased without fear of rebuke or dismissal in a court where law and order had broken down. The man who frequently offered sweets to lackeys or peeled an orange for some less exalted companion now became excessively auto-cratic, meting out punishments (albeit never severe and in fact rarely carried out) for disobedience or insubordination which, in the light of later events, were not unjustified. One member of his staff was said to have been ordered to wear a mask in the presence of the King who said that he could no longer bear the sight of the man's stupid face. In the main, these tales were spread by servants who were already in the pay of Max Holnstein and Ludwig's small transgressions and eccentricities were magnified a hundredfold before they reached the taverns of Munich.

Yearning for affection, Ludwig debased himself occasionally with young *Chevauxlègers*, resorting afterwards to self-castigation in the diary as for example when he wrote "Terribly near to the brink of a complete fall, night of the 12–13th September, 1877; *damned* by the *blinding apparition* which *oppresses* our *senses.*"

CHAPTER TWELVE

JOSEF KAINZ

BY the late 1870s Ludwig had virtually lost contact with the outside world although he remained more closely informed both on domestic and foreign matters than people supposed. Owing to his aversion to being stared at he now avoided the public theatre together and his enforced economies had greatly curtailed his separate performances. Obsessed still with the romantic dream of finding some solitary haven abroad he sent his new secretary, Bürkel, who had recently replaced Ziegler, to seek such a place. Bürkel was no more successful than Loher, probably because he did not look very hard. Some of Ludwig's more discerning staff had at last discovered that when he had taken chloralhydrate he was inclined to say things he did not mean, on which basis his orders were not always carried out.

During his term of office Ziegler had become very fond of the King who on his side had a warm regard for him. On May 10th, 1879, the King wrote affectionately to him, "Today, on (St.) Friedrich's Day, your name day which will be forever be symbolically entwined, my heart has need to beat for you." It was a *cri de coeur* from a desperately lonely man. Ziegler, exhausted by his efforts to look after the demanding Ludwig, at last resigned on health grounds. Since the abortive attempt on Count Bismarck's life by a man called Küllmann at the time of the 1874 troop review and, indeed, the painful discovery that he himself had many enemies among his political and religious adversaries, Ludwig had become extremely nervous and was constantly haunted by fears of assassination. To Bürkel he had written some time earlier, "I am sending you herewith an *Augsburger Zeitung* in which I have underlined an article which is discussed an organisation which exists in Russia for the protection of the Tzar. That so necessary "coalition" about whose establishment I have indicated to you both verbally and in writing, should be established similarly to the article in which such an institution is the theme, but to a different end, not so much for personal protection as for the combating of evil elements which everywhere are unfortunately very cleverly organising a network which extends through the country, is very necessary."

Ludwig's feelings on the subject became so heated that Bürkel was eventually forced to tender his resignation as his own principles would not allow him to accept an organisation of the type which he considered to be detrimental to the well-being of Bavaria. In the event, Ludwig's fears were later to prove justified. At every conference for many weeks, the subject of the coalition was raised, discussed and finally put discreetly to one side by Bürkel until eventually, Ludwig's rages became too much for him. Ziegler had also quarrelled with the King on the same subject and while he was certainly a sick man, the seal on his resignation was certainly placed there following one of these arguments. Ludwig had rashly accepted it although he was soon to regret having done so for with Ziegler's departure he was again bereft of a companion on a similar intellectual plane to his own. The reason why he was forced to match his mentality to that of the grooms and lackeys with whom he spent most of his time was not due to any mental failing on his part but because they were unable to rise to his level. The result was a chaotic existence in which the court as such no longer existed except when the efficient Hornig was available to restore order. Still a friend and adviser but obviously no longer the romantic companion of 1867, Hornig spent much of his time negotiating loans and bravely manipulating the Civil List in order to stretch the King's resources to the utmost. Forgotten was "Richard of my Heart", the man whose charm and wit had made no small contribution to Ludwig's decision to jilt Sophie.

Once a week, the King was in the habit of spending the day at Seeleiten where Richard Hornig and his family afforded him a warm welcome. He was fond of Hornig's children and invariably arrived with an armful of presents. After a meal and a discussion on Hornig's efforts to find the finance for the building programme, he and his Stallmeister would stroll by the lakeside and afterwards sit smoking in the garden. In spite of their disagreements the two men were still on good terms and the King doubtless found a sympathetic listener in Hornig who was aware of the root causes of most of Ludwig's troubles, namely his financial difficulties and the latent homosexuality which he tried so hard to suppress. The time spent with the Hornigs was only a fleeting pleasure, and he invariably returned to Berg with an even more pronounced feeling of loneliness.

Ludwig's prolonged absences from Munich continued to cause so much comment that he was again urged strongly by a deputation to show himself in the capital. After a lapse of some years, he agreed in April to officiate at the Festival of St.George, but apart from the elaborate ceremony itself, which had a strong appeal for him, it was an agonising ordeal for him to appear before so many people, especially since he deeply distrusted an assembled crowd. Immediately the ceremony was over he fled to the mountains and stayed there until he heard news of Elisabeth's arrival in Bavaria. His outlook brightened immediately as he set out to meet her, but when she saw his pitiable condition Elisabeth was even more shocked and worried than before. Whether they were of a spiritual or a physical nature, Elisabeth's relationships with Julius Andrássy, with Captain Middleton or a young man with whom she correspondend for years under the pseudonym of "Domino" had never replaced her profound feeling for Ludwig and she was as deeply upset by his depressed state of mind as by his seriously reduced physical appearance. When she left the family home at Possenhofen, she sadly expressed her fears as to their next meeting.

Although there is no doubt that Elisabeth was deeply attached to Ludwig, she seemed constantly impelled to run away again whenever they met, as if, having found him after a long search, she discovered that she was, after all, a little afraid of him. It is possible that she thought too much of those who might be hurt should she become too openly involved with him. Whatever her reason, it was certainly not the suspicion that the King might not be normal or, indeed, that her affection for him had died for at the end she was his only remaining intimate friend. Elisabeth was to protest his sanity to the last and even beyond his death until her own end at an assassin's hand in 1898.

Scarcely recognisable as the beautiful boy who had so captivated his people in 1864 when he could not avoid going to Munich in 1864, Ludwig would now take a solitary walk in the Hofgarten or even openly in the streets in the vicinity of the Residenz, aware tht he could go unrecognised and unmolested. Noticeably, on these occasions he had no fear of being assassinated which would indicate that his suspicions lay only with those inside the Residenz; it further indicates that his insistence that such a plot existed was not the product of a sick mind or the anxiety would have remained with him when he left the Residenz. When he walked in the mountains and in the Bavarian countryside and forests, he was always instantly recognised and greeted adoringly by any peasant or woodman but he now appeared so rarely in his capital that, without the trappings of royalty he received no more than the occasional curious glance.

While he was prepared to promenade openly in the capital, he refused adamantly to make an official appearance on the occasion of the 700th anniversary of Wittelsbach rule, shrugging off Bürkel's efforts to persuade him: "But what would happen if I didn't go? There wouldn't be a revolution!" And of course it was true that his absence made little difference to the ceremony and festivities themselves but the people were naturally critical and disappointed when he failed to appear. While there was no revolution, there was a further distinct wane in the King's popularity in the capital, if not in the countryside.

At last the long-promised *Parsifal* was pronounced ready for pro-duction and, filled with desire to hear the related earlier work *Lohen-grin* once more, Ludwig invited Wagner to Munich to conduct a private performance of this and other works. He placed the entire orchestra at Wagner's disposal with the instruction that he could do anything he liked so long as he produced *Lohengrin* which, in the light all previous events, seems to have been a somewhat foolhardy offer.

During the first two months of the composer's visit, Ludwig came out of seclusion to spend some time with him, but one glance at the ageing Wagner must have warned him that it might well be their last meeting. The composer was invited to dine with the King in his Wintergarden and, as he afterwards noted in his diary, they "enjoyed intimate precious hours." It was as if Ludwig had received a blood transfusion. The first diary entry had announced "News! Richard Wagner here. Considered special things for Schloss Chiemsee. Was present with Richard Wagner at the performance of *Lohengrin*; very successful and beautiful. He present. With him in the apartment. Supped in the Wintergarden, a long time together (...) In the afternoon on the 12th heard the miraculous and glorious prelude to *Parsifal* conducted by the creator himself. Profoundly magnificent. Also the prelude to *Lohengrin*."

Nevertheless, the reunion as a whole was by no means as idyllic as the diary entry would suggest and the afternoon referred to was actually something of a disaster. Commanded specifically to give Ludwig the opportunity to hear the prelude to the new opera for the first time in its orchestrated form, as customary, the audience would consist of the favoured few including the now eminently respectable Cosima and the artist Lenbach. The guests as usual were to sit immediately beneath the King so that host and guests would not actually see each other. Ludwig had agreed to appear in the Royal box when the bell sounded but while Wagner waited on the rostrum, baton in hand, the box remained empty and the furious composer was obliged to wait for fifteen minutes, wondering if the King had forgotten him. He did his best to hide his humiliation but his Royal patron had made it apparent to all that his "boy", as Wagner had once indecorously referred to his Sovereign, was no longer his slave. In recent years he had become increasingly aware of Ludwig's declining amiability towards him, but to be kept waiting in public for all the world to see how little the King thought of him could only be regarded as a direct affront. When Ludwig did appear it was with a noticeable lack of haste and he further irritated the composer by taking longer than usual to settle himself before finally giving the signal for the concert to begin.

Wagner nevertheless conducted the haunting prelude to *Parsifal* as only he could and Ludwig was enraptured but it was not enough: he wanted to hear also the prelude to *Lohengrin* which was not on the programme. This was too much for Wagner. Furious that anyone could be so musically insensitive as to want two such totally different pieces of music to be played one after the other, he refused to commit the sacrilege himself and handing his baton to the director, stormed out of the auditorium. Unmoved, Ludwig sent a message saying that if he cared to present himself at the Residenz for an audience or for their previously arranged visit to the theatre, he would be graciously received. In the face of such regal courtesy Wagner could only swallow his pride and comply. Two days later they enjoyed a performance of Verdi's *Aida* together and the rift, at least on the surface, was repaired.

In the long term, Wagner's visit brought home to Ludwig how much he missed the company of intellectuals. In particular, he longed for the erudite company of Friedrich von Ziegler. The sophisticated, part-time poet's services as a cabinet secretary had been so invaluable that Ludwig had often sent a lackey to fetch him at dead of night after the poor man had staggered home exhausted, having already spent a long day at the King's beck and call. Flattering as it was, Ziegler was so insensed by Ludwig's habit that he instructed the lackeys that next time this happened, they were to remain in their quarters for a reasonable time before reporting back to the King that they were "Not able to enter the Herr Hofrat's house because of the attentions of a ferocious dog." Although Ludwig was never so naïve as to believe this, he is said to have taken the hint. Whether or not it is true, this anecdote has a curiously similar ring to Festetics' story concerning Elisabeth of Austria.

Notwithstanding his earlier troubles, Ziegler was now reinstated but the earlier warmth between the two men had gone, eroded by bitter quarrels over money and government policy in the past. Possibly at the same time, Ziegler did not want to be scorched by the flames of Ludwig's love or perhaps he feared another breakdown in health if he worked too closely with the King for, although he was a kind and generous man, to work for him was no sinecure and he expected 24 hour attention from his staff at all levels. While Ziegler worked willingly for the demanding and unpredictable King, their discussions now were limited to professional matters. Ludwig, who had been expecting a wealth of intellectual conversation to emerge from Ziegler's reinstatement, was sorely disappointed.

The new production of *Lohengrin* and the fragments of *Parsifal* which Ludwig had heard during Wagner's guest appearance had rea-wakened his appetite for music and drama and at the end of April, he heard a revival of *Tristan und Isolde*, describing it in his diary as "imperishably beloved and glorious; it sounds so old and yet so new, like the song of the birds in May." Immersed in Wagner's genius he was able to recapture if only briefly the spiritual comfort of something he had found lacking for so long. Sadly, his buoyancy did not last and he soon sank back into his old apathetic lifestyle, travelling constantly to one or other of his alpine retreats but having little contact with the outside world. He spent a great deal of time at Hohenschwangau, overjoyed to watch the rise of his new castle which, when completed, was to provide a breathtaking spectacle from every angle. Perched high on its rock, it could be seen for several miles. The outer splendour was more than equalled by the glories within or at least, in accordance with Ludwig's idea of matchless splendour. With his equally well-beloved Linderhof already completed, he also had other plans in mind, yet still he was tormented by a sense of unfulfilment.

As if aware of his problem, the actor-manager, Ernst Possart, who was as shocked and upset by Ludwig's unhappy looks and distraught behaviour as everyone else who loved him, tried his best to help. He sent the King a photograph of Joef Kainz, a young actor whom he had recently engaged, in the hope that the King might show a spark of interest in him, thus satisfying both the King's longing for a new and stimulating companion and the young man's ambition to make his way in the world.

The 23 year old Kainz, known to his family as "Seppel", was of Hungarian extraction, born in Wieselburg on January 2nd, 1858. He had already made a promising start in the theatre in Vienna, and had newly arrived with a string of solid classical parts behind him and the glint of ambition in his eyes. He was of slight build and somewhat unprepossessing appearance with huge, heavy-lidded eyes and a pointed elfin chin. Kainz was one of those actors who get into the skin of their role but have very little personality of their own. He had a high opinion of his own ability and, indeed, a serious attitude towards his art. Shortly after his arrival in Munich,* he wrote home to his mother in the Viennese suburb of Klosterneuburg, "The Munich people have been performing without a juvenile lead for two years but the theatre has held up very well. Could they have held out any longer? Wasn't I right? As Romeo I had five curtain calls, and the role is not exactly the most thankful one for a juvenile, and is the most difficult of all since it needs much study, much understanding; it requires tragic strength and the whispering tone of the most enamoured lover, and then again the extrovert humour of the *bonvivant* and added to that the routine delicacy and elegance in the approach and the movements, and finally the ability to be able to fence elegantly and be somewhat athletic as he has two duels and spends the entire evening jumping over garden walls and balconies. Last but not least, Juliet, whose part is much lighter and less thankless, takes away from him all the best entrances and exits. On top of that I have to learn the part in seven days with three days of rehearsal, and then perform in front of a foreign audience ..."

* September 11th. 1880

Although Kainz was scarcely Ludwig's idea of a classical actor, he was anxious to see what Possart's protegé could do and commanded Baron von Perfall, the theatre intendant in Munich to mount one of the contemporary Victor Hugo's plays, *Marion de Lorme*, casting the newcomer in the role of Didier. In his wisdom, Possart was perfectly well aware that Lohengrin was being temporarily transformed into the Marquis de Saverny and that, while another man would play the part on stage, Ludwig would be watching a facsimile of himself in a close relationship with the Didier. It was unhealthy but it was harmless. Possart's prime consideration was to please the lonely King who had done so much for him in the past and Perfall wanted only a successful production.

In the event, Ludwig was so delighted both with the play and with Didier/Kainz that he commanded another performance after which he sent Kainz a valuable ring. The gift was accompanied by an invitation to a private performance of another play. Predictably, the King noted in his diary, "Didier deep impression." His spring awakening had come.

Each May, as if seeking to find himself, Ludwig would embark upon some new friendship and occasionally, May had brought him a friend of enduring strength such as he had found in Richard Hornig. At the time of his discovery of Kainz, the little actor was merely one of many diversions and the gifts no more splendid than those received and treasured by many artistes whom Ludwig held in esteem. Kainz, a raw newcomer to Ludwig's strange little court, did not realise that his token was the customary reward for a worthy artistic performance and his little head swelled accordingly. Possart, who had no wish to see his star fall to earth before it had reached its zenith, advised him that if he wanted to remain in Royal favour, he should write immediately to thank the King; the result was a ridiculously fulsome and sycophantic missive which was excessive even in the 19th century when such effusion was the norm: "Most gracious, most powerful King! Most gracious King and Master! In profound humility I take the liberty of laying at Your Most Gracious Majesty's feet my profound thanks for the precious ring which Your Most Gracious Majesty did me the honour of sending me. Your Most Gracious Majesty may be convinced that I shall do my best to prove worthy of the gift which Your Most Gracious Majesty has honoured me and that I shall always try to earn Your Majesty's satisfaction. Dying in the profoundest humility, Your Most Exalted Majesty's most humble and faithfully obedient servant, Josef Kainz, Königl. Bayr. Schauspieler."

If Kainz' prose was not all it might have been, his acting at least was of a high standard and he was reputed to have a particularly pleasing stage voice. The private performance which he had been invited to watch was *La Marquise de Pompadour* with Frau Levinsky. Kainz could hardly contain his nervous excitement but if he had expected to be presented to his Royal admirer he was disappointed for Ludwig remained inaccessible and, indeed, invisible, in the royal box while Kainz was seated with the other guests in the stalls beneath him. As a compensation, Ludwig sent him some opera glasses, secure in the knowledge that they would not be turned inquisitively upon himself.

So intrigued was Ludwig by the actor's portrayal of Didier that a few days later he commanded a repeat performance of Hugo's drama in the Royal Court Theatre instead of *Die Meistersinger von Nürnberg* as originally scheduled. The gossips were not slow in speculating as to whether the railwayman's son had ousted Wagner who had been publicly snubbed by the King during his last visit to Munich. This juicy piece of gossip, which already enjoyed wide circulation, was manna to the scandalmongers but it was a little premature. The King had still not actually met the young man. In any case, the change of programme was of no particular significance since the King often changed his mind at the last moment. In fact, despite his euphoric praise at its première, *Die Meistersinger* had never had the same mystic appeal for him as Wagner's other works.

Ludwig enjoyed the season of 1881 enormously but twenty Didiers could not have made him truly happy. His castles were allegedly still draining his financial resources and the increasing debts outlined by his advisers were driving him to despair. The unfavourable attitude of the people towards his building projects upset him and he was piqued by reports of the strange rumours which circulated concerning the three castles. The chief difficulty was that, owing to their isolated locations, few had even seen them except the workmen who were employed on their construction and the privileged minority who were invited to inspect them. The bitter realisation that the Munich burghers hated him more than ever pushed him back into his old melancholy and inevitably, his thoughts turned again towards abdication. The gossips were delighted, quickly attributing these disturbing ideas to the King's love for little Kainz and indeed, at a much later date, Ludwig himself was not above saying as much when, for his own purposes, he wanted to flatter the actor, just as he had used the same ruse to flatter Wagner, but like so many of his exotic compliments, they were merely words.

His notions of abdication never lasted for long and when he made threat to put aside the crown to such lowly beings as artistes, we can be sure that he never seriously considered such a step. If Ludwig had wanted to quit the Throne it would have been on the grounds that he had failed in his task, his financial inadequacy, the feeling that he had failed in his task or that the Munich townspeople no longer loved him. It would certainly never have been for the sake of a young commoner of lowly birth whom he had not, at that point, even met personally. There is some basis in the idea that he occasionally "cried wolf" although interestingly, it was usually for a totally different reason from the one he averred. In 1866, for example, when he had written to say that the was "ready to abdicate or die" for Wagner, he had been at the time hard-pressed by his cabinet over his refusal to involve himself in the Schleswig-Holstein question with its strong connotations of war; at the same time, they had been making his life a misery with their criticism of the amount of money he was expending on Wagner. Now, in 1881, he was still lavishing every penny on his current interest - not a human being this time but on his building programme. Sixteen years after Wagner had enjoyed his heyday in Royal favour, Ludwig's Ministers were still complaining about his expenditure – if anything, their complaints were louder than those of his alleged creditors.

Although he was aware of the gossip, Ludwig was too proud to deny the charge that his threat to abdicate was over a nondescript little Hungarian. That Kainz himself believed he had turned the King's head is certain: in any event, the King had turned his especially when, as a reward for his performance he received another valuable gift in the form of a golden watch fob in the shape of a swan on a chain. Intoxicated, he wrote to Ludwig "Great psychic emotions make a man speechless. In vain he wrestles with words in order to give some shape to the feelings in his head – but does not find them. And when at last he has found the words and imagines that the feelings of his heart are expressed in sound, they appear cold, stiff and desecrated. 'The word kills', it says in the Bible. And I feel today as I take up my pen in order to lay before Your Most Gracious Majesty my very humble thanks for the most gracious rounds of applause which Your Majesty did me the favour of giving me last night – also for the beautifully made watch covered with brilliants and the picture representing poesie. Joy, happiness and enchantment threaten to burst my bosom. Oh, if only I could do a great deed in order to give Your Most Gracious Majesty a proof of how profoundly I feel I am penetrated by the feelings of gratitude towards Your Most Gracious Majesty, oh, I could die for Your Majesty!"

Whatever, in his vanity, Kainz may have imagined the King felt for him, his protestations were by no means mutual. Ludwig's interest in the young man was purely that of an ardent theatregoer who saw personified in Kainz a fictitious character whom, owing to the unpleasant circumstances surrounding his own life, Ludwig preferred for the moment to look upon as real. We all have our fantasies but Ludwig's crime was to let the world know of them.

As if seeking comfort in an existence more acceptable than his own, Ludwig became so obsessed with *Marion de Lorme* that he wanted to see it performed over and over again. But the pull of the mountains was too strong and by the end of the following week he was back at Linderhof. Seeing no reason why he should not enjoy the best of both worlds he invited Kainz to appear at Linderhof. Encouraged by the actor's reaction to the news that he had been selected to act in the new production of *Hernani*, in which he promised "to fulfil the task with the greatest love and diligence in order that Your Gracious Majesty may be pleased with my representation of that magnificent part" he thought that their meeting would be portentious. After an adventurous journey Kainz duly appeared hours late, tired, terrified by the ordeal before him and overwhelmed by his opulent surroundings. The combination of poor offstage deportment and ill fitting clothes did nothing for him and the sceptical Bürkel, whose job it was to see that he did as the King asked, must have wondered what Ludwig saw in him.

The Grotto where the King awaited him was reached by means of a path leading from one of the tree lined avenues in the Schlosspark. This manmade piece of ingenuity in cement and wire was modelled faithfully on the famous Blue Grotto on Capri and Ludwig loved it dearly. Fascinated also by lighting effects he satisfied another whim by having in the grotto a changing display of diffused light ranging from purple, red, pink and blue. On the waters of an artificial lake floated a small, shell-shaped canoe drawn by the inevitable artificial swan inside which a lackey was obliged to paddle furiously in order to make the vessel move.

To complete the effect, there was a flock of real swans who looked constantly for the bread which Ludwig always carried in his pocket. He never lost his reverence for these graceful creatures which remained to him the symbol of purity. As a backdrop to the whole of this fantastic place was a huge, brilliantly painted mural depicting the Venusberg from *Tannhäuser*. It was Ludwig's custom to take his evening meal in this solitary place, seated at a small table in the gallery where he could be unseen and uninterrupted in his thoughts. It was here also that Baron von Varicourt had so far forgotten himself as to nod off while the King was talking to him.

In such surroundings Kainz' offstage persona paled into insignificance and when he replied to Ludwig's questions his voice was considerably higher in pitch than usual. He had scarcely embarked upon his ordeal when Ludwig, appalled, called out to his secretary that the actor had his leave to withdraw. Fortunately for Kainz, the kindly Bürkel understood his problem and spoke up for him, suggesting that he might be given another chance. Carefully primed, Kainz gave a better account of himself the following evening; "Act, man, act!" Bürkel told him. When the young man began to declaim his part from *Marion de Lorme*, Ludwig responded with the lines of the Comte de Saverny. When he was ordered to recite from Schiller, Shakespeare and Goethe as well as the part he had just been given in *Hernani,* he regained his confidence and performed so well that the delighted King kept him at his recitations in the grotto for most of the night.

Although he expected his guest to work hard, Ludwig could not do enough to keep his Didier happy; he had been saved from a night of lonely insomnia and from the dreadful nightmares which tormented him when he did sleep. He escorted Kainz personally on a tour of Schloss Linderhof and the surrounding parkland and, under the gaze of the exotic, enamelled peacocks in the Turkish kiosk, the overawed railwayman's son was plied with coffee and sweets until his brain was addled and his head swelled to twice its normal size. Very full of himself, he wrote to his mother on June 3rd, 1881, "...I am to remain here for a few days and need a change of clothes: cravats, shirts, stockings and my little book. I am also required to wear a suit. Send me a jacket suit (brown) which I shall need for the return journey." Clearly, he already saw himself attaining giant importance in the the King's circle and began to behave accordingly.

Even the most modestly brought up person can accustom himself to more elevated surroundings with surprising speed, and after only a few days of this new life, Kainz relaxed under Ludwig's spellbinding charm. He soon discovered that he could converse with his Sovereign without resorting to ridiculous sycophancy and was as overawed as everyone else by Ludwig's erudition. His own efforts were rewarded by a visit to the Hundingshütte and he was taken rowing on the beautiful Plansee with its heightened colours and intoxicating aroma of pinewood. He was even taken to Hohenschwangau to see Ludwig's castles there. Spoiled and generally treated by Ludwig as an equal, he was in his element but inevitably, like so many who are given too much too soon, Kainz quickly forgot himself and grew bored and arrogant. He found it all too easy to accept presents and favours but something of a strain to reciprocate by doing what the King had sent for him to do, namely, to read and recite to him.

Ludwig, who possessed a photographic mind, already knew most of the plays and books better than the actor himself, and always savoured an opportunity to air his knowledge when Kainz misquoted or "dried" and this, of course, wounded the actor's vanity. Nevertheless, the pair were on good enough terms by this time for Ludwig to record in his diary that having climbed the Säuling* he and "... Didier went down arm in arm."

The ambitious little actor had still not quite grasped the fact that the King believed in him only as Didier and not as Josef Kainz, a very ordinary being; he was deeply flattered by the attentions bestowed upon him by the kindly Ludwig he imagined himself being raised to dizzy heights by his august patron. He had never known such luxury and opulence as he found at the castles and summer houses where the King entertained him but neither had he experienced such spartan simplicity as Ludwig himself happily endured in some of the huts and hunting boxes in the Ammerwald and Graswangtal.

Together, the ill-assorted pair covered a good deal of ground, both in mileage and in literary explorations. What had begun as a three day escape from boredom for the King and a kind of holiday for Kainz had somehow become something of a honeymoon lasting eleven days. But even basking in Royal favour as he was, the actor's time was not his own; he had a contract to honour and eventually his professional commitments as well as the now rampant gossip about his absence drew him back to Munich. The homebound mail now contained somewhat different requests: "Yesterday the King and I drank to your health and he asked me to tell you that further thanks are unnecessary. Don't tell anybody in town that I am here. Say I am in Vienna! Say the same to my colleagues. This morning I was in Oberammergau (...) I have had from the King three watches and a splendid ivory cigarette case ...". And on the night of the 5th/6th, "...The King wants to know the reason why the people are angry as you expressed in your note. Have the goodness to report in as much detail as possible about the events during my absence! But tell the truth! Who is angry? Write comprehensively about everything! Which parts are being taken? What is being said? Who is saying it? And in what manner? (...) The King has again made me some expensive gifts! Four large French lilies of brilliants! In 15 minutes we are going for a walk, then to the swan grotto..."

Kainz had at least the grace – and good sense – to write to the King after his return "The time from May 31st to June 11th was the most beautiful in my whole life and if anything could belittle the joy and all the favours which Your Most Gracious Majesty heaped upon me it is the thought that I was helped by my luck rather than my merit. I still cannot quite believe that everything happened; I feel as if I had awakened to dry, cold reality after creating a beautiful dream." This was exactly what Ludwig wanted to read but he was less pleased when Kainz could not resist telling his new patron "My colleagues received me very amiably – though I could not look into their hearts. To explain

* At Hohenschwangau.

my absence by saying that I had been in Vienna was impossible; the ladies and gentlemen knew almost more about the grotto, the Hundingshütte and all the marvels of the Linderhof than I did; they also knew about the excursion to the Plansee. I do not know who told them." But obviously his proud parents had lost no time in babbling to everyone they met of their son's good fortune. Now, he was clearly trying, somewhat ingenuously, to cover himself before the King discovered his indiscretion. The hypersensitive Ludwig would undoubtedly have spent some time ruminating on the point and quizzing Kainz as to the truth.

Despite the effusion of Kainz' letter and the apparent euphoria of Ludwig's mood, the visit, like that of Wagner, had not been entirely successful. Gauche and unaccustomed to being entertained by Royalty, the actor who had at first been too sycophantic even for Ludwig had quickly become over familiar which was far more unacceptable. He had already discovered that, when he was not playing the part of Didier, little Kainz had some very unpleasant traits. On June 16th, for example, we find the new favourite plummeting to earth with undignified speed: "I am very sorry indeed that Your Majesty has not yet forgiven me for the words I spoke on June 9th. Your Majesty shall always punish me by recalling that unhappy day," he wailed in his letter of appeasement, "If I only knew by what I had hurt Your Majesty so much." The offender was at last forgiven and, in the exhilaration of the moment, Ludwig had made all kinds of plans which were never to come to fruition. After they read *Phaeton* together on the mountainside, Ludwig had been gripped with the sudden ambition to visit Spain although the plan was quickly abandoned as "impractical"; having seen a memorable production of Schiller's *Wilhelm Tell* at the Court Theatre, he conceived instead the notion of re-tracing Tell's footsteps in Switzerland with little Kainz in tow. The actor was given no choice but was told bluntly to be ready for departure on the 27th. There was nothing Kainz could do but pen his gratitude and aver that he was "looking forward to it like a child," which was undoubtedly true. The inevitable request for fresh clothes was despatched his parents and he prepared himself for what for him would have been an event quite out of the ordinary.

There was something strongly theatrical about the whole expedition. The party set out for Lucerne on the King's special train with attendants chosen for their willingness to comply with Ludwig's every whim. These included Hoppé, the King's hairdresser, and Karl Hesselschwerdt, who was officially termed as a "forage quartermaster" but who actually worked for Ludwig on a full time basis, his duties encompassing a number of strange tasks many of which were of a somewhat

dubious nature. No one ever trusted him except Ludwig. Hesselschwerdt selected the King's guard, such as it was, and knowing Ludwig's
preference for having young and handsome boys about him, pandered
to his whim by selecting only those who came into this category. He
also made the hotel arrangements for the party at the Hotel Ahrenstein
Benziger where Ludwig stayed as the "Count von Berg". He was easily
recognised, of course, and was invited to move to the more comforable
Villa Cautenberg by the owner who knew of Ludwig's interest in
Wilhelm Tell.

Although the King rarely travelled abroad, the widely-read intellectual knew a great deal about countries other than his own and when he
did leave Bavaria he always enjoyed himself to the full until something
occurred to mar his pleasure as, fatefully, something always did. The
fly in the ointment on this occasion was Kainz, the guest of honour.
Sure of his importance to the King, the actor was becoming increasingly
temperamental. Forgotten was his plaintive letter to the King following
his earlier offence. He now believed that he could do exactly as he
pleased. However indulgent and generous Ludwig might be to those
who obeyed him implicitly, he would not tolerate anyone who did not
know how to conduct himself, nor would he allow any man to make a
fool of him.

Kainz paved his own road to disaster with his foolishness, demon-
strating repeatedly that those who become elevated overnight to positions of some importance rarely deserve it. In the intoxicating Swiss
air, Ludwig had been quite carried away; he expected Kainz to recite
the part of Mechtel in the moonlight, perched high on the Rütli. It was
the reason why he had been invited and even if it seemed an eccentric
request to the little Hungarian, he must surely have expected to give
something in return for all the expensive gifts he had received, not to
mention a free holiday in Switzerland. Kainz protested that he was
tired and proved it by making the same presumptuous mistake as
Varicourt: he fell asleep in the Royal presence. Ludwig appeared to
be complacent and forgiving, merely telling the actor that he "snored
beautifully" but the following morning the deflated Kainz awoke to find
that the King had abandoned him and left him to find his way back from
Switzerland alone. Belatedly realising how stupid he had been, little
Josef eulogised profusely to the King, adding slyly with an eye to the
future, "I would like to lay before Your Majesty's glorious feet my
heartfelt and most profound thanks for all that I enjoyed by Your
Majesty's favour during the last sixteen days." But the damage was
done and Ludwig never again felt the same about Didier/Kainz.

The fiasco of the Swiss holiday and the disappointment of another
unsatisfactory friendship were forgotten when Elisabeth reappeared

at Feldafing. As in the past, they met frequently in private, isolated places where no one could disturb them. Owing to a hernia which he had sustained during a riding accident some time before, Ludwig no longer rode on horseback but would arrive for his rendezvous with Elisabeth in a carriage and then dismiss the coachman and groom in order that he might be "completely alone" with his adored Sisi. Noticeably, there are no sour references by Marie Festetics to these clandestine meetings and it is clear that Elisabeth, who would appear unattended on horseback, failed to inform her lady-in-waiting where she was going. When Elisabeth went to meet Ludwig the most notoriously unpunctual woman in Europe would arrive on time, usually with her Saint Bernard dog loping along at her side. Despite Festetics' assertion to the contrary, Ludwig seems to have been quite happy to tolerate her menagerie.

Far from thinking less of the King now that he was no longer as handsome and outgoing as in his earlier years, Elisabeth grew even more attached to him and was always quick to defend him when their relations commented about his strange lifestyle. Her 14 day visit passed all too quickly; their last hours together they spent on the Roseninsel when they were accompanied for once by her new personal attendant, a Moor who had been given to her by an Oriental potentate. This strange gift had caused endless comment, but Elisabeth liked him and Ludwig was so diverted by his talented, multi-lingual singing that he afterwards gave him the gold ring from his own hand. After their farewells, a stream of bouquets and books followed the Empress on her travels. The pair corresponded occasionally but when one considers the vast profusion of letters and documents which both Ludwig and Elisabeth cast constantly at their friends and relatives, surprisingly few letters between them have survived apart from those of the most prosaic nature, which would suggest that such letters were deliberately destroyed or placed in the secret Archives.

The year 1881 like so many other years, dwindled finally into an morass of unsatisfactory relationships with the most unsuitable of companions to cloud both his life and his judgement. He was also being made increasingly miserable by his headaches, for which his idea of relief was the excessive use of chloralhydrate. Such treatment naturally only excacerbated the problem and his resultant erratic behaviour cleaarly only bewildered the new and inferior breed of staff who now served him. Their limited intellect took no account of the fact that it was the effects of the drug which led him to do such strange things and caused him to lose his temper with increasing frequency.

Much has been written about Ludwig's hallucinations and here again, it is logical to connect them with his drug-taking. It was said after his death that these hallucinations "entailed discussions which sometimes lasted for a whole day." In 1876 for example, his valet Mayr told the secretary, Klug, "It is deplorable when the King imagines something and absolutely refuses to argue about it. If he begins, for example, 'Take the knife (or some other thing) away' and then I say 'Majesty, there is nothing there', then he continues to look for it for hours on end. 'There must be something there. Where would it go? You have taken it away. Where have you taken it? Put it back immediately'." Not surprisingly, some of his staff began to whisper of the "tyrant" and the "despot" while others, unfortunately, chose to tell people that they thought he was mad, which he was not. What does emerge is that it suited people on all levels to regard these discussions as the result of too much chloral. On another level some of the servants' outpourings may have been tissues of lies bearing in mind that most of them were in the pay of either Holnstein or Hesselschwerdt. Sadly, his erratic behaviour only encouraged such opinions. He kept extraordinary hours, rarely rising before five or six in the afternoon and after a hurriedly eaten meal would go off on one of his excursions from which he rarely returned before morning.

If the more honest domestics were puzzled by all this, Ziegler was far from mystified. He was later to testify "His Majesty often held his hand against the back of his head and complained of a dull pain in his brain. Majesty regularly took chloralhydrate before going to bed. I had often warned him against this substance but Majesty always replied that he could not otherwise sleep at all." To indicate the resultant changes in Ludwig's behaviour, Ziegler added, "The whole year through Majesty avoided being seen. Travel and excursions were increasingly deferred until the lonely time of the night. Majesty saw almost only his body servants. Even they were watched suspiciously, andone had to guard every glance, every word. Not once but often, Majesty suspected that I had regarded him with an unseemly look during our conference. Immediately after the conference, I would receive the command that I must justify myself for this, and in order to make these justifications I required an enormous amount of time." More damning still, after the King's death, Ziegler also testified, "Towards 1883, in my position as cabinet secretary it became increasingly difficult to answer all the questions he posed. Scarcely had I begun to speak than Majesty did likewise. That was interpreted by Majesty as an interruption and I received many reproofs that I had again interrupted Majesty."

Despite such adverse and disloyal comments by a man regarded by all including Ludwig himself as the King's friend, the Sovereign still liked Ziegler and if he was exacting in his demands it was because he valued his secretary's opinion. At one point in their relationship they had been extremely close and it seems puzzling that only during Ziegler's second term of office did he feel the King's interest in him to be "unhealthy". Alternatively, the old reversal of feeling and his ultimate testimony against Ludwig might also indicate that Ziegler, like so many others on the King's staff, had also been bought by the Prussians. Nevertheless, despite his endless complaints against his Royal master, he remained in his highly confidential post until his energy flagged and he resigned for the second time.

Growing sadly adept at putting himself on bad terms with friends and staff alike, Ludwig again quarrelled with Richard Wagner in the summer of 1882 over the first production of *Parsifal* which the King wished to take place in Munich and which Wagner naturally intended to produce in his new theatre at Bayreuth. Feelings ran high with both parties bitterly unforgiving and uncompromising in their attitude. It was to be their last disagreement.

CHAPTER THIRTEEN

RETREAT INTO LONELINESS

ZIEGLER'S final departure from the King's service was inevitable. On January 8th, 1883, the secretary wrote to Bürkel who, having held the same position, had a good idea of what was entailed: "Mayr has just been here with me. He is going to write to you that you must come here on the 10th in order to go over the Court affairs and that you shall remain here on the 11th and 12th so that we might also discuss State affairs. I am, at the moment, in the most peculiar state of disgrace: on New Year's Day, ie, at the close of the year, I received three reprimands: (1) Because I looked penetratingly at His Majesty several times previous to our Conference (2) Because of the question as to whether the lady-in-waiting, Baroness Reichlin should have for her living not only the agreed sum of her pension but also that it is agreed that she should also have accommodation at the Residenz; (3) Because I was not lively enough the day before. For all these things I have to apologise in writing. On New Year's Day Hornig confided to me that if I behaved as the King would like me to, he might perhaps confer an honour on me in 1884. For this I put my thanks in writing and promised to do all possible to give satisfaction to the All Highest."

Ziegler's accusations were somewhat exaggerated: to imagine slights where none were intended was not necessarily a disease but merely a sign of the deep depression from which Ludwig undoubtedly suffered. He was introspective and he was uncomfortably aware that he had very few real friends. Knowing that his Uncle Luitpold was waiting only for a chance to take his throne, he was justifiably suspicious and critical of everything. The slights themselves were in any case real enough since many of his staff saw fit to show their Sovereign their contempt for his intellect which was so different from their own, for with the exception of Ziegler and Hornig, this highly erudite man was surrounded by petty bureaucrats and he made no attempt to hide his impatience with them. They in their turn did not bother to conceal the inbred contempt which the ignorant often have for their intellectual betters.

Still determined not to involve himself in politics and State affairs now that he knew for certain that his Ministerium was pro-Prussian, Ludwig would refer to State affairs as "State dullnesses". On one occasion when the deputation of Ministers arrived from Munich to present their report, they were rewarded with the message that "The All Highness would like to see the whole pack thrown out again."

On February 13th, 1883, the 69-year old Richard Wagner died in Venice of a heart attack in Venice, thus bringing to an end the difficult but stimulating and, in the long-term, productive relationship whose waves had engulfed Bavaria for so long. Their friendship had not been an easy one but it had given works of immeasurable value to the world and to posterity, and on this account if on no other, Ludwig was shocked and upset. Nevertheless, it would be wrong to suppose that he was broken hearted, despite the wild protestations made in his youth when he had asserted that when Wagner died his life would also end. The King was to survive the composer by only three years but it is unlikely that Ludwig's melodramatic assertion regarding his boyhood hero was ever meant to be taken seriously.

The King did not attend Richard Wagner's funeral but instead sent Bürkel to represent him, giving him a letter for the distraught Frau Cosima in which he assured her, "It is impossible for me to express to you the deep pain which overspills from my soul over this awful loss which you have suffered. What an irrevocable stroke of fate that you and the poor children should have had the pleasure and numerous miracles of the great, unforgettable friend and master." Intimate with the workings of the King's mind, Bürkel knew how to sugar the pill by describing to Ludwig in glorious detail the "dignified obsequies" of the funeral and the "many flattering comments made by people of all Nations" about Ludwig for having been "pleased to inspire his genius for the creation of his greatest works" which in spite of the eulogy was no more than the truth. "During the last few days before he died the Master was very occupied with the thought of how it might be possible to give a private performance of *Parsifal* before Your Majesty and said to the Kapellmeister Levi how unhappy he was not to be able to fulfil Majesty's commands."

*   *   *   *   *

THE rift between the King and Wagner had been too deep and of too long a duration for Ludwig to be totally shattered by his death, but he was not entirely disaffected. Despite Wagner's shortcomings, his cavalier insouciance towards other people's money and his perpetual attempts to interfere in Bavarian politics, Germany as a whole had lost a genius.

As a mark of respect the King covered with black crêpe all the pianos which Wagner had used in the various residences and none of them was ever played again. Contrary to popular supposition, his had never been a blind adoration. In many ways, Ludwig had disapproved ot Wagner who was sometimes moved to use "the most appalling language", in the presence of his Sovereign. The King once confided to Josef Kainz that, when Wagner flew into a rage - something which occurred with deplorable frequency - he would "pound the table with his fists" which Ludwig told the actor he considered "very unseemly".

Ironically, many mutual acquaintances sympathised more with Ludwig than with Wagner's widow and even the prosaic anti-Wagnerian Marie wrote her condolences to her son and sent him flowers, a gesture which did much to forge a new bond between them. During Wagner's lifetime, she had been one of his loudest opponents but in later years she appears to have mellowed. Ludwig in his turn grew more tolerant of his mother and, touched by her unexpected gesture, he warmed even more to her. Perhaps he was reminded of the gentle creature of his early childhood years who had grown away from him as his tastes moved beyond her comprehension.

Shunning all the inevitable public ceremonies connected with the composer's death, Ludwig waited for some days before visiting the grave in Bayreuth. Now it was no longer possible to hear Wagner's masterworks except under the baton of lesser lights, his enthusiasm for the opera diminished and he channeled all his energies into his building.

Although his resources were already said to be considerably drained by the other castles, a plan for a new castle to be built on the site of the Falkenstein near Pfronten in the Allgäu and a Chinese Pagoda at Plansee were on the drawing board. As with all his projects the site he had chosen was superb, attracting as it did panoramic views of the Wetterstein, Karwendel and Kaisergebirge and above all, the "mighty Watzmann" so dear to his heart. He had commissioned the theatrical designer , Christian Jank, whose work on Neuschwanstein had so pleased him, to plan the new castle and a large papier mâché model of the new Falkenburg now stood in the vestibule at Hohenschwangau.

Anxious to make a beginning, he refused to listen to his advisers who reminded him with monotonous frequency that he still had a frightening number of unpaid bills to settle for the existing building work. All efforts of the more loyal members of his staff to obtain loans for his plans had apparently failed and although he had a small squad of patient negotiators busily attempting to find money in all quarters of Europe, none was forthcoming. He was thus feeling acutely miserable and frustrated and his mood was further blackened by the departure of Josef Kainz from Munich.

In his farewell letter to the King, the opportunist actor explained "Before long I shall have to say goodbye to the kindly walls of Munich. Fresh developments call me to Berlin; a great project is to be realised in which all the first class German actors have been engaged and I have been considered worthy to take part in this work which will some day stand by the side of the Théâtre Français; I am deeply sorry to leave Munich where the beams of the gracious sun of Ludwig of Bavaria warmed and strengthened this modest plant in the garden of art." Prudently, the modest plant remembered to add "I shall never forget what you did for me, the poor unknown, and I shall certainly remember with loving gratitude the benevolence and love whch were poured over me." It is doubtful whether Ludwig considered gratitude to be demonstrated by Kainz' admission that he proposed to go, of all places, to Prussia.

Although it was the year of Wagner's death, 1883 proved to be one of the happier of Ludwig's later years. In January, a close personal friend of his, Prince Ludwig Ferdinand, the elder son of Ludwig's uncle Adalbert, married the Infanta of Spain in Madrid. Paz was the third daughter of Queen Isabella II and in April the Prince proudly brought his bride to Munich where Ludwig, who had already heard a great deal about her from his enthusiastic relatives, was anxious to meet her. He was as captivated by her as everyone else and she brought back to his sad life a small ray of invigorating light just as little Maria Josepha, Gackl's wife, had done. The King enjoyed the company of the bridal pair so much that he emerged unexpectedly from his seclusion, attending receptions and banquets with a combination of dignity and benign good humour which surprised and overjoyed everyone who had been led by malicious Court gossip to expect another Otto to preside over the festivities.

As always, Ludwig was lavish with his wedding gifts and with the bombardment of flowers on the astonished Paz. Before her first presentation, she had been warned that she must always treat the misanthropic King with great deference and that he would become extremely angry if she did not. Less ingenuous than the other teenage bride Maria Josepha, who had been given similar instructions, she replied crisply "But how does one treat a King? The only Kings I know are my father and my brother." As soon as he smiled down upon her from the top of the Emperor's staircase in the great cold Residenz and gave her his arm to escort her in his courteous way to his personal paradise, she realised that she had nothing to fear from him. The kindly Ludwig talked to her in French although, because he always walked with his head thrown back in his highly theatrical manner, she had some difficulty in hearing what he had to say to her. With his deep understanding of shyness and of children, he expected little of her. He was delighted by the obvious pleasure and enthusiasm with which she rewarded his efforts to please her and this naturally inspired him to do even more. As it drawing new life from Paz, he astounded everyone by devoting most of the summer to her and even invited her to view the incompleted Schloss Chiemsee (later called Herrenchiemsee) a favour rarely conferred on anyone although he did not accompany her on the visit.

Deeply impressed by the magnificence of the building and the mystique of its surroundings, Paz afterwards wrote of Ludwig "This man has something great and poetic about him and he has powers of imagination such as one rarely finds in anyone." She also said she did not understand why people found him unapproachable, for she did not find him so, particularly since she shared his appreciation of the arts. Together, they discussed the theatre, literature, painting and the opera; he even discussed with her his protegé Josef Kainz whose memorable performance in *Marion de Lorme* was still vivid in his mind, proving that he bore the defector no rancour.

Paz was amazed by Ludwig's meticulous attention to detail in his building projects. Schloss Chiemsee, virtually based on Versailles, was intended to be absolutely authentic. It was for this reason that the building costs had already reached such giant proportions although by today's standards they would appear minimal. With great trepidation Bürkel had approached Ludwig in October with his mighty collection of bills and insisted that the financial situation should be discussed forthwith. There was at this time a sum outstanding for the lavish embroideries alone of some 200,000 Marks.

All four of the workshops engaged on the work commissioned by the King were clamouring for payment and Döllmann, the chief architect, himself threatened to take action to recover his weekly overheads. Ludwig was at first unbelieving, then furious. Whatever his reaction, however, he was obliged to accept the fact that a sum of 800,000 Marks was required for the painting and a further 1million for the facsimiles of pictures and *objets d'art* from the Hertford collection would have to be found. In all, for the existing work only, a minimum of 4million Marks was required. This was aside from what was needed for the work on Neuschwanstein, which continued to eat its way through the Civil List with the most voracious of appetites. Yet was it really so much when one considers the artistry contained in these three masterpieces? Was it really so wrong to want to leave his mark on Bavaria in such a manner? In any case, it was not the country's money which Ludwig spent, but only that set aside for his own personal use. His error was to spend it in advance and to leave the accounting to men whom he could not altogether trust. If he had been a little more careful when dealing with his financial matters he would, in any case, undoubtedly discovered that he was not in debt at all but merely told so by Lutz and his cronies as an additional step in the plan to bring about his downfall.

Completely out of his depth, the King sought solutions in unlikely places. Aware that he must find a great deal of cash to pay for the alleged arrears he was gripped by such feverish compulsion to complete the works that he could not stop. As other men gamble so Ludwig spent on building. The money was never wasted yet he was rewarded only with criticism for his efforts and his castles were at that time dismissed by his Ministerium as "products of a sick mind". His grandfather Ludwig I, himself an avid builder, obssessed by the same desire to create something for posterity, would have understood but old Ludwig was long dead and the King thus found little sympathy anywhere except among the workmen for whom he provided a steady living over a number of years in an otherwise impoverished region. Only the greedy and sycophantic artists were ever made to wait for their money: he made sure that none of the common labourers were out of pocket for his sake.

For all this Bürkel found it impossible to reason with him on financial matters. His fluctuating and mercurial moods made it impossible to foresee his reaction to a report or to the man who presented it. Without the constant ingestion of chloralhydrate, he might have set about solving his problems in a logical manner but under its hallucinatory influence he became a different person. Many of his staff assumed that he was mentally disturbed and he was too proud to dispel this impression. Rather than approach him, the minions now took their problems to the apparently sympathetic Minister Lutz.

Opinion within the Ministerium was that things could not continue as they were with the King rarely, if ever, available to attend to affairs of State but always ready for consultations on the building work. Ruthless, ambitious and determined that he himself should rule Bavaria, Lutz was in complete agreement with the other Ministers but at the same time he had no wish to fall foul of the King at this stage and expressed the opinion that something could only be done if the Sovereign on his part did something which actively "endangered the wellbeing of the country" and thus "rendered the continuancy of the State impossible." Sadly, Lutz was not above helping Ludwig to bring such a condition to fruition.

Trained as a lawyer, Lutz had an agile brain and an elephantine memory tempered with a taste for intrigue. He had been prominent in the fight against the validity of the Dogma of Papal Infallibility in 1878 and there were bitter disputes in the Landtag. Despite his enthusiastic efforts he had been unable to bring down the Government. Ludwig had followed these disputes closely; although he was himself a Catholic, he disagreed with the Dogma which conflicted with some of Bavaria's own autonomous laws His unpopularity in Munich did not stem solely from his interest in the arts, his dislike of public life and his mania for building expensive castles but ironically from his enlightened and all-too-reasonable views on burning political issues. Men like Lutz, Count Holnstein, Baron Crailsheim and Colonel Baron Washington found it all too easy to fan the flames of hatred by means provided by the King himself and they never lost an opportunity to do so.

Because Ludwig stubbornly refused to discuss his finances, presumably because he knew in his heart that they were sound, Bürkel like his predecessors collapsed under the strain and, at the end of February, Franz von Pfistermeister resumed the post he had vacated years before. An unimaginative, second rate bureaucrat was how Ludwig had accurately described him, but he had usually been able to reason with the King in the past, and knowing of Ludwig's unfortunate predilection for chloralhydrate, was therefore fully aware of what he was up against. Long accustomed to the King's lack of business acumen, it came as no surprise to him to find that he had taken on something of a dead horse. During the past months, negotiations had been opened in various quarters of Europe to acquire loans for the King, one of which, with a Berlin banker, had seemingly come to fruition. At the same time, a firm offer of 6 million Marks had been put forward by the London-based Baring Brothers, but owing to the unacceptability of the terms and conditions, the latter was never taken up.

Instead of showing improvement under Pfistermeister's "guidance" things went from bad to worse; the official trustees of the estate of Maximilian II, Baron von Mahlsen and Baron von Prankh were approached in March 1884, but these gentlemen, for reasons of their own, categorically refused to allow Ludwig to have his own money. Both somewhat impertinently disapproved strongly of the King's building activities which they considered to be little more than follies, or playthings of the type currently being built all over Europe by eccentric millionaires and monarchs who had nothing better on which to spend their money. (The countryside in England, for example, abounded with "ruined" castles and abbeys). Even the entreaties of Queen Marie on her son's behalf brought no softening of attitude and to Ludwig's indignation, the lower paid workmen had threatened, with the encouragement of their superiors, to go on strike if they were not paid at once. With alleged debts now outstanding of some 8 million Marks, he was at last obliged to concede that the situation was desperate.

Filled with loneliness and despair, with frustration and the feeling that time was slipping away Ludwig's health, never robust, again began to suffer. His head- and toothaches became worse and he continued to dose himself with the deadliest of drugs. Whether from genuine concern or whether from some more sinister motive, Pfistermieister, who had in the past occasionally engaged in court intrigue, persuaded Marie to arrange for Ludwig to consult a doctor. Vacillating as ever, she could not make up her mind to do so and when eventually she was pushed into a decision, foolishly left the choice of doctor to the conspirators.

The "physician" initially called in was Dr. Franz Karl, a mental specialist who visited Ludwig ostensibly to make a "dental inspection". But Ludwig was nobody's fool and the moment the consultation began, he was alerted by the man's manner and knew instinctively the nature of his qualifications. The long-dreaded moment had arrived; foreseeing the possibility that he might find himself locked away for ever like Otto, he set out to dazzle Dr. Karl with the brilliance and rationality of his conversation. Since this entailed only behaving naturally, he was entirely successful. When Ludwig abstained from taking Chloral, there was nothing wrong with his mind that a little human warmth could not have cured. The method of introducing the doctor was shabby and unprofessional but Ludwig gave no indication that he thought so and Karl fell completely under the spell of his charm, thus thwarting the expectations of his adversaries. The King on his side confided that he was worried about his sight, a subject which he was too vain and proud to mention even to his closest associates. In fact, his poor vision was common knowledge although no one attempted to help him.

The interview with Dr. Karl lasted for almost three hours and when it ended the doctor was the more exhausted of the two. When his report was presented it left no hope for Ludwig's furious adversaries. Relieved but conscience-stricken, Marie tried to atone for what she had done by writing more frequently to her son and by suddenly showering him with gifts. Ludwig was deeply touched and sent her a note of thanks on February 12th: "I feel urged to thank you once more for the wonderful presents which made me so happy. I admire them very much and offer you my deepest thanks for them." This was a normal note from a normal man, but if Ludwig himself was normal, his Court was far from being so, and by the spring life in all the residences had become a travesty. Things had deteriorated to the extent where even the humblest of lackeys would refuse to obey an order if it did not suit them to carry it out.

Pfistermeister cannot be blamed for giving up in the face of such hopeless odds, whether or not he was in Ludwig's camp. He left the post open to a retired army captain and momentary favourite, Herman Gresser. This latest recruit to Ludwig's motley entourage was comparatively lively, well-educated and worldly, but scarcely equipped to deal with the chaos and complication of the King's financial dealings and general business affairs. After an initial half-hearted effort to put the Sovereign's affairs in order, Gresser made only the lightest of impacts; the servants, ignoring him completely, continued to do as they pleased. So little was poor Gresser respected that when Ludwig sent him to the Treasury to appropriate some diamonds and other precious stones for conversion to cash, Count Castell-Castell, who was responsible for the Wittelsbach valuables, rudely sent him away with a flea in his ear.

The King spent the summer of 1884 at Berg and Hohenschwangau, hoping for a sight of the Empress, longing for love or cultural satisfaction but finding none. He no longer went to the theatre and there is more than a note of regret in his tone when, in a reply to a letter from Ludwig Ferdinand in which the latter had mentioned *Parsifal,* he recalled, "The last time I heard this wonderful work was in spring and it moved me in an extraordinary way. Truly it is uniquely beautiful. It has a purifying effect and one is carried away in wonder and admiration". On his birthday he visited Herrenwörth but finding that "everything there was behindhand" he left, piqued and disappointed, after only a short stay in the lodge.

Although they had seen nothing of each other he was constantly on Elisabeth's mind. The Empress had been seriously ill and in the spring she had taken a sciatica cure in Zandvoort on the North Sea coast where, in the solitude of the sand dunes, she thought wistfully of Ludwig, writing a poem to him:

> Du Adler dort hoch auf den Bergen,
> Einst sind wir einander begegnet
> Am spiegel des lieblichsten Sees,
> Zur blühenden Rosenzeit.

> Du Adler dort hoch auf den Bergen,
> Dir schicht die Möwe der See,
> Einen Grüss von schaumenden Wogen
> Hinauf zum ewigen Schnee.

> [Thou Eagle up there in the mountains,
> Once we would meet
> In the reflection of the beloved lake,
> When the roses were in bloom.

> Thou Eagle, up there in the mountains,

The ocean seagull
Sends a greeting from the foaming waves
Up to the eternal snows.]

With their mutual love of fantasie Elisabeth had often described
Ludwig as her "eagle" while he called her his "dove"; in her restless
odyssey across Europe, she now saw herself as a seagull. When she
returned to Bavaria she took her poem with her, hoping to find the King
at Berg but he had given up waiting for her and returned to his Alpine
seclusion. In spite of the obvious longing on both sides their paths did
not cross. Disappointed that Ludwig could not be found she left her
verse in the rosewood bureau in the summerhouse on the Roseninsel
to which only she and Ludwig held keys. When Ludwig found it in
September 1885, he left an answer: "I hadn't visited the Roseninsel for
years until a few days ago when I experienced great pleasure there.
When I heard the news [ie, of her arrival], I hurried to the idyllic island
and found there the seagull's dear offering. Deepest, most profound
thanks!" Underneath, he added:

> Der Möwe Grüss von fernen Strand
> Zu Adlers Horst den Weg wohl fand
> Er trug auf leisem Fittigschwung
> Der alten Zeit Erinnerung
> Du Rosenduft umwehte Buchten
> Möwe und Adler zugleich besuchten
> Und sich begegnend in stolzen Bogen
> Grüssend an einander vor überzogen ...

> [The seagull's greeting from a distant beach
> Found its way to the eagle's eyrie
> Pinioned gently in its wings
> It brought memories of old times
> Thou bay in scent of roses wrapped
> Where seagull and eagle were together
> Proudly meeting one another
> Greeting each other before the parting...]

In fact, Elisabeth had waited in vain at their former trysting place
three times before she finally lost hope and left Bavaria without meeting him at all. Had she known of the uproar which now reigned in
Ludwig's curious menage she might well have waited longer and saved
him from the inevitable retrogressive path on which he now trod. But

sadly, at that time, no one saw fit to inform her of the true state of affairs and it is likely that she merely assumed him to be occupied with his building projects.

Gresser had already been dismissed for "incompetence" which, as always, meant that he had failed to obtain a loan from any source on the King's behalf. In his place was now appointed a man of even less distinction with the somewhat inappropriate name of Klug ['clever']. Determined to have no initial difficulties with him, Ludwig astutely allowed him only half-an-hour's conference with Gresser before he officially took over the post of Cabinet Secretary. Evidently the King was afraid that, if Klug knew in advance how bad things really were, he might refuse to take the job. His biggest headache in Ludwig's service was, inevitably, that of trying to balance the books.

As it was, Klug found written negotiations from all kinds of people: bankers, moneylenders, politicians and of course, an assortment of embarrassed or indignant monarchs. These letters included the firm offer of a large personal loan from Kaiser Wilhelm I who had heard of Ludwig's predicament from Bismarck. Ten million Marks would have been extremely useful but Ludwig's dislike of the Hohenzollerns was so intense (and not without reason) that he could not bring himself to accept, proudly declining both the loan and the attaching conditions with the single word "Impossible!" The conditions mentioned were that the money should be used only to pay arrears. Ludwig spent hours brooding on the fact that his grandfather had been given *carte blanche* for his building and had never been subjected to the humiliation of refusal or of clauses and conditions. Furthermore, Ludwig I, who had never been called mad, had drawn his building funds from public money without curb or criticism, and much as he had loved his grandfather it was this which infuriated Ludwig more than anything else.

In the spring of 1881, with an alleged deficit of some 7 million Marks in the building accounts Emil von Riedel, a man said to be a financial genius had been brought in to put Ludwig's affairs in order. After remonstrating with the King he embarked on a tour of all the monetary institutions. He was no more successful than any of his predecessors since he evidently came up against the same ultimate obstacles, namely, members of Ludwig's own staff who deftly vetoed any plan before it could come to fruition. Three years later he was still struggling and, presumably still unaware of the root cause of Ludwig's problems, on April 10th, 1884, he wrote to the Cabinet Secretary, "The position in the Privy Purse is very serious, so serious that, since I am closely occupied with it, I am almost weighted down with the heavy troubles it causes. If the debt is not honoured at the earliest possible date, it is to be feared that hundreds, perhaps even more, will fall into economic ruin and this fact alone generally brings great danger because the justified complaints will find an echo not only throughout Bavaria but far over her borders which will not be able to be kept from the steps of the Throne by any means and which, at a time like the present where social relationships are more and more undermined, appears doubly critical." He added ominously, "To this is added an extremely unpleasant circumstance. According to Bavarian law, a Civil List can have legal proceedings taken against it in a court of law and can be, at least to some extent, legally seized. Now, scarcely any loyal subject can be deterred from bringing legal action. As far as most people are concerned, only a necessity can repress the feeling of loyalty, but others who do not know the meaning of the word 'loyalty', will seize upon a way out of their difficulties (...). In no way can the State impede the course of legal procedure (...). These disciplinary measures can, in my opinion, only be absolved by the acquisition of a speedy loan to quicken the discharge of the debt, in the systematic removal of the creditors and in the strict avoidance of new debts."

Having diagnosed the trouble as he saw it, Riedel then went ahead in his efforts to effect the cure by trying, on June 1st, to arrange a bank loan of 7 million Marks, but unfortunately, in order to do this he had first to obtain the permission of Ludwig's uncle, Prince Luitpold, who was the first male heir after the allegedly incapacitated Otto, before any agreement could be finalised. The curious basis for this stipulation was that such a loan could only be repaid by 1901 when the opposition was said to regard it as "unreasonable" to suppose that Ludwig, who was not quite 40, would still be on the Throne after the turn of the Century. This would seem to be the most extraordinary excuse of all to avoid helping the King, since Luitpold himself was 22 years Ludwig's senior. Predictably, the "wicked uncle" declined to give his permission. To complete the King's misery, Riedel informed him in no uncertain terms that no further building work, or completion of any existing work, could even be considered. This effectively curtailed his plans for a Chinese palace at Plansee and the new castle on the Falkenstein. Another dream had been brutally shattered by harsh reality.

Restrained from building curbed in his joy of reading by failing sight, unable to continue with the building or to command theatrical performances, Ludwig inevitably found that time began to hang even more heavily on his hands. Forgetting his resolution, he resorted again to the company of young *Chevauxlègers* and servants to his own humiliation and occasionally to theirs.

Some of these ephemeral liaisons were undoubtedly base and unsavoury enough to cause him considerable heartache and regret, but occasionally his fancy would be caught by a better type as for example, Chevauxlegèr Thomas Osterhauer. This young soldier's birthday fell while he was on guard at Hohenschwangau and, summoned to present himself to the King, he found a benign Ludwig standing by a small table on which were arranged delicacies of the type which a boy in his position rarely saw. Besides a large bouquet of flowers was a large and elaborate torte, a beautifully garnished mayonnaïse of two pike, two boxes of cigars and a photograph of the donor. The King then wished Osterhauer a happy birthday and offered the lavish display as a birthday treat. Osterhauer's enraptured note of thanks so pleased Ludwig that he invited him to visit the grotto at Linderhof. While it was a great honour, one cannot help wondering what Osterhauer made of this eerie place. Whatever it was, he evidently said and did the right thing for this intelligent and lively soul later accompanied the King on many of his nocturnal jaunts.

During one of these, they came to a small country inn at the deserted centre of a small village, the hardworking peasants having retired for the night. Outside the inn was a bowling alley so beloved of Bavarians and Ludwig, in a good humour, was unable to resist a game of skittles. The noise they made while trying their luck soon brought the irate innkeeper from his slumbers. He appeared in his nightshirt, brandishing a shotgun, swearing loudly and threatening to kill the intruders. Laughing heartily, Ludwig fled across the village green and got into his carriage, an ungainly figure in his heavy topcoat, but poor Osterhauer was too near the inkeeper to escape and found himself grasped roughly by the collar to receive a stinging blow across the ear.

Only when his helmet fell to the ground did the innkeeper notice that he was wearing the uniform of the King's personal guard and that his companion had climbed into a royal equipage. The following day, doubtless after a sleepless night, he wrote posthaste to the King apologising for spoiling his sport and for inadvertently committing treason by threatening his Sovereign with a shotgun. Predictably, he received a silver watch by return of post.

Apart from such harmless diversions, the year was a grim and tedious one for Ludwig. Thwarted in everything he tried to do, he had become increasingly misanthropic and eccentric. Despite the official request to stop building, he had continued in a defiance born of desperation, thus incurring new debts of six million Marks. This allegedly brought the grand total to almost 14 million. He longed to see the completion of Schloss Chiemsee and ordered Riedel to renew his efforts to raise money. "It is my Royal command that, in accordance with my orders, an appropriate means is found to complete the building work which I have undertaken. However, my intentions suffer considerable frustration arising from the condition of the Privy Purse. I authorise you, Herr Minister, to take the necessary steps to regulate the finance so as to enable me to carry through my project."

Riedel's reply merely emphasised the need to exercise "the strictest economy measures" and in doing do, reminded the King once more that the Sovereign could be sued for default. Ludwig was furious and decided to avenge the insult by dismissing the writer of the letter. As the removal of the Minister for Finance made it impossible for the other Ministers to continue their business – or so they asserted – it was held that the "dismissal was intended for them also."

With or without Riedel, the wrangling over money continued. Ludwig received little help from Lutz who, threatening lackeys or Chevaux-légers with punishment or army service in the most undesirable postings, instructed them that, if any bankers or moneylenders should beg audience of the King, "Such persons were to be sent away with the information that the King was not in residence." One Jakob Lidl, who left behind him an extremely interesting testament*, stated, for example, that when in 1884 two gentlemen arrived from France to see Ludwig, a friend of his employed by the Crown at Schloss Berg was told by Lutz, "under threat of being drafted into the pioneers"**, that he was to say "the King is not at home" and that the same should apply to any other visitors. It thus becomes clear that, even at this early date, King Ludwig was virtually a prisoner in his own palace.

At last, the desperate Klug, presumably unaware of Lutz' intrigues, sent a message to the King through Mayr, Ludwig's personal valet, on December 10th, to the effect that he had at last succeeded in finding a moneylender, a certain Herr Schühelein who was prepared to loan the sum of 400 thousand Marks for the continued building work at Schloss Chiemsee and Schloss Neuschwanstein on the understanding that he could expect a title in exchange. With great reluctance, the high-minded Ludwig was obliged to concede, having used up his entire Civil List for the year. Lutz, who had placed him in this invidious position, then made great political capital from his action.

Aside from the building debts, the King had incurred a variety of other debts for living expenses and for gifts; the latter involved considerable outlay owing to his incurable habit of bestowing presents on anyone who took his fancy. He was, and remained, hopeless over money and all Europe knew it. With his affairs in such poor condition, Ludwig laid the blame for the chaos firmly at the feet of his staff and refused to have anything further to do with them, thus not only flouting convention but also greatly annoying the gentlemen in question. Soon he had dismissed all his secretaries and Court officials of any standing, outraging everyone by insisting upon conducting highly confidential

---

* See page 312   ** A very tough and unpopular regiment.

State affairs through guardsmen or lackeys. In fact, this was not quite as outrageous as it sounds; aside from the fact that he could not trust his senior staff, what would have been more logical than to trust those whom he knew to love him and at the same time did not always fully appreciate the full import of the messages they carried? In the days before the telephone was invented it was common practice for this method of transmission to be employed. Queen Victoria of England did exactly the same thing over a period of many years and provided the lackey was trustworthy, the system never failed.

Only Mayr retained Ludwig's complete trust although ironically, even he appears to have spied upon his master, as had Hesselschwerdt who had long since been reporting Ludwig's every move to Max Holnstein. Encouraged by the former Oberstallmeister with promises of financial reward if he complied or physical violence if he did not, Mayr began at this time to glean tidbits from Ludwig's waste paper basket. It is evident also that he retrieved notes to the domestic staff from their recipients.

Increasingly desperate for human warmth, surrounded by traitors and enemies, Ludwig's only solace was debauchery with soldiers and grooms until he hated himself so much that he could no longer be looked at for fear of seeing signs of criticism in the expressions of those who silently watched his escapades. Nor could he bring himself to look into a mirror now that his famous good looks had virtually disappeared. He was now a heavy, middle-aged man, pale and unhealthy looking owing to the irregularity of his lifestyle and the dangerous substances which, on his own admission, he habitually consumed with the uncomfortable admixture of rum and cloves, in the fruitless effort to rid himself of his tormenting headaches.

This is probably the basis also of his refusal to allow his bodyservants to look directly at him and they were ordered to scratch upon the doors because the sound of loud knocking was agonising when he had a headache. Obsessed by Oriental autocratic custom and seeking perhaps to prove at least to himself that he had not quite lost the aura of autocracy which had meant so much to him, after a large dose of chloral, he would insist upon lackeys performing the kow-tow. Wherever possible, he would avoid having servants in the room at all, preferring to leave notes of instruction. In the main, these notes were highly prosaic requests, albeit somewhat dramatically phrased, for meals and clothes to be prepared, innocent and logical enough within their context but extremely damaging when later produced as "evidence" of a sick mind. As on many occasions in the past, Ludwig now proved to be his own worst enemy.

On May 12th, 1885, the last of the separate performances took place.

Such luxuries were now for the most part beyond his reach but this one exception appears to have been in the nature of a farewell. An additional reason for the cessation of what had once given him enormous pleasure and satisfaction as well as artistic stimulation was his dislike of being seen in his depleted state. Even the prospect of being observed by the few people he was likely to encounter on his way from his apartments at the Residenz to the Royal Court Theatre was too much for him. Annoyed with Richard Hornig for his failure to produce building funds, Ludwig quarrelled at last with "Richard, beloved of my heart," thus severing a friendship which had endured for some 18 years. Hornig had been dismissed on the spot by Ludwig who had not waited to learn that he had, in fact, found a banker willing to loan him money. Following Hornig's visit, the banker had presented himself at the Residenz only to be told, on Lutz' instruction, that the King was not in Munich.

By the end of 1885, Ludwig must have deeply regretted the loss of his dearest and most loyal friend, but his obssession with losing face had become such that he was no longer able to make the first move towards reconciliation, as he would have done in his earlier years. He now had to make his own decisions. In December, he wrote commanding the President of the Cabinet Council to comment on the position in the Privy Purse, not realising that by doing so he was quite literally signing his own death warrant.

Within the next few weeks the position was fully discussed both verbally and in writing, among the various officials who saw the opportunity for advantageous action. Lutz wrote to secretary Klug on the subject, emphasising that despite the existing debt, Ludwig had demanded a further 20 million Marks to complete his castles. Joyfully believing that his long-awaited opportunity had arrived, Lutz stated boldly in his letter "I hold it for quite impossible to obtain this amount by means of a private loan (...). It goes without saying that an advance from State funds as the easiest way out without legal powers is unthinkable (...). There remains only the question as to whether Majesty should appeal to the Bavarian people, or whether it is possible for the sum of 20 Million Marks to be allocated by the Landtag as desired by His Majesty the King in order to secure the requisite six million Marks necessary for the liquidation of the debts."

He went on "After receiving the initial command from His Majesty I have spoken repeatedly with all the Ministers setting out this question; also I have put out feelers in many suitable places in order to make a reconnaissance. The result of this reconnaissance and the discussion is that all of the Ministers are of the firm and unwavering conviction that the Landtag must make every effort to agree some amount above the amount of the Civil List to be acquired will be met with defeat, through which at the most the prestige of the Throne is damaged.(...). Without the liquidation of newly incurred debts the taking of legal steps by the creditors against the Privy Purse are to be feared and could even lead to a seizure of the Royal Estates (...). If His Majesty would graciously condescend to suspend for a time the building and decoration of the castles which have begun then, through an experienced businessman (...) a precise catalogue of the contracted debts might be presented to establish the amount required, the type of loan and the time of repayment, so that this might be re-examined, and it can be decided what economy measures might be taken by the Court staff, thereby facilitating a stricter means of paying back the loan. In this way, I am convinced we can return to order the financial circumstances of the privy purse despite the amount of the burden in hand, but although painful a great sacrifice is called for on the part of His Majesty; however, it is the only way to reach our goal and escape from the serious financial embarrassment which now makes all our hearts heavy."

Ludwig, who disliked both Lutz and his methods, ignored this missive which, although apparently reasonable, displayed all too clearly his innate contempt for his Sovereign and the fact that he did not propose to assist him in any way. On January 17th 1886, Baron von Bruck reported "The memorandum of Lutz' Ministers has been in the hands of His Majesty since the 6th instant. It has certainly aroused a storm of indignation but has brought no decision."

It did, however, bring a great deal of heartbreak to the sensitive King, a fact totally disregarded by the prosaic Cabinet who considered him to be at an age where he should have the fortitude to bear both censure and suggestion. Such was not the case. Ludwig would never become so old that he could learn to accept the untenable, and he was particularly horrified by the prospect of being sued by a commoner or having his castles seized. At heart he was immature and lacking in confidence but perhaps the only person ever to appreciate this was Elisabeth, whose childhood had also been lost for a crown.

Totally engulfed by shame and despair, Ludwig wrote to Klug on January 5th, "I enjoin you to take care to see that things are really going forward and that you procure what I want in the shortest possible time (...) If I am only told the truth the trouble you have taken will quickly bring results. It is also expected of you that, by means of the correct manipulation on your part, the seizure of the Royal estates will be rendered impossible. As you have decided on your plan, you must stand firm."

The beaten King could still speak with the voice of autocracy.

CHAPTER FOURTEEN

THE PLOT

IN a desperate attempt to uphold his honour and with the fear of a moral "fall" constantly with him, Ludwig commenced a new volume of his secret diary on January 19th, 1886, with the words: "It is in the name of God, and thinking of the Great King, the Immortal King, that I begin this book and may the Almighty give me power: may the memory of the King sanctify me so that I may conquer the evil, subdue the senses, so that not once can there be any question in this book of a relapse (the last in the 40th year). Given at Hohenschwangau, January 19th, 1886, before the portrait of the King."

For all his good intentions, his path continued downhill and things were not improved by the repeated threat of legal action against him. In a panic, he wrote to Dürkheim on January 28th, "If it (...) is not possible to succeed in getting a certain sum in about four weeks, the Linderhof and Herrenchiemsee, even my Kingdom, will be seized. If this is not stopped right away, I shall either kill myself immediately or, at any rate, leave this damned country where such an atrocious thing could happen. I beg you now, my dear Count, to bring together a contingent who will stand by me, true and firm, allowing nothing to intimidate it, and if it really comes to the worst and the necessary sum does not flow in, the rebellious scoundrels must be thrown out. I know that I can leave you to accomplish this in a discreet and efficient manner. Because Ministers, Gendarmerie, can achieve nothing; secretaries (Klug, Schneider), would not dare to have anything to do with it; they are officials who fear the Chamber, legal decisions and public opinion and are consequently old women and not the King's loyal subjects as they should be."

Sensible, down-to-earth and deeply concerned about the King, Dürkheim replied that Ludwig must put all such ideas out of his mind because "the carrying out of such plans would result in the most difficult possible consequences for the authority of the All Highest and must result in dire consequences for the Most Royal Person of Your Majesty and might even lead to disastrous discussions in the Bundesrat and in the Reichtag." After reading this, Ludwig demanded waspishly, "I am anxious to learn what you mean and why you see the possibility of these things because I only do what has to be done and such affairs certainly have nothing to do either with the Bundesrat or the Reichtag and whoever said it to you must be very democratic."

His only consolation was the fact that the castles had been built at all; even if they were incomplete, all three of them stood as tangible evidence of his genius. Linderhof, his "glowing jewel", set in the depths of the Alpine countryside so dear to his heart; Herrenchiemsee, a poem of symmetry on the Island in the Chiemsee and Neuschwanstein which soared in splendour towards the sky at Hohenschwangau, dwarfing his father's contribution to the Wittelsbach heritage which stood almost directly opposite. All in their different ways were incomparable. He had also undertaken various smaller projects, which were equally unique: the hunting lodge at Schachen, the Hundingshütte, built in 1876, the renovations at Trausnitz and his much-discussed Wintergarden in the Residenz with the unused bridal apartments directly underneath. The latter were ostensibly intended for his bride, but to Ludwig they were merely part of another creative project and were, in fact, only completed several years after his rejection of Sophie. After all the excitement of 1867 had died down, he had had the winding staircase to Sophie's dressing room boarded up and only a small inlay of wood marked the spot from which the staircase led. Over the years his own apartments in the Residenz had been altered to suit his taste, the colours being the ones he always favoured: blue, green and red. His desk was leather topped and a blue velvet chair bore his crown and cypher, the motif which was repeated on all his accessories. To the left of his desk was the ingress to the Wintergarden.

In his bedroom the canopy of the inevitable great bed behind a gilded ceremonial balustrade was blue and gold, and the adjoining room which served as an audience chamber and dining room combined was decorated in crimson and gold, a colour combination which was also employed on the great chair of State.

The effect of the whole was somewhat oppressive and it is small wonder that Ludwig himself disliked living there. All-consuming as his difficulties seemed, he clung stubbornly to the hope that all his projects, most of which were intended to attest to the autocracy of Monarchy, would somehow be completed. He was always touchingly pleased when a member of his family enquired as to their progress and would reply with enthusiasm, as when Ludwig Ferdinand asked about Neuschwanstein and Herrenchiemsee. In this particular case he gave a transparent hint that monetary contributions would be welcome: "I am infinitely concerned that, as I was always promised, the new castle here as well as the castle and gardens at Herrenwörth should be finished by 1889. For the new castle at Neuschwanstein, the architect tells me that he will require five, for the Herrenwörth six, million Marks. My bedroom at Linderhof - which is as sumptuous as the Reichszimmer in the Residenz and which they promised to have finished by November 1883 are, alas, also very far behind. The paintings on the ceiling are, however, nearly completed and is an apotheosis of Louis XIV after Le Brun."

He went on to describe Neuschwanstein: "In my study here, from which I am writing to you, are pictures from the Tannhäuser saga, in the dining room the pictures are of the Wartburg in all its fluorescence; in my bedroom are pictures from *Tristan und Isolde* and at the head of the bed is a painting of the Blessed Mother of God after a picture in the church of St.Sophia in Constantinople; on the bedhead is a representation in relief of the Ascension of our Saviour. The next room is a small oratory with a picture of St.Ludwig as an altarpiece. In the dressing room are depicted events from the life and writings of Walther von der Vogelweide and Hans Sachs. The sitting room is adorned with representations from the saga of the Knight of the Swan and in the large Sängersaal on the fourth floor with paintings illustrating the poetic version of *Parsifal* by Wolfram von Eschenbach."

After reading this glowing account, Ludwig Ferdinand might have been justifiably surprised to see the lodge at Neuschwanstein where the King actually spent most of his time rather than in his own comfortable rooms at nearby Hohenschwangau or in the more uncomfortable grandeur of the ceremonial apartments at Neuschwanstein which he so lovingly described. Probably, he took refuge in this simple lodge in order to avoid his mother whom he could still only tolerate in small doses. The temporary quarters in the lodge consisted of a simple, peasant-style room with a wooden bench fixed at right angles in the corner of the room with a wooden table hard against it, the very ordinary but comfortable *Sitzecke* to be found in every peasant's home. There were two other rooms, even smaller and simpler, where Ludwig and his Aide could sleep. The simplest and cheapest of furnishings provided a sharp contrast to the overpowering grandeur of the new castle yet, oblivious to this noticeable lack of comfort, Ludwig seemed content to hide away in the company of the workmen who still toiled to finish his castle.

Despite his inability to pay these few remaining common labourers, they were the ones who remained behind, wholeheartedly loyal. Not one of them would hear a word against their *Kini*, yet these were the very men who were allegedly ready to go on strike, although possibly this was another invention by his staff to destroy his confidence.

Among the very few of Ludwig's staff who felt the same way about him as the peasants was his namesake, Ludwig von Bürkel. His life in the King's service had been difficult and frustrating and a good deal of his time had been spent in trying to curtail Ludwig's spending, yet he still found himself able to speak more than kindly of his autocratic master. Describing the King's increasing shyness and loneliness, Bürkel said, "I had to present to him the invitation of his capital to a Jubilee Celebration. I knew from experience that it would be refused but it was my duty to submit the application to him. Naturally he declined.

I urged him and explained to him how his people loved him and with what joy they would receive him in Munich after so many long years. 'I cannot, I cannot,' he replied, rubbing his forehead, 'It is a terrible thing but I can no longer bear to be stared at before thousands of people, to be laughed at and to greet people a thousand times and to put questions to people who are intolerable to me and to have to listen to answers which don't interest me! No, no, I cannot now emerge from my solitude!' And, in a whisper full of pain, he added, 'Sometimes, when I have read myself to exhaustion and everything is so quiet, I have the overpowering longing to hear a human voice. Then I send for some lackeys and grooms to tell me about their homes and families.' And with a sadness which cut me to the heart, he continued, 'I would otherwise have to learn to speak again.' There was no other explanation: an awful demon held him back from a return to the world; he struggled with this gloomy power but still succumbed to it." This epitaph might well have applied to his homosexuality as much as to his loneliness, but far from proving him to be mad, it clearly offers us a picture of unhappy sanity.

Giving a character reference in 1886, the same official stated, "Three years ago when I still had a function with him, I was often amazed by the precision of his thoughts. He only appeared disordered when he was talking about his building projects; then he lost all semblance of reality and it was difficult to conclude anything with him. Then he would write unreasonable letters and speak unreasonable words and then it seemed to me that the wilful, autocratic despot emerged. But I also remember with genuine pleasure the many conversations which he had with me about literature, theatre and people. It was a pleasure to listen to him and he still had the power to enchant one; when he looked at me with his dreamy eyes which, through shortsightedness were a little hazy and were often raised upwards, when an attractive almost childlike smile played around his lips and he would put to me some completely unworldly, touchingly naïve question, then I was really enchanted with this man and I realised the rare and fascinating effect which he had for a long time on the masses when he appeared; then – I do not conceal it from you – there were moments when – and I am an otherwise calm and circumspect man – I would have given up my life for him. Two souls lived in his breast: one a tyrant and the other a child; harsh and tender, high and low, shallow and deep, a shyness yet a fondness for splendour blended in a character of (…) rare nuances."

Despite such testimonials from men such as Bürkel and the loyal support of the simple people who were powerless to put their love to any practical purpose, it was impossible for Ludwig's alleged financial difficulties to remain a secret from the public for long. The Press and the Court gossips were quick to see to that. For some years reports concerning the King of Bavaria's financial troubles had appeared regularly in the foreign press but, growing bolder now when it was apparent to all that Ludwig had few supporters within his own Ministerium, the Bavarian press also began to publish articles and detrimental comment on the subject. With depressing frequency these slurs began to appear, each one naturally offering some solution to the problem.

Why were Ludwig's debts which, if they existed, were no worse than those of his grandfather, considered to be so disastrous? Ludwig I's buildings were paid for to a large extent from public funds without demur, but no such concession was made to Ludwig whose castles, even in his lifetime, were acknowledged works of art.

As early as 1885, Ludwig's financial difficulties were discussed by both sides of the family and Dürkheim was even despatched to Berlin to put the King's Hohenzollern relatives in the picture. The latter decided among themselves that Ludwig must be assisted, but predictably, Bismarck stepped in and insisted that funds could only come from the family coffers, that only the outstanding bills were to be paid and that there was insufficient left in the Welffenfonds to give the King what he needed from that source. Since, under the pretext of providing Ludwig with the agreed annual sum following the institution of the Reich, Max Holnstein had been steadily diverting it into his own bank account (and Ludwig's staff denied ever seeing a penny of it), this could well have been true. Since Bismarck was fully aware of what was going on, we may assume that he knew from the start that assistance for Ludwig was unlikely to be forthcoming.

Already acutely hypersensitive, Ludwig's further loss of face over the public discussion of his private affairs drew him yet further from his staff and closer to his Chevauxlègers who knew better than to criticise. Most of the domestic staff was now recruited from this regiment, mainly because no professional servant would now accept a post in the Royal Household owing to the many strange stories which circulated concerning debts and debauchery. On the other hand, a soldier eager for promotion or reward to boost his meagre pay would gladly obey a command, whatever it was. The crafty Hesselschwerdt, well paid by both Ludwig and Holnstein, thus had the double post of spying for Prussia and, in the absence of a *bona fide* Stallmeister, was virtually the holder of this important position, grasping the reins both figuratively and professionally speaking. Unfortunately, Ludwig was more or less at Hesselschwerdt's mercy and, indeed, at that of many other unscrupulous rogues who were quick to seize an opportunity to take advantage of the ailing and unhappy King.

With the bitter realisation that he could no longer count on his servants but afraid to accuse them openly in case his outburst was misconstrued, the King found himself in a dilemma. No one was more aware of his eccentricities than Ludwig himself – and he was certainly eccentric in the way that artists and writers are inevitably branded as "different" or "eccentric" by their more prosaic fellows. But he was at the same time considerably saner than many who walked the streets in peace and he was deeply wounded that people thought such ill of him.

For years he had tolerated the gossip and spiteful jokes, but now a new element had crept into his sad existence with which he was powerless – and probably too proud – to deal. Aware that everything he said and did would ultimately be transmitted to Prussia, he must have known that, by continuing with his current lifestyle, he was helping his enemies to their ends, yet strangely, he did nothing to help himself. He still hid away from the world, taking only the occasional nocturnal excursion to one of his favourite haunts and continuing to behave in an autocratic manner which no longer fitted his circumstances.

Night after night he would sit patiently writing commands to Hesselschwerdt, his valet or his secretary to attend to the building works. It was useless for them to remind him that there was no possibility of his orders being carried out until the alleged arrears were paid. Ludwig on his side remained unshakeably convinced that no begging should have been necessary for the heritage which he was to leave to Germany after his death and that the money should automatically have been forthcoming from public funds, as indeed it should.

It was a bitter pill for the crumbling man to swallow and it was the final straw. The combination of insomnia, drug taking, constant debauches and an irregular routine combined with everyday worries was taking its toll on his general health. When he induced sleep by artificial means he was subject to horrendous nightmares. Tortured since his boyhood with this phenomenon, the nightmares naturally grew worse after he had tried his usual cure for the insomnia which was the alternative to the bad dreams and his nocturnal hours were frequently coloured with scenes of violence in which the central focus was often his mother. He would regale his bodyservants with descriptions of these dreams in which he had thrown the Queen down a flight of stairs or torn out her heart with his bare hands. Probably many of his listeners had experienced similar dreams at one time or another, but what made Ludwig's dreams so fascinating was the titillating fact that he was the Sovereign speaking slightingly of the Queen Mother. With Hesselschwerdt ever ready to pay handsomely for the recounting of such lurid tales, it suited people to describe the King's outpourings as the rantings of a lunatic. It was some time before Ludwig realised what a poor turn he had done himself by describing his dreams so readily to lackeys and the like, and when he did it was already too late and half of Germany had condemned his dreams as further expressions of his abnormality.

At the end of January 1886, he received a long letter from Feilitzsch, the Minister for the Interior, extolling the virtues of economy. This was actually in response to his own letter asking for money in which he had complained bitterly and not unreasonably, "During the reign of Ludwig I, 20 million was diverted from the reserves for his building projects. When I now make a claim for the same thing, when I make eager representations for it to be made possible for me, such burdensome conditions should not be imposed which, for the King, would be extremely undignified, and I would become desperate. Even if only the sum needed to cover the arrears were to be forthcoming and not the sum I so urgently need in order to continue the building, I would be served and helped in no small way. I therefore charge you urgently once more to do everything possible to contribute to the fulfilment of my longing wishes and to silence opposing elements."

The reply, which annoyed Ludwig intensely, contained various disturbing pieces of information, including the ominous paragraph which read "The truly obedient undersigned has also given much consideration to the question whether the Landtag might see their way clear to consenting to the agreed sum. Unfortunately, there is absolutely no hope in this direction. Regrettable information received on this subject leaves no doubts; there is an agreed opinion that the majority will not take responsibility in the country and especially for Your Majesty. A prominent member of the Patriotic Party has already put this question to a public meeting of peasants many weeks ago and there was, on that occasion, 'verbal refusal'. And he certainly did not do this because he had already been informed of the mood of the majority Patriotic faction."

But who were these "peasants"? They were certainly not the ones who lived in Schwangau or Hohenschwangau in Prien, Oberammergau or Garmisch or, indeed, from any of the other small villages in the vicinity of any of the royal residences for all the peasants, farmers, herdsmen and foresters were fond of the King and proud of his castles and were for the most part as keen to see their completion as the King himself. Ludwig was perfectly well aware of this and, indeed, took great comfort from it. He considered the whole affair of the funds to be a slight on his honour and understandably could not accept that the Privy Purse was in the lamentable condition described. He stubbornly refused to see why he must economise so drastically or, indeed, how one could economise on the building of a castle except by using inferior materials and workmanship - and in the past years he had had many a dispute with dishonest suppliers over the former. A castle was, after all, built to last as long as a Monarchy, if not longer.

Having met with so poor a response from official quarters, Ludwig began to search around within his own family and among the other crowned heads of Europe. He instructed Hesselschwerdt to go to Duke Max in Bavaria,* for example, to ask him to approach the Emperor of Austria for a loan on his behalf. Brash and resourceful by nature, Hesselschwerdt would have had no qualms about carrying out such an order had he not been well primed by Holnstein. He was accustomed to mixing with the nobility and well-versed in the art of carrying messages between the King and his Cabinet, and the fact that he made no attempt to do as he was told lies not with any sense of delicacy or embarrassment but with the fact that Holnstein had instructed him not to do so.

Possibly aware that Hesselschwerdt did not deliver this message, Ludwig tried again, offering him alternatives in the shape of Prince Maximilian von Thurn und Taxis, the King of Sweden and various Oriental rulers who were known to be open handed. To other more reliable messengers he gave the task of approaching and merchant bankers in Paris, Frankfurt, Berlin and Zurich. When told of the failure of all these missions, Ludwig was heard to remark wryly that he would soon be reduced to holding the bank managers at pistol point and taking the money by force, but instead of being greeted with the laughter he obviously expected, the joke misfired and was meticulously added to the growing store of "evidence" now being accumulated against him.

Undaunted, he despatched a fresh wave of agents to a new selection of prospects, instructing each man to ask for two million but informing Hesselschwerdt at the same time that each man was not to know of the other's commission. In this way, if more than one of the agents was successful, he would acquire a minimum of four million marks or a maximum of 20 million. There was no discussion as to how the money would be repaid. There was a puzzling naïveté in Ludwig's whole attitude to money which lasted throughout his life. He was a man whose whole existence was based upon honour; it is unlikely that he was scheming to get money under false pretences and, indeed, such vast sums that he could never have hoped to repay them from the Privy Purse alone during his lifetime. It seems not to have occurred to him that what he was now doing, even if the loans did not actually materialise, was less than honest and over the next few weeks after he had had time to digest Feilitzsch's letter, he threw caution to the winds and approached all manner of unlikely people, despatching Klug and others to various parts of Europe while he himself waited hopefully for success in his mountain eyries.

Unfortunately, Klug proved to be as useless in the art of obtaining

* Empress Elisabeth's father.

loans without security as his predecessors, while the efforts of Prince Ludwig Ferdinand, who was deeply attached to the King and would certainly have liked to have helped him, were too discreetly made to obtain results. Hesselschwerdt and his underlings, however, made no genuine effort whatever. In view of the futility of the operation, even the faithful Dürkheim was unwilling to go a-begging. On one occasion, Hesselschwerdt arrived at Dürkheim's quarters with the message that he was to travel to London and ask the Duke of Westminster for a loan of 10 million Marks; Dürkheim told him to tell the King that to make such a request to a foreign power could only damage the prestige of the throne, whereupon the Hesselschwerdt promptly replied that he could not deliver the message "until Wednesday" because he was "actually in Naples." When the astonished Chamberlain demanded an explanation, the Quartermaster replied "The King has sent me to Naples but I would achieve nothing by going there and therefore I have remained here. But I have said I am going there and that I will return on Wednesday and therefore I cannot report to the King before that time."

Klug at least put himself out to undertake the journey, fruitless though he knew it would be. He arrived home a day early and reported to the waiting King that his last words had been with the bankers, Bleichroder, who had held out no hope whatever after discussions with Bismarck, who stated baldly, "Without any guarantee it is impossible to raise one million in Germany. Even if His Majesty the King of Bavaria wrote to me personally I should not be able to give him any other advice than this: stop the building and go to the Ministers." Klug also pointed out that this would enable Ludwig to borrow the money more cheaply than if he went elsewhere. In his reply to the King, the wily Bismarck did not fail to hold out his usual false ray of hope: "I am taking up the possibility of fulfilling the wishes of the All Highest without delay, and find that the present financial crisis is already known to my trusted special employees. After your declaration of the pressing monetary need of six million Marks it is believed it may be possible to procure this sum but only against security and only on condition that, only by the abandonment of further building can the means be found of paying interest and paying back the loan. As such an abandonment of the continuation of the building is not Your Majesty's intention, we have no possibility of administering the necessary sum either from the circle of moneylenders or from the Home Ministerium of His Majesty the Emperor. I have also carefully weighed up the possibilities by which I might offer assistance to Your Majesty by which, under open representation of the circumstances in the Landtag, I could make a motion for the granting by the Ministerium of the necessary sum. In my humble and all-submissive opinion, there is no doubt that the national representation will confirm the fact that the Bavarian people will not only grant a concession of the outstanding debts of the Privy Purse, but will also make an allowance for the conclusion of the buildings which have been begun."

Realising that he could expect no real help from Bismarck, who was anythig but "humble and all submissive" Ludwig decided at least to take up the Chancellor's suggestion and put his case to the Landtag, unfortunately failing to see that even this was, in fact, a carefully laid trap. He accordingly wrote to Minister Lutz, "It is my will that an advance should be made to my Privy Purse by my Government in the form of the combined Landtag with all possible speed and the sum referred to submitted to me." He then instructed Klug to give the Chancellor's letter to Hesselschwerdt together with a note which read "Read this very sensible letter from Bismarck and give it to Ziegler to read. He must force an issue on this affair. Summon everything in his power."

But although Bismarck's letter was in fact read by at least six persons empowered to take action, and Ludwig's accompanying instructions were quite explicit, Lutz had other plans and it did not suit him to carry out Ludwig's orders. His purpose was far better served by mentioning the matter, almost in the course of mere social conversation, to one or two carefully selected Ministers who shared his own views; unsurprisingly, nothing came of it. The King had by this time given up all pretence of reading the Parliamentary reports, and was inclined to leave them, together with other purportedly "highly confidential" documents lying opened on his desk for days or even weeks for anyone to read at whim. When one considers that such reports had usually been seen by everyone else before they ever reached Ludwig, this was not quite as scandalous as it might appear.

One report which he did respect was that concerned with his brother, and he always gave this his close attention. Ironically, in the light of ensuing events, even these may have been no more than an elaborate fiction.

In spite of his naturally suspicious nature and the fact that he was aware there were very few loyal officials left in his cabinet, he was probably still impervious to the dangerous direction in which he was heading. In addition to impending loans from outside sources, Holnstein had long since instructed treasury minions that no bills were to be paid and that the world was to be given the impression that the King was bankrupt. In reality, the King was by no means penniless and funds could easily have been found to settle all the outstanding accounts. This is obvious from the fact that Ludwig's coffers magically refilled the moment Luitpold became Regent; it indicates also that the plot to get rid of Ludwig had been afoot for some time. Having thus effectively

placed the King in an invidious position Lutz, in company with Holnstein, Crailsheim and Eulenburg, and with the bribed connivance of
many of Ludwig's body servants, now began to put into action the
ambitious plan to depose the King. Numbers of Ludwig's notes and
instructions, innocuous and straightforward enough to those for whom
they were intended became, when taken out of context, damaging and
seemingly conclusive evidence of the King's abnormality.

Even Bismarck, who was ever the master of the double game and
would lose nothing by Ludwig's deposition, was quick to aver publicly
that the Bavarian ministers were "butchering their King to maintain
themselves in office" and that their means to this end were not as
honourable as it could have been since those involved "did not shrink
from collecting their evidence from the King's waste basket" which of
course, he was in a good position to know at first hand since he himself
was the final recipient of these unfortunate scraps of paper.

Only on March 6th, when a brutally frank and damaging article
appeared in the *Bayerische Vaterland* concerning the situation in the
Privy Purse, did Ludwig realise the full implications of the situation.
He felt trapped and forsaken and, perhaps for the first time for many
years, remembered his father. On March 9th he wrote to Marie, "In
remembrance of tomorrow's anniversary of father's death and because
I am not in Munich as usual at this time of year, I feel urged to get in
touch with you in this way. For the near future I shall remain here
anyhow, as what ought to have happened has not happened. Because
of profoundly sad experiences I am unhappy and must wait for the
reason for it (the earlier the better) to disappear. It is disagreeable to
write or to say more about it, and I beseech you not to say anything to
anybody. I very much enjoyed the winter here, but would rather like
to go to town as usual now."

Encouraged, Marie wrote back telling him of her proposed visit to
see Otto and asking Ludwig after his own health and well being. In his
reply, he said, "I do hope you found Otto reasonably well. Today I
dreamed I spoke to him for a long time. It is deplorable that it isn't
possible in reality. I thank you heartily for your kind wishes that I
should be happy. That I have not been happy for some months has to
do with the building." Following Ludwig's admission Marie made a
gesture which at last vindicated much of her past behaviour; she offered
him all her money and her jewels to help pay his debts. Naturally he
declined but he was deeply touched. In any case, what Marie had to
offer would scarcely have skimmed the surface of the sea of debts by
which he thought he was now totally engulfed. The plot had now
progressed too far for anyone to help him. While Ludwig was writing
cordially to his mother, Lutz' well-laid plans were crystallising. Dr.
Bernhard Gudden, whom he had approached with a view to examining

the mental health of the King with the understood intention of finding it to be deficient, had seen only the written testimonials of those members of Ludwig's staff who had been bribed to say anything they could think of which might damage the King's image and reputation. He had not even examined Ludwig personally and had previously met him only once when he had personally presented the report on Otto some years earlier. He was nevertheless quite prepared to report officially to Lutz that the King was mad.

The situation was exacerbated by the appearance of another vitriolic article in the *Bayerische Vaterland* which announced sanctimoniously "the financial embarrassment in the Privy Purse has occupied the Press both at home and abroad for some considerable time now in such a manner that these affairs can no longer be regarded as private affairs and have gained a very serious importance. Now, not only the newspapers but all the world speaks about it and the way in which the world speaks about it is, for the Bavarian people, neither flattering nor pleasant." This is somewhat strong criticism coming from the press, whose omission to balance the books by mentioning any of the excellent things which Ludwig had done throughout his reign broke the heart of their much-maligned target.

In fact, the King had never been as thoughtless and idle as people had been led to believe. He was responsible for the separation of church and education when Hohenlohe had first put the idea forward and thereafter had founded a number of schools and colleges as well as the Munich Academy of Fine Arts and the Institute of Technology. He was deeply and actively interested in all the arts and sciences and had he had the opportunity in his youth to attend the University as had originally been planned, he would have studied under the great Professor Liebig himself, and we may be sure that he would have grasped such an opportunity with eager hands. Ludwig was a firm believer in education for all, without the restrictions imposed by the church on whatever subject was being taught, and was also among the first active supporters of Henri Dunant's Relief Action of the Red Cross. Above all, despite the storm of protest which it had provoked at the time, his patronage of Richard Wagner when no one else would have anything to do with him gave incalculable pleasure to the world. Expert in matters aesthetic, Ludwig perceived Wagner's genius many years before the rest of the world recognised it or indeed comprehended the immense value of his work. Further, Ludwig's castles themselves were to add further lustre to Bavaria's already glowing beauty, giving enormous pleasure to the many thousands who continue to visit the castles today, thus providing the German government with a healthy revenue. Finally, against the dictates of his own conscience, he was instrumental in creating the German Empire, an act for which he never forgave himself. Yet for all these positive achievements, at the beginning of 1886 only the peasants could see any good in Ludwig at all.

On April 11th, the report of Baron von Bruck announced that the long-expected disaster had finally struck: "As I have just telegraphed, the first complaint against the Civil List has just been brought. Complainants are the Gas and Water Installation Companies from Wachter and Morstadt regarding an advance of over 100,000 Marks. The Court of Justice in Munich has fixed a date for the hearing of this case on May 9th. Doubtless this example will shortly be emulated and one can look forward to further complaints against the Royal Civil List within the next few days."

A sure sign of the extent of Ludwig's desperation was his approach to Prince Hohenlohe, a man in whom he had long since lost faith and also, for the second time he approached the sympathetic but ineffectual Prince Ludwig Ferdinand. The former, forgetting Ludwig's many kindnesses to him, did nothing; the latter approached his mother-in-law, Queen Isabella of Spain, on the King's behalf, but to no avail.

Defeated, Ludwig sought solace in his usual manner and afterwards, full of remorse and self-contempt, wrote in the diary "Never again (sensual kisses) the morning of April 16th definitely the last fall, which I deplore with all my heart and of which I repent sincerely." His troubles were now spiritual and physical as well as financial. Only days before, he had written to his mother at Elbigenalp, where she was staying for a while, "A few days ago the dentist was here and instead of putting everything right, I now have more toothache than before. Please forgive the bad writing but in consequence of a sleepless night and the medicine, I am very agitated." And again, on the 21st, "My toothache has gone; unfortunately, not the cause of my melancholy because instead of getting better, the latter is becoming worse and worse."

In addition to the constant public airing of his financial difficulties it was now common knowledge throughout Bavaria that Ludwig's ménage bore little resemblance to a Royal household. His strange life had become a cheap music hall joke, something to be satirised in the raucous songs of the tavern singers. His servants, far from being the victims of a cruel tyrant as so many of them were later to testify, now treated him with an insolence and neglect which they would never have dared accord a less exalted master and generally made his life a misery by giving him the poorest of service and by showing unfeeling inattention to his simplest needs. But his notes of protest, written in moments of sheer desperation by the hypersensitive man who could no longer endure direct confrontation with his unruly staff, continued to be avidly snapped up by Hesselschwerdt to add to his nefarious collection of "evidence".

Hoping to find things more amenable at Berg, Ludwig left the Residenz in May, anxious as always to enjoy this particular month as in former times, in the place where he had been happiest with Elisabeth and with Richard Hornig. Unfortunately, the only improvement appears to have been in the food, for Berg was fortunate in having a resident major domo and chef, one Friedrich Zanders. Things were otherwise much the same as elsewhere and he spent his time poring over the building reports and the ever-increasing file of correspondence with the Berlin Chancellery, including letters from Bismarck himself which had grown continually more emphatic as to his recommended course of action. On May 19th, Bismarck wrote "It appears without doubt that the grant of the Landtag at the present moment and above all in the future can only be brought to fruition if the Landtag are of the conviction that the replenishing of the Privy Purse will prevent the future exhaustion of the same. Also, as far as the acquisition of any loan from outside is concerned, there would be imperative preconditions concerning increase of economy without which capital cannot be raised under reasonable help than that which Majesty can find within his own means and decision.

"What we need," Ludwig confessed to his hairdresser, "Is a new cabinet secretary." He then sent the highly flattered Hoppé to Karl Hesselschwerdt with the order to find one. Although the situation was largely of their own making, the Ministers were enraged by the fact that Ludwig put more faith in his hairdresser than in those in high places who should have been performing the functions now being carried out with such blissful exhuberance by the semi-educated little man most of whose life until now had been devoted to the application of pomade and curling tongs.

The Prussian attaché, Phillipp, Count von Eulenburg who, for reasons of his own, wished to ridicule the King as much as possible, reported "The latter [Hoppé], a genuine if foolish soul of a hairdresser, felt extremely elevated by his political role. I myself had direct knowledge of the proceedings through hairdresser Hoppé when I visited his business premises one day and, as it happened, was alone in his salon: he told me (in a whisper) that he had given the Minister of Justice, Fäustle, his dismissal in the name of the King. 'And what did the Minister say?' I asked. 'Nothin', replied Hoppé, before concluding, 'I've offered the position to Herr Schwiegersohn now'."

This unsatisfactory state of affairs continued until the beginning of June when Lutz, Bismarck, Prince Luitpold and Holnstein as well as Eulenburg, Washington and Crailsheim, having clearly agreed among themselves that the time was ripe for a change, now saw their opportunity. Ever with an eye to the main chance, Lutz was well to the fore. Four months earlier, in February, Baron von Bruck had reported to

Vienna, "It has recently been said that Ludwig II is ill; in Ministerial circles it is even said that he is very ill; outbreaks of rage are increasing in a most alarming manner. Highly confidential discussions have therefore taken place between Prince Luitpold and Herr von Lutz which have resulted in Prince Luitpold agreeing, in the event of his taking over the Regency, to retain the present Ministerium and to undertake absolutely no changes in the personnel of the same. Since Herr von Lutz has succeeded in winning the complete confidence of Prince Luitpold, the possibility of a regency has become much more imminent." It was the most blatant treason; it was a political deal not unworthy of a present day Third World manipulator.

Echoing the sentiments of the rebels, however, the *Nürnberger Zeitung* openly voiced the opinion that it was inconceivable "that subordinate men should undertake to be offered ministers' posts and give themselves as as the spokesmen for the will of the All Highest. While it is clear that similar commands given to a hairdresser or a lackey cannot be taken seriously, they must unfortunately be regarded as symptoms of a serious illness." Surely such information could only have come from Count Eulenburg, who was certainly not averse to this kind of sublimation and was, as we shall later see, an expert in the art? The article continued "the position is serious and can no longer be maintained. It concerns the prestige of the Dynasty, the bearing and consciousness of the Monarchy and of the orderly continuation of the Government. It is unthinkable that the relationship between crown and ministerium has to rely exclusively upon the unreliable mediations of subordinate servants." All of which sounds very reasonable if the reader is unaware of the full picture.

The article provided Lutz with his cue to take matters into his own hands. He approached Luitpold officially now with the welcome suggestion that Ludwig must be removed from the throne, asserting that the King was insane and must be dethroned *in favour of Prince Otto* [Author's italics]. The latter is surely the most extraordinary pronouncement in view of the fact that Otto, who had been certified in 1878, was allegedly no more than a vegetable. This fact, aside from any other consideration, would offer conclusive proof that Ludwig was the hapless if largely unprotesting victim of a *coup*. He was to be deposed purely for political and financial reasons which had nothing to do with his health. His shy and nervous disposition provided his enemies wth an extra flag to wave – and undoubtedly the way he was being treated by so-called responsible officials must certainly have made him appear worse.

It is quite clear that his staff knew the effect of their attitude upon him and played ruthlessly upon their victim's feelings. Ludwig on his side knew that something was going on, although probably not exactly what was being planned, for after all, he had been complaining about court intrigues against him for some time.

Childlike, he tried to close his eyes and will the trouble to go away but the knowledge that he was surrounded by enemies kept him awake at night and gave him headaches. The now obligatory "medicine", the chloralhydrate, unfortunately left him unfit and unwilling to carry out his duties, but it was certainly not a permanent condition and when he was not thus affected he was a perfectly normal man, a fact well known to all who were personally acquainted with him and certainly by those who now persecuted him.

However, it suited the King's adversaries to ignore the truth and in order to render respectable what was tantamount to a *coup d'état*, Luitpold now acted out his part with the same somewhat histrionic technique used by Julius Caesar: although in private he had already accepted the Regency, for the sake of appearances he piously refused it three times in public. This of course pleased the Munich people to whom he immediately became a hero and they accordingly placed him far higher in their estimation than he deserved. Predictably, after lengthy discussions with those who shared his hopes for the future, he at last put pen to paper on June 1st: "My dear Ministerialrat Dr.von Ziegler, The serious illness of His Majesty the King has, as you know, put the country into a very sad predicament so I consider it my duty to consider taking measures which -within the constitution - would guarantee the continuity of the Government. For this purpose, it is absolutely necessary to get as exact a picture as possible of the mental state of His Majesty the King. As you have been in the immediate circle of His Majesty for a long time, you should be in a position to give trustworthy facts which would be valuable as phsychological evidence and I therefore request you to let me have a memorandum with the observations which you have made in that direction. With the assurance of my esteem I am, Your gracious Luitpold, Prince of Bavaria."

He was coolly asking Ziegler to betray one of his oldest friends, a man who had never shown him anything but kindness. It is no credit to Ziegler that he complied with Luitpold's request and afterwards did irreparable damage to with his biased and not altogether truthful testimony against the King.

Luitpold next called a meeting of the Landtag to announce the appointments of Max Holnstein and Clemenz von Törring-Jettenbach as "special advisers" to Berlin "in the best personal and private interests of Your Royal Majesty". Needless to say, the first priority of these two gentlemen was to institute Luitpold officially as Regent. Everything was now neat and tidy, if totally illegal.

Apparently unaware that his days were numbered, Ludwig moved on to Linderhof and on the same day as Luitpold wrote to Ziegler,

Ludwig noted in his diary "June 1st, definitely the last fall, two months and three weeks before the 41st birthday." Having signed this statement and appended the great seal, he ordered Albert Welcker to sign with him. This current favourite was no more loyal than the others and was quick to offer evidence of the King's "madness" when the time came, his pockets still heavy with the money which the King had given him. Everything that Ludwig now said, wrote and did was carefully reported to Holnstein who avidly collected every shred of "evidence": every rumour, every note he had written, every excursion he made, every appeal for money he put forward, every casual friendship he struck. No stone was left unturned.

Although Holnstein's personal relationship with the King had long since ceased, he had never officially relinquished his post as Oberstallmeister and no other official had taken his place. He had meantime taken a new position on Bismarck's personal staff but technically he could legally resume his post with the Bavarian King at any time and thus found that he could to advantage fill two posts at once.

When he was in Berlin, he kept himself informed of events in Munich by Hesselschwerdt. The quartermaster thus found himself in the position of go-between when Ludwig was in the process of negotiating a loan from the Banker Rothschild in Paris. In this respect, Ludwig ordered him to go to the French capital with a note authorising him to accept the loan on his behalf. At the same time, Ludwig was in touch with the French Royal family and the Orleans were prepared to do what they could to assist him in his predicament. But Hesselschwerdt knew that it would not suit Holnstein if the King were to be released from his monetary difficulties and before setting out on his mission, telegraphed to the former Oberstallmeister who was taking a cure at Karlsbad*, telling him of the King's instructions. Holnstein replied forthwith to the effect that he must not finalise arrangements for such a loan, "or he would pay heavily for it." Holnstein himself then returned to Munich forthwith, arriving before Hesseschwerdt's departure, took the King's sealed letter to Rothschild and delivered it instead to Lutz, who in turn took it to Luitpold. Infamously, none of these "gentlemen" saw anything wrong with opening another man's letters or interfering in the King's personal business.

The next move in this unpleasant game was for Lutz to seek the advice of four medical practitioners who, with the exception of Dr.Bernhard von Gudden, who had met the King briefly, did not even know Ludwig personally and would therefore seem ill qualified to pass medical judgment on him.

Gudden, a Prussian, made his name in the Lower Saxonian Hospital Foundation Werneck and the University of Munich and had been a

* Now Karlovy Vary.

professor at that establishment since 1872. He was also a director of the Munich Health Foundation of Upper Bavaria. Lutz knew immediately where to go in order to get what he wanted but Gudden later made such incredible mistakes in the treatment of his "patient" that it is difficult to believe that he was called on to the case in his capacity as a doctor rather than as a conspirator.

When putting together his initial report on Ludwig without a personal examination he was careful to outline only those eccentricities which had been with him since childhood, notably his love of solitude, his shyness and his deep suspicion of his fellows and when one considers how he was treated by most of his friends, his attitude is perfectly understandable. Nowhere in Gudden's report was it mentioned that except when he was stupefied with chloralhydrate, Ludwig was charming, erudite and pacific. His foibles were no worse than anyone else's and, as Bürkel had asserted, the only time he ever appeared to be anything but normal was when he was dealing with his building projects.

Nevertheless, after a meeting in Munich on June 8th, 1886, a statement was issued bearing the signatures of Gudden (*Obermedizinalrat*), Dr. Hagena, Dr. Grashey and Dr. Hubrich, attesting that the King was suffering from paranoia and that he was thus prevented from ruling "as his impediment will last not only for a year (the specified time by which, according to the Bavarian Consitition, a mentally sick monarch could remain on the Throne), but for the whole of his lifetime. Ludwig's fate was thus sealed without his knowledge and without the courtesy of an opportunity to defend himself. On the following day, a deputation representing the Government, together with the medical commission, began preparations to travel to Hohenschwangau that afternoon by special train.

Predictably, the leader of this expedition was the ubiquitous Max Holnstein. At his side was Krafft, Baron von Crailsheim, the Master of the King's Household, Clemenz, Count Törring-Jettenbach, a prominent nobleman, Colonel Baron Karl-Theodor von Washington, a former aide de camp of the King, Dr. Bernhard Gudden and his assistant, Dr. Karl-Franz Muller. Flanking the party were two mental nurses with privy counsellor Karl von Rumpel to perform the curious function of "secretary".

Armed with Luitpold's signature on the medical report together with a further "authorisation" from Lutz, the party completed their preparations in good spirits and with a good appetite: Gudden ordered supper for himself and his colleagues with remarks which indicated that he considered the occasion to be a festive one. When questioned by his colleagues during the meal as to what would happen next, he replied pompously, "The King is ill and *we must inform him of the fact*"

[Author's italics], a reply which should have produced a startled reaction but which, revealingly, did not.

Gudden then expounded his theories as to their course of action, saying that the party members should present themselves at Hohenschwangau and inform Ludwig of Luitpold's declaration of the taking over of the regency "because of the King's sick condition". At this point, Ludwig would be told that his medical treatment was to begin immediately, and that a carriage would take him to Linderhof.* Gudden explained that this particular residence had been chosen on the grounds of its inaccessibility and because it was thought that because he was so attached to it he would not try to escape!

The plan was to convey Ludwig by means of a specially prepared carriage with the handles removed from the inside so that he would not be able to escape. He would have two nurses to guard him and, in case of some objection on his part, one doctor would travel in front and one behind. Baron Washington was to travel in the last carriage. The obtuse and unfeeling Gudden had decided in his wisdom that, as Washington had been known personally to the King for many years he was "the most suitable" choice of companion, regardless of the fact that Ludwig disliked him and, indeed, had dismissed him from service for that reason some years before.

The younger doctor, Karl-Franz Müller, afterwards admitted to being shocked by the "calm and callous way in which Gudden spoke of the King" and that "all the gentlemen in spite of themselves felt a certain unease over the fact that the plans *seemed too well made to have been entirely spontaneous suggestions on the part of Dr. Gudden* [Author's italics]. Holnstein remarked, "Gentlemen, if you will permit me, I would suggest that you amend these travel arrangements. I for one cannot take upon myself the responsibility of allowing nurses to travel in the carriage with His Majesty. I will not allow these *Schwarze Hände* [Black Hands] to be let loose upon His Majesty." This apparent *volte face* on Holnstein's part is puzzling, a possible explanation being that at that point he had other reasons for considering the attendants to be in the way. Gudden replied, "Your Excellency chooses to joke."

Gudden was clearly put out by the opposition which he had encountered. Following up Holnstein's comment, he wanted to know "what the Herr Graf has to suggest as an acceptable alternative". Holnstein said "I can only repeat that the King must travel alone, but it would, I think, be acceptable to all, including His Majesty himself, if either a nurse or a doctor were to sit on the box." There were instant cries of "Ridiculous! Shame! Imbecile!" followed by a heated and lengthy argument which would suggest that even among these obvious plotters there were two separate factions, the one who knew the King to be sane

* Later discarded in favour of Berg.

and wanted him out of the way and the other the medicos who had been told that the King was mentally ill and obviously expected to treat him as a dangerous lunatic. At all events, it is clear that throughout the extraordinary proceedings the members of the Commission did not understand each other at all.

Holnstein behaved very strangely altogether and here again there are two possible explanations: either he had been hoping to carry out the assassination plan *en route* while the King was alone in the carriage and saw his plans being thwarted by Gudden's interference, or he was genuinely embarrassed by the thought of a personal confrontation with the King who by this time must certainly have been aware of the former Oberstallmeister's change of political affiliation. Holnstein would naturally want to appear in as favourable a light as possible in order to escape Ludwig's understandable wrath when he laid eyes on him. Max Holnstein had done very well out of the *Kaiserbrief* affair, having received by devious means from Bismarck no less than the equivalent of 10% of the entire war damages from the Franco-Prussian conflict. As we know, he also received a Prussian decoration and a post on Bismarck's staff. Interestingly, both he and Philipp Eulenburg were later involved in the removal from office in Berlin of Bismarck himself.

Whatever his reasons, during the discussion concerning Ludwig's abduction, Holnstein certainly became very agitated and the argument continued until Gudden said firmly, "Gentlemen, please! We cannot remain here like this indefinitely. I myself will travel in front in case something happens on the journey." "But what could possibly happen?" Holnstein snapped and Gudden, after regarding him "for some considerable time" replied with great deliberation and, indeed, most enigmatically, "My dear Count Holnstein, you must appreciate that it might be that measures have to be taken to protect the King from himself."

There was no more to be said.

CHAPTER FIFTEEN

DEPOSITION AND ABDUCTION

ON arrival, the party of men from Munich discovered that the King was not at Hohenschwangau but at nearby Neuschwanstein. Holnstein, who was well acquainted both with the castles and with Ludwig's routines, such as they were, took it upon himself to reassume his former mantle and departed to inspect the stables where he found Osterholzer harnessing a team of horses in preparation for the customary nocturnal carriage ride. It was Ludwig's custom to drive out in all weathers and he was unperturbed by the heavy mist which completely obscured both castles.

Holnstein called roughly across to Osterholzer to stop what he was doing and walking swiftly towards the astounded coachman added, "The King will not be needing that carriage. You may put it away again."

"But Excellency, Majesty always goes out at this hour." To this Holnstein replied that "another carriage and another coachman" awaited the Sovereign. Osterholzer, knowing that the detested *Ross-Ober* was out of favour with Ludwig, immediately feared the worst and his anxiety was confirmed when, after objecting, "Begging your pardon, Excellency, but I only obey the commands of His Majesty and he has told me to harness the horses," he received the brusque rejoinder "The King can no longer give commands but only His Royal Highness Prince Luitpold."

Afraid that the King's life might be in danger, Osterholzer's only thought was to find a way of preventing such a catastrophe. To allay Holnstein's suspicions, he did as he was told and led the horses back to the stables which were situated below Schloss Hohenschwangau before setting off for Neuschwanstein by the side track to alert the King to the danger. Although extremely steep, this track was often used for expediency but it was a hard climb especially since the heavy rain had turned it into a river of mud. His errand left him wet and exhausted but to have used the new carriageway would have taken some 15 minutes longer and instinct told him that there was not a minute to lose.

Niggl, the Major Domo, admitted him quickly, alarmed by his frenzied hammering on the doors and by his frightened appearance. Even before the coachman demanded to speak to the King urgently, Niggl had realised that something was very wrong and complied without demur. When Osterholzer was announced, the valet Weber was helping Ludwig into his topcoat and the coachman delivered his news so incoherently that the King could not understand his heavy Allgäuer dialect. "What does this mean? What is he saying?" Ludwig asked Niggl, although in his heart he must have guessed why the coachman had come. When the horrified Niggl explained, the servants in unison told Ludwig that they feared for his life and that he must flee, reminding him that by using the Kitzburg path he could be in Austria in ten minutes. Indeed, there was an even quicker path* which ended at Schluxen just over the Austrian border, but as this led from the edge of the Alpsee and the entrance to Schloss Hohenschwangau, he could not have taken this route without going directly towards his pursuers. The essence of any escape operation was speed.

While Ludwig was touched by their concern, when he heard the word "flee", he drew himself up proudly, "Flee? Why should I flee my own castle? If there was any real, imminent danger, Karl would have written immediately." Erroneously, he still trusted Hesselschwerdt. Persuaded at last that the danger was real enough, he was still only ready to concede "You may give the order to barricade the castle; bring some guards to me and have some messengers sent down to Füssen to get the Gendarmerie and the Fire Brigade." He also suggested reinforcements from Schwangau and Walthenhofen but he had already procrastinated for too long. The Commission members were by this time waiting directly below in the courtyard where stood their own carriages as well as that prepared for the King. It was almost four in the morning and a mist hung heavily over the woods; cold and heavy rain continued to beat down, chilling all the men to the bone but apparently not cooling their zeal.

When they arrived at the gatehouse they were turned away politely enough by some Gendarmes who were on duty there. In vain they offered their credentials but the Gendarmes, being typically rational countrymen, refused to take them seriously. They all knew Ludwig personally and were aware that whatever else he was, he was certainly not mad. They could only repeat to Holnstein, "The King has commanded us not to allow anybody into the castle and we shall obey without consideration for the consequences." When the furious Holnstein tried to brush past them, they also moved forward, determined not to let the interlopers have their way. All of these men loved Ludwig deeply and were ready to kill anyone who tried to abduct or harm him in any way, although in fact, they had not the means to prevent such a disaster. In the face of all argument and threat they nevertheless continued to resist, "The King has commanded and we shall obey." Seemingly, it had not occured to the conspirators that they might encounter opposition.

* Now known as the Fürstenstrasse.

As dawn broke, a number of people from the surrounding villages had come, despite the incessant rain, to defend their Sovereign and some 50 firemen from Schwangau alone arrived to join Kommandant Hainzl who was already there. To the discomfort of the Commission, the numbers began to swell alarmingly as the news spread and they became even more disturbed by the sudden appearance of a well-dressed aristocrat who stood up in her carriage and began to berate the Munich party. "Herr von Gudden! Herr von Gudden! I am going to protect the King!" Her appearance in particular upset Gudden deeply.

The lady in question, Spera, Baroness von Truschess, was one of Ludwig's most fervent admirers; she had followed him everywhere for some time and for the moment had taken Schloss Bullachberg, a large villa which lay directly across the fields from Hohenschwangau in the direction of Horn, simply in order to be near the King when he was in residence. Several of the Commission members knew her personally as she was prominent in Munich society and always appeared at Court if she thought Ludwig was likely to be there. Unfortunately, she had once been a patient of Gudden's and on this basis he advised his companions not to take her too seriously. It was an ugly breach of professional etiquette on his part to describe her as "mad", but he used the word repeatedly and as with his other patients, showed little tact or discretion. It is hard to imagine how this clumsy, unprofessional man came to be so greatly revered.

At the time in question, the Baroness did not show symptoms of madness but only those of very natural fury at the idea of her adored Sovereign being treated like a criminal. She was as unwelcome as the ghost at the wedding: "Graf Törring!" she screamed, "Your children will be ashamed of you forever! Baron Washington, how can you treat your King in this way when he has shown you nothing but kindness! Minister Crailsheim, I shall never play the piano with you again! You are traitors, all of you! A finer man than His Majesty does not live!" Her expostulations may seem a little wild but they were more the outraged expletions of one who is too angry to think of appropriate expressions rather than the incoherent ramblings of a madwoman. By this time she had alighted from her carriage and with her servant was trying to force an entry into the castle. The villagers certainly did not regard her as deranged and had listened to her taunts in sympathetic agreement, applauding loudly as she berated each man in turn. Holnstein restrained her from reaching her goal and as she drew close to him, she said, "Ah yes, you, Oberstallmeister! It is no surprise to find you here for you were always a traitor to His Majesty." This, as we know, was no more than the truth. Holnstein was extremely put out to

hear her say it in public, however, and let her go immediately, remark-
ing angrily to Gudden, "That madwoman would have to arrive now!"

As the minutes passed the crowd began to grow, tempers became
frayed and many heated words were exchanged. Neither the Commission members nor the Gendarmerie had expected such a scene
since the village would normally be deserted at this hour, but the
plotters had greatly underestimated the love which Ludwig's peasants
bore him. If only the King himself had realised it earlier, and had known
exactly what was happening, and if only he had been able to rouse
himself from his apathy, he could have taken direct action to avoid
deposition by appealing for the help of these people who would
certainly have come to his assistance as indeed so many of them had
done voluntarily when the news spread that he was in difficulties. But
without leadership or weapons they were powerless to do anything
constructive and could only demonstrate their angry protest.

Holnstein was furious to find such strong loyalty and snatching the
papers from Gudden, who had been making a further ineffectual
attempt to offer them to the guard, said: "I have written authority. Do
your duty, man!"

"I need no authority and I need nothing in writing. I recognise only
one order and that comes from the King." Holnstein pushed forward towards the man upon which Wachtmeister Heinz raised his
pistol, his face set and determined, "Come no step nearer or I fire!"
Angered by the aggressive attitude of these city dwellers and, in
particular, Holnstein, the other Gendarmes came forward with him
and as they did so, a rifle butt brushed against one of the nurses,
knocking a small, dark-coloured bottle from the man's hand.
Everyone present saw it and guessed from its general appearance
what it contained. Equally, there could be no doubt as to its intended
purpose. "My God!" Heinz shouted, "What have you come to do?"
"We have come to do our duty, as you should be doing! The King
is mad and must be restrained!"

"What nonsense!" Heinz countered, "I myself passed the time of
day with His Majesty only yesterday and you may have my word no
saner man lives! It is clear you mean some mischief. Nothing will
persuade me to let you pass now!"

The whole affair had been incredibly mismanaged. The Commission members looked indecisively at each other for a few moments,
Holnstein glaring angrily at the nurse who had inadvertently betrayed
the purpose of the expedition. After a short discussion it was agreed
that it was pointless to wait any longer and the party returned dejec-
tedly to Hohenschwangau, followed by a barrage of colourful insults
from the crowd. Once back in the village, they telegraphed news of

their failure to Munich. Nevertheless, they had caused a sensation. Although it was still only six o'clock in the morning, the tiny village was full of angry people and a number of firemen from Füssen had now joined their colleagues from Schwangau. Contemptuously, Holnstein called out to them, "Go home, do you hear? There is nothing on fire, nothing for you to do! Go back to your homes, I say!" But the voice which had for years struck fear into the hearts of the peasants now seemed to have little effect.

Meanwhile, Baroness Truschess had managed to find her way into the King's presence, determined to be of service to him. With so few people remaining in the castle it was not too difficult for her to do this but Ludwig was bewildered to find her standing before him, leaning heavily on her stick, her pointed chin jutting forward with determination. "Madam, what do you want? What are you doing here?" he asked. She replied that she had come to assist him, to die for him if necessary. She was extremely excited, so much so that she had forgotten the usual proprieties and while Ludwig was touched by her declaration of loyalty, he felt uneasy in her presence, being of the opinion, as he later told Dürkheim, that if either of them was mad, it was the Baroness. Too well bred and gallant to make her aware of his feeling, he spoke calmly and politely to her, "Madam, I beg you to calm yourself. I need no protection. Indeed, if there is any protecting of my person required, I am perfectly capable of doing it for myself, for I would never lay claim to help from a woman." [Interestingly, he did not take this view where Elisabeth was concerned, which again suggests that he placed her in a different category from the other ladies of his acquaintance – Author] He paused for a moment before adding, "And in any case, what do you imagine they intend to do with me? They can scarcely treat me like my brother." With Weber's assistance Ludwig finally persuaded her to leave but not before he had thanked her courteously for her loyalty. Was this the behaviour of a normal man or the deranged action of a lunatic?

While Baroness Truschess was with the King, Gendarme Bruckner had gone on horseback to the Master of the Watch of the Füssen Gendarmerie, Poppeler, with the message that the King commanded him to present himself at Neuschwanstein. As alarmed as everyone else by the appearance of the men from Munich, Poppeler complied forthwith, taking with him District Officer Sonntag and eight Gendarmes. Sonntag then remained at Hohenschwangau while Poppeler was in private audience with the King. "Herr Wachtmeister," Ludwig said, his voice low yet, according to Poppeler, calm and firm, "You must advise me. What shall I do? A Commission has come from Munich to legally restrain me and want to declare me mad and bury me alive like my brother Otto. I couldn't bear that. Please give me some advice for I am poorer in that than a beggar. The law can demand it but I as the King cannot."

Poppeler was horrified by the events of the past few hours but did his best to oblige the King. "Majesty, if it please you, my advice would be for Your Honour to go to Munich immediately and summon the Landtag."

"No, I will safeguard my rights and will not go. I will see who can declare me to be mad when I am not. Now the main thing, Herr Wachtmeister, is that you must arrest the whole Commission and bring them to the castle."

"Majesty, that would be extremely difficult to do."

"Indeed? And why is that?"

"For one thing, Majesty, before I could do anything I would have to have an order for imprisonment from Your Majesty, with seal and signature."

"An order for imprisonment? Good Heavens, man, I have never seen such a thing in my life – I had no idea that such a thing existed."

Such was the mad tyrant! He had never even heard of an order for imprisonment. Eventually, Ludwig acceded, "Well, if you will propose one then I will sign and seal it." Poppeler readily agreed and, leaving six of his men to stand guard over Ludwig, he returned to Hohenschwangau with the remaining Gendarmes.

And so the farce began again. When Poppeler arrived at the other castle he found the Commission members gathered there. By this time they had acquired the requisite injunction and were discussing their best course of action. Poppeler said he "looked at the gentlemen with ill concealed contempt" and especially at Holnstein, whom he regarded as a traitor of the first order. Poppeler told the Commission that he held a Royal command in Ludwig's own handwriting to the effect that "persons who had that day tried to forcibly enter the new castle were to be arrested and brought to the castle." Holnstein answered that the order was "Ridiculous" but Poppeler insisted: "No, Excellency, with respect: I obey the commands of my King and must therefore arrest you! It is my duty!"

Holnstein came towards him with a sneer on his face, "Herr Wachtmeister, you are in error. You have no authority to carry out this command to arrest me because you have no legal grounds for doing so."

"The King has ordered it," Poppeler insisted stubbornly; Holnstein was equally adamant. "You are in error, Herr Wachtmeister, for His Royal Highness Prince Luitpold has taken over the Regency. We also have documents but ours carry weight." Holnstein then produced these and the sight of Luitpold's signature struck a chill through Poppeler's heart.

"My God," he said, "So it has come to this (...). What harm has His Honour ever done you that you should so dishonour him?"

"You forget yourself, Herr Wachtmeister."

"I am loyal to my Sovereign, with respect to Your Excellency, I cannot be reproached for that, and having made that avowal, I must carry out my duty and arrest you gentlemen." Holnstein at last agreed that they would go to the castle but of their own free will. He evidently believed that the King had no remaining power and that he was not committing treason. At the same time, he appeared still to be playing some kind of double game. It was part of his makeup and he could no more help it than he could help breathing.

During the exchange between Poppeler and Holnstein, Gudden was growing steadily more impatient. With an intensity one might have associated more with one of his patients, he said: "Come now, are we going to spend the whole day arguing here?" After further discussion, Crailsheim, Törring-Jettenbach and Holnstein decided to go to Neuschwanstein accompanied by some of the Gendarmes while their colleagues remained under watch at Hohenschwangau. Twelve of the Schwangau firemen followed the prisoners to the castle.

When the disordered little party emerged into the cold, wet air, they found a large number of people gathered in the courtyard: fireman, peasants and foresters, all standing so closely knit as to force them to push their way through, ignoring as best they could the abuse which was being hurled at them from all sides. They were conducted to three small rooms in the gatehouse where, shortly afterwards they were joined by the rest of the party with the exception of Hofrat von Rumpler. The next to arrive were Gudden and Washington with the apprehensive Dr. Müller close behind; they too found themselves in difficulties with the local inhabitants, especially when they passed the Alpenrose Inn in the village and again when they reached the castle courtyard where the crowd was still growing steadily. The district officer was doing his best to keep order but he was afraid that this unwarranted invasion by so many pompous city folk who were openly regarded by the locals as traitors would end in an affray or worse. Quite apart from their love for Ludwig and their ferocious determination to defend him at all costs, they harboured the traditional dislike of the countryman for the sophisticated city dweller.

When the new arrivals were at last ushered into the gatehouse, they found Holnstein lying comfortably on the bed in his shirtsleeves; his watch hung on the wall and he was staring speculatively at it as if deciding how long his "imprisonment" would last. With a sarcastic

smile he told his colleagues, "Noble Majesty has been threatening us
(...) our lives are in danger." He could not resist adding that the King
had ordered their eyes to be gauged out, the skin torn from their backs
and hands, that they were not to be given anything to eat and that they
were to be "left to decay in their own filth." His words merely made
them roar with laughter for every one of them knew well enough that
Ludwig would never have harmed them physically. He was also well
known to be given to verbal and written extravagance and as Holnstein's derogatory manner indicates, if Ludwig had made such statements they were not intended to be taken seriously. Who has not, in a
moment of anger or exasperation, said "I'll kill you" or "I'll have the
hide off your back"?

Ludwig was angry, despairing and frustrated. He knew why these
men had come and there was nothing he could do about it. A strictly
non-violent man, he could only express himself in these feeble terms,
well aware that if there was any punishment to be meted out that day,
he himself would be the victim. Throughout the long hours of waiting,
he had remained strangely lethargic, as if he knew that he was already
beaten and that he could not divert these men from their intention.
Only the remains of his Wittelsbach pride led him to put on a show,
however ineffectual.

The "prisoners" remained in the gatehouse for two hours, after
which they were released and, with an escort of Gendarmes to ensure
their safety from the angry villagers, returned to Munich. Meantime,
Alfred, Count Dürkheim-Montmartin had arrived at Neuschwanstein,
having received the telegram which Ludwig had had despatched to him
from Steingaden. Ludwig received him immediately, knowing that he
could count on the support of the friend who in better days had vowed
to give his life for his king should it ever become necessary. He gave
Dürkheim a resumé of all that had gone on before, with the plea "Help
me out of my dilemma (...). What did they intend to do with me? They
could scarcely treat me like a madman. The whole thing is only a
question of money. If someone would only lay before me on the table
here a few million Marks, we should soon see whether or not I was
mad!" This is surely a strange statement to come from the lips of a
"lunatic"?

Dürkheim was later to insist that the King was "completely lucid"
and spoke exhaustively of what had happened. The Chamberlain, like
Poppeler, had considered that Ludwig's best course was to go to the
capital immediately and show himself to the people, that everyone
would cheer him and it would be apparent that he was alive and well
and, above all, perfectly sane and capable of ruling his country. It is
unlikely that the level-headed Dürkheim would have suggested such a

thing if he had thought for a moment that Ludwig was not in his right mind, particularly in view of Otto's problems. Yet still Ludwig remained stubbornly proud as ever on this point. "He said that he was tired, that the atmosphere in the city did not suit him." In short, Dürkheim summed up, "He waved away my suggestions."

Determined not to give up, he offered the King an alternative, namely, to order the carriage and cross the border to nearby Tirol, where he would be safe and where the Empress and the autocratic Franz Josef would offer him protection and assistance. "What would I do in Tirol?" Ludwig protested wearily and, momentarily nonplussed, Dürkheim had no solution. He had no further suggestion to offer except that it was "now or never". Only when he reminded the King that the new government had proclaimed the Regency in Munich did he rouse himself sufficiently to agree to a number of telegrams being despatched with a view to enlisting aid and, more importantly, for a counter-proclamation to be issued. Still irresolute, Ludwig continued to sit apathetically in his high-backed leather chair smoking, his eyes turned upwards in a characteristic pose. No one could ever accuse Dürkheim of being lethargic, however; while the King looked on, he busied himself with a series of telegrams, some of which were despatched from Hohenschwangau. Others were sent from the Austrian border village of Reutte where, in fact, a force of Austrian troops already waited, ready to help if necessary, indicating that at least one of Ludwig's earlier messages had produced results.

Dürkheim had also called upon the troops at the garrison at Pfrondten, the troops at Kempten, Prince Ludwig Ferdinand and Baron Franckenstein, the leader of the opposition. Other telegrams found their way to Franz-Josef, Elisabeth and Bismarck (this latter, of course, was a waste of time since it was he who was later dismiss Ludwig by saying that he had "reckoned that (...) either the King is healthy and will follow my advice [ie, to stop the building and show himself in Munich] or he really is mad and his shyness of the public will prevail. The King did not go to Munich. He reached no decision. He no longer had the spirit or the strength and permitted events to break over his head." This seems a somewhat harsh judgement on Bismarck's part since shyness and indecision are not necessarily signs of insanity. In any case, Bismarck himself had already effectively vetoed any real assistance being given to the King.

With Dürkheim's persuasion and assistance, a counter proclamation was at last issued and although it was immediately suppressed in South Germany it appeared in the *Bamberger Journal*. It stated:

"I, Ludwig, King of Bavaria, feel myself constrained to make the following manifesto to my beloved Bavarians and to the collective German people: the Prince Luitpold desires, against my will, to make himself ruler of my land. My former Ministerium has deceived my beloved people by erroneous representations as to the state of my health and has been guilty of high treason. I feel physically and mentally in as good health as any monarch. The projected treason has come in a manner so surprising that I have not been given time to defeat the base intentions of the Ministerium. Should the projected deeds of violence be put into operation and Prince Luitpold should seize the reins of office against my will, I give my faithful friends the task of protecting my rights with all their means and under all circumstances. I expect that all the officials of Bavaria, above all, all the gallant Bavarian officers and the soldiers of Bavaria in remembrance of the solemn oath with which they swore allegiance to me, remain faithful to me and stand by me in this difficult hour. Every loyal citizen is called upon to brand Prince Luitpold and the former Ministers as traitors. I am at the will of my beloved people and cherish the firm belief that they will all protect me. At the same time I turn to the rest of the German people and to the allied Princes. As much as it was in my power, I contributed to the building up of the German Empire. Therefore, I dare to expect of Germany that she will not allow a German prince to be wrongfully displaced. If I am not granted time to address myself directly to the German Emperor, I am confident that no objection will be raised to my delivering up to the law the traitors of my country. My good Bavarians will certainly not fail me. In the event that I may be prevented by force from protecting my rights, I shall call upon every faithful Bavarian to gather around my adherents and help them to defeat the projected treason against King and country. Given at Hohenschwangau, June 9th, 1886.

Ludwig II, King of Bavaria, Prince Palatinate, etc, etc.

Unfortunately, in his depressed and depleted condition Ludwig took a prodigiously long time to do anything and by the time Dürkheim left Schloss Neuschwanstein in the early hours of the 11th with the counter-proclamation in his pocket, Ludwig was already virtually a prisoner in his own castle.

In the early evening, a posse of Munich Gendarmes met at Hohenschwangau where they had been sent to mount guard over Neuschwanstein. Some hours later, two of the Commission members, Senior Privy Counsellor Koppelstätter and Ludwig von Müller, a former cabinet secretary, had been assigned to keep law and order. But in spite of this, the people of Schwangau continued feverishly to to make eager if ineffectual plans for the King's escape. They were determined to send him to safety in Austria where they knew that his honour and dignity would be as revered as his person. Every villager present had met Ludwig personally and felt a fierce protective instinct and love towards him. The tragedy was that they totally lacked leadership, equipment and cool-headed planning.

Osterholzer, who had remained in the castle, and Alfons Weber, the *Chevauxlèger* turned valet, still insisted that their plan for escape could succeed if only the King would stir himself but Ludwig, fearing bloodshed, still refused. "No blood shall be spilled for my sake," he insisted, "I make my reckoning with heaven and with He who watches over us. I am pushed from the greatest heights into nothing. My life is destroyed. I am living, declared for dead. And that I cannot endure. If I was merely deprived of my crown, I could have endured it, but that I am deprived of my freedom and my life and treated like my brother, no, that I cannot endure. I will escape this destiny. I am driven to my death." But was this necessarily a declaration of his intent to commit suicide? His words merely temporarily eased his pain; exhausted and out of his depth he was casting half-heartedly around in his mind seeking an honourable solution. Of course he did not mean it. He never did. Even his words "deprived of my freedom and my life" do not suggest a true intention to die. Throughout his life in moments of stress he had frequently resorted to threats of suicide or abdication as a means of getting his own way or solving the immediate problem but he never once meant it seriously. His Royal person and his innate autonomous and religious instincts were too strong. On this ground alone, to actually commit suicide as opposed to threatening to do it would have been unthinkable.

Unable to settle, he roamed the castle looking with despairing love on his creation, lingering in the unfinished rooms, the incomplete Throne room with its inlaid mosaic walls, floor and ceiling, their profusion of saints, flora and fauna glowing with brilliant colour. Under the golden cupola the dais was still bare of a throne. Lorenz Mayr followed him around but we have no way of knowing his motive for doing so. He could have been genuinely worried about the King's threat to do himself an injury, although in the light of his subsequent behaviour it is more likely that he was merely keeping watch on the King on behalf of the conspirators.

"Do you believe in the mortality of the soul?" Ludwig asked suddenly. "Yes Majesty, I do." Mayr replied. "I also believe in it," Ludwig told him, "I believe in the mortality of the soul and in the justice of God. I have read a great deal about materialism; it does not appease. It is not munificent because it places man on the same level as the animals."

He went on for some time in the same vein although most of what he said went far above the valet's head, and using almost the same words as he had previously used to Dürkheim, he added, "To slip from the highest steps of life is to become nothing; it is a lost life and this I cannot bear (...). I would be grieved if they were to take my crown, but I couldn't bear them to declare me insane nor can I bear the thought of being treated like my brother Otto, to whom every attendant can give orders and who is threatened with the fist if he does not follow."

As his depression deepened Ludwig convinced himself that this was to be his fate and looking gloomily out of the castle at the rushing waters of the gorge through which the Pöllat flowed almost a thousand feet below he told Mayr "When Hoppé comes tomorrow to dress my hair you might as well tell him that he can look for my head in the Pöllat. I only hope that God will graciously forgive me for doing it. I cannot spare my mother the pain which I have previously given her - they have driven me to it but my blood will cover all those who have betrayed me." When Mayr tried to reassure him on this point, somewhat superfluously one might think, he insisted, "And I tell you that there are many who have. My own uncle! Have I ever harmed him? He is not a Prince Regent but a Prince Rebel!" This was no more than the truth. No matter how, in his despair, he chose to express himself, he was in no way blind to the current situation or how it had arisen. He knew the cause, the effect and the course which events would now inevitably take. Above all, he knew how it would end. He was aware that, if he did not take his own life then someone else would undoubtedly do it for him.

After a while, he embarked upon yet another tour of Neuschwanstein, caressing as he went the panelling, the pictures and the dark, heavy furniture which had been specially commissioned and designed for its ornate Gothic surroundings. Finally, he went on to the balcony and looked across the flat plain towards Füssen. The storm clouds which had temporarily dispersed had now begun to gather again as if presaging the inevitable. With his long, fur-trimmed robe slung across his shoulders, Ludwig continued to wander from room to room for some hours, drinking the equivalent of a bottle of rum mixed with champagne and cloves, but he could not eat anything. At last he came to a decision.

"Niggl," he said, "I have changed my mind. Perhaps from the Tirol I could, after all, work towards bringing down this riff-raff." Niggl was at first startled, then uncomfortable. The plan which had been discussed many hours before might have been successful and even comparatively easy had it been carried through at the moment of instigation, but the man most essential to its expedition was no longer at Neuschwanstein.

Niggl told the King that after his contretemps with Max Holnstein the coachman had wisely made himself scarce although he only did so when he thought the King had no need of him. "The Commission from Munich knew that he had helped Your Honour and Count Holnstein especially would remember that," the Major Domo added. Ludwig took the point and after some thought asked, "Tell me, Niggl, to your knowledge, would the people do anything at all towards the peace of their Sovereign?" Niggl replied carefully, "Majesty, the people are without arms." Ludwig digested this: how could they defend him when they had nothing but a few shotguns for hunting game and a collection of sharp-ended agricultural implements? Without further preamble, Ludwig reached his gloomy conclusion "Well then, just as I was born at half past twelve, I shall die at half past twelve."

Niggl, who was devoted to the King, was deeply upset by all this and concerned for his welfare. Mayr also professed to be so although like so many other members of Ludwig's personal staff, he seems to have played a somewhat ambiguous role towards the end and there is good cause for supposing that he had long since changed his colours. All the servants disliked and distrusted Holnstein, the hard, brusque and ambitious man who was generally regarded as being full of evil intentions, a man to whom loyalty and honour meant nothing. The prospect of Holnstein's reaction to opposition must certainly have crystallised many a servant's decision to desert the King.

After so many hours of confinement Ludwig was beginning to feel claustrophobic, longing for some fresh mountain air and expressing the desire to go for a walk, asked Mayr to bring his topcoat. Mayr objected, "Majesty, with respect, that is impossible."

"Impossible? Why so?"

"The castle is surrounded, Majesty. Your Honour will not be able to pass the gate." Exasperated, the King suggested one of the forest paths which had been marked and laid down on the instructions of his energetic mother. When this idea met with no response, he suggested a walk around the Alpsee, the Schwansee or the Gumpe*. In view of Ludwig's earlier maudlin ramblings, which were undoubtedly due more to the rum and cloves which he had imbibed than from any real desire to die, Mayr seemed convinced that Ludwig meant to do himself a mischief, and would only repeat "Majesty, we cannot leave the castle."

It is probable that Mayr had been instructed by Holnstein to make

* Another name for the Pöllat Gorge.

sure the King stayed where he was. What is certain is that the valet now had more power of decision than his master. Ludwig asked him for the key to the tower and was told that it had been mislaid. He afterwards said that he thought the King intended to jump from the window of the tower but since he knew Ludwig so well, it seems incredible that he would not have realised that, whatever wild remarks he might make in a moment of anguish, so vain, fastidious and honourable man would never seriously have considered so ignominious an end.

Drunk or sober, Ludwig was nobody's fool and naturally did not believe him. With a sad look at the valet, accompanied by the slow nodding of his head, he acknowledged his acceptance of the fact that he could no longer count on Mayr's loyalty.

CHAPTER SIXTEEN

IMPRISONED AT BERG

IN Munich that morning the commission members, still smarting over the fiasco of the previous day, again discussed their plans for Ludwig. Gudden was opposed to the initial proposals and put forward some suggestions of his own. He was convinced that a deputation consisting only of doctors and nursing personnel might find it easier to convey Ludwig to Linderhof than a posse of armed men. His remark gave Holnstein the perfect cue to explode his own bombshell: he told his colleagues that he had had second thoughts about Linderhof as a suitable place of detention and now averred "it was not to be considered" for the same reasons as he had earlier objected to the use one of the castles at Hohenschwangau, namely, because of the deep love and loyalty of the local peasants and because of the "unsuitability" of the structure of the castles.

Interestingly, despite all the criticism and ridicule to which Ludwig had been subjected during the building of Linderhof, nobody now suggested that its structure should be altered to suit the proposed purpose or damaged during such an operation. All were obviously deeply aware of the fact that Linderhof was a priceless masterpiece and that to deface its beauty would have been unthinkable.

The question as to where the "prisoner" should be detained was discussed at length and the propensities of almost all the Royal residences considered, including Schloss Fürstenried where Prince Otto was already incarcerated. Inevitably, Holnstein got his way and it was decided that Schloss Berg would be more convenient venue than any of the other residences since it was only 25 kilometers from Munich and being structurally simple any necessary alterations could be made without damaging anything of value!

The attitude of the Commission members thoroughout these discussions, and in particular that of Holnstein and Gudden, left much to be desired. Holnstein's attitude is, perhaps, understandable if not forgivable since it is clear that he bore the King a personal grudge and also quite obviously went through life with a chip on his illegitimate shoulder which urged him to torment anybody who got in his way.

It is equally apparent that Holnstein had already laid plans before the subject came under general discussion, the whole ensuing charade, the discussions, the abduction, the King's sudden death and the result of the ensuing autopsy probably having already been arranged with his Prussian masters. For Gudden there is no justifiable excuse. When it was agreed that it would be too easy for the King to escape from Neuschwanstein or Hohenschwangau because he had known every inch of the forest and mountains of the region since childhood, the question "Then why has he not attempted to escape already?" could only be met with a baffled silence. Why indeed? To remain defiantly to face his adversaries with the comment "Why should I flee my own castle?" was scarcely the reaction of a raving lunatic and it was only one of many such questions which were cast aside unanswered when Ludwig asked them directly of his tormenters, all of whom were impatient to put him away with no questions asked and above all, no objections from the victim.

Berg had many advantages not least of which it considerably enhanced Holnstein's hopes for personal revenge against the King for no one knew better than he that Ludwig had the happiest memories of the place. It was here that for many years he had enjoyed the company of Empress Elisabeth and Richard Hornig, and spent stimulating days in the company of the volatile Richard Wagner. Holnstein was well aware that it would be torture for Ludwig to be locked up there. It was an act of deliberate cruelty and Holnstein's malcious joy was observed by all even though, as events proved, the King's stay was to be of short duration. Having convinced the other men that Berg was the ideal place for Ludwig, it was decided that Dr. Gudden was to make occasional visits for "consultations" while his subordinate, Dr.Müller, was to remain in residence as the King's personal physician. Their plans satisfactorily cemented, they set forth from Munich for the second time.

While the plotters had been busy in the capital, Ludwig had sent the counter-proclamation asserting his legal right to the Throne although as yet, Luitpold's own proclamation had not been fully distributed. Immediate action was essential but only after Dürkheim had appealed to Ludwig's Wittelsbach pride and royal dignity did he agree to despatch the telegrams to Bismarck, Franz-Josef and Elisabeth. In order to maintain secrecy, the counter proclamation had been despatched from Basel across the Swiss border.

Unfortunately, just as Dürkheim had begun to make an impression on the King, a telegram arrived from the Minister for War ordering the Chamberlain to return to Munich immediately. Dürkheim showed it to Ludwig who implored him not to go and predictably, he at once offered to reply saying that he would not leave the King. While Ludwig appreciated the gesture, he knew in hs heart that Dürkheim would not be able to remain with him; this was confirmed when a second telegram arrived with the explicit message from Prince Luitpold that if Dürkheim did not return forthwith the new Regent would regard him as "a person guilty of high treason." When he showed this to the bewildered King, Ludwig said "But Alfred, you cannot go after you have given me your word that you will stay."

Thrown into despair at the thought of being deprived of his last remaining friend and ally, Ludwig continued to beg him not to go until it suddenly occurred to him that he could not impose such a duty on anyone and particularly not on a man whom he liked and respected. "Yes, you are right," he conceded finally, showing that in spite of everything, he was still the most rational and responsible of men, "I can see that you must go back; otherwise your career and your future are lost."

Dürkheim gave the King his assurance that he would continue the fight in Munich, reminding him that he was not totally without friends and that in just a few days the nightmare would be over. Realising that Dürkheim's last words were probably the only ones with a ring of truth, even if perhaps not the way he intended them, Ludwig sadly shook his head. Before the chamberlain left Neuschwanstein, Ludwig made a startling request: he asked for some poison and when Dürkheim, greatly alarmed, enquired as to its purpose, he replied that it was a "useful commodity to have about one's person." He refused but Ludwig continued to wear him down until, weakening, the Chamberlain asked "But where would I get poison, even if I could bring myself to commit such a crime?" Ludwig answered "From the nearest apothecary. There is poison everywhere and I cannot live any longer."

Terrified at the idea of what the King might do after his departure Dürkheim was tempted to ignore Luitpold's command and remain with Ludwig but in the end his sense of duty to his uniform overcame his personal wishes for as he was still in the army he was subject to military law. He had no choice but to obey. The moment he arrived at Munich station on June 11th, Alfred Dürkheim-Montmartin was arrested and sent to a military prison*.

This alone indicates not only that someone at Neuschwanstein was sending messages to Munich but also shows the extent to which the word and, indeed, the honour of those now struggling for power was to be trusted. The new Government had acted with almost unseemly haste to remove Dürkheim simply because he was loyal to the legitimate Sovereign and presumably every official in Munich had full knowledge of what was going on.

Unaware of the fate which had overtaken Dürkheim, Ludwig continued to sit patiently waiting for assistance to come, having in the meantime sent Mayr to look for the "lost" key to the great tower. He also sent for Alfons Weber and gave him a present of 1,200 Marks in

---

* He was released on June 15th after making a complaint of wrongful detention but proceedings were taken against him four days later on the grounds of "treason" towards Luitpold.

gold pieces with the words "This is all I have. You have earned it. You were my most faithful servant. Just take it – I shall have no further need of money." To the undeserving Mayr he gave the famous diamond agraffe from his hat, together with a written deed of gift to the effect that, should the new owner be ordered to return it to the Treasury, he was to receive the sum of 25,000 Marks in lieu – another strangely rational act on the part of a raving lunatic.

It was midnight when the little party of conspirators set out way to Neuschwanstein for the second time. As they wound their way along the undulating carriageway, the light from their torch flares was visible to the waiting monarch. This time the Commission consisted of Doctors Gudden and Müller flanked by five mental nurses and a captain of gendarmes from Munich. When they reached the courtyard, Mayr rushed towards them, "God be praised that you have come," he called out to Gudden, "Come at once to His Majesty's apartments if you will, Your Honour. He is very agitated and upset and I fear he wants to throw himself from the window."

If Ludwig was agitated then he had good reason to be, but it does seem strange that Mayr should describe him as "agitated" when previously, all those around him had complained unceasingly of his total apathy. Significantly, Mayr added as if reading from a script that the King "knew there was something in progress against him" and that he [Mayr] "thought he might commit suicide." The men followed Mayr through the still-incomplete part of the castle until finally they reached a spiral staircase which led to the tower. Gudden and Müller stopped to inspect it. "Where does that go?"

"To the tower, sir."

"The one from which the King has threatened to jump?"

"The one to which Majesty has asked for the key."

"And where does this corridor lead?"

"Directly to Majesty's apartments, sir. The King's chamber lies here...". There is a curiously rehearsed sound to this and other conversations which have been reported to have taken place between various people during this dreadful night, as if it had been agreed that certain things must be said "for the record" regardless as to whether or not they fitted the circumstances; this is a noticeable factor throughout the later "Enquiry" which was also a farcical affair.

Like automatons, some of the nurses stationed themselves by the access to the tower while others followed Gudden and Müller. The Gendarmes were strategically placed so that no one could have gone past them without being apprehended but in such a way that when the King emerged he would not see them until it was too late. His architectural masterpiece had been more cleverly designed than even he had realised and there is an unhappy irony in the fact that Ludwig's own castle was to trap him in this way. Gudden ordered Mayr to go to the King and give him the key to the tower. The valet now seemed torn between shame and the desire to be on the winning side. In the end, he decided there was nothing for it but to obey, and going to the King's room, told him that the key had been found. "Then give it to me," Ludwig ordered quietly, probably suspecting that all was not what it seemed. "At least I may after all survey my kingdom for the last time." He knew that he must be apprehended now and that he would never see his beloved Allgäu again. Despite his erlier threats of taking poison or leaping from a window into the Pöllat, it cannot be emphasised strongly enough that, apart from his horror of abusing his Royal person, his religious beliefs would have precluded taking his own life. His captors, most of whom had been embroiled for years in the religious disputes between the Ultramontanes and the Particularists, must have been well aware of this.

Mayr, however, was an obtuse or insensitive man who, despite his long and intimate service with the King, either did not realise what was going on, or had already been coerced into assisting the plotters. His story was that he heard the King threatening to kill himself – and it must be admitted that, when Ludwig was under the influence of Chloral, he was likely to say anything – and had accepted the statement at its face value. If this was so, it seems extraordinary that Mayr did not realise that the King's word was not necessarily his deed since, like everyone else in the King's employ, he was quite accustomed to his verbal extravagances.

The men waiting in the corridor suddenly heard "slightly faltering" footsteps. The door to the King's room opened and Ludwig stood framed in the doorway, a giant even in the overpowering surroundings of Schloss Neuschwanstein. Niggl, who waited outside the door with the others, bowed deeply to him, realising that it might be for the last time and Ludwig, probably with the same emotion, spoke to him in a low voice using "short, clipped-off sentences." He was calm, lucid and surprisingly well in command of the situation which instinct now told him existed. He exhuded a strong aroma of rum and cloves and for all his dignity and obvious clear-headed calm gave the impression of having been drinking heavily for which, in the circumstances, no one could blame him.

As he stood talking to his servant, all the hidden men appeared, surrounding Ludwig and cutting off any possible means of escape. Two of the nurses speedily grasped the King under the arms in a manner unfitting both to his rank and his dignity as a man, and fitted him with a straitjacket. "What does this mean?" he asked, "What do you want?" Gudden stepped forward officiously and "with a faint smile on his lips" made an extraordinary pronouncement, "Majesty, it is the saddest duty of my life which I have undertaken to perform. Majesty has been diagnosed by four mental doctors and on their recommendation, His Royal Highness Prince Luitpold has taken over the Regency. I have been commanded to accompany Majesty to Schloss Berg and this is to be done tonight. If it please Majesty to command it, the carriage will depart at four o'clock." Ludwig drew in his breath and emitted one soul-rending "Ach...." He looked "as if he had received a single blow to both body and soul." There was a long silence before, accepting his fate as inevitable, he added, "Yes, and then what will you do? What will happen then?" Gudden made no reply to this but, after the King had been led back to his room, with ill-placed sycophancy and a monumental lack of tact, Gudden, having introduced all present by name, actually reminded the King that he himself had been favoured with an audience in 1874. "Yes," replied Ludwig somewhat ruefully but with admirable self control, "I remember it exactly", as well he might since on that occasion Gudden had intruded upon the King's family birthday celebration in order to present his first report on Otto. It would hardly seem the best time to remind Ludwig of this, yet he did, following this gem with another curious observation, namely, that he had had "only the most troublesome of reigns".

The King naturally had nothing to say to this but instead very sensibly enquired "How can you declare me insane? You have never even previously seen or examined me."

"Majesty, it was unnecessary. The documentary evidence is very copious and completely substantiated. It is overwhelming."

"So, so.... Well, it has proved very fortunate for Prince Luitpold, but he did not need to go to such great cost to his cunning. He needed only to have said the word and I would have laid aside the crown and moved abroad."

Silence. No one dared to speak or to interrupt the regal, most extraordinarily calm, logical and courteous "madman" as he questioned the doctor: "How long will this 'cure' last?"

"Majesty, it stands in the Constitution that, when the King is prevented from ruling for various reasons, then the Regency is instituted; a year would therefore be the shortest time."

"Na, it might have been done much quicker. It can be done as with the Sultan*. It is very easy to remove a man from this world," to which Gudden no less interestingly replied, "Majesty, to answer such a statement would cost me my honour." What could he poss-

---

* A reference to a recent assassination.

ibly have meant by that? Did he, in fact, know or suspect that the King was about to be assassinated? Was he part of the conspiracy? He certainly did not appear to regard Ludwig's remark to be that of a man deranged although he might justifiably have picked it up as proof of Ludwig's "illness"; instead, he conversed with him as he might have done with any man, except that he was considerably more deferential.

Ludwig nodded, "A great many perjuries will now be sworn, I suppose..." He added that he already knew that there was a conspiracy and that he was sure the affair had been arranged by Luitpold. Again, nobody contradicted him or tried to pass off his observations as delusions despite the fact that it was the very type of comment to be seized upon as proof of his "paranoia". Ludwig then made some "further comments about his uncle, saying that it was a 'fine comedy' and that Luitpold should have been an actor". The King knew everything that had been written about him yet puzzlingly, he made no move to stop the escalation of events before they went too far.

Their conversation continued for some time with Ludwig asking his inevitable question: "You are Prussian, are you not?"

"Majesty, I am a Bavarian citizen now and indeed, all my children were born in Bavaria."

"Indeed? To me you are still a Prussian, Herr Doctor. (...) Would you have the goodness to leave me alone for a while."

"Majesty, you are not to be left alone. Dr. Müller and I will leave you with your permission as we have some business to attend to, but the nurses are to remain with you."

At the mention of the name "Müller", Ludwig turned away from Gudden and wandered over to the other side of the room where Dr. Müller stood; he accorded the latter a faint smile. In fact, he was to establish a good rapport with the younger doctor. Having ascertained that it was he who usually prepared the monthly reports on Otto, Ludwig thanked him graciously for his trouble and assured him that he always read them, indicating at the same time one such report which lay on his desk. Then he nodded again to Müller, this time in cordial dismissal.

Although he knew that the battle was lost and, indeed, he had made no attempt even to put up a fight, Ludwig seemed determined to get someone to admit that he was the victim of a conspiracy and began to question each of the nurses in turn. As was afterwards reported, they were already surprised and disturbed to find so rational a "madman" in their charge and had difficulty in finding their tongues to reply to his questions. They were no less surprised by the sycophantic demeanour of Gudden, who was well known to treat his patients with a marked lack of respect and consideration, regardless of their rank or the degree of their illness. At the end of each conversation Ludwig would ask, almost offhandedly, "Why do you not go out of the room now? I would like to be alone. It is so very unpleasant." But from each man he received only the stereotyped reply, "The *Herr Medizinalrat* has so ordered."

Then Ludwig repeated to Gudden his earlier question, "How is it that you come here to give a medical opinion on my condition when you have never examined me? Can one do that?"

"Majesty, one can certainly do that. If certain facts can be conclusively proved, one can arrive at dependable conclusions. All medical opinions which are being given in evidence can only support that of the documentary evidence and will be followed by a personal examination. And in any case, it is not always necessary to examine the patient personally in order to give an opinion." When Ludwig asked for a second time what they proposed to do with him, Gudden repeated that Schloss Berg had been chosen as the place of incarceration. Noticeably, it was no longer referred to as "detention". "And I shall find myself eternally surrounded at Berg as I am here?" he asked, indicating the attendants.

"Majesty," Gudden replied, "That will depend entirely upon whether you go freely and unwatched in the Schlosspark."

Ludwig's only reply to this was "So, so..."

Left alone with the attendants, the King questioned them repeatedly, staring hard at each one in turn as he did so, but he soon tired of this unproductive occupation, apparently concluding that they were as much in the dark as to the true situation as he himself was. He then asked for Mayr and Weber, who brought him Glühwein and water and helped him to lie down. There was no question of his orders being disregarded now, although all were aware that he would issue no more orders in the future. There would be no more notes complaining "Cutlets, beer, ham bad; the latter badly cooked," or verbal requests to his valet for hat or umbrella, no more commands for the coach to be prepared to take him to one of his other residences.

Niggl pottered around putting things in order as usual, dusting and cleaning the King's commode; all the time, Ludwig paced the floor, whistling absentmindedly, presumably unable to sleep now that he had the chance. He appeared to be trying to make a decision. The hours passed and with a slightly quizzical air he watched the frenzied comings and goings of the Commission members. Repeatedly he consulted his watch. By this time, the effects of his unusually heavy intake of alcohol had worn off and he wanted only coffee and peace and quiet.

While the final preparations for the journey were being made he tormented Gudden with an endless stream of questions concerning his forthcoming imprisonment, his future companions, the means of transferring him to Berg and a number of other matters concerning the arrangements until the doctor became as nervous and intense as one of his own patients. At last, to Gudden's [reported] relief, it was time to go. Ludwig remained quiet, dignified and regal; his head was still erect but his eyes were no longer those of an autocrat. He knew he was beaten. Nevertheless, he was still able to fix his captors with a look of such enquiring intensity as to oblige them to drop their own eyes and in fact, this was something he had been unable to do for years.

It was almost four o'clock when Mayr helped Ludwig on with his topcoat while the few remaining domestics stood waiting awkwardly, not knowing what they should do or say. The King looked for the last time on his beloved Neuschwanstein, and as he gazed around he saw the Master of the Watch of the Füssen Gendarmerie, a man he had known for many years and to whom he had appealed for help only a few hours before.

Going towards Poppeler in his habitually cordial manner, he held out the customary two fingers towards him, a friendly if rather sad smile on his face. "Herr Wachtmeister, please accept my thanks for the loyal service which you have always given me. It saddens my soul not to be able to thank you in a more suitable manner." Everyone present had, at some time or another received a gift from the King or benefited in some other way from his generosity, his kindness and even from his vast knowledge which he had ever been willing to share without the condescension which often goes hand in hand with the imparting of information to a less erudite person. Many people described Ludwig as being "a pleasure to listen to". Poppeler, the recipient of many a Christmas gift and a man who genuinely liked Ludwig for himself, could only stand wordlessly staring at him, his eyes full of tears. "Farewell, my friend," Ludwig said, looking at him for the last time, "I shall never see you again."

The domestic, Stichel, his face also wet with tears, came into the vestibule and Ludwig went towards him with an outstretched hand. Only now did he realise that, after all, by no means all of his staff were as disloyal as he had thought and, in the main, those closest to him were the most unfaithful. The tragedy was that, with a total lack of organisation and weapons, he could not hope to put into action any defence other than the newspaper proclamation which, unfortunately, had only a limited circulation before the rebels suppressed it."Sticherl, farewell," he said, "Keep these rooms as a shrine. Don't let them be profaned by the curious because I have lived through my bitterest hours in them. I shall never come here again." He stood staring for a while at the model of the Falkenstein, the dream which he could no longer hope to see realised, and as he lifted his gaze, his eyes met those of his former cabinet secretary, Ludwig von Müller, who was now acting for his enemies. His expression changed to one of contempt and he passed by without a word.

When the little procession reached the courtyard, the King stood for some time bidding farewell to Mayr. He had plenty of time in which to do this since there was still a great deal of frenetic activity with orders being given and rescinded, fresh ones given and plans revised. The whole thing was a fiasco; even now, the parties involved could not seem to agree on the simplest detail.

Ludwig on his side never once lost his composure. At last everything was ready and the final order for departure given. In the first carriage were Dr. Müller and the two nurses; then came Ludwig's carriage from which the door handles had been removed so that the door could only be opened from the outside. Ludwig was especially offended by this. On the box sat the head nurse and a stable servant rode alongside with the instruction to watch the carriage and if he had "the slightest ground for suspicion" he was to inform the men in the other carriages immediately. Full of self-importance, Gudden rode in the third carriage with the Gendarme Captain Horn and the other two nurses.

If Gudden had expected some sort of disturbance during the journey he was to be disappointed, for the King was still too stunned and unhappy even to change his position as he sat looking out at the rain and the heavy mist which hung over the Bavarian countryside. It was as if the whole of his kingdom wept for him. The May had gone for ever.

During the journey of some 75 kilometers, the horses were changed three times, the last being at the post and telegraph office in Starnberg where Ludwig asked the postmaster's wife for a drink of water. She also knew him personally and burst into tears when he returned the glass with his usual courteous thanks. Like all the country people she was willing but powerless to help him. No one knew better than they that the King was perfectly sane and normal and many of them, like Poppeler, could testify to the fact that the King had "only recently stopped to pass the time of day" with them – a phrase which was later to occur with some frequency in evidence – and to exchange a few pleasantries about local affairs. To them, he was more of a beloved squire or laird than a remote and autocratic Monarch. He had always been someone to whom they could confide their problems with every expectation of receiving good advice or more tangible assistance. He was an understanding friend in time of crisis with an ever-open hand when it came to need or celebration. Small wonder then, that when these people were told that the King was mad they had difficulty in believing it.

The party finally arrived at Schloss Berg on Whit Sunday, June 12th, travelling via Seeshaupt, this being the final insult inflicted deliberately upon Ludwig in view of the fact that Richard Hornig's villa was located here and passing it would thus have brought back a thousand memories of happier times.

At Schloss Berg, it was decided that the King could keep his own bedroom and sitting room but the small anteroom connecting the two had been fitted in such a way as to allow the nurses to watch him constantly. To his horror and indignation, peepholes had been cut out of the doors, which would mean that he would be under 24-hour surveillance. Sensitive for years to being stared at and intent on maintaining a state of deepest solitude as a better alternative to being surrounded by those exhuding hostile vibrations, this particular torment was especially noxious and his "medical advisers", well primed by Holnstein, knew it. An additional blow to his pride was the discovery that the doorhandles and locking mechanisms had been treated in exactly the same way as those on his carriage. Ludwig complained immediately to the most congenial looking of the nurses, one Bruno Mauder, about the peepholes, saying that he found it "very unpleasant if somebody was always looking in." Genuinely sympathetic, Mauder replied that the holes had been ordered to be made by Gudden and Grashey, and that he personally had no part in it. He promised that he and his colleagues would forebear from looking in, but this must have been cold comfort to the King, to whom it was enough to know that such holes existed. Resigned to this, he turned his attention to the shutters of the bedroom window which were also closed, and asked for them to be opened. This request at least was granted.

Bored, he began to watch the other two nurses, Hack and Schneller, as they went about their business. He asked who they were and Mauder introduced them as the nurses who would share the task of looking after him with Mauder himself. The thought of assassination was still very much in the King's mind and he was determined to be taken in by nobody. "Where do they come from?" he enquired, "Are they Prussians?"

"No, Majesty, they are both Bavarian."

"And what is their religion?"

"Why, they are both Catholic, Majesty."

"Did you know them already?" But interestingly Mauder, who was quite obviously a trained nurse, did not reply directly to this question but only murmured that he "knew them to have the highest qualifications." This did not satisfy Ludwig. At one thirty, the King dined and to his further mortification he found that there were no sharp knives on the table but only the small fruit knives which were not usually placed until the end of the meal. "What?" he asked sarcastically, "Surely we are not going to start with the fruit course?" "Majesty," came the apologetic reply, "Those are the orders."

Despite the unsatisfactory answers to his questions, Ludwig liked Mauder, finding in him a kindliness which was conspicuously lacking in his colleagues and, indeed, in his superiors. Mauder was sensitive and intelligent and the two conversed socially for some time until Ludwig said he was tired and asked to lie down. There was nothing extraordinary about this since, although it was only three o'clock in the afternoon he had been up all night and had undergone a traumatic journey which must have taken its physical as well as spiritual toll. He removed his clothes and settled down to sleep, asking Mauder to put out the light and draw the curtains and for two candles to be lit. There was in any case very little daylight owing to the bad weather. Mauder complied and Ludwig then said quietly, "You must wake me in nine hours' time, that is to say, at midnight."

Mauder bowed himself out and went to report to Dr.Müller. He told the doctor every detail of the luncheon and of the King's final instructions. Müller said firmly, "Of course you will not wake him. You will leave him to sleep until tomorrow morning. It is imperative that the King be brought to order and day turned into day, night turned into night."

On the face of it this was reasonable enough, but Mauder with his sharp intelligence was already comparing the vindictive, highly excitable and unsympathetic medicos with his "paranoid" charge, the calm and gentle being who had submitted to bitter insults and unfeeling treatment with such regal dignity. As the evidence was later to show, Mauder was no longer convinced that the situation was as simple and straightforward as he had been led to believe.

CHAPTER SEVENTEEN

INTRIGUE AND DEATH

ON June 12th, Schloss Berg swarmed with people; owing to Ludwig's dislike of social activity it had for many years been almost deserted and the sudden inundation was far too great for so small a building. At its best, it was little more than a country villa never intended for more than modest use and the sudden influx imposed a considerable burden on the establishment.

A surprising number of people were foregathered to control one extremely docile man: Gudden, Müller, Grashey, Holnstein, Törring, Mahlsen and Washington were all present, supported by various other gentlemen, nurses and other officials as well as a few Gendarmes and the usual collection of domestics. All continued to rush around in a state of chaotic indecision and the only person continuing normally with his work was Friedrich Zanders, the combined chef and major domo. This was fortunate for all concerned since to this efficient and well-balanced man fell the task of running the Schloss and the catering arrangements.

Those who had declared themselves to be in command had spent a prodigious time discussing a situation with which they seemed totally unable to cope and with the exception of Gudden's junior colleagues and the nurses, everyone seemed all too uncomfortably aware that the King was as sane and normal as any man present. Their greatest uncertainty was the length to which they could take their charade in order to convince the public of Ludwig's incapacity.

Seated together over a glass of wine the conspirators discussed possible precautions to prevent Ludwig from escaping. Why did they take so long over this and why did they wait until he was actually in the building before deciding what to do with him? Was it because they had expected something to happen to him during the journey from Hohenschwangau or because they had suddenly got wind of an escape plan? Aside from personal spite on Holnstein's part, why did they choose Berg at all as a place of "detention"? Only if they knew that the King's stay would be of short duration was it a logical choice: Berg's proximity to the capital would have made it easier for Ludwig to escape and appeal to the Landtag, which of course was the last thing they wanted. The explanation that it was adaptable, easily accessible and of no especially architectural value seems somewhat feeble when balanced against the inaccessibility of some other residences which would have made rescue difficult.

Confronted by the posssibility that the King might escape it was obviously assumed that his intention was to make his way across the lake to his family or loyalist friends who lived at various points along the lake shores. The Commission members' first consideration was thus to erect some sort of fencing, though it is hard to see how they imagined this would stop him from defecting. Grashey suggested that "some light iron bars should be placed in a sloping direction in the lake and linked up to two meters in height with barbed wire (...) so that the view would not be spoiled" asserting only *en passant* that it would be "impossible to climb over it."

Gudden's contribution clearly puzzled the others: "I think we can safely say that no further precautions are necessary". Why was he so sure? Was he already aware that no amount of "protection" could prolong Ludwig's life, whether or not he attempted to evade his gaolers? Were they perhaps more interested in finding a means of keeping rescuers out than keeping Ludwig in? Gudden added intriguingly "Except perhaps that special attention should be given to the area by the kiosk and the rocky place I have observed on the way to it where there is a high, firm area."

Holnstein said that closer attention should be paid to the Schloss itself, where he thought the first necessity was to have bars placed upon all the windows, but since bars had already been placed on the King's own windows and he was not allowed to move around freely, this seems to have been little more than waffle.

At last the meeting ended and Gudden, accompanied by Grashey, returned to his room; the two continued to discuss the situation. Gudden expressed his satisfaction with the way in which things were going, saying how pleased he was by the King's acceptance of his detention and the announcement of the Regency. Above all, he marvelled over the King's "quiet demeanour". Grashey, who by this time seemed as puzzled as some of the others involved, could not help commenting on the difference between Ludwig and Otto. "That madman!", retorted Gudden unprofessionally.

When Ludwig awoke at midnight, refreshed by his long sleep and anxious to get up, his clothes were denied him. "But I have been in my bed for nine hours. I want to get up."

"Majesty, I have to obey my orders." Feeling understandably sorry for himself, Ludwig nevertheless controlled his anger and walked around the room wearing only his shirt but his repeated requests for his clothes met only with refusal. He was at least allowed to have his socks after complaining that his feet were cold, and was also permitted an orange and the bread for which he asked. After this he agreed to go back to bed, possibly realising that as well as conserving his energy until such time as he could escape, he could also avoid the indignity of being stared at. And so he lay waiting for dawn to break, probably surprised to find that he was still alive, for throughout his long ordeal at Berg, the feeling that he was about to be assassinated never left him.

At six o'clock Mauder took over from Braun and Ludwig told him with a smile that he was annoyed with him because he had not carried out the instruction to wake him at midnight. Mauder protested that orders from his superiors precluded him from doing so and, reasonable as ever, Ludwig accepted this. He then asked to see Dr. Gudden. In spite of his innate dislike and distrust of the man, Ludwig enjoyed conversing with him, probably because he liked to engage in a battle of wits. His questions and remarks to Gudden on this occasion would certainly indicate that he was attempting to discover how deeply the doctor was involved in the conspiracy. And there is no doubt that the doctor was involved.

Gudden was a hard, unsympathetic man, bigoted, dogmatic and lacking the deep understanding so necessary to a man of his calling. At the same time he appears to have retained some faint vestige of honour and it is unlikely that even he would have broken his Hyppocratic oath and committed murder with his own hands. When Ludwig summoned him at 8.15 am, he went with undignified haste to find out what the King wanted. Cold and miserable, Ludwig had again taken to his bed and Gudden seated himself in an armchair nearby. They talked for some 15 minutes or so until at last, embarrassed by Ludwig's probing, highly pertinent questions, Gudden sent for his son-in-law to take over.

While Grashey was apparently as deferential in his manner as Gudden, he was equally cold and charmless with the same inherent bigotry and lack of personal warmth towards the patient. Ludwig disliked him on sight. When Gudden left, Grashey began to question the King who replied with his customary charm and courtesy and again Grashey, who had been led to believe that the King was a dangerous lunatic, was surprised and disturbed to find that the voice which answered his questions with "short, clipped sentences" was firm, steady and lacking any of the peculiarities which might be expected in a man who had just been declared insane and unfit to rule.

Grashey was further put out when Ludwig reversed the proceedings and began to question him as to his nationality, his family, his religion and his professional qualifications. Firmly convinced that he was the victim of a Prussian or a Jesuit plot, all of Ludwig's balanced, well-phrased and deeply penetrating questions were directed towards picking up a direct clue. It was clear also that he could not satisfy himself as to the source of the danger. While it is true that both these phenomena are symptoms of schizophrenia, the patient does not usually confine his delusions to so single-minded a path; nor are they confined to such prosaic circumstances. Ludwig's convictions were of quite a different nature from the schizophrenic norm. They were in no way fantastic or improbable and centred solely on the people whom he knew from experience he could not trust. At the same time he was aware from reading his brother's medical reports that any complaints concerning his treatment would be construed as "symptoms".

More for their own sakes than for his, the Commission members decided that Ludwig should be made to adhere to a strict routine, that he was to be allowed no drugs or alcohol and while the latter deprivations can be considered as reasonable medical measures, the institution of a strict routine could well have been to assist an assassin, for what could be more convenient than to know exactly where Ludwig would be at a given time and place? A means of preventing him from becoming too interested in what was going on about him was that he should be kept occupied, probably by means of his favourite hobby, reading. Pushed by necessity the King at last overcame his vanity and confessed that his sight was poor. Eagerly, Grashey offered to arrange for his eyes to be tested, whereupon Ludwig made the counter-suggestion that a messenger might be sent to Neuschwanstein for some books from his library.

Later, when Grashey was discussing with his colleagues the conversation which he had had with the King, he announced that Ludwig had said "Count Törring is very pleasant but I find the choice of Count Holnstein untenable." Continuing in the same vein, Gudden expressed the opinion that Ludwig should be constantly accompanied "by at least one gentleman", adding that when he had suggested this to the King, Ludwig's reply had been "No, no. Even one is too many." It seems extraordinary then, that the doctor did not realise that by deliberately throwing the shy misanthrope into the company of people not of his own choosing, and in particular with one with whom he was well known to be at loggerheads, he was likely to do more harm than good. Such torment could only have made a man like Ludwig more miserable and neurotic than before.

After Gudden left, Mauder came to help Ludwig to wash and dress as Ludwig's regular personal staff had been left behind at Neuschwanstein. The King was reasonably content with the present arrangement as he had taken an instant liking to the quiet, well-balanced Mauder who in turn obviously liked him. Mauder was, in fact, the type of man whom Ludwig might have chosen to employ and he trusted him sufficiently to ask him what he thought of his superiors. Confounded, the nurse could only reply "They are both qualified and at the top of their profession, Majesty. It is not for me to give an opinion." He refused to be drawn further on the subject but when Ludwig asked if Gudden was "serious in his flattering words" Mauder replied that he "believed the *Herr Obermedizinalrat* meant what he said" which was not particularly encouraging. "And Grashey?" Ludwig pressed, "Is this Grashey also party to the conspiracy?" Mauder did not know how to answer and the King added, "This person has made a bad impression on me. Do you know him?"

"No, Majesty. I saw him for the first time this morning." Closely supervised by the King, Mauder then dressed his hair for him. When his toilet was completed, he again looked regal, dignified and considerably saner than any of his captors.

Shortly after this Friedrich Zanders was summoned to take Ludwig's order for breakfast and the King sat watching as Mauder prepared the table. Perhaps the man's expertise in domestic matters emphasised the lack of these accomplishments in his colleagues for Ludwig again began to question him about the other nurses. In particular he asked about Schneller's nationality, religion and politics.

After many hours of reflection, he had become even more firmly convinced that the plot he suspected was either religious or political, but more probably Prussian in origin; he did not seek confirmation of this, but instead, set out with determination to find out by whose hand he was to die. It was no easy task to do this without further condemning himself as paranoid in the eyes of those who were at Schloss Berg in their true capacities. Revealingly, in all the time Ludwig directly accused his doctors and his own former staff members who now served on the Commission to depose him, not once did any of them denounce his remarks as symptomatic of the illness from which he was alleged to be suffering, although he certainly provided them with more than enough ammunition with which to do so. Only those who were apparently NOT a part of the conspiracy assumed his accusations to be confirmation that he was ill, and their bewilderment to find that he was otherwise the most rational of men is well documented.

While Ludwig had servants of the calibre of Zanders about him there was still hope for escape but he knew that he must distinguish between friends and enemies before any plan could be put into operation. This was the second time he had enquired about Schneller; it was not absentmindedness on his part but the hope that constant repetition might trap someone into an unguarded truth. What one would today describe as "vibrations" told the King that Schneller in particular was unsympathetic and so clumsy in his work as to suggest that he was doing a job for which he was not qualified and, indeed, which he did not normally do at all.

On the other hand he did not suspect Mauder whom he had observed to be kindly, efficient, polite and professionally competent and conscientious as well as being familiar with the various aspects of medical care. By comparison the rough and incompetent Schneller made a poor showing. The King told Mauder to go and ask the man again what his religion was and by the time Mauder had returned, he was enjoying a good breakfast. The King finished his meal at 10 o'clock, completed his ritual of dressing and gave Mauder his watch to wind, whereupon Schneller, deeply suspicious of the rapport which had sprung up between the two, intercepted it. Ludwig was annoyed with Schneller and he allowed it to show. He then asked to see Gudden again and that gentleman was sufficiently eager to do the bidding of the man whom only half an hour before he had said should be "brought to order" to come running. To the nurse's surprise, he sent back an invitation to Ludwig that he might like to converse while taking a walk in the Schlosspark. Ludwig agreed with alacrity; he was not only longing for some fresh air but undoubtedly welcomed also the opportunity to explore his plans for escape.

Mauder was clearly worried and puzzled when he was asked to bring the King's coat and umbrella since up until then. Gudden had gone on *ad nauseum* about Ludwig's "dangerous condition". Although he himself found the King to be a calm and balanced man, no one could blame him for thinking it strange that his eminent superior, having made loud assertions as to the patient's insanity, did not shrink from taking an unattended walk with him.

At approximately 11.30 am, Ludwig and the doctor set off at a leisurely pace through the Schlosspark; their walk lasted until 12.15pm, during which time they conversed on a number of topics but Ludwig continually reverted to the question as to whether anyone was ready to strive for his life or whether he would have to remain at Berg until he was "disposed of". It is strange that he gave every appearance of trusting Gudden with his private thoughts and not Grashey, unless he was simply testing Gudden to see if he would make a slip. This was a favourite ruse of the King's. [He would describe this colourfully as "lathering them up." *(Einseifen)*.] Gudden, of course, dismissed what the King said as "Nonsense", but it does seem odd that the doctor who had spent so long trying to convince Ludwig and, indeed, everyone else, of the fact that he was suffering from paranoia, did not seize upon the point which Ludwig made so persistently in order to illustrate the "patient's" most prominent symptom.

Nurse Hack, who had been ordered to accompany the two men, had been told by Gudden to walk "some hundred paces" behind them, a command which came as an unpleasant surprise to the second nurse who had also been led to believe that the King was a dangerous lunatic not to be trusted. It might be conjectured that, finding that the conversation was taking a dangerous turn, Gudden simply did not want the nurse to overhear what was being said.

From a more sinister viewpoint, it is just possible that Gudden, as one of the plotters to assassinate the King, had been instructed to lead him into a vulnerable situation at a given time - and remember, all of the Commission members were seemingly addicted to this burning question of time, despite the apparent haphazardness and general confusion of the King's abduction. Was this first walk a kind of "dummy run", a rehearsal for what was to occur later? To nurse Hack, who to all intents and purposes had been sent with them either to protect Gudden from Ludwig or to protect Ludwig from himself, it must have seemed strange indeed when the doctor suddenly swung round and waved him back even further. With so many trees and bends in the path, and with so much dense shrubbery and with the additional hazard afforded by the heavy mist, Hack soon lost sight of them altogether although the sound of their voices carried across to him in the damp air. It had stopped raining by that time and the walk proved to be both pleasant and uneventful, so much so, apparently, that Gudden suggested they might repeat the exercise later in the day, to which Ludwig again agreed with alacrity.

Despite the inclement weather, the projected excursion appeared to suit both men if perhaps for very different reasons. Having come to an understanding about a second walk, the two men returned to Berg in time for lunch.

Served by Mauder, Ludwig ate alone in his room while Gudden joined Grashey, Washington and Müller in the Kavalierhaus, a small villa situated on the lakeside some 500 feet from the Schloss itself and connected to it by a tree-lined avenue. It had been requisitioned by the Commission as quarters for Baron Washington, who had been selected to remain in attendance on the King for the duration of his captivity. During the meal, Gudden was in a good humour, well-satisfied with the walk, for whatever reason, boasting loudly to his colleagues that he thought the King "had settled down wonderfully well" in his new surroundings. Washington viewed this comment with some scepticism, doubtless recalling how often the King had stayed at Berg in the past under less stressful conditions and, of course, without the indignity of constant surveillance. He remarked that, knowing the King as he did, he found this hard to believe. The others then questioned Gudden concerning the walk and he replied eagerly, adding that he intended to go for another walk in the evening as he "could see no danger in it" since the King "was like a child." This was reasonable enough since no man knew better than he that Ludwig was perfectly sane and therefore harmless.

Dr. Müller, however, was very much in opposition to Gudden's plan if for different reasons from Washington's. Unlike the adjutant, he seemed to have no idea of the true situation, and looked upon Ludwig as a temporarily well behaved patient who was likely to become violent on the slightest provocation. Müller said, "I could never take the responsibility on myself of going walking alone with the King. I wouldn't do it if I were you." He added that Gudden was making it very difficult for him to carry out his work. Müller's reaction, his testy manner and undisguised annoyance with his superiors are understandable when one considers that, like the nurses Mauder and Hack, he had been led to believe that the King was raving mad and unfit to be left unguarded.

However strange he found Gudden's behaviour and general attitude towards the case, he could scarcely go too far in his criticism of his superior. He did venture to say that he proposed to leave such unattended walks to Gudden with his "fascinating power over the patient" and repeated that he himself would never dare to do it, to which Gudden merely laughed "You pessimist!" As the discussion progressed, both Müller and Washington professed to being increasingly uneasy and astounded by Gudden's complacent attitude towards the man who, hours before, had been diagnosed as paranoid.

If there was a plot (and who can believe that there was not?) it is probable that, at least at the outset, Müller was not part of it and Grashey may also have been brought in as a red herring to disguise the political purpose behind the removal of King Ludwig from his throne. In spite of some of the remarks and attitudes attributed to him, there is some evidence that Washington was a participant in the charade. Gudden's role in the affair is ambiguous. His junior staff, in particular Dr. Müller and nurse Mauder, were constantly puzzled by his curious behaviour and inexplicable attitude towards his "patient", his nauseating sycophancy and endless boasting as to the ease with which he was handling the case. Equally noteworthy was the King's demeanour, his affability and unswerving good humour which never for a moment faltered or displayed the schizoid tendencies which his enemies had stated he possessed.

When Gudden was questioned by his outraged colleagues as to the reason for the walk, he explained that, in the past, the King had been much in the company of servants and stable personnel and he thought the time had come for him to be led back into the company of more erudite men. The modest doctor did not neglect to add that Ludwig had greatly enjoyed this facility during their morning walk together.

After lunch Gudden went in search of Friedrich Zanders to tell him that the King wished to see him but during their conversation he warned the major domo that, while he might go to the King as requested, it was with the proviso that he first gave his "word of honour" that he "would not discuss with him a plan of escape or otherwise awaken in him hopes of release." Zanders gave his word but he was no fool: he afterwards admitted that, having given his smiling assurance to Gudden that he would not speak on the subject of escape on this occasion, he told himself, "from now on, he will permit me to see him often and he will not make me repeat my promise every time." In fact, Zanders was said to have in his possession a note which he held with his other papers, his Menus and Orders of the Day, which he could hand to the King without breaking his word to the doctor.

Gudden, who was short-sighted in more ways than one, took Zanders at his face value, failing totally to grasp that, like other staff members of long standing, he was more of a personal friend than a servant to Ludwig. Zanders had held his post for over 15 years and had frequently accompanied the King on his travels to France, Switzerland and to various parts of Bavaria although for some reason not to Neuschwanstein. [Noticeably, it was only there that Ludwig had occasion to complain about the catering and domestic service.] Because Ludwig had spent so long in the Allgäu, Zanders had not seen him for some weeks and like everyone else, he was initially surprised by the King's general appearance for the horde of officious-looking men who had descended upon Schloss Berg had led him to anticipate a dull, bewildered creature stupefied by drink and drugs and perhaps even a raving lunatic; Ludwig was quite obviously neither of these. On the contrary, Zanders was relieved to see that the man who came towards him with a smile was: "Balanced, civilised and as charming as ever" and that his eyes "sparkled with pleasure" as if he anticipated some happy event or, more probably, as if he knew that Zanders would have brought some encouraging news. He showed the major domo the locks and bars on the windows and the peepholes which had been cut in the doors saying that everything "was bound to remind him that he was regarded as a raving lunatic". He recounted the awful events of the past days and asked "Do you think that, throughout the years, I shall still be imprisoned as I am today?" and Zanders* said that he replied that "perhaps less time would be needed to cure Majesty of his nervous disorder" but that "there would be no further reason for keeping him under medical treatment."

"Do you really believe that?", Ludwig countered, *"L'appétit vient en*

---

* Giving evidence at the eventual Protocol.

mangéant*. My uncle Luitpold will find so much pleasure in it that
he will never want to let me out again."

Zanders properly forbore from responding to this observation and
Ludwig, possibly realising that he might be placing his friend in an
invidious position, did not pursue the topic but instead asked how many
Gendarmes he had seen in the park. Zanders answered that there were
"six to eight".

"Would they shoot me, given the oportunity?"

"How could Majesty think that?"

"Are they armed with something sharp?"

"They are not armed at all," was Zanders' somewhat surprising
assertion. The King then led him to the window niche from where
it was possible to see the keepers in the area outside his door.

"I could not fail to notice that he wanted to tell me something very
important", Zanders said carefully at the enquiry.

Remembering his promise to Gudden, he then asked the King's
permission to withdraw and perhaps thinking that his old friend had
defected to the other side Ludwig agreed "with a gloomy expression in
his eyes". Nevertheless, when the major domo handed him the papers
he had brought, the King's mood brightened considerably. This might
well indicate the moment when a note from Elisabeth or from the
Emperor, probably the former, was handed to him. Certainly at about
this time his whole demeanour underwent a change. [In view of his own
precarious position, it is unlikely that Zanders would afterwards have
admitted to being the bearer of the good tidings.] Moments later the
King suddenly asked Zanders to go to Munich for him to get a new
surgical belt**, adding that he felt sure that Gudden would permit him
to go. "At the same time, you will not deny me the courtesy of going to
Duke Max and giving him or one of his sons this letter for the Empress.
If you are able to see the Empress yourself so much the better. It is
sealed; a personal note. There is no need for you to know the contents."

This is Zanders' report of the conversation and, far from Ludwig's
letter to Elisabeth being merely "a personal note", it was more probably
concerned with a plan of escape. Curiously, no one seemed to associ-
ate Elisabeth with any escape plan despite the fact that, years before,
she had risked not only life and limb but also her reputation for the
sake of Julius Andrássy, and their plans for a better Hungary. Why
should she not have similarly embroiled herself in order to help someone who was far closer than the Hungarian patriot?

If Ludwig's captors knew of the note, they made no effort to persuade Zanders to relinquish it, but since everyone at Court was aware
of the affinity between Elisabeth and Ludwig they evidently took the

---

* The appetite increases with eating.
** Ludwig had suffered a hernia following a riding accident some years before.

note to be what Ludwig said it was. The King then gave Zanders two envelopes, one addressed to the Empress and the other containing the instructions for his purchase. Zanders was then dismissed and Ludwig sent for Dr. Müller, who like his superior, hurried to the King. Ironically, Ludwig's captors seemed more anxious to attend to his needs than were some of his personal staff.

When Müller entered he found Ludwig standing by the window still staring out at the park and watching the patrolling Gendarmes. He inspected the doctor thoroughly, but characteristically dropped his eyes as soon as Müller returned his stare. He was still uncertain whether or not the doctor could be trusted but was clearly determined to find out. The conversation began prosaically enough but cleverly sandwiched between his generalities were far more searching questions: "Where did you study?"

"In Würzberg, Majesty."

"You are with my brother, I believe? How is he?"

"No noticeable changes have taken place in the last few weeks, Majesty."

"Is it not true that you have also now made a report about me and are writing to Prince Luitpold about me?"

"I have not yet been informed of any order in that respect, Majesty."

"Ah, but if you do, things will go badly for me, I think? Will the people be pleased when they hear that it will be the worse for me?"

"Majesty, I am firmly convinced that not only Prince Luitpold but also the Bavarian people will be very pleased when they hear that things are going better with the King."

"Yes, but it is still very easy to put something in a man's soup from which he will never awake."

Embarrassed, Müller made no reply to this. By this time he was deeply uneasy and there was a strong doubt in his mind as to whether the King's obsession with assassination was, as Gudden had told him, a symptom of mental disorder or whether there was in fact a plot in progress to depose and assassinate the King. Müller was in an invidious position for he could scarcely ask his superior who, despite his strange working methods, was regarded as a man of impeccable medical reputation, if he was involved in a political plot to kill one of the calmest and most charming "madmen" he had ever encountered in his professional life. Equally unwelcome to him was the only other alternative, namely that Gudden had gullibly allowed himself to be duped and used by a coven of rogues. From Müller's later comments it would seem that from the moment he had arrived at Neuschwanstein and met the King with a view to apprehending him he had been disturbed by certain puzzling elements, but after the bodies of the King and the doctor were found, Müller's attitude and, indeed, the tone of his later testimony, underwent a definite change. His earlier criticism of his superiors had not endeared him to Gudden; the simplest way of silencing him was obviously to implicate him. Afterwards, at the enquiry, Müller's own safest course was to emphasise his earlier unease without stressing what later occurred. This at least explains his self-contradictory behaviour.

Unfortunately, Ludwig was ever his own worst enemy: his questions and comments were frequently so ambiguous as to indicate either that he expected to be poisoned or that he intended to take his own life and was sounding out everyone in the vicinity with a view to finding a willing accomplice to provide him with the facility to do so. Ludwig had always been somewhat enigmatic in his remarks and this was no exception. Müller also found his questions to be so ambiguously phrased that he found it impossible even now to make up his mind about the King.

"What kind of things are there to make one sleep?" Ludwig probed. "There are many, Majesty: opium, morphine, chloralhydrate; there are baths, washing, gymnastics, exercises, etc." The King nodded and, changing the subject abruptly, enquired about Müller's eyesight and about his education before asking him if he would care to put his library in order for him. Müller was clearly flattered by this unexpected invitation which was a compliment not only to his knowledge of French,* but was also Ludwig's way of showing that he liked him. Having ascertained the doctor's agreement he then enquired as to his anticipated duration of service at Berg.

"Will you remain here permanently?"
"Majesty, it is agreed that I shall change monthly with another colleague."
"And who is that?"
"He has not yet been named, Majesty."
"Na, no doubt he will know a little about removing me unnoticed from the world."
"Majesty, I can vouch for any of my colleagues you care to name, as well as for myself, that it is the duty of doctors to heal and make better, not to destroy."
"Yes, I trust you but not the others."

To Müller's discomfort Ludwig now began to elaborate on his theories as to his removal from the throne and undignified abduction from the Allgäu to Berg. But the doctor, who knew little about politics and less about his patient, failed to appreciate even now the true state of affairs in the Treasury and Ludwig's difficulties with the Ultramon-

* Ludwig's vast library collection included a multitude of books in French, mostly concerning the Bourbons, but also the literary classics.

tane Party. He had merely been told that the King had been diagnosed by four doctors as suffering from Paranoia.

Müller's basic training told him that he must look upon the King's apparent ramblings as "delusions of persecution" - symptoms which, unfortunately, fitted all too well the picture which Gudden had been at pains to paint in the younger doctor's mind of a man completely unhinged. Unlike genuine paranoids, Ludwig at no time expressed the fear that everyone was against him. On the contrary, he continued to the last to trust people who were most definitely his enemies. He merely pinpointed a small minority group and stuck to his story, and this was what most disturbed Müller who had naturally encountered many paranoids and schizophrenics in the course of his work and was accustomed to persecution complexes. At the same time, Ludwig's withdrawal from society and nocturnal lifestyle together with his apparent inability to look his doctor in the eye appeared to indicate some kind of abnormality. No one had seen fit to tell him of the King's acute natural shyness coupled with the fact that he could no longer bear to see reflected in people's eyes criticism or ridicule because his good looks had disappeared. He had for some years preferred to gaze at the heavens or the floor and, like an actor, found it easier to fix his eyes on some distant point and pretend the critics were not there.

Knowing all too well what Müller's reaction must be, Ludwig was understandably nervous. He paced back and forth in the room wondering how he could convince this young man that he was not mad. It is a great pity that at this early stage he did not sense Müller's own dilemma for in the end, despite the fact that he had taken a great liking to the King, the doctor felt obliged to accept the pronouncement of his betters and put aside his own fears that Ludwig might, after all, be sane. He had been too well trained and, more recently, too carefully briefed, on his present case to be taken in by the King's "rationality". It was on this ground alone that he could not allow himself to be totally convinced of Ludwig's normality. The tragedy was that he had not been allowed to acquaint himself sufficiently with the facts of Ludwig's life before blindly accepting his senior colleagues' version of them.

After the two men had talked for some time, the King looked at his watch and walked to the window again, looking out with mounting anxiety. It was again raining heavily and grey clouds hung over the lake and trees. In the distance was the barely discernable outline of a canoe going in the diction of Leoni, its occupants bowed against the force of the wind. Ludwig turned suddenly to find Müller watching him closely and dismissed the young doctor "with a genial nod". Müller afterwards said of the interview, "I was with the King for about three-quarters of an hour and during that time I had more questions put to me than in the State Examinations. If I had not already been informed of the patient's bearing by Dr. Gudden and convinced of his illness during our first and second visits to Neuschwanstein, then *I would never have had occasion to make my diagnosis.*" [Author's italics].

But he did not explain whether this meant that he himself had earlier been convinced of Ludwig's illness or that his colleagues had convinced him. The statement remains as ambiguous as some of his later remarks yet there is no doubt that Müller's feelings remained an uncomfortable admixture of doubt, puzzlement and the determination to do his duty as it had been outlined to him by his senior colleagues. It is, of course, possible that he had been advised by those who knew of his doubts to refrain from "making waves". On the other hand, Müller had clearly been impressed by the King's demeanour, his bearing, his lucidity, the clarity of his mind and the interrogation to which he had subjected his doctor. Ludwig's failure to comply with the accepted picture of a madman must have been especially noticeable to Müller who had worked predominantly with the totally insane.

The only remaining point to count heavily against the King was his longing to be alone and his frequent requests to be freed from the surveillance of his keepers. But was this an indication of madness? Surely Müller himself, or indeed any normal person, would have been extremely upset to have found himself so closely watched or, indeed, to have been subjected to any of the other indignities to which Ludwig had submitted over the past hours without complaint or any sign of anger.

At four in the afternoon, the doctors and the other members of the Commission met for coffee and further discussions and Müller repeated to his colleagues the main body of his conversation with the King. There was still a certain amount of dissention. Despite his own mixed feelings as to the King's true condition, Müller was becoming increasingly disturbed by Gudden's strange attitude towards the patient. For years Gudden, considered to be an expert in his field, had advocated that a mental patient should never at any time be trusted, however calm and lucid he might appear to be. Yet Gudden showed towards Ludwig a sycophantic deference and a measure of freedom during their morning walk which clearly worried his colleagues who knew his usual working methods.

Casting aside all his own basic principles, Gudden had gone walking alone in a vulnerable location with a man declared to be dangerously insane, and had deliberately sent back the keeper who had been provided for his protection. Surely he would only have done that if he had known without any doubt that the "patient" was perfectly normal or, more sinister still if he had known that some third person, armed with a weapon of some kind, already waited in the vicinity for a suitable opportunity to present itself or alternatively, carrying out a rehearsal for some later attack. It is unlikely that suspicion of anything like this would have entered Müller's head. What did disturb him was the fact that Gudden now boasted of his intention to take another walk later in the day, in failing light and again without attendants. Why should he have taken this extraordinarily lax attitude towards his reputedly dangerous patient?

Müller was also worried by the fact that Ludwig had been officially deposed in favour of his brother Otto, whose condition was considerably worse than Ludwig's. The newly-appointed Prince Luitpold stepped into the role of Regent immediately, fully prepared and with such men as Max Holnstein and Philipp Eulenburg, both of whom were directly employed by Bismarck in Berlin, as his advisers.

There was every justification for Ludwig's distrust of this unpleasant trinity. Many years earlier, Prince Hohenlohe, when writing to the Imperial Chancellor in Berlin, had stated revealingly, "I cannot, in view of King Ludwig's individuality, definitely confirm that the King deliberately aims for the same goals as ourselves. I can only say that His Majesty is clever enough to estimate the danger which the clerical policy in Bavaria might prepare for him. Whether this intelligence goes sufficiently far for him to parry the consequences of the policy which would arise from the formation of a Catholic ministry, I am not at the moment able to judge. The leaders of the Ultramontane Party are, moreover, as I believe, more concerned with the question whether, at a given moment, Prince Luitpold or Prince Ludwig might be substituted for the King at the helm of the State. Possibly in this connection, they have also taken into consideration the right of the Pope, which gives him the power to depose princes. The reserve to which the King, in spite of the fact that the Ultramontane Party programme appeals to him, has formerly observed to this Party suggests that this plan has become known to His Majesty. On the other hand this reserve may be due to the King's natural distrust or to the realisation of the objective difficulties. Be this as it may, the King's resolutions are not to be foreseen." This proves that, many years earlier, the King's expectancy of reprisal from the Ultramontanes was strong. Dr. Müller, of course, would have been unaware of all this.

In the late afternoon of the 13th, Grashey returned to Munich and Müller, more dissatisfied than ever, went to his room to write letters. Nurse Mauder, who also had the King's welfare at heart, bitterly resented the callous treatment which this charming being was receiving from the senior medicos. He was clearly upset because the Commission members appeared to have little or no respect for the King's feelings and comfort. For example, although Ludwig had only just had his lunch Gudden, with his almost psychotic passion for "strict routine", expected him to eat another main meal only three hours later, simply to fit in with his own arrangements to bring Ludwig's life "back to order".

Outraged by this lack of consideration, the kindly nurse asked Gudden if the King could postpone his next meal until later; surprised and annoyed but evidently not eager to upset Mauder, Gudden agreed and, pleased by this small triumph on the King's behalf, Mauder went to tell Ludwig, whom he found pacing the floor and still staring out anxiously at the lake. The rain beat incessantly on the windows and Mauder later reported his impression that the King feared his walk would have to be cancelled, the possibility of which appeared not to suit him. This would indicate that the King knew that he had friends waiting to rescue him and did not want to lose his opportunity.

Despite the continued inclemency of the weather, the three small boats earlier observed were still sailing doggedly back and forth along the shore. Ludwig asked Mauder to go to his bureau and find his opera glasses, and the good-natured nurse obediently complied. Was he aware of Ludwig's keen interest in the canoes and the weather, or was he merely anxious to keep the King amused? Ludwig immediately trained the glasses on the misty waters "with the gloomy comment that it was still raining." This, of course, was no rarity since June weather in Bavaria is notoriously bad, but again, Mauder got the strong impression that Ludwig was annoyed by it because it would hamper some personal plan, and as it afterwards transpired, this was exactly the case. The King then added "and such weather for the consecration of the church at Grosshessenloh' – the new church there, you know. Such bad luck." Another curiously normal, even prosaic, remark on the part of the "raving lunatic". There was a long silence while Ludwig scanned the lake and the Schlosspark through the glasses and then suddenly, like a cat pouncing on a mouse, he said, "Tell me, Mauder, have the Gendarmes received fresh instructions?"

"I have no idea, Majesty. That side of the administration has nothing to do with me. Has Majesty some special reason for asking?"

"Yes, two of them have just taken up positions outside the Schloss. Can you think of any reason why they should do that, Mauder?"

Mauder could not. When the King noticed this phenomenon, however, he seemed to come to a decision. He consulted his watch again and asked when his dinner would be served. Mauder said that he could have it any time he wanted and in the event the soup was served at four o'clock. To Mauder's surprise, Ludwig ate a great deal although he had quite recently eaten a large meal. It was as if he was systematically packing himself with food in preparation for some ordeal – as if, for instance, he was anticipating a long journey and knew that it would be some time before he had the opportunity to eat again. He also drank a prodigious amount, although his thirst might well have been the result of the combination of champagne, rum and chloralhydrate which he had consumed at Neuschwanstein the day before. By the time the coffee was served, he had become so restless that he could hardly bring himself to remain at the table for long enough to drink it but, interestingly, Mauder regarded this as a symptom of impatience rather than mental disturbance.

The moment the meal was finished, he sent for Gudden with a view to taking the projected walk, regardless of the weather. From this we know that he himself elected to go out at this particular time, as if he had made an arrangement to meet his rescuers and his consumption of the large meal which he did not really want confirms this possibility. It is difficult to believe that a potential suicide would eat so heartily before ending it all.

Another puzzling factor now arises: either Gudden and Washington belonged to different groups of conspirators or they were playing some macabre game of charades. There is no escaping the fact that both men perjured themselves at the subsequent enquiry in the affair. The stories of the Commission members did not even tally. The following account is gleaned from the testimonies of the ensuing events given by the people directly involved.

While Ludwig prepared for his walk, Gudden was in Washington's room having yet another discussion about the King. Leaning back characteristically in his chair, Gudden confessed pompously that he was completely bewildered as to the King's docility, his amiability and calm, and that he agreed "to all suggestions (...) without demur". His somewhat curious conclusion was that "the King knew he was ill and hoped by such rational behaviour he might recover" is scarcely the anticipated comment of an eminent medico. Before he had the opportunity for any further observations, an American newspaper reporter was announced. Although they had already made a statement to the Munich press, they had not yet prepared something suitable for the foreign newspapers. On their own admission, they were dismayed to find that the news had travelled so quickly.

The journalist naturally wanted full details of such a sensational event as the King's deposition and of the journey from Neuschwanstein but he received only the reply that there was no additional statement or information available to that already published in the *Allgemeine Zeitung*. He then asked for further details concerning the King's condition and Gudden, proud of his undoubted prominence in the whole sordid affair, had no objection to replying to this: "His Majesty survived the difficult journey extremely well. He has enjoyed a good night's rest and in general his condition is very satisfactory. There is really nothing further I can add to this statement." But the journalist had one final if somewhat more embarrassing question to which even the glib Gudden had no ready answer:

"Is it true that the King will appear in Munich early tomorrow morning, that is to say, on Whit Sunday?"

"Where on earth did you hear such nonsense?"

"The peasants in Leoni told me." After they had assured the journalist that any such appearance was out of the question, he took his leave but he was unconvinced by what he had been told and his informants themselves were uneasy.

After he had gone Gudden told Washington that he wished the King would let him off going for the walk adding, despite all his previous boasting, "The man's questions are such a frightful strain on one." From his earlier experience as one of Ludwig's aides and from his presence at Court over a period of many years, Washington had already been subjected to the King's endless stream of rapidly-fired questions and well knew that this could be traumatic. Noticeably, neither pursued the possibility of cancelling the walk. Gudden left the room shortly afterwards to prepare for his "ordeal", saying to Washington, "Dinner at eight o'clock."

The disconcerting visit from the American journalist had clearly indicated that the peasants in Leoni expected the King to escape; Gudden was intelligent enough to realise that there must be some substance to this rumour since most of the locals were employed by the Crown or by members of the Wittelsbach and Rambaldi families and by members of the nobility who had their summer homes nearby. As if to reassure himself, Gudden sent a telegram to Minister Lutz timed at 6.35 pm in Berg. It read confidently, "Hagena and Hubrich ordered for Tuesday morning at 9 o'clock. The diagnosis on Prince Otto [sic] expected ready for presentation on Tuesday evening. Here it is going wonderfully well. Incidentally, personal examination only confirms written medical opinion." This, of course, was blatantly untrue and the contents of the telegram as a whole must be one of the most perjurous and, indeed, curious documents produced in the whole sordid affair, yet it caused little comment.

The King's name was not mentioned but since it was common knowledge that Otto was unlikely to be released from his convenient incarceration at Fürstenried, it is improbable that the members of the Commission were considering his ascending the Throne. By bringing his name into the proceedings the conspirators were merely satisfying protocol. The telegram may therefore be safely taken as a euphemism for "Luitpold may usurp the Throne as arranged."

Dr. Müller meantime had settled down to write letters in his room; just before six o'clock there was a tap on his door and, imagining it to be Mauder coming to report, he said "Come in" without looking up. A heavy hand descended on his shoulder. It was Gudden. Müller apologised and in a sudden burst of deference which seems at odds with his rather discordant relationship with his superior, made to stand politely but Gudden held him firmly in his seat with the words "Do not disturb yourself." He seemed to have something on his mind and wandered about the room as restlessly as Ludwig himself, inspecting various objects in the room and especially the portraits of Wagner and scenes from his operas, of which he "greatly disapproved". At last he confided "If only I was not commanded to an audience. The eternal questioning is almost painful. The King wants to know everything and then, when he has the answer, goes on to ask 'Why?' "

This is almost word for word what Gudden was purported to have said to Washington. Was he merely a tedious man apt to repeat every utterance to anyone who would listen or was he, for whatever reason, making it clear that the walk was not his idea – which would make nonsense of his earlier statement regarding the walks? Noticeably, he still referred to the King as "giving audience": as Ludwig's gaoler, he had him totally in his hands, yet still he was the one "commanded to an audience".

Müller himself sensed some anachronism here and again felt "deeply uneasy". For all Gudden's loud assertions concerning the King's illness as diagnosed by himself before he had seen Ludwig personally, and the mode of "treatment" to be employed or rather, imposed, the doctor continued to display a sycophantic deference towards him bordering on idolatry. It seemed not to occur to him that, since he had total charge of the King (or so we are told), he had the power to ignore his commands – for example, to refuse to accompany him on the walk or even to choose not to reply to the "endless questions" which were clearly a source of great anxiety to him. Small wonder that Müller felt so perplexed.

At this moment, Mauder appeared and announced that the King was ready to go. When Gudden left the room to prepare for the walk in the rain, Müller asked Mauder which of the nurses was to accompany them and was told that, since Hack had gone in the morning, it was now Schneller's turn. Schneller was the nurse who seemed so clumsy and inexperienced in the matter of nursing care and whom Ludwig immediately pinpointed as the "odd man out" among the nursing staff.

Müller instructed Schneller to follow at a discreet distance, but Gudden overheard and again insisted that they were not to be accompanied by nurses at all, not even at a distance. This caused some consternation, particularly in view of the failing light but it also casts further doubt on Gudden's credibility.

Mauder then helped Ludwig on with his heavy velours topcoat and seeing Gudden, the King nodded amiably to him. Good-tempered and reasonable, Ludwig was at the same time evidently eager, even impatient, to make a start. He walked briskly down the staircase with Mauder close behind in willing attendance, carrying his umbrella for him. In just a few hours he had become very attached to the King and would have done anything for him. He would, in fact, have liked to accompany him on his walk, to watch over him, as it were, not as a mental nurse guarding a dangerous patient but purely as a companion to one who needed protection for despite his exalted rank, Ludwig was not the most forceful or self-reliant of men. Helpless as a baby when it came to looking after himself, it soon became clear to Mauder that all Ludwig needed was a caring and reliable body servant and someone with whom he could converse amicably.

He had quickly found the King to be a kindly and charming man whose intelligence and witty conversation endeared him to all who were privileged to see him as he really was. In his fascinating, cultured voice, he could discuss anything, trivial or profound, in an articulate manner and was interested in scientific as well as artistic topics. With his love of nature, Ludwig had spent a lifetime in the open air and was well-grounded in the problems as well as the joys of peasant life. He loved to watch the wildlife which abounded in the forests and meadows of Bavaria; apart from the occasional fish which he had proudly caught in his youth, Ludwig had never knowingly killed a living thing and disapproved strongly of hunting. What quickly transpired to the personnel at Schloss Berg in June 1886 apart from the fanatic few who were out for his blood, was that this so-called "raving madman" was an enthralling companion and except for his complaints about the "endless questions" it is clear that Gudden himself enjoyed his company.

When the men reached the courtyard and emerged into the cold, damp air of the park, the King asked Mauder to roll his umbrella for him, since it had momentarily stopped raining. Mauder complied and handed it back to Ludwig who then walked unchecked down the small stone stairway which led into the Schlosspark, without waiting for Gudden who, having come face to face with Mauder at that moment, repeated the curious instruction "No nurses are to go with us."

The ageing doctor then had to walk at some speed to catch up with the King who, still unguarded, had walked a considerable way ahead, himself choosing the route which was, predictably, the path going towards Leoni. Again, Mauder admitted to feeling very puzzled by the excessive freedom allowed to the alleged lunatic whose incarceration had required such lengthy discussion over the past hours. Somewhat unusually, Gudden's instructions were spoken quietly so there was presumably no question of Ludwig himself having overheard. After watching them go, Mauder returned to Dr.Müller to report that the King and his doctor had set off for their walk.

Ludwig and the doctor were never seen alive again. Not until some hours later, after a half-hearted and incredibly ill-organised search, were their bodies found floating on the waters of Lake Starnberg. What had happened in the meantime?

* * * * *

WHEN the King was first apprehended at Neuschwanstein, he had been overtaken by physical and mental exhaustion, and doubtless his feeling of frustration and failure had contributed to make him feel worse. He had been too pessimistic and unhappy to do anything but wait for his captors to claim him but now, reasonably certain of at least two escape possibilities, his old energy returned.

The recent satisfying meal had fortified him against the chilly air and against the ordeal before him and to cheer him further was the thought that on the other side of the lake awaited Empress Elisabeth and her daughters. The canoes and their occupants were still waiting for him, coming as close as they dared to the shore; if he was obliged to wade or swim a short distance in order to reach them, this would present no problem since he was a powerful swimmer although in any case the water at this point was relatively shallow. He would first have to remove the heavy topcoat which, when wet, would considerably hamper his progress. He therefore carefully unbuttoned it in readiness so that he could tear it off quickly. He also undid the buttons of his inner jacket presumably so that he could remove two coats simultaneously, thus leaving his arms and trunk unimpeded for swimming. Mauder had watched him do this.

As he set out on this final walk with Gudden that evening, Ludwig was thus acutely aware that help was at hand when the right moment came. When Gudden had caught up with him the two set off down the path together. Out of breath, the doctor walked on the King's left at the water's edge since they were going towards Leoni and interestingly, Gudden unquestioningly adopted the direction which the King had chosen, indicating that the American reporter's remarks may well have been discussed between the conspirators and taken to heart. It was now a quarter to seven and because of the heavy rainclouds, it was growing very dark.

In the cold, fresh air, with freedom in sight, Ludwig's spirits rose further, and he may have regarded as a blessing the heavy mist which fell as it darkened. Although it was impossible to see anything with total clarity, he knew that a carriage waited outside the gates at the edge of the Schlosspark, but had apparently decided to abandon that particular means of escape, possibly since he had noticed the extra Gendarmes on whose presence he had earlier remarked to Mauder. The prospect of reaching one of the canoes was much better, particularly in view of the mist and gloom at the lakeside. Ludwig of course knew every step of the path around the shore while Gudden had been there only once before. The three canoes were not hallucinations. They were observed (with some astonishment) by a number of people as they plied their way back and forth along the shore between Berg and Leoni throughout the whole of that appallingly wet day. In addition a carriage, also seen by a number of people including Washington, had waited for some hours at the gate to Schloss Berg with a team of fresh horses ready to take the King to safety. But the moment Ludwig saw those extra Gendarmes he realised that this means of egress was no longer open to him. Everything now depended upon his reaching the lake.

For many years Empress Elisabeth had been acquainted with all the noblemen who lived along the lakeside near to her own childhood home, Schloss Possenhofen. She therefore knew exactly whom she could trust and whom she could not. From Ludwig's earlier telegram she knew of the plot to depose him. When she received news from Dürkheim and Zanders of the King's plight, in all probability she sent one of her brothers to Major Hornig, the brother of Ludwig's old friend and Stallmeister. In his biography of Prince Karl Theodor in Bayern, Richard Sexus states: "Graf Dürkheim, the King's adjutant, was in communication with the Empress when he arranged with Baron Beck for that vehicle to come from Eurasberg* to fetch the King." He added that Dürkheim himself had told the son of the owner of the carriage (Baron Beck) and Count Rambaldi who lived at Schloss Allmannshausen near Seeleiten, south of Berg. Baron Eugen von Beck-Peccoz, a kinsman of Baron Beck, was also alerted and he waited in the carriage. This was no spur of the moment rescue operation, for the Baron is said to have earlier sent specially to Munich for a team of his best and sturdiest horses to be sent to his lakeside home, as if he had heard of the *coup* and had somehow got wind of where Ludwig was to be taken. Meantime, Count Rambaldi and Major Hornig had set off in two canoes (the third probably carried Elisabeth's brothers).

---

* Some 14 kms from Berg.

Although the rain had beaten down incessantly throughout the day and the mist was now so heavy that it was at times impossible to see the shore, the men in their canoes had continued to row back and forth between Berg and Leoni. As the King and his companion walked further along the path, whenever there was a break in the mist he cannot have failed to see them but it is possible that Gudden, who was considerably more myopic than the nearsighted Ludwig, had not. Thinking that his rescuers were still too far away, he continued further with Gudden along the path which drew gradually nearer to the water, he clearly anticipated an opportunity to make his bid for freedom.

As on their earlier walk, Ludwig and Gudden chatted intermittently and when they had reached the point where a bench offered an uninterrupted view of the water, Ludwig suggested that despite the bad weather they might sit for a moment – surely a welcome idea to the out-of-condition doctor. Unfortunately, by doing this Ludwig inadvertently played into his enemies' hands for if one or more assassin had been lying in wait or, more probably, had been following the King and Gudden, this would have provided them with an excellent opportunity to trap their quarry. Now, on the choppy waters of Lake Starnberg, the final act of the drama was now played out.

From the moment the Commission members appeared at Neuschwanstein Ludwig had been well aware that he was to be first discredited and then assassinated, either by the Ultramontanes or by the Prussians-possibly even by a combined effort of the two, which would account for the extraordinary mismanagement of the affair. There is little doubt that those two ubiquitous and unsavoury gentlemen, Max Holnstein and Philipp zu Eulenburg were deeply involved in the plot. (Both, incidentally, received generous rewards from a grateful Prussia and both afterwards enjoyed careers in Berlin which were littered with intrigue and deception.)

Ludwig's time had come. Several times he had remarked to the doctors and the Commission members on how easy it would be to kill him – an observation which had met only with an embarrassed silence or an averted gaze. He had obviously been waiting for something of the sort to happen for many hours; it would have been all too easy for them to accost Ludwig at some deserted spot and dispose of him in a convenient manner, possibly first stunning him with chloroform as they had earlier attempted to do and then shooting him.

The only real obstruction to the plot to assassinate King Ludwig was the proposed victim, who had neither the wish nor the intention to die at that particular moment. No longer befuddled by alcohol or soporifics, he knew that he had only to spring quickly into the water and swim or wade towards one of the waiting canoes before the more elderly

Gudden had time to apprehend him or raise the alarm, and all his troubles would be at an end.

Assassination theories have always been unpopular, especially with the authorities and the possibility – adamantly denied – that Ludwig had a definite escape route equally so, but the testimonies of on-the-spot witnesses seem curiously at variance, a hotch-potch of hastily-put-together yarns and opinions, few of which ring true and few of which even agreed with each other on the most fundamental of points. Whether or not the confusion was deliberate, this must surely be the clumsiest and most ill-organised *coup* in history.

What exactly happened to Ludwig and Dr.Gudden can only be conjectured, despite copious testimony of varying quality and reliability. The existing evidence and statements are set out below, together with some of the many theories propounded, including that of the author. Readers must draw their own conclusions as to the truth about Ludwig's undignified end. The whole story can neither be confirmed nor disproved since the relevant documents in the private Archives of the Bavarian State and of the Wittelsbach family will not become available until the year 2000, and it is generally supposed that even then their contents will remain secret. This fact in itself suggests direct family involvement in the affair.

One thing is certain, however: King Ludwig I's prophecy proved to be all too accurate for Ludwig II, a man of honour, integrity and good intention, did indeed dig the grave of the Bavarian monarchy.

CHAPTER EIGHTEEN

A MYSTERIOUS END

HOW did King Ludwig die? There were several contemporary theories which were widely discussed in the press and elsewhere, the most popular being that the King had committed suicide after murdering Dr. Gudden. This was sensational enough, but nowhere in the press was the assertion that Ludwig was murdered although this is undoubtedly what happened to him.

The peasants from the villages near his castles were less coy: they firmly believed that his death was neither natural nor accidental and to a man favoured the theory that he had been shot while attempting to reach the Roseninsel where Empress Elisabeth waited for him with protagonists ready to escort him over the border to safety in Austria. Everyone who lived on the banks of Lake Starnberg knew of Ludwig and Elisabeth's long-standing attachment, whether it was of a physical or a spiritual nature and further, the peasants knew their *Kini* too well to believe that he had taken his own life.

There is no doubt that his enemies went to great lengths to cloud or suppress much vital evidence, but they could not destroy all of it and there remains copious evidence that Ludwig was murdered. The abovementioned theory, put out by the new Regent and his acolytes, is so full of holes that one can only wonder that it has been taken seriously for so long. The statements of witnesses, hostile and otherwise, were disjointed, unsatisfactory, contradictory, confused and confusing. The clearest thing about them is that they were deliberately ambiguous and even, in some cases, totally false, as if the conspirators were using the best means at their disposal to cover their traces. They were greatly assisted in this by the fact that even genuine witnesses proved unreliable while others had undoubtedly been encouraged by means of threats either to say nothing or to perjure themselves.

According to the evidence of the domestic and medical staff and the Gendarmerie (later revealed to have been composed largely of members of the Prussian secret police), some time passed since the King and his doctor had set out on their second walk of the day. Their failure to return was at last remarked by the curiously apathetic staff and search parties half-heartedly organised, but by this time it was almost completely dark and again raining heavily which would scarcely have assisted these all-too-incompetent "searchers".

According to the official reports, by ten o'clock on the night of June 12th, the park was swarming with Gendarmes and officials who at last discovered a hat, claimed by the finder as being the King's hat because he recognised the agraffe which adorned it. But we know that, almost immediately before being apprehended at Neuschwanstein, Ludwig removed the agraffe and gave it to Mayr as a present together with a deed of gift entitling his servant to claim its value in hard cash should he later be required to return it to the Treasury. Is it likely that, at such a traumatic moment, with a posse of men clearly visible on the approach to the castle, either the King or his servant would have had the presence of mind to replace the ornament with another? The hat found at the lakeside was described as having in it "a tear about 2 cms in size (...) and also torn and frayed at the back." Could these not have been bullet holes?

Nurse Schneller, whether he was a real nurse or merely one of Holnstein's men, testified that the King's hat was "absolutely wet through, and it could be seen that the brim which was trimmed with a silk band, had a tear of about 2 cms in it, and was also torn and frayed in two other places at the back, each tear about 2 cms wide." Almost as if a bullet had passed through it, in fact. The only other reasonable explanation for the holes would be that they were made by Ludwig's diamond agraffe, but this was always inserted at the side; no one wears a brooch at the back of his hat and in view of the style of the hat itself which was of the curled brim type, it is unlikely that he wore it the wrong way round. Curiously, in regard to this agraffe, Schneller was the only witness to mention it at all, the others attesting only to the holes in the hat.

One of Count Rambaldi's servants who had been told to wait in the park to direct the King to the waiting carriage or to one of the canoes which had been plying up and down the lake, came to tell his master the news. Rambaldi, however, was already aware of the tragedy which had taken place, having been one of the occupants of the canoes in question. Earlier, when Rambaldi's wife, puzzled by his sudden enthusiasm for sailing in such inclement weather enquired as to the reason, she was given the surprising explanation that it "gave him pleasure". Later, after a few more hours' "pleasure" taken in the same manner, he returned home soaked to the skin and clearly distressed. He offered his wife no more than the inadequate comment, "They have found a hat. The secret is out" but, we are told, aggravatingly failed to elucidate.

At the alleged scene of the tragedy itself, two coats belonging to the King were found with the arms of the jacket inside those of the topcoat, suggesting that they had been drawn off together, either by an assassin attempting to pinion the King's arms by drawing off both coats from behind, or by the King himself in order to facilitiate movement. Since

Ludwig was seen to unbutton his coats before setting off on his walk – and it was unlikely in view of the bad weather that he would have done so without good reason – we may assume that such was his intention. A sickly man, he had always complained of feeling the cold and this is evidenced by the fact that he wore a heavy topcoat in mid-June. Two umbrellas belonging to Ludwig and Gudden next came to light and shortly afterwards, whether by accident or design, the bodies were discovered.

During the sketchy and ill-managed enquiry, Dr.Karl-Franz Müller stated that he and Leonhard Huber, the Schloss steward, went to the fisherman, Jakob Lidl, whose cottage was on the King's estate, and told him to row them along the shore to look for the King and it was not long before Müller shouted that he could see a body floating in the water and "without a second thought" jumped into the icy waters of the lake in the misplaced hope of recovering the King alive. Ludwig was discovered face downwards in his shirtsleeves and Gudden was then found some seven paces away from him, still wearing his topcoat and floating in a curious, half-kneeling, half-crouching position. Both men were said to have their eyes open in an unnatural stare which seemed, according to several witnesses, to be "more artificial than the stare of death."

Müller and Huber pulled both bodies into the boat and some of the nurses (or whatever they were) hauled them on to dry land. The King's watch was hanging from his waistcoat pocket but, as Lidl somewhat acrimoniously asserted, "it disappeared into someone's pocket", the someone in question being Baron Washington, whose behaviour throughout was curious to say the least. The watch was afterwards said to have stopped at 6.45 pm; water had seeped between glass and dial which would indicate this to be the time when the watch and its owner came in contact with the water. Nevertheless, if Washington was less innocent than he purported to be, there was nothing to prevent him from altering the time to suit his own purposes after he had appropriated the watch.

Rigor mortis had already set in and both bodies were described as being "extremely stiff" yet before any further examination was carried out, Baron Washington rushed away to telegraph to Munich, "The King and Gudden both alive. Müller carrying out artificial respiration." The wording of this telegram is extraordinary: what could an innocent recipient have made of it? If he had sent an earlier [unrecorded] telegram, why should he have declared that both were alive when it had already been ascertained by all present that both men were already dead and indeed had been so for some time before they were discovered? Artificial respiration was nevertheless doggedly carried out and the charade purposefully continued.

Many strange rumours surrounded the bodies themselves and, indeed, Lidl the fisherman, afraid for years to speak his mind, left a sworn testimony from his deathbed in 1935* to the effect that what he saw floating on the choppy waters of the lake at midnight that night were two dummies or, at the very least, two corpses wearing masks over their features. Lidl attested that he knew this to be the case because he had, some hours earlier, seen with his own eyes what actually happened that night.

Quite obviously, the secrets which Lidl carried around with him for so many years preyed on his mind. For instance, in his testament he averred that when, in 1884, two gentlemen arrived from France to see Ludwig, a friend of his who was employed at Schloss Berg was told by Minister Lutz, "under threat of being drafted into the Pioneers", that he was to say that "The King is not in residence" and that the same instruction was to apply should any other visitors appear. This clearly indicates a definite plan to isolate the King totally from his people and, indeed, from reality. The man in question had further informed Lidl that, after 1886, he kept quiet about his knowledge (as indeed had Lidl himself) because – and they had both seen for themselves how true this could be – "It was all too easy to send a man to Haar."**

Lidl further asserted that Ludwig was fully aware of the intrigues which abounded within the Court and Cabinet. The King had always been in the habit of chatting democratically with his boatman when he went across to the Roseninsel and it was probably on one of these occasions that he had confided to Lidl his suspicion of an imminent assassination attempt. Comments of this nature made to the wrong listener sometimes added weight to the stories of Ludwig's abnormality, but Lidl knew that he could take what Ludwig told him in confidence to be no more than the truth. Lidl's revelations ended with the information that yet another friend of his of his, a fisherman from the nearby Ammerland, had been told to take two wooden shoes and a stick and form with them two sets of footprints close together in the lakebed, as if to indicate that a struggle had taken place (see page 321). He was ordered to do this, he said, under pain of imprisonment. What possible motive could this simple man have for inventing such a story on his deathbed some 50 years after the event? Further credence is added by the fact that pro-Prussian Prime Minister Lutz summoned everyone who had been concerned, however tenuously, with the events of the night of June 12/13th to the Munich Residenz and made them swear an oath never to divulge anything or to repeat a single word of

---

* See page 234.   ** A Munich mental institution.

what had happened, "even on their deathbeds to a priest"? Lutz, having come to an arrangement with Luitpold, remained in office for a further four years but died, it is reported, "a tormented man" in 1890, while other Court and Government officials were said to have suffered from such guilty consciences afterwards that they "could not bring themselves to function at Luitpold's Court".

To return to the events of the night of the 12th/13th, Dr. Müller, commenting on the somewhat rash "both alive" telegram, afterwards stated, "It is not clear to me how this came to be observed. It is possible that, during one of the resuscitation attempts, one eyelid was raised higher than the other in pupil reaction. Probably a mechanical reaction caused by changing the position of the body. I don't know. But so much was clear to me right away and that was that both had been dead for some hours, and I made the attempt to revive them only in order to cover myself in this connection." Again, this is a very curious statement to come from a medical man.

Lidl had known the King personally over a period of many years and had frequently ferried him to the Roseninsel when he went to meet Elisabeth there. If there was anything strange about the body found in the lake, then he of all people would have noticed it, as would a qualified medical practitioner who purported to have already attempted artificial respiration. If there was any truth in the testimony, the men knew of the charade and the reason for it. Lidl was quite obviously convinced that the whole thing had been engineered by Baron Washington, whom he did not trust. He also averred that Washington's telegram was "falsified".

According to another contemporary, a friend of Jakob Lidl who died in 1963, even more startling occurrences took place that night. According to this person, "Lidl knew that the King wanted to escape on the evening of June 13th, 1866. To this end he received instructions that he was to wait in his canoe some meters away from the shore, hidden in the bushes. When he had thus positioned himself, the King began to embark but, with his weight of about 200 lbs. the canoe sat fast on the shore and hasty flight became impossible. The King already had one foot in the canoe when a shot was fired which obviously killed him instantly. In his bewilderment and in fear of his own death, Jakob Lidl then pushed the King, who had fallen across the end of the boat, back into the water and rowed back panic-stricken towards his own house (...) and crouched gasping and weeping on his bed. When, towards 11 that night, he was awoken by Assistant-Doctor Karl-Franz Müller (...). The terrified Lidl thought that he was being arrested for helping the King to escape, but it seems that they only wanted him to row them along the shore in search of the King who had apparently been missing 'since eight o'clock'."

The narrative continued to the effect that Lidl, who "since about 7 o'clock already knew the place of death", immediately found the King and Dr.v.Gudden in spite of the darkness and the weather. The two bodies were then lifted into the canoes and rowed not to Schloss Berg but to the boathouse and laid out on the wooden-planked floor. *There they lay for exactly four hours* [Author's italics] and not before this were they moved into the Schloss."

Interesting as this is, the informant does not offer us a reason for the hiding of the bodies. He does, however, refer to a convoy of "five or six large canoes each with about 20 armed mountain artillerymen" whom, he said, would attempt to land with the King at Leoni, Ammerland, Ambach or Seeshaupt where a four horse carriage provided by the Baron von Beck-Peccoz from Eurasberg was waiting for the King's use in case it was necessary." This confirms the story that the Baron suddenly had a number of his best horses from his Munich stable transferred to his villa at Starnberg.

If all this is true, why did Müller hide the bodies? Was he implicated in the conspiracy? His earlier reports and behaviour would suggest otherwise, unless he also was indulging in some elaborate charade. The most likely explanation is that he was drawn into the affair at the last moment. If, having joined the conspirators, he then persuaded the boatman to help him to conceal the bodies in the boathouse, it is easy to accept that the horrified peasant could be easily silenced by threats. But if this was the case, why did not the conspirators, who were ruthless, powerful and determined men, not simply dispatch the unimportant Lidl in the same way as they had just done away with their King?

The testimony concerning Gudden is equally unsatisfactory. If he outlived the King by an hour, why did the fisherman fail to mention this, although he does concede, "the bodIES were laid out in the boathouse", which might well indicate, as is averred in yet another newly-discovered testimony, that there were considerably more bodies than two, following a fracas. There were persistent whispers to the effect that there had been "six to eight" or "eleven" other sudden deaths and disappearances that night. Rumour had it that some of Ludwig's loyal supporters were also killed when the King met his end: could the vagueness of the Commission members and witnesses concerning other casualties be a further attempt to conceal what really happened? According to the local records, eleven other able-bodied men died suddenly that night, which seems somewhat excessive for such a small village. Sinister rumblings were also heard concerning the boathouse itself which was ordered by Minister Lutz to be destroyed by fire shortly afterwards.

While Ludwig's watch was reported to have stopped at a time which accorded with Lidl's statement, Gudden's watch stopped at 8.00 pm; his colleagues explained this away by asserting that he notoriously forgot to wind his watch, but this seems unlikely in a man as obsessed with time and routines as he.

However, we still have Lidl's final assertion concerning the event, namely, that the King had been shot after the body (or bodies) had been removed and had remained in the boathouse "for exactly four hours", they were brought out again and left to float on the rain-swollen waters with masks over their faces so that they might be found in suitably "mysterious" circumstances in order, as Lidl put it, "to satisfy Lutz' or Luitpold's lust for power". This is a strange statement to come from the lips of a simple peasant fisherman; indeed, it has about it the distinct ring of some untutored person repeating a phrase which he has heard used by someone more erudite, probably Ludwig himself.

The suicide theory discounted, Ludwig certainly could not have drowned. The water at the point where the body was officially found is only four feet or so deep; no adult person could possibly drown there and certainly not a powerful swimmer well over six feet in height such as Ludwig. Lidl's statement, albeit not the most scholarly of efforts (which actually lends weight to its authenticity), also states that he had "taken some 40 souls from the water" in his time and that "this was the first one I had ever seen with his eyes open." He made the same observation to Müller at the time and the doctor told him sharply to be silent and get on with his work, which consisted of hauling the boat on to dry land. Even the local priest who kept vigil over the King's body that night pronounced that the King's features and general aspect were not those of a man who had met his end by drowning.

Lidl's statement contained other interesting remarks which conflicted with other testimonies, but the greatest point in their favour is that he knew the King better than anyone else present. Furthermore, he had no reason, especially so many years after the event, to lie about the circumstances of the King's death. Müller's testimony, on the other hand, frequently contradicts itself. Of the discovery of the bodies he attested, "Both, I ascertained right away, were without pulse and without breath. *Rigor mortis* had set in; both were face downwards." Yet in contradiction to this he also stated, "After we had quickly opened their clothes we now made the necessary attempts to revive them, during which time I carried out artificial respiration and in between times massaged their chests. A stable servant called Baron Washington over because one of them had shown signs of life but this

was quickly dismissed as "final nerve spasms". Puzzling, then, is that
telegram in which Washington stated categorically "Both live! Müller
carrying out artificial respiration!" Can Washington really have been
so irresponsible as to despatch such a message to the Cabinet without
ascertaining for himself the true situation? More puzzling still is
Müller's statement that he attempted resuscitation "only to cover
myself" having much earlier expressed the opinion that "both men had
been dead for some hours" (and if Lidl's assertion was true, no one
knew better than Müller that this was the case). Somewhat superfluously, Müller added "Naturally, all attempts were useless".

According to the accepted statements concerning the discovery of
the King's body, Müller pronounced loudly "Lieutenant Colonel
[Washington], I confirm the death of His Majesty and *Obermedizinalrat*
von Gudden! All attempts to revive them are futile!" Again, why did
he bother to make such a dramatic announcement when he had earlier
told everyone present that he had ascertained the lifelessness of both
men? Was he still "covering himself" for the benefit of the servants
and Gendarmes so that he could be seen to be doing his duty? Most
of those milling around in the Park and the Schloss must have been
aware of the unsavoury atmosphere which pervaded the place, and of
the strange goings-on of the past hours. Was this merely Müller's way
of satisfying protocol or was he, in fact, covering for someone else? If
what Lidl said was true, he was all too uncomfortably aware that
Ludwig had been dead for several hours – had Müller become part of
the conspiracy or was he simply trying to save his own skin, knowing
that if he did not go along with the conspirators he would undoubtedly
come to the same end? It may sound unlikely but it is not impossible.
Müller certainly seemed unreasonably angry with Lidl for pointing out
the inappropriate aspect of the King's face when his body was removed
from the water – was he annoyed because he disliked being treated as
an equal by a peasant? Was he distraught and tense owing to the
pressures of the situation? Was he himself overstressed because he
knew what was happening but was powerless to do anything about it?
Or was he angry because, as one of the conspirators, he saw Lidl as a
hazard to the success of the plan? The latter is unlikely because it
would not have been difficult to dispose of Lidl if necessary. The
speculations as to Dr. Müller's role are endless.

The two corpses were carried back into Schloss Berg where they
were laid out in two adjoining rooms. Some hours later Müller testified
that Gudden had a bruise over one eye "almost certainly caused by a
blow from a fist" (and this precludes the use of a mask on Gudden)
and a crack in his hat "as if he had been struck by a blunt instrument",
but he did not go so far as to say that the King himself might have been

Gudden's assailant. In any case, Ludwig had no "blunt instrument" except for his umbrella which had been found undamaged nearby.

Müller further stated that, although there was no visible damage to the King's hat, there was a fresh tear (elsewhere described as "a small hole") in it. On Gudden's face, on his features and nose, according to Müller, "there were several diagonally running scratches over his right eye and a not-unimportant blue fleck certainly caused by a blow from a fist" – but whose fist? Surely not the pacific Ludwig's?

*   *   *   *   *

AFTER the initial excitement had died down, an enquiry ensued at which the various Commission members, their staff and Ludwig's own staff were called upon to give an account of themselves.

The obtuse or more probably, implicated, Baron Washington stated "Now I decided that the time had come to let HRH The Prince Regent know and also the Ministers. My first despatch was addressed to Colonel Freytag [Luitpold's adjutant]. Then I despatched another to the ministers. Scarcely had these despatches been sent when some Gendarmes came and announced that the middle gate of the park was closed yet there were fresh carriage tracks to be seen going in the direction of Munich. Immediately, I gave the order for the horses to be harnessed and enquries made in the next village to see whether a carriage had come through, and the information brought to me." He did not say what information, if any, was forthcoming and he naturally had no need to amend the wording of his somewhat ambiguous statement in order to conceal the real reason for the instruction, namely, to find out exactly who was attempting to help the King to escape.

In addition to all the doubts which must inevitably surround the actions and behaviour of Max Holnstein over the last few years of the King's life, the activities of another figure are worthy of mention, namely Count Eulenburg; the latter had much to say at the enquiry concerning the King's death and he looms repeatedly on the horizon in a way which suggests that he was more – or rather, less, than the respected aristocrat he purported to be.

Philipp, Count zu Eulenburg* was born at Königsberg, Prussia, in 1847. Landowner, music lover, sportsman, man of letters and diplomat, he became a confidant of King Wilhelm in the fateful year 1886, and during the latter course of his career seems to have had a nefarious hand in the deposition of various favourites within the Prussian Court. Notable among these – and here is a certain irony – was the final brusque removal from office of Bismarck himself who had of course been responsible in his turn for the removal of so many others. One might almost say that this particular activity was Eulenburg's speciality,

---

* Later zu Eulenburg und Hertefeld.

but he himself received his come-uppance when he was disgraced some years later after his involvement in a monumental homosexual scandal was widely publicised in the press.

At Whitsun 1886, when he was the Prussian Envoy to Bavaria, he had rented a villa from a friend and was ostensibly enjoying a holiday weekend at Starnberg in common with many others. On the preceding day, when the King was first brought to Berg, he was nowhere to be seen although this was the very time when his presence in his official capacity might have been justified. No one would have thought it strange had he arrived at Schloss Berg out of sheer curiosity like everyone else who had heard of the upheaval taking place within the Bavarian Court. Nor did Eulenburg show his face during the night of the 13th when, for whatever reason, every able bodied man in the vicinity had been alerted to join the search for the two missing men. Yet he was the first to offer testimony "as an eyewitness" the following morning and in view of his exalted and responsible position, what he said was accepted as irrefutable. His ensuing statement thus coloured public opinion and acceptance of what had actually taken place. Giving his description of the corpses, for example, he was the only person to observe "marks of strangulation" on Gudden's throat, marks which should certainly have been noticed by Müller and the bevy of other medicos who performed the somewhat sketchy post-mortem. Such marks were not mentioned in the official medical and legal report – a strange omission if they had really existed.

Eulenburg asserted that the King had attacked Gudden in a blind rage (itself an unlikely occurrence since Ludwig's anger was invariably verbal) and strangled him before suffering a stroke or heart attack moments later. Eulenburg put other thoughts into people's heads by stating, somewhat histrionically, that in death Ludwig "wore a smile (...) of madness" whereas official photographs of the King both in his coffin and laid out on his bed shortly after the accident show a calm though unsmiling countenance. Lidl had been firm about the "staring eyes" but said nothing about a smile, nor would he have expected to see one in the circumstances.

After the tragedy, Eulenburg wrote a curious letter to his friend, Fritz von Farenheid-Baynuhnen and if it proves nothing else it shows his unreliability as a witness: "I have stood up well to the unbelieveable excitement which the drama of the King has brought me. It was extremely interesting to experience this, the most unbelievable of all recent catastrophes, while it was actually happening. *Let into the secret of the previously prepared proclamation, by which the unfortunate King was put under restraint, I afterwards experienced the events at Hohenschwangau* where the mad King, whose deposition was being promulgated

by the Commission, was caused to die [Author's italics]. I was also
awoken during the night at Starnberg when the King with Gudden had
been found dead in the water across in Berg. Never will I forget the
impression as I rowed alone with the fisherman, Jakob Ernst, across
the lake in the mist. The stillness of death lay over Schloss Berg and
white as death, as if paralysed, incapable of words, the Court servants
stood along the paths as I hurried with a beating heart into the room
where the myth-surrounded King, a mad smile on his pale lips, the
black locks curling dashingly on his white forehead, had already been
laid out on his bed. I received scarcely any replies to my questions. I
myself had to piece together what had happened. In the neighbouring
room, Dr. Gudden lay dead, an expression of gloomy vitality on his face.
I saw the scar on his forehead. *The frightful marks of strangulation on
his broad neck. He had been strangled by the King because he had tried
to stop him from putting an end to himself* [Author's italics]. I was the
first to examine in broad daylight the traces of the struggle which had
taken place at the water's edge. There I saw the impression of the
King's footprints, so deep beneath the surface of the water that only a
person who had forcibly pulled himself down could have made such
marks. No one fleeing would have been able to leave traces at this place
which led to the middle of the lake, and from this place a fugitive could
have reached the shore from right or left and a strong swimmer like the
King would leave no trace beneath the surface of the water had he not
been overcome by the intention to die. From the place where the
struggle took place, the further hurrying footsteps of the King were
clearly visible leading downwards towards the shoreline to his death."

This was presumptuous nonsense clearly calculated to confuse or
mislead. It was wrong in almost every respect for at the place of which
Eulenburg spoke, far from being "unfathomable" as he had stated in
yet another testimony, the water is only 12 inches deep and even the
most determined of suicides could not manage to do away with himself
in the face of such poor resources. Eulenburg went out of his way to
assert that Ludwig's death had been suicide and coloured his tale with
the most lurid of prose, yet he constructed his story with surprising
carelessness, presumably in the expectation that most people who read
the nobleman's testimony would believe what he said and in any case
would never find themselves in a position to check it. His story, in fact,
did not even agree with the testimony of other hostile witnesses,
namely, the members of the Commission. His official testimony was in
some respects similar to that addressed to his friend and in it he had
described his visit to the King's bedroom to view the corpses: "Deeply
moved, I looked closely at the dead man. His dark locks hung in
confusion over the white forehead. Death had stretched back the

bloated features of the King and the great beauty of his noble mien was apparent once more. Only an extraordinary, strange smile played about his pale lips, a smile which perhaps I might call mad. There were no injuries on the corpse." He had earlier stated that "both bodies were covered up to the neck in blue silk, but when I went back to poor dead Gudden, I noticed small scratches on his forehead. I then looked more closely at the head of the corpse. There on his neck I observed clear flecks like the impression made by nails. It became clear to me that the unfortunate man had suffered a violent death and I began to piece together the puzzle."

Interesting also is Eulenburg's boast to his friend that he had "experienced the events which had taken place at Hohenschwangau" for nowhere in any of the accounts and lists of persons who were in the Schloss or in the area is there any reference, official or otherwise, to his presence there in any capacity – as Prussian Envoy, had he been there, he would certainly have been mentioned.

To return to the theory concerning Ludwig's death it is not beyond the bounds of credibility that the body found in the waters of Lake Starnberg that night was wearing a mask to temporarily disguise a bullet wound or even to disguise the fact that a totally different body, that of some poor unknown, had been substituted. Several people handled Ludwig's body on the way back to Schloss Berg. A mask might just possibly have gone unnoticed at least for a while in the darkness and confusion especially if, as is often the custom, the face of the dead person is covered. Further, it must be remembered that, despite his curiously extended efforts towards resuscitation. Dr. Müller did not seem to pay any particular regard to the body, apart from what Lidl has told us, and again, this might indicate implication in the King's death.

Such a ruse as has been suggested would serve a number of purposes. Several of those who afterwards viewed the body as it lay in the gloom at Schloss Berg remarked that his features wore "a waxy look", and while this is by no means an unusual description of the dead, in Ludwig's case it occurs with an almost monotonous frequency, together with the equally repetitive observation that his face "had regained its youthful beauty" of some years before. But the body which was later on view to the public in Munich, carefully prepared and arranged on the catafalque was in no way youthful or beautiful. Is it possible that for the sake of expediency, one of Elisabeth Ney's working models for the King's portrait had been used as a model for a mask to hide a bullet wound until such time as the King's body could be tidied up and rendered respectable before it was seen by too many people?

Eulenburg described Ludwig's hair as "curling dashingly on his forehead" (and remember that he was purportedly viewing the body after it had been prepared), while the photographs taken at the time show it to be swept well away from his face although not in the way in which he wore it in life. In any case, Ludwig's hair was naturally straight and he had it curled with tongs every day. Is it not strange that the apparently long exposure to rain, wind and lakewater had not straightened it? Was it, after all a specially prepared wig, possibly used in conjunction with a wax mask, as a further expedient to hide a wound? Further, even if submersion in water had swept his hair forward in an unruly manner, it seems surprising that no one thought to push it back into position, either as a reflex action or during examination? Yet if Eulenburg is to be believed, nobody in authority touched it and no other person was allowed to go near enough to the body to be able to do so.

Interestingly, when paying her last respects to Ludwig as his body later lay in the Residenz chapel, Princess Maria Josepha was to observe that his body, in it's 16th Century Knight's Robes, was "almost completely covered with concealing flowers, carefully arranged, especially about the head".

When the park and lakeside were again deserted at 4 o'clock the following morning, Eulenburg decided to visit the scene of the "accident" in a canoe; this seems an odd time to choose but even more curious was the fanciful report which he produced shortly afterwards, a contradictory and largely inaccurate report of what he saw or what he surmised or what he wanted people to think he had seen. He offered detailed descriptions of the much-discussed footprints in the lakebed which, in view of the terrain and prevailing weather conditions could only have been a figment of his imagination unless he had waited until the peasant ordered to make the marks with his wooden shoe had finished his strange task before making an inspection.

His description of the "still visible footprints of the King and Gudden in the bright sand through the clear water" is scarcely believable. At this rather exposed place in the lake the constant shifting of the water and loose stones during the storm would have rendered it impossible to see anything clearly and would certainly have obliterated any genuine footsteps after so many hours of rain. "Through my assessment," he reported, "I was able to prove the following picture: from the path near the bench were to be seen the broken reeds of the path which the King had trodden while the doctor followed him. In the water, Gudden reached the King and grasped him by the coat. Here the footprints within the area of about four feet in diameter were visible in great profusion. The King had undoubtedly struggled with Gudden at this point and probably brought about the wounds on his forehead.

As the King now let his coat fall in order to free himself from Gudden, he made some deeper steps into the water while Gudden followed him. Here there were two sets of footprints side by side - but no further than about six steps. Then countless footprints become visible in the place of about five feet in diameter; in the middle of them were two holes. This is where Gudden slipped. The King would have to free himself if he wanted either to escape or take his own life, and in this knowledge grasped the doctor, who was close on his heels, around his neck and pushed him under the water with such demonaical force that the big, strong man sank to his knees in the loamy lake bed. I saw the marks of strangulation on the body. Under the water it may well have been possible to do this on firm ground. At this point the water would have gone to the waist level of the struggling man. From here on, the footprints of the King, who now felt himself to be 'free', went vertically into the lake. With long steps almost like those of a man running, the King went into the deep water. The last impression was clearly visible on the border where the ground drops sharply, probably to 100 feet. And where this impression was visible, even a tall man would have no more ground on which to stand. The King must therefore have pulled himself down forcibly into the water. He did not intend to flee either – otherwise after murdering Gudden he could easily have reached the gate to Leoni and got help from the fishermen there (…). The supposition still held by many people that the King, who was an excellent swimmer, wanted to be rescued by swimming and was drowned instead, is false. The impressions made by his feet led vertically from the lakeside path to the place where there was no more ground. This factor excludes absolutely any other supposition than his intention to die."

All of this sounds reasonable enough, and indeed Eulenburg's report was widely accepted, contradicted openly only by the local people on lake Starnberg. Unfortunately, it is totally inaccurate and in the various letters and reports issuing from Eulenburg himself in the ensuing weeks and at the enquiry, he himself made many more observations and comments which contradicted each other and indeed even conflicted wildly with the above. Although a great deal has been written and speculated about the footprints in the lakebed, what Eulenburg reported was what he wanted people to believe, not what had actually occurred. At the point where Eulenburg insisted that the water was so clear that he could still see the footprints, he apparently also consulted his crystal ball in order to describe exactly what had happened.

Even in the Protocol of the Starnberger Gerichtskommission it is stated "on the night of June 12-13th the wind, rain and strong waves made conditions such that *no footprints could possibly have remained undisturbed"* [Author's italics] for the four hours between the removal of the corpses and the visit to the scene of Eulenburg which took place hours after the event and in the calm of the morning. Even so, at that time it was scarcely light and it is unlikely that he could have seen "bright sand" as the water would still have been cloudy after the turbulence of the night before and would in any case only appear "bright" if the sun shone directly on to it. Only if Lidl's story of the order given to his friend to falsify the footprints (conveniently, immediately before his visit so that he might "truthfully" record having seen them) was true and his account of the prevailing conditions, likely to be in any way accurate.

Further, the lakebed at this point is not as Eulenburg described it, although everyone who had not been there accepted his word for it. There are some very large cobbles somewhat brighter in colour than the smaller, grit-like stones which are often associated with this type of shoreline, and the lake bed is actually covered with *Schwemmkies*, that is to say, loose stones which shift around when the water is disturbed and not *Schlick,* a more solid mass of small gritty sandlike stones as Eulenburg asserted. He was believed because he was the Prussian Envoy in the same way as they unquestioningly accepted that the King's hat had shown a mysterious tear without asking what had caused it, and that Gudden's throat had borne marks of strangulation although the doctors who actually examined the bodies made no mention of any such marks.

Otto Schleusinger, the young son of the local district judge, however, made an investigation of his own of the lakebed and it was his contention that there were signs that Gudden had fallen, or been pushed, into a yew bush to the right of the path just at the point where the footprints led down to the lake "because the remains of twigs and leaves were sticking to his coat and umbrella", an important observation which the official searchers either overlooked or intentionally ignored. The bright 16 year old also observed, "About ten meters from the shore were footprints clearly showing a struggle during which Gudden was submerged. From there onwards, the King went on alone for some eight or ten paces in the direction of the Roseninsel (...) the footprints, therefore, did not go, as F. von Müller states, towards the shore, that is to say, in a Northerly or even Southeasterly direction, but South West, in the direction of the Roseninsel." This supports the theory that Elisabeth was waiting for him and expecting him to go either to Possenhofen opposite or to their usual haunt, the Roseninsel, where it is possible that more rescuers waited for him.

Young Schleusinger's examination was carried out while all the excitement was going on and he was clearly able to go about his sleuthing unnoticed by the crowds of shouting men, but he does not say whether he used a torchlight or lantern to help him to see what he was doing. Clearly, it had not occurred to the searchers to look anywhere but in one particular place for footprints – or perhaps they thought that no one else would trouble to examine the lakebed in a more sheltered place where the effects of weather and tide were likely to be less intense. His observations were made long before anyone thought of falsifying any footprints and might thus be taken more seriously than certain other statements.

Various other people had comments to make concerning the footprints and most of them disagreed with what Eulenburg had to say, yet all were ignored in favour of the highly dramatic statement of the Prussian envoy. Another point concerning those footprints is the astonishing fact that, between the wild action of the wind and rain in the place in question, and the countless numbers of people who had trampled over this spot, it apparently remained possible for two distinct sets of identifiable prints to be so clearly discernable hours after the event, and this was the very valid point made by the local Authorities and which, although it was the most logical remark made, was totally ignored by everyone.

If those footprints existed at all, they could equally have been those of Ludwig and his assailant or of Gudden and the assailant. Indeed, they could have been prints made by the many people who were milling around in the area. Whatever the truth, Eulenburg had prepared a piece of sublimation worthy of any present-day adman. He was determined to implant in people's minds the idea that Ludwig, a dangerous paranoid, had murdered his doctor and committed suicide – a theory which, when considered seriously, is nonsense but like so many other false interpretations of history and historic fact, has been readily accepted for posterity.

If ever a man had genuine ground for taking his own life, it was King Ludwig. In his 41 years he had encountered many a crisis: the handing over of the Kaiser's throne to a Hohenzollern and the loss of Bavaria's autonomy; the incarceration of his brother Otto; the impossibility of his relationship with Elisabeth; the realisation that he would never be able totally to overcome the sexual proclivities which troubled his spirit so deeply; last but not least, the alleged accumulation of debts which had brought about his downfall.

In the knowledge that fate had caught up with him, he had every opportunity during the night of June 11-12th June to put an end to himself had such been his true intention. But having spent hours with Dürkheim vigorously despatching telegrams to a variety of people from

whom he hoped to gain assistance in a projected escape, it is scarcely
logical that he then took his own life without waiting to see if help was
to be forthcoming. The key to all this lies in the official denials either
of an assassination plot or of a counter-plot to rescue the King. Earlier
at Neuschwanstein, when he had called for the key to the tower (and
was there really only one set of keys to that huge castle?) despite his
gloomy comment to Mayr that the hairdresser might "look for his head
in the Pöllat", vanity, pride and commonsense alone would have
prevented him from jumping a thousand feet to an ugly death, quite
apart from the other considerations already mentioned. It is far more
likely that, from such a vantage point, he would have a panoramic view
of the surrounding countryside and would thus be able to see the
advance of friends and enemies alike. Hohenschwangau was the place
he loved most in the world: whether he saw death or exile before him,
the romantic Ludwig would, in any case, have been unable to resist one
last look at his paradise.

When he had earlier asked so many questions about poison, it is
possible that he was considering this as a last resort, but since he
already had in his possession unlimited quantities of such substances
as chloralhydrate, laudenum and the like, of whose dangerous properties he was already more than well aware, it is more probable that,
deeply suspicious of most of those in his direct employ, he was trying
to weigh the likelihood that his enemies would try to poison him. He
may also simply have wanted to have poison by him for use in the last
resort for, of course, he had no idea whether or not the conspirators
intended to do away with him immediately or whether they had some
other frightful plan in store.

Where Dr. Gudden is concerned, it is difficult also to accept that
Ludwig would have murdered even a man whom he fundamentally
disliked and mistrusted since he was a known pacificist with a horror
of blood and violence. Early on in the proceedings, he had actually
said "No blood shall be spilt on my account". Punishments alleged by
spiteful servants to have been meted out to them by the King were
mostly figments of the imagination; he would never have stooped to
such demeaning acts or to physical force although his verbal extravagances – a characteristic well known to all throughout his life – would
give lie to this. The reaction of the Commission members when they
were put into the guardroom and told that Ludwig proposed to have
them "skinned and their eyes gauged out" was greeted with derisive
laughter: they considered the very suggestion to be hilarious, since they
were all aware he would not hurt a fly.

The probable reason for Ludwig's assassination was that, with his expensive building mania and his stubborn refusal to give in to the demands of the Prussians and the Ultramontanes, he was an annoying embarrassment to a great many people. His Uncle Luitpold appears to have been something of a dark horse for he certainly had some prior discussions and correspondence on the question of the Bavarian Throne and Ludwig on his side was certainly aware of his scheming for did he not refer to him openly as a "Prince Rebel"? After Ludwig's death, Empress Elisabeth wrote a poem accusing Luitpold of murdering him and for the rest of her life went to great lengths to avoid meeting him, even though her daughter Gisela was married to his son Leopold.

Ludwig disliked Minister Lutz and often disagreed with him on matters of State; he had quarrelled with Holnstein after bearing his unwelcome presence for years in his capacity of Oberstallmeister and he would have disliked Philipp Eulenburg on principle, simply because he was Prussian – this was not a sign of madness, however, but one of blind prejudice.

This leaves only Gudden himself, another Prussian, albeit one who had for many years been resident in Bavaria. Almost excessively sycophantic towards the man whom he had just delcared to be insane, he was probably obeying orders from a higher quarter. Having spent most of his professional years working among the mentally ill it seems incredible that he would agree to go out walking on a stormy evening in poor light with a dangerous patient, allowing him even to choose a path which, while secluded, lay in places directly at the water's edge, deliberately and explicitly instructing the staff that no one was to follow: *Es darf keiner mitgehen – not "no one need* come with us" but "no one *must* come with us". The question still remains as to why Gudden should have given such an order and, unpleasant though it is, the logical solution is that Gudden knew that the King was shortly to be assassinated and more importantly, by whom. Is it really likely that he would otherwise deliberately place himself in such a vulnerable position with a large, powerfully built man whom he had recently diagnosed as being dangerous unless he knew that the King was not ill at all and that they would in any case be followed by someone other than a nurse? Dr. Müller was earlier vociferous in his annoyance over Gudden's apparent foolhardiness in going out alone with the King and permitting him so much freedom. On his own admission he became very angry indeed at the beginning of the second walk when Gudden was so adamant that they should go unaccompanied. If Müller on his side had a change of heart, how can we account for it? Was he persuaded by means of threats to help the conspirators or was he merely trying to cover himself?

From Ludwig's earlier conversation with Mauder we know that he was aware of the presence on the lake of Count Rambaldi and the canoes, and he must have realised that various other people had observed them. Time was of the essence. He knew that, if he was to escape at all, now was the moment, whether or not the canoes were near enough for him to reach one of them before the alarm was raised. It is possible that at this moment, he saw Lidl hidden in the bushes, removed his coats in one movement and ran as swiftly as he could towards Lidl's boat, but failing because of his own weight to launch it into the black and angry waters of the lake. The assassin, close behind, then shot the King through the head, killing him instantly before – as a logical sequel – dispatching Gudden who had now served his purpose, perhaps knocking him into the yew bush during the struggle. But who was the assassin? It is hard to desist from pointing the finger of accusation towards Max Holnstein, with his strange background, his unsavoury reputation and personal animosity towards Ludwig. There is also the question of the extent of Gudden's implication: was he prepared to disregard his Hyppocratic Oath and assist in the killing of the King? Not all doctors are perfect; in the same era, for example, Dr. Pritchard and Dr. Gully in England similarly disgraced themselves – the former for gain and the latter for a woman. Was Gudden cast in a similar mould? The only other explanations are (a) that Gudden himself shot Ludwig and was then attacked by one of Ludwig's horri-fied rescuers nearby or (b) that Gudden had no part in the affair and was killed while trying to defend the King, although in view of his very obvious earlier involvement in the *coup*, the latter theory does not seem the most likely one.

Assuming that Holnstein, physically powerful and a crackshot, had disposed of Ludwig, to kill the elderly doctor would have been even simpler, particularly since he would not have been expecting an attack from a fellow conspirator. His demise would not only silence his tongue but would leave the indelible impression that the King himself was the murderer of his doctor. Eulenburg's blatantly inaccurate but widely accepted theory was clearly designed to uphold this impression and, at the same time, to refute the possibility of the existence of an escape plan.

Whatever happened on that terrible night, we may be certain that King Ludwig's death was neither an accident nor suicide. We can also be sure that he was not removed because he was mad. It would be ludicrous in the extreme to depose a man like Ludwig in favour of his brother Otto who, whether or not he was truly insane, was certified as such in 1878, unless the conspirators had already agreed that Luitpold was to act as Regent on the understanding that he would have full

powers.* This has indeed been discussed in the earliest years of
Ludwig's reign before anyone had suggested that there was something
wrong with him.

*   *   *   *   *

ALMOST as great a puzzle in the affair as the King's end was the
clumsy and ineffectual nature of the proceedings both before and
after his death.

The King and Gudden were said to have set out on their walk shortly
before six o'clock. By eight o'clock, with another stormy night presaged, they had still not returned but only then did it occur to the large
numbers of people at Berg, who had hitherto never let the King out of
their sight, to wonder where they were. Before the King and the doctor
set off, there had been general dissention about the walk itself yet no
one, including the men who had deposed Ludwig, seemed unduly
worried by their continued absence.

Why was no one concerned and further, why was no one alerted
earlier? Contrary to Ludwig's earlier suspicions, the Gendarmes asserted that they had not even been informed that the King had gone
out, but were only sent out on a further routine patrol of the park. One
of these, Lauterbach, even said that during his patrol from 7.25 pm to
8.00 pm, he noticed "nothing but three or four canoes plying up and
down between Berg and Leoni some 20-30 paces from the shore". How
could he have regarded such a sight as being "in no way suspicious"?

Dr.Müller said that he continued to write letters in his room until
about 7.45 pm when he went to the Kavalierhaus chiefly to complain
that Gudden had permitted Ludwig "an unprecedented measure of
freedom" which he himself "would never have allowed had he been in
charge of the case". He had aired the same views to the doctor himself
at lunch, yet now, with every apparent likelihood of his fears having
come to fruition, he did nothing about it except to remark that the
doctor was "nowhere to be seen" – although shortly after this his
suspicions were aroused sufficiently for him to send a patrol out to look
for the missing men. Müller averred that, subsequent to this, he
remained for some time standing at the entrance to the Schloss before
organising a search of the park in collaboration with Baron Washington
and the Schloss Steward, Huber. According to Müller, from about 8.30
pm virtually the entire domestic, gardening and nursing staff as well as
the Gendarmes were engaged on a somewhat disorganised search for
the two men. But what on earth were they all doing prior to that? Why

---

* In a recent history of the Wittelsbach family, Georg Lohmeier states that he has
found evidence of contemporary witnesses who insisted that Otto had been placed
for years under damaging drugs and kept sedated although he was perfectly sane and
further that, according to a letter in the Secret Archives, "noble relatives" had visited
Otto in Schloss Fürstenried in 1913-1914 and "conversed with him for hours about
art and literature."

wait so long before thinking to go to look for their "dangerous lunatic" and the senior medical official? Curiously, it was stated that nobody wanted to search the park and lakeshore with nets "for fear of attracting too much attention from the number of small boats crossing". What an extraordinary statement! An equally strange comment came from Washington who, while admitting to "growing anxious" about the absence of the two men said that he could "Hardly imagine that an accident count happen in the lake" because he "had seen some little boats crossing continually which either came from Leoni or went there." Unless he was perfectly well aware why they were there - and of course he was - surely an intelligent man might not only have sought their assistance but also stopped to wonder why they had continued to sail up and down so patiently for a whole day in atrocious weather and why their occupants continued to show such dogged persistence with night drawing on. Surely not, as Count Rambaldi asserted, "Because it gave him pleasure"?

The report also stated quite adamantly that, during all this time, namely between six and nine o'clock, none of the Gendarmes in the park could recall hearing any noise – by which was presumably meant sounds of a struggle, for Ludwig and Gudden, both of whom enjoyed intelligent conversation, would have chatted together sporadically as they walked, and we know from their earlier discussion that the nurse could hear them talking, Ludwig's voice was soft and low, often described as "well modulated", while that of the doctor was notoriously strident and pompous. Yet despite the clarity of the air and the fact that sound often carries across water, the noise of the waves and the wind in the trees might possibly have drowned the sound of their conversation, and equally it would probably have been loud enough to disguise the sound of a shot. However, the general attitude of the strange assortment of personnel who abounded in the area that night would suggest that they heard only what they wanted to hear. Zanders, who alone seems to have been genuinely concerned for the personal safety of the King, ordered the shore to be combed, presumably in the foreknowledge of where the King was headed, and it was he who at last summoned the entire domestic staff and sent them to join the search with lamps and torches.

Washington stated that at 9.00 pm he decided it was time to inform Luitpold and the Ministerium, hence those rash and oddly worded telegraphs. Scarcely had these been despatched than some Gendarmes announced to Dr. Müller that they had found the carriage tracks at the middle gate. But it was Washington who, having overheard them, sent the men to investigate. It was now 10 o'clock and raining hard. Next, the King's two coats were found with sleeves interlocking and, nearby, his hat and umbrella. Gudden's hat was found some paces nearer to Schloss Berg, but it could have been blown by the wind to that position from elsewhere (as could that of Ludwig). Only after all these objects had been recovered did the staff show any real concern. By this time it was 11 o'clock and almost another hour of aimless coming and going ensued before the bodies themselves were recovered in time for what can only be described as a macabre pantomime.

* * * * *

LUDWIG must have encountered his assailant, possibly Holnstein or Eulenburg, perhaps even both, at about 6.54 pm when his watch had stopped (presumably on contact with the water). To re-iterate, Gudden's watch was found to have stopped at 8.00 pm, but this was pronounced by his colleagues as having "no significance since he often forgot to wind it". This conflicts with Gudden's all-too-obvious obsession with schedules and routines. Throughout the evidence it was stated that he consulted his watch frequently, which was no more than one would expect. Another explanation is that Gudden outlived the King by an hour, but if this was the case, what occurred during that time?

Logically, Gudden was an accessory and having performed his function might well have become a victim of the same ruthless man who had put an end to the troublesome King. It would have been all too easy for a brutal, ruthless man such as Holnstein to overpower the elderly doctor and hold his head under the water for a few minutes. This would certainly account for the curious, bent-kneed position in which he was found and perhaps also for the scratches on his face. The famous "marks of strangulation", however, did not really exist.

It was now time for the assassin(s) to leave the scene, fully intending the circumstances of the discovery of the bodies to be so ambiguous as to render the deaths of the two men shrouded for ever in mystery. If Jakob Lidl's testament is to be believed, it was 6.54 pm when Ludwig tried to get into the boat and met his end. At this time, everyone in the Schloss was going about his business and, not expecting to hear anything unusual, such as a shot, would not have noticed a shot: The only member of the Commission who disappeared from sight in the midst of all ensuing turmoil at the very time when one might reasonably have expected him to be very much in evidence was Max Holnstein, who would now have returned to Munich to await the "news" of the King's death.

Although no official acknowledgement has ever been made of Empress Elisabeth's participation in an attempt to rescue Ludwig, certain puzzling facts lead one to the conclusion that the unsuccessful bid to free the King was carried out with her knowledge and probably with her active participation.

According to Elisabeth's lady-in-waiting Marie Festetics (who, it will be remembered, disliked Ludwig intensely, probably because she was jealous of his close bond with the Empress) on Whit Monday, when Elisabeth was driving back to her hotel at the nearby village of Feldafing following a visit to her mother, she seemed greatly upset and "had obviously been crying". Festetics' explanation for this was that there had been heated altercations concerning Ludwig and his deposition. The Empress insisted hat he was not mad but merely "an eccentric living in a world of dreams" while the Archduchess who, understandably, had never forgiven him for jilting her daughter Sophie, criticised him for "bringing the country to bankruptcy with his building schemes". This, of course, was nonsense since there had never been any question of Ludwig using public funds; he had utilised only his personal monies and his allowance from the Civil List and Ludovika, with her taste for minding other people's business, would have been perfectly well aware of the fact, particularly since his engineered request for Government funds had been the official immediate cause of his deposition. In any case, far from wreaking ruin, Ludwig had brought great prosperity to the country people by providing them with a long period of regular work of various kinds. When there was no building work, he even occasionally ordered road repairs to be carried out simply in order to provide the men with a living. Ludovika's acrimony was based solely on his refusal to marry Sophie and it was for this reason alone that she could find no sympathy for his predicament. *

According to Festetics, neither Elisabeth nor her mother had any idea of Ludwig's deposition until a day or so after the event, but Festetics had already contradicted herself by repeating the story of their argument and the reason for it before the King's body was found and further discredits herself by stating that the Empress had spent the evening of the 13th sending telegrams to the Emperor and to her son Rudolf, asking them to protest against the enforced abdication of the Bavarian King. Festetics cannot have it both ways.

Of course Elisabeth knew that Ludwig was at Berg. Festetics further contradicted herself by saying that, on the following day, Duke Karl Theodor brought his sister the news that Ludwig had been subjected to the indignity of being arrested and placed under restraint at Berg. Describing Elisabeth's reaction, Festetics says "She hardly spoke all day and in spite of the extremely inclement weather insisted

---

* Ludwig would doubtless have appreciated the irony of the fact that nowadays visitors flock to Bavaria from all corners of the world to visit his architectural creations. A whole industry has grown up around them and the German people as well as the Government have good reason to be grateful for the prosperity he has brought them.

upon remaining out of doors, *walking for hours by the lake, looking across the grey waters to the Roseninsel and the woods of Berg* [Author's italics]. Would Elisabeth, who had spent a fortune trying to combat her rheumatism and sciatica, really have passed her time thus in such bad weather unless she had an impelling reason for so doing?

Festetics asserted that, on June 14th, Elisabeth was having breakfast with Valerie when Gisela arrived, her distraught manner presaging the bad news which she had brought. Without waiting to hear what her elder daughter had to say, Elisabeth whispered "Ludwig is dead (...) They might have treated him more gently and so spared him such a terrible end." If she knew nothing of what had happened, what could have prompted her to make such a remark and how, indeed, did she know that he had not been treated gently or that his end had been "terrible" if, as Festetics insisted elsewhere, she had had no contact with the King? We know that Ludwig wrote her a note from Berg and therefore she had first hand knowledge of his treatment during those last hours. She was shocked and grieved beyond solace, not only by Ludwig's death and the loss of her dearest friend and relative, but also by the manner of his end. After placing a nosegay of jasmine, the King's favourite flower, in his dead hand, Elisabeth fainted on the spot; she never recovered from his death. Her feeling for Ludwig is undisputed; only its depth and the exact nature of their relationship has given rise to speculation. After his death, her whole lifestyle and attitude to life changed and she had little real interest in anything.

Shortly after the tragedy, Elisabeth left Starnberg and while she occasionally visited her beloved childhood home, the visits were rare; she never again set foot on the Roseninsel, which had long been regarded as their exclusive territory. Lost and lonely, she wrote poems to Ludwig's memory and a vituperative poetic offering to prince Luitpold, whom she openly accused of murdering him. Her grief was to be extended when, only three years later, she was crushed by her son's death in equally mysterious and horrible circumstances. This was the final blow and on her subsequent nomadic wanderings across Europe, dressed always in black and heavily veiled, she became known as the *Mater Dolorosa*. Her quest for peace was never to be fulfilled until she herself was stuck down by an assassin's dagger in Geneva in 1898.

His mother fared little better, surviving only three years longer than Ludwig. At the time of his death she was still at Elbigenalp. Was she aware of the *coup d'état*? Ludwig himself did not approach her for assistance and although she knew of his earlier difficulties, she did not renew her offer of help. Their naturally cool relationship was a boon to Ludwig's enemies, who were quick to see the advantage of keeping them apart. Nevertheless, she was appalled by his untimely end and the lengths to which his enemies had gone to dispose of him. "All the waters of the seas would not be enough to wash away the stain of this brutal violation of the King," she averred, somewhat belatedly.

The endless speculation concerning the death of King Ludwig II continues. Contemporaries of the tragedy never stopped wondering; countless witnesses, reliable and otherwise, expressed their views on the occurrence, on the location and significance of the personal effects found near the supposed scene of the tragedy and above all, those footprints in the lakebed which were probably not even genuine. Despite all the conjecture, the surmise and guesswork, the dramatic, erroneous and highly suspect statements – and especially those made by Philipp Eulenburg – mean little or nothing. Significantly, the one man who might have shed a great deal of light on the affair, Max Holnstein, remained silent. Strangely, in view of his prominence in the affair, he was not even asked for a statement. The persistent official dismissal of the affair as "a mystery", "suicide", "an accident" or "drowning, following a stroke or heart attack" add up to no more than a clumsy attempt to suppress the truth.

Political motives apart, despite his innate shyness and very expensive hobbies, and assuming that Otto's instability had not been artificially induced, Ludwig was definitely the lesser of two evils. Luitpold, a Prussian-loving man of mature years would, in the normal way, have stood little chance of ascending the throne since the King was a comparatively healthy 41 year old with a life expectancy of anything up to another 40 years or so, by which time Luitpold himself would be long since dead. Only if Luitpold had pressing aspirations to rule does Ludwig's deposition in favour of Otto make sense. As another of Ludwig's former servants, Fritz Schwegler, said of him, "The King mad? No, never! He was perfectly normal. Only cleverer than all the rest put together!"

Even today, large numbers of people remain adamant in their belief that Ludwig was murdered. Legends, hearsay and rumour persist with such dogged similarity to this effect that it is impossible to believe that the hypersensitive, nobly-minded man with his staunch autocratic belief in the sanctity of his Royal body would ever have desecrated it, betrayed his people and his religion or cast shame upon the name of Wittelsbach by taking his own life or that of another.

As someone once said, it is all politics.

THE END

PICTURE ACKNOWLEDGEMENTS

Hohenschwangau, Neuschwanstein, Linderhof and Nymphenburg – Feature Pix/Mauritius Bild. Richard Wagner, and Wagner with Cosima Wagner – the Hulton Picture Company. Empress Elisabeth of Austria – Bildarchiv der Oest. Nationalbibliothek, Vienna. All other photographs – Bayerische Verwaltung der Staatl. Schlösser, Gärten und Seen. Dust wrapper: (Front) Ludwig II – Bayerische Verwaltung der Staatl. Schlösser, Gärten und Seen; (Back) Feature-Pix.

Selected Bibliography

Adalbert, Prinz von Bayern: Die Wittelsbacher (Munich 1980)
Bayerns König Ludwig II – Wahnsinn oder Intrige? (Munich 1984)
Beckenbauer, Alfons: Ludwig III von Bayern – 1845-1921 (Munich 1987)
Bismarck, Prince Otto: Reminiscences (1898)
Böhm, Gottfried von: Ludwig II, König von Bayern – Sein Leben und seine Zeit (Berlin 1924)
Chapman Houston, Major Desmond: Bavarian Fantasy (London 1955)
Corti, Count Egon: Elisabeth, die Seltsame Frau (1934)
Corti, Count Egon: Ludwig I von Bayern (1937)
Cosima Wagner's Diaries (2 volumes, London 1978 & 1980)
Derry & Jarman: The European World (London 1968)
Dirrigl, M: Maximilian von Bayern (Munich, 1984); Ludwig I (Munich 1984)
Ebenthal, H: The Tragedy of a Throne (1917)
Eisert, B: Ludwig II – Leben, Wirken, Sterben (Munich 1979)
Erloesser, D, ed: Der Junge Kainz – Briefe an seine Eltern (Berlin 1924)
Gebhardt, H: König Ludwig II und seine Verbrannte Braut (Munich 1986)
Gutman, R: Richard Wagner; The Man, His Mind and His Music (New York 1968)
Hacker, Rupert: Ludwig II in Augenzeugenberichten (Düsseldorf 1966)
Haslip, Joan: The Lonely Empress (London 1963)
Hierneis: Der König Speist (Munich 1953)
Hohenlohe-Schillingfürst, Prince Chlodwig: Memoirs (London 1907)
Kobell, Luise von: Unter den vier ersten Königen Bayerns (Munich1894)
König Ludwig und Richard Wagner Briefwechsel (5 volumes, Karlsruhe 1936)
Larisch, Marie Wallersee-Wittelsbach: My Past (1913), Secrets of a Royal House (1934), My Royal Relatives (1936)
Leeb, Herman: 100 Jahre Freiwillige Feuerwehr Schwangau 1874-1974
Lohmeier, Georg: Die Ahnen des Hauses Bayern – die Geschichte der Wittels-bacher (Munich 1980)
Mommsen, W: Otto von Bismarck (Rowohlt 1966)
Newman, E: The Life of Richard Wagner (London 1941 & 1946)
Nostitz, Georg, ed: Briefe Franz-Josefs an Kaiserin Elisabeth (2 vols, Vienna 1966)
Obermeier, S, ed: Das Geheime Tagebuch König Ludwigs II (Munich 1986)
Rall, M: König Ludwig II und Bismarcks Rangen um Bayern 1870-71 (Munich 1973)
Rall & Petzet: König Ludwig II–Wirklichkeit und Rätsel (Munich 1980)
Rall, Hans u Marga: Die Wittelsbacher in Lebensbildern (1986)
Richter, Werner: Ludwig II von Bayern (Munich 1970)
Röckl, Sebastian: Ludwig II und Richard Wagner (Munich 1903)
Schmidtauer & Kemper: Ein ewiges Rätsel will ich bleiben mir und anderen: Wie Krank war Ludwig II wirklich? (Munich 1986)
Wagner, Richard: Letters selected by W Altmann (2 volumes, London 1927)
Wagner, Richard: Mein Leben (1911)
Welcome, J: The Sporting Empress (London 1975)
Witzleben & Vignau: Die Herzöge von Bayern (1986)
Wöbking, Wilhelm: Der Tod König Ludwigs II von Bayern (Munich 1986)

BAVARIAN ROYAL HOUSE OF WITTELSBACH

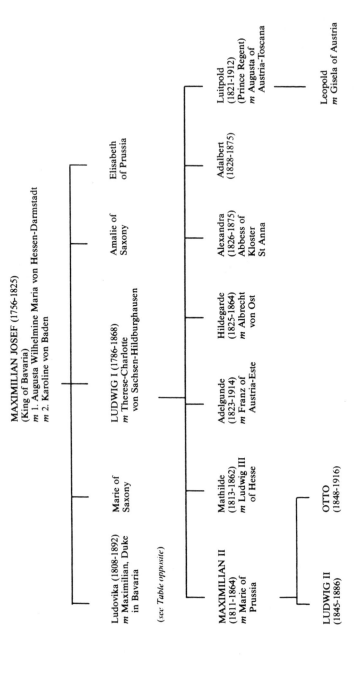

MAXIMILIAN JOSEF (1756-1825)
(King of Bavaria)
m 1. Augusta Wilhelmine Maria von Hessen-Darmstadt
m 2. Karoline von Baden

Ludovika (1808-1892)
m Maximilian, Duke
in Bavaria

(*see Table opposite*)

Marie of
Saxony

LUDWIG I (1786-1868)
m Therese-Charlotte
von Sachsen-Hildburghausen

Amalie of
Saxony

Elisabeth
of Prussia

MAXIMILIAN II
(1811-1864)
m Marie of
Prussia

Mathilde
(1813-1862)
m Ludwig III
of Hesse

Adelgunde
(1823-1914)
m Franz of
Austria-Este

Hildegarde
(1825-1864)
m Albrecht
von Ost

Alexandra
(1826-1875)
Abbess of
Kloster
St Anna

Adalbert
(1828-1875)

Luitpold
(1821-1912)
(Prince Regent)
m Augusta of
Austria-Toscana

LUDWIG II
(1845-1886)

OTTO
(1848-1916)

Leopold
m Gisela of Austria

BAVARIAN ROYAL HOUSE

BIRKENFELD-GELNHAUSEN LINE (DUKES IN BAVARIA)

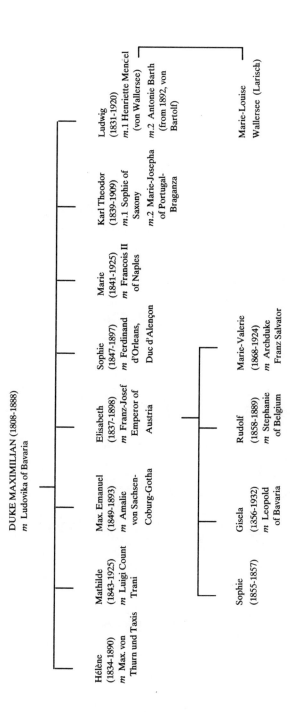

DUKE MAXIMILIAN (1808-1888)
m Ludovika of Bavaria

Hélène
(1834-1890)
m Max. von
Thurn und Taxis

Mathilde
(1843-1925)
m Luigi Count
Trani

Max. Emanuel
(1849-1893)
m Amalie
von Sachsen-
Coburg-Gotha

Elisabeth
(1837-1898)
m Franz-Josef
Emperor of
Austria

Sophie
(1847-1897)
m Ferdinand
d'Orleans,
Duc d'Alençon

Marie
(1841-1925)
m Francois II
of Naples

Karl Theodor
(1839-1909)
m.1 Sophie of
Saxony
m.2 Marie-Josepha
of Portugal-
Braganza

Ludwig
(1831-1920)
m.1 Henriette Mendel
(von Wallersee)
m.2 Antonie Barth
(from 1892, von
Bartolf)

Sophie
(1855-1857)

Gisela
(1856-1932)
m Leopold
of Bavaria

Rudolf
(1858-1889)
m Stephanie
of Belgium

Marie-Valerie
(1868-1924)
m Archduke
Franz Salvator

Marie-Louise
Wallersee (Larisch)